Movies at Home

ALSO BY KERRY SEGRAVE AND FROM MCFARLAND

Film Actors Organize: Union Formation Efforts in America, 1912–1937 (2009)

*Actors Organize:
A History of Union Formation Efforts in America, 1880–1919* (2008)

*Obesity in America, 1850–1939:
A History of Social Attitudes and Treatment* (2008)

*Women and Capital Punishment in America, 1840-1899: Death Sentences
and Executions in the United States and Canada* (2008)

Women Swindlers in America, 1860–1920 (2007)

Ticket Scalping: An American History, 1850–2005 (2007)

America on Foot: Walking and Pedestrianism in the 20th Century (2006)

Suntanning in 20th Century America (2005)

Endorsements in Advertising: A Social History (2005)

Women and Smoking in America, 1880 to 1950 (2005)

Foreign Films in America: A History (2004)

Lie Detectors: A Social History (2004)

Product Placement in Hollywood Films: A History (2004)

Piracy in the Motion Picture Industry (2003)

Jukeboxes: An American Social History (2002)

Vending Machines: An American Social History (2002)

Age Discrimination by Employers (2001)

Shoplifting: A Social History (2001)

*American Television Abroad:
Hollywood's Attempt to Dominate World Television* (1998)

Tipping: An American Social History of Gratuities (1998; paperback 2009)

*American Films Abroad: Hollywood's Domination of
the World's Movie Screens from the 1890s to the Present* (1997)

Baldness: A Social History (1996; paperback 2009)

Policewomen: A History (1995)

Payola in the Music Industry: A History, 1880–1991 (1994)

The Sexual Harassment of Women in the Workplace, 1600 to 1993 (1994)

*Women Serial and Mass Murderers:
A Worldwide Reference, 1580 through 1990* (1992)

*Drive-in Theaters: A History
from Their Inception in 1933* (1992; paperback 2006)

BY KERRY SEGRAVE AND LINDA MARTIN AND FROM MCFARLAND

*The Continental Actress: European Film Stars of the Postwar Era;
Biographies, Criticism, Filmographies, Bibliographies* (1990)

*The Post-Feminist Hollywood Actress: Biographies and
Filmographies of Stars Born After 1939* (1990)

Movies at Home

How Hollywood Came to Television

by KERRY SEGRAVE

McFarland & Company, Inc., Publishers
Jefferson, North Carolina, and London

The present work is a reprint of the library bound edition of Movies at Home: How Hollywood Came to Television, *first published in 1999 by McFarland.*

LIBRARY OF CONGRESS CATALOGUING-IN-PUBLICATION DATA

Segrave, Kerry, 1944–
  Movies at home : how Hollywood came to television / by Kerry Segrave.
    p. cm.
  Includes bibliographical references and index.

  ISBN 978-0-7864-4080-1
  softcover : 50# alkaline paper ∞

  1. Television broadcasting of films. I. Title.
  PN1992.8.F5S45   2009
  791.45′0973′09045—dc21
                                              99-24239

British Library cataloguing data are available

©1999 Kerry Segrave. All rights reserved

No part of this book may be reproduced or transmitted in any form or by any means, electronic or mechanical, including photocopying or recording, or by any information storage and retrieval system, without permission in writing from the publisher.

Cover image ©2009 Shutterstock

Manufactured in the United States of America

McFarland & Company, Inc., Publishers
  Box 611, Jefferson, North Carolina 28640
  www.mcfarlandpub.com

Contents

Preface	1
1. Hollywood Sits on Its Assets, 1940s–1955	3
2. Hollywood Launches Its Assets, 1940s–1955	21
3. TV Surrenders, 5,000 Times a Week, 1956–1961	45
4. Television Defends Its Honor, 1956–1961	63
5. Hollywood Goes Primetime on the Networks, 1961–1975	79
6. A New Genre: The Made-for-TV Movie, 1961–1975	105
7. Cut, Colorized, Panned and Scanned, 1976–1998	123
8. Movies from the Sky, or the Corner Store, 1976–1998	159
Notes	201
Bibliography	229
Index	251

Preface

The response of the major Hollywood motion picture studios to the arrival of television in America was mixed. Initially they tried to buy into the new rival by acquiring ownership interests in outlets. When they were effectively blocked from that goal in any meaningful fashion the majors turned to an attempt to establish alternatives to television. The first was theater television, which failed quickly for a variety of reasons. A second alternative was the early experiments in subscription television, or toll television, a forerunner of what we have today in premium cable and pay-per-view. Hollywood strongly favored toll television as an alternative because it held the potential of giving them greater control, compared to theater television, which remained located in cinemas. If theater audiences were declining as television spread across the land—and they were—toll television gave Hollywood the hope it could transfer the box office into each person's home, if those people would not make the trip to the cinema box office. Subscription television also failed in its early incarnations.

While all that was going on, Hollywood's majors steadfastly withheld their prime assets, thousands of movies, from the new medium. As well, they tended to bar most of their contract stars from appearing on television. As the financial potential of the new medium made itself evident, that resolve began to weaken. Once the first major released to television, the others quickly followed. Soon, independent television stations were screening old movies throughout the day, and into the night. Stations affiliated with networks telecast those films at all hours, except primetime, in the beginning. It all had the effect of driving local, and live, programs off the air. Nothing could compete with the low price of an old film, which had long recovered its cost. Also, those old movies had the added benefit of being known quantities, usually with actors well known to the public. They needed little publicity. Films on television sped up the process of going to filmed material, from the mostly live programs with which television began. This made it easier for Hollywood to move into the production of series fare for television, and to come to dominate that area, at the expense of the independent program suppliers who rapidly dwindled in number. Networks initially held out against telecasting old movies in primetime, feeling that it was not in television's interests, or part of its mandate, to air used product. They soon succumbed to the balance sheet argument. Television's hunger for old movies, and its ability to devour them much more rapidly than they were created, led to the birth of a new genre, the made-for-television movies.

Before the point of exhaustion was reached, movies came to dominate the ratings battles between the three networks. Given the state of reruns on television today, it is hard to believe that in the beginning industry executives worried about telecasting reruns: would the public accept them? The early, and repeated, use of movies on television was one of the factors that helped convince the industry that indeed the public would.

As the dominance of old movies on the networks began to decline, any income loss to Hollywood was more than offset by new technology: cable TV; satellite pickup of distant stations transmitted to cablers who delivered them to customers; satellite delivery direct to the home. It all meant more and more outlets for Hollywood on which to screen its old films. And the biggest development of all for Hollywood was the video-cassette recorder. Today Hollywood's movies are available from the networks, the independent stations, the basic cable networks, the premium cable channels, the pay-per-view systems. They are available from the sky, and from the corner store. Everywhere, movies on television, for free—sometimes.

Chapter 1

Hollywood Sits on Its Assets, 1940s–1955

> "We shudder to think what might be the result ... if MGM should ever unload its collection of technicolored junk on the unsuspecting home viewer."
> Hugh Garner, 1955.

> "Old pictures never die. Their audience slowly fades away."
> Sylvester "Pat" Weaver,
> NBC president, 1954.

The Hollywood film industry—dominated by the eight major conglomerates, 20th Century–Fox, Universal, Columbia, Warner Bros., RKO, United Artists, Paramount and MGM—entered the post–World War II period in good shape. Business had been good throughout the war period, and prior to that in the 1930s. Compared to most industries the film industry passed through the Depression era comparatively untouched. In fact, Hollywood had never experienced a prolonged or severe economic downturn and looked forward to increased prosperity for itself as America returned to a peacetime economy. Those first two years, 1946 and 1947, rewarded Hollywood handsomely for its optimism. But then the industry went into a steep two-year decline; panic began to take hold. Although television was often blamed for Hollywood's decline of this period it played no role at all, in the beginning. The rapid spread of television into American homes at the very end of the

1940s and into the early 1950s ensured Hollywood would never return to its former glory. Hollywood did not ignore television in its early stages; it tried to buy into the new arrival. However, Hollywood was in the midst of a lengthy antitrust action begun against it by the Justice Department in the 1930s. A consent decree signed by the majors at the beginning of the 1940s was ignored by the majors, which infuriated Justice further. War delayed court action but finally the case was on the docket again with a decision by the U.S. Supreme Court in 1948 ordering the majors to divest themselves of their theater chains (five of the eight majors were involved in that aspect), thus breaking up the cartel's production/distribution/exhibition control of the industry. Other practices of the cartel were also voided, such as block booking and fixing the admission rates charged by theaters. All this happened when the FCC was developing its plan for television station ownership, spectrum allocation, and so forth. Justice made it clear to that regulatory commission that it would not be pleased to see Hollywood exert the same control over the television industry as it had in motion pictures. The FCC obliged. Under the divestiture provisions the cinema-owning majors had to file a proposal for selling off theaters, have it approved by Justice, then implement it. Almost ten years passed before the last of the involved majors had formally shed its movie houses. Denied any significant ownership in the new medium the film capital fought back by using its movies as a wedge to gain access to television, but not right away. In time it would dominate the new medium. If it could not own the hardware it would control the software. Somehow the cinema owners, who shuddered at the thought of motion pictures on television, had to be placated. Initially there weren't many television stations and they didn't have much money. Those two facts would be used by Hollywood to shield itself against any complaints from Justice that it was involved in any conspiracy to deny movies to television. Given the state of reruns on television today it is hard to believe that Hollywood worried that once a film was sold its value was severely damaged, with respect to future sales. Why sell early if it had to be cheap? And, after ownership of stations was denied and before movies were sold to "free" television, the majors tried to come up with some type of early pay-television.

As 1948 began hard times were noticeably affecting Hollywood film production. MGM cut its payroll by 40 percent, Columbia Pictures laid off 25 percent of its employees, RKO's studio had been dark for ten days, an unheard of length of time. That first full week of 1948 saw Hollywood shooting just 25 movies, not quite half as many as were underway at the same time in 1947. Judged on profits, though, the movie capital was still doing very well with an estimated net profit in 1947 of $100 million, down from the all-time peak registered in 1946, yet still far better than in any other previous year.[1]

One year later employment in the film industry was estimated to be down some 25 percent from the 1946 peak. Only 370 stars were then under regular studio contract, compared to 750 in 1946. Still, observed a reporter, "Profits, while down from 1946 and 1947, remain large." By late in 1949 employment of production workers in the industry stood at 14,700, substantially below the 24,000 workers employed in 1946. A low point of 12,100 employed had been reached earlier that year. From a peak of more than 80 million paid admissions to movies each week in 1946 film attendance dropped into the 50-something million per week range in 1949. By then the five affected majors were grappling with the fact they had to dispose of their theater chains. Those "Big Five" were Paramount, RKO, Warner, MGM and 20th Century–Fox (hereinafter Fox). The "Little Three," Columbia, UA and Universal, along with the other five, were enjoined from block and blind booking, fixing ticket prices, and other practices.[2]

The picture industry accounted for only 18.8 percent of household expenditures for entertainment in 1952, compared with 36 percent in 1946. During those years average weekly attendance declined from 82.4 million weekly in 1946 to 46 million in 1952. Corporate income after taxes for the industry fell from $187 million in 1946 to a "meagre" $31 million in 1952. During that same period the presence of television sets in U.S. homes rose from 0.2 percent to over 34 percent.[3]

An early study of movie attendance among television set owners was conducted early in 1949 by Audience Research, headed by George Gallup. It found that television was cutting into movie attendance at the rate of 500,000 admissions per week. With the average ticket price at 48.5¢ it amounted to a loss of $243,000 at the box office. Still, this figure represented less than one percent of the total number of tickets sold each week. While the loss was concentrated in television areas the alleged inroads of television, even in those areas, was judged "too slight" to permit a really accurate measurement of its extent.[4]

About 56 stations were on the air in early 1949 with 66 others then in various stages of construction. There were about 1 million sets in U.S. homes. Television service was available to around 40 percent of the country's population. Leading the way, as might be expected, was the nation's biggest metropolis, New York City. In the spring of 1948 the area was served by three stations offering a total of 75 hours a week of programming. One year later six outlets provided a total of 225 hours per week. One or more stations began telecasting as early as 10 A.M. while one or more continued broadcasting past 11 P.M. In the week ending April 16 229 hours were broadcast, of which 47.5 were movies, 35.5 hours of comedy/variety and 35 hours of children's fare. Regarding those movies columnist Jack Gould reported that "Most of the motion pictures are some years old, though there is a sprinkling of more recent films from England." Those U.S. films that were shown were all from independent producers and studios; not a single one came from Hollywood's major studios.[5]

By the spring of 1951 there were 11.7 million television sets in the U.S. A total of 63 markets had a combined 107 television stations operating. Forty-seven of those markets, with 80 stations and 9.9 million sets, were connected by coaxial cable or microwave relay; that is, they were in a network. The remaining 16 markets, with 27 stations and 1.8 million sets, were not yet interconnected. A true coast-to-coast national network was still a year or so away. Largest of the markets were New York City, 7 outlets and 2.2 million sets; Los Angeles, 7 stations and 877,000 receivers; Chicago, 4 stations and 890,000 sets; Philadelphia, with 3 television stations reaching 814,000 sets.[6]

Hollywood grew increasingly worried over television and its possible effects on the movie industry. Paramount conducted its own study in the New York City area, finding television set ownership cut family moviegoing between 20 and 30 percent. Another survey of television owners in Washington, D.C., claimed to have found a 74 percent cut in attendance. Making matters worse was the bad publicity Hollywood received in 1948 when the U.S. Supreme Court found the industry guilty of monopolistic practices and ordered theater divestment. Hollywood had fallen in public esteem. An article in the February 1949 issue of *Consumer Reports* voiced concern over possible film inroads into television. Objections were based on several grounds: the simple bigness of the film industry with fears of placing both film and television production into single hands; the known record of monopolistic practices; the possible attempt of Hollywood to slow up development of television; the inadequacy of the Federal Communications Commission (FCC) to tackle regulation of such a large industry as that of motion pictures; and the "deterioration of public service standards" sure to result if Hollywood—as opposed to radio corporations—took over television programming.[7]

Questions that Hollywood grappled with in the late 1940s, and beyond, had to do with what effects television would have on the movie industry and what part Hollywood should play in television. Should it buy into the new medium? Should it produce material for television? Selling its motion pictures, new or old, to television was never one of those questions, at least not in the early stages. Hollywood had no intention of releasing its product to television.

Director Reuben Mamoulian declared, late in 1948, that television would not exert a harmful effect on the motion picture industry, but instead would depend upon movies for its material. He told a meeting of the American Television Society that television's adverse influence would fall on radio whose destiny "is going downhill." Television, he said, would become more closely allied to films, adding that the use of movies for television thus far had been "largely uninvestigated."[8]

Taking a similar position around the same time was independent producer Samuel Goldwyn who also believed movies were television's destiny, although he had a different type of film in mind. He thought the quality of theatrical films would have to improve since it was certain that people would be unwilling to pay to see poor movies when they could stay home and see something which was, at least, no worse. Goldwyn declared that "nothing will stand in the way of full-length feature pictures in the home produced expressly for that purpose." The key to that would be in "phone-vision" whereby a patron could dial a number, tell what film he wanted to see, and have it transmitted to his set over the phone lines. The fee would appear on the monthly phone bill. Confidently he predicted the production of full-length movies especially for home television would become a practical reality in five to ten years. New films would have to be created especially for television since as the novelty of television quickly wore off "the public is not going to be satisfied to look at the flickering shadows of old films which have reposed in their producers' vaults for many years." Goldwyn was equally convinced the public would not be content to spend an evening watching series programming on television.[9]

Paramount executive Paul Raibourn predicted that "B" pictures (second half of a double-bill) would find competition in television and were "likely to disappear from our screens." In fact, they soon did. He added that "television has, as yet, produced no serious competition for the 'A' pictures." Raibourn stated Hollywood would be able to increase its attendance by showing its trailers on television: "We believe there is no way of making a person hungry as completely effective as that of giving him a small taste of a delectable dish. Through a television broadcast we will come into your home to show you just enough of a picture to make you hungry for the rest of it."[10]

Television industry consultant Ralph Austrian also said Hollywood could arrest the theater decline by using television to advertise its movies. As well he urged Hollywood to utilize "closed circuit" television to augment regular film fare and to greater activity in producing television shows. As early as 1949 that recommended use of large-screen television in the cinemas was already a reality, at least in a limited, experimental way. Movies and television had been married in a double bill on Broadway in a process still being perfected. In one method the RCA instantaneous system used a receiver much like a home television set, plus a projector that threw those images on a theater screen as they were received. In a second system incoming images were photographed, the film was developed and then projected on the screen by the regular movie projector, a process that was said to take only 20 minutes.[11]

When business publication *U.S. News & World Report* looked at the situation at the beginning of 1949 it declared there were only two ways to meet the competition of television. "One is for the movie producers to invest heavily in television itself, and in that manner help to control television programs and share in the profits. Another way is to make movies to be broadcast on television programs." What was meant by movies was any material for television, such as series. However, each of these methods had its drawbacks. The

"FCC apparently wants to avoid a tie-up between television and movies similar to that existing between the movie producers and the theaters." If, instead of investing heavily in television stations Hollywood turned to television as a market and source of new revenue, it would find few television advertisers could afford to pay for films as then produced; then, thought the magazine, "advertisers are likely to be wary of spending that kind of money for a film that can be shown only a limited number of times." Even shorter material such as series-length would be too costly for most program sponsors: "The industry has a long way to go in working out new techniques before it can make a profit out of selling new movies to television stations for home broadcasts." Despite the problems this observer felt had to be overcome before television provided a profitable outlet for Hollywood, he was still confident that the film capital would eventually provide 60 to 70 percent of all television material.[12]

Some in Hollywood saw opportunity where others saw a threat. Believing that few sponsors could afford "live" shows some film executives felt TV would have to soon turn to filmed material. Those in this camp also noted with satisfaction that attendance at Hopalong Cassidy theatrical westerns rose sharply after the cowboy appeared on television. That strengthened their opinion that TV was turning out to tbe less of a threat to the box office.[13]

In 1951 Goldwyn declared that despite the box office decline Hollywood would survive and thrive because it was the best storyteller, had the most technical expertise, and so on. Therefore "television must turn to Hollywood for entertainment of a kind and quality it cannot itself produce; and we, on the other hand, will find through television, a large new audience." He did acknowledge that Hollywood's major studios "have, generally, fought or shied away from television." As well, he agreed Hollywood had bound its topflight performers who were under contract not to appear in that medium. He thought there was a sound reason for that: the studios didn't want to expose their glamorous stars to the flat lighting, the inadequate makeup, the imperfect cameras—all factors in early television—which made even the most glamorous film star look like an "anemic ghost" on a viewer's screen. And more importantly, the studios did not want "to give aid and comfort to their strongest competitor." They reasoned also that if a motion picture star was appearing on the home screen for nothing, "the family is not so apt to rush out to buy tickets to see him in a theater." In fact, concluded Goldwyn, "To my knowledge, none of the major production companies or principal independent producers in Hollywood has so far sold a foot of film to television."[14]

Business Week announced in 1951 that some movie men thought they might be able to use their lots to make new films specifically for television, and old films carried on the books at little or no value would bring in new revenue from television. One major problem with that idea, thought the business magazine, was the fact that "the $1-million-plus features made by

Hollywood are rarely suitable for home TV as we know it today, unless sponsors can be found who will pay huge fees for a few minutes of commercials. That's not likely; so some kind of subscription TV must be developed." However, estimating a base of 20 to 25 million television households in the near future, "how many could be relied upon to pay 50¢ or $1 to see a new pix— once the novelty has worn off—when they can see older ones for nothing." If some producers released their films to television, not just old ones, but movies only a few years old, would their attempts to push subscription television be affected, the magazine wondered. Such questions were indeed running through the minds of Hollywood moguls.[15]

When 30 delegates representing film exhibitors and film producers met in closed-door session in Hollywood in the summer of 1951 the topic was the present and potential impact of television on the film industry. Reportedly general agreement was reached on three points. One was that the industry had nothing to fear as long as it provided enough good products. A second point was the declaration that competition from television had by then reached its maximum. Lastly came the statement, "Films made expressly for theatrical distribution should not be funneled into television, nor should big-name personalities be encouraged to appear too frequently on video, because the public will tire of seeing them and thus their pictures will suffer at the box office."[16]

Early in 1952 RCA (parent of NBC-TV) board chair David Sarnoff expressed his annoyance over Hollywood sitting on its film assets. The longer Hollywood refused to sell its movies to television, the less valuable they would be, he argued. Those films would become more and more dated. Agreeing that people willingly watched airings of the old B films, Sarnoff believed that within a few short years viewers' standards would rise considerably, as television passed the novelty stage. He added, "I envision pictures produced especially for television as the real 'better entertainment' of TV's future. And if that comes to pass, as I think it must, these specially produced vidpix will prove Hollywood's stiffest competition."[17]

If, on the one hand, Hollywood was interested in getting a piece of the new medium, on the other hand, fear and loathing of television was another common reaction within Hollywood. Around 1950 Jack Warner reportedly banned the appearance of a television set in any Warner films. Stars were routinely banned from appearing on television. MGM and independent producer Stanley Kramer reached agreement in principle in 1950 whereby the studio would "loan-out" its contract actor Arlene Dahl to Kramer to appear in his movie *Cyrano de Bergerac*. When the actual contract drawing began MGM required the inclusion of a clause that Kramer would never permit his *Cyrano* to be transmitted on television. As a matter of principle Kramer declined to accept any outside limitations of his exhibition rights, and so the deal died. An MGM spokesman declared the television prohibition clause "is standard policy in all studio loanouts as protection for our players."[18]

Years later superstar Bette Davis recalled, "In all our studio contracts ... there was a little last line: 'You must have permission to go on television.'"[19]

Back in the 1940s Paramount treasurer Paul Raiburn said: When the telecasters are ready to buy films and can pay what that are worth, we will be ready to talk with them, but not for the mere glory of television." Expressing the same sentiment in 1955 was David Selznick who declared, "When television is willing to pay more than the amount made in reissues, then we'll go into television."[20]

Early in 1951 both the Justice Department and the FCC were actively looking into Hollywood's relations, or lack thereof, with television. Justice was then undertaking its own study of the studios' video ban. H. G. Morrison, Assistant Attorney General in charge of the department's antitrust section told the press that the film industry's attitude regarding the new medium was "a matter of continuing interest" to the government. Justice planned to keep its eye on the situation with a view to bringing antitrust action, if warranted, regarding "the Hollywood policy barring players and pix from TV."[21]

At the same time the FCC warned Hollywood producers to make their leading players and films available to television if they expected favorable consideration of their own bids to enter video as owners of stations. Executives in the film industry expressed astonishment that the FCC could expect them to come to the aid of their foremost competitor. It was all part of a process whereby the FCC was adopting a policy toward station applicants who had been convicted of antitrust violations. In its statement the agency said, "It has come to the commission's attention that many motion-picture companies refuse to make copies of their films available for use by television stations. Similarly, restrictions are imposed by these companies as to the appearance of actors under contract to the studios on television programs and to the use on television of stories or plays whose rights have been acquired by the studio." In the view of the FCC the success of television would depend to a large measure on the ability of stations to acquire the best films, talent and stories available. Without expressing an opinion whether such practices were or were not in violation of antitrust laws the FCC said that whether or not such practices were a violation of a law they were considered by the regulatory body to be relevant in determining the qualifications of applicants utilizing such practices.[22]

Editorializing on the matter the *New York Times* thundered that "The Federal Communications Commission has overreached itself," calling its position "an arbitrary and capricious action that flouts the elementary principles of a competitive economy and raises serious questions of law." Pointing out that Hollywood's least expensive film required a gross of $1 million or more to make a profit while the most expensive show on television then cost around $85,000 (for 90 minutes) the editorial concluded, "Apparently the F.C.C. is unconcerned, however, whether Hollywood goes broke in serving as the involuntary sugar daddy of television."[23]

Columnist Jack Gould pointed out another reason why Hollywood was not releasing actors to television, after agreeing that many did indeed impose such bans while others had no objection if the player "can take care of himself." A number of Hollywood stars, he thought, needed protection when it came to memorizing lines, ad libbing, picking a part that was not beyond their talents, or selecting a supporting cast. "The backstage trials of Hollywood have glamorized more than one personality who otherwise would be poison at the box office," said Gould. Hollywood was not anxious to trust such chores to parties without the same economic incentives to be careful.[24]

Late in 1951 independent producers James and George Nasser filed suit in U.S. District Court in Los Angeles against United Artists seeking to force it into selling some of their movies to television. Joining the Nassers in the suit was the Bank of America which attached assets of the Nassers in a bankruptcy proceeding the previous year. Involved in the dispute were 4 films, *Don't Trust Your Husband* (Fred McMurray), *Kiss for Corliss* (Shirley Temple), *Cover Up* (William Bendix) and *Without Honor* (Laraine Day). The Bank was acting to recover unpaid loans totaling $829,628. Plaintiffs' petition sought a ruling to affirm the right of the Nassers to sell the films for television exhibition. They contended their contract with UA as distributor provided that, in the event television became a commercial reality, the company would, after major sources of theatrical revenue had been exhausted, sell the films on the television market, or permit the Nassers to have the pictures sold in that fashion. UA had refused to do that, stated the petitioners.[25]

Dore Schary, MGM production head, was asked in 1953 about the release of old movies to television: "There isn't even any prospect that films will be taken off the shelf and dusted off for television reissue because video just can't pay enough. We probably couldn't even get more than $75,000 the way things are now. But if we re-release something like *Mutiny on the Bounty* to the theatres it would probably bring in upwards of $200,000."[26]

However, the firm resolve to withhold films was starting to weaken. At a Fox company stockholders' meeting in spring 1953 president Spyros Skouras told the meeting that the sale of Fox oldies to television was no more than a year away, maybe even less. It made Fox the first of the majors to announce plans of selling to the new medium, albeit with no details. Skouras thought the time would come as soon as 75 percent of the 2,500 to 3,000 theaters from which it got more than 80 percent of its revenue had been converted to Cinemascope. He said: "Up to this time, for our own sound business reasons, we have refrained from disposing of these pictures to television stations. However, with the advent of CinemaScope and other new techniques, it is anticipated that the theater demand for motion pictures will be generally for pictures of the new types. The demand for older pictures will greatly decrease for theatres. Therefore, it is likely these older pictures will then be made available to television." One other way Hollywood tried to fight television was with new production techniques in its theatrical releases ranging from items such as wide screen (cinemascope), to 3D effects, to casts of thousands (such as in *Ben Hur* or *The Alamo*). All were designed to produce an effect you could not experience in front of your television.[27]

Only independent producers were selling films to television, such as Republic, a prolific B producer. Practically all of the majors had had what were termed "fabulous offers" for their old movies. In its first 15 months of operation Republic's television arm had earned about $4 million. It was virtually all profit. The majors were getting interested.[28]

Contradicting that report somewhat were comments by Sylvester "Pat" Weaver, president of NBC, who said his network had been offered the backlog of two major studios but had declined to buy. He argued there was a revolt among local advertisers and viewers against the old movies that were on television being played over and over again and that stations were willing to take anything live the network had to offer in lieu of old pictures, "senile celluloid." Even if the majors were to try and unload their backlogs on the open market there would be no rush to buy them, thought Weaver. He quipped, "Old pictures never die, their audience slowly fades away." It was all, of course, head games, as the two sides jockeyed for psychological position and supremacy for negotiations between them which Hollywood and the television industry understood would take place between them sooner or later.[29]

External barriers to Hollywood releasing its product to television came primarily from the exhibitors and the talent unions. There was even a question over who owned the legal rights to Hollywood's old films for television as nothing was mentioned in contracts of the era. It was an issue that would not be clarified until a 1954 court decision ruled the studios did hold implied television rights to their films. When those old films were finally sold to television none of the money would go to any talent involved since none of those union contracts contained any mention of television either. In a major contract agreement reached in 1946 by the American Federation of Musicians (AFM) and the studios one clause prohibited the release to television of movies containing AFM-produced soundtracks made after that year, unless the films were rescored using AFM musicians. Or, of course, financial compensation of some sort was paid to the AFM. It was the first step for the talent unions in establishing their right to some of the revenue the studios would receive from television sales. In this case the AFM left the status of pre-1946 films unclear and controversial, in order to get the post-46 clause in the agreement.[30]

When independent producer Sam Bischoff tried to sell a package of four recent films to television in June 1950 (all were theatrically released between 1947 and 1949) he explained that any buyer had to clear the musical scores of the movies with the AFM by some agreement or replace the musical soundtracks with substitute "canned" recordings, over which the musicians' union had no contractual hold.[31]

Robert Lippert, another independent film producer and distributor, reached a precedent-setting agreement with AFM president James Petrillo in the spring of 1951, which would permit the release of films made for theaters to television. It was a deal open to any other producer who wanted to take it, although other producers were not bound to it. They could negotiate other terms with the AFM. Lippert's deal provided that musical scores of affected films be rerecorded for television and that the producer pay five percent of his video revenue to the AFM recording fund. The same number of musicians who recorded the track originally had to be used and they had to work the same amount of time. That newly recorded track had to be used on the television version even though it was exactly the same as the original score. Partly that was to comply with the Taft-Hartley law prohibition on featherbedding. Cost of rerecording the score on a dramatic film (as distinguished from a musical movie) varied from $2,500 to $11,000, depending on the length of the picture and number of musicians used. Lippert said he would immediately rerecord the music for 26 movies made in 1946, 1947 and 1948, for the 1951 television market.[32]

Within weeks of that deal being struck Petrillo came to terms with both Republic Pictures and Monogram studio on the same terms. Back in the fall of 1950 the AFM had flexed its muscle by prohibiting the scoring of any Monogram-produced movies because of an alleged breach of contract involving the release of a group of Monogram pictures to television, without an AFM agreement. For some seven months Monogram was unable to turn out any movies in its own name. As a consequence of the ban the studio had to rely on independent producers financed indirectly by the studio to maintain its flow of produce.[33]

During its contract negotiations with the producers in the late 1940s the Screen Actors Guild (SAG) had a clause inserted which provided that should a producer permit television use of its films made for the theaters and completed after August 1, 1948, SAG could notify its members not to work for him. As all Hollywood actors belonged to SAG it would have been impossible to operate under such a ban. Like the AFM, SAG left open the status of pre–48 films (pre–46 for the AFM). Both unions concentrated on the more recently made movies feeling those were the ones that would most likely be sold to television first. It proved to be a mistake as the producers would later come to financial terms for television release of post–48s, but at the price of the union abandoning monetary claims on the pre–48s. That, in turn, would lead the Hollywood studios to first offload all those pre–48s. Robert Lippert did indeed rescore and release those 26 movies, selling them to Los Angeles television station KTLA, then owed by Paramount Studios. All had been theatrically released within the previous five years. When SAG determined that four of the films were shot in 1949 and five in 1950 the union set out to enforce its clause preventing such release.[34]

The Screen Actors Guild notified Lippert in the fall of 1951 that it was canceling its contract with the producer, effective 60 days hence, because of violation of the television clause. As well SAG served notice on the film industry as a whole that the guild would stand firm. In its coming contract negotiations SAG would unsuccessfully seek an outright ban on television exhibition of movies made after August 1, 1948, until producers agreed to a formula by which performers would receive extra pay from income derived by producers from such showings.[35]

Although the majors held firm in refusing to offer the unions any share of television revenue from the sale of their theatrical movies they began to yield in other areas. Four majors entered into an agreement with SAG in 1952 recognizing the principle of additional payment to performers for repeat showings on television of material made especially for that medium. Columbia, Universal, RKO and Republic each had a wholly owned subsidiary then active in the making of material designed specifically for television showings; that is, series. While no specific sums of money were mentioned, or then negotiated, it marked the first time any of the majors publicly accepted the idea of actors sharing in revenue from repeat telecasts.[36]

Also opposed to the release to television of movies were some of the stars. Action by two of them would determine just where ownership rights resided. The stars were not actors from the lots of the majors, since they weren't releasing to television. Rather, they were cowboy stars from Republic studios. When Republic announced it was set to offer 52 of Roy Rogers's old films to television, along with those of other western stars, including Gene Autry, the two men were no longer employed at Republic. Rogers filed suit against the producer in Los Angeles Federal Court in June 1951, asking for an injunction to restrain Republic from selling or licensing his old films for video transmission on the grounds that their use under commercial sponsorship would involve the "name or likeness of Roy Rogers and his horse Tigger," in commercial advertising. Attorneys for the western star had obtained a preliminary order against Republic temporarily halting any sale. Rogers alleged Republic's announcement of its intention to sell the old movies had damaged him and had caused cancellation of his radio program. Rogers was about to produce a series for television in which he would also star and telecasting of old Republic pictures would seriously interfere with the success of that enterprise, he argued. His old films on television would make it appear he was endorsing the products involved. Thus it would greatly damage a business he himself had built up in merchandising and advertising tie-ins, which for years had produced substantially more income than his films, said Rogers.[37]

Within days of the launch of the Rogers suit, Autry said he would also take legal action to prevent the showing of his Republic pictures on television. Autry made 72 westerns for the studio between 1934 and 1945. At the time of his suit he was producing and starring in his own television western series, then carried on 90 stations.[38]

Late in 1951 Judge Pierson Hall granted a permanent injunction to Rogers preventing Republic from selling or licensing any of his old Republic films for use on television. Hall held that while under contract to that studio Rogers had reserved his right to control the association of his name with the sale or advertising of any commercial product. When Autry launched his suit, in addition to causes of action cited by Rogers, he contended that Republic together with all the Hollywood studios, had conspired to require actors in signing contracts with the producing companies to surrender all rights, among them television rights, as a condition of employment, in violation of the Sherman Anti-Trust Act. Also, Autry argued the quality of films on television suffered from editing, commercial interruptions, and so on, damaging his image.[39]

District Court Judge Ben Harrison denied Autry's petition in 1952, ruling his position to be "untenable" and "unfair" in seeking to prevent Republic "from enjoying the full share of the profits to be derived from said photoplays." Seemingly this contradicted the Rogers's decision. One difference was that Rogers did have a specific clause reserving his right to commercial use of his name while Autry did not. The latter had a far more standard contract. In any case the losers in both cases appealed.[40]

In mid-1954 the U.S. Court of Appeals (Ninth District, San Francisco) cleared the way for Republic to release to television a group of Rogers and Autry movies. Distinctive points of contracts and interpretations were involved. Rogers's victory was reversed when the Court held, on the basis of contracts between Rogers and Republic signed in 1937 and 1948, that the company was entitled to exercise its "ownership and rights to the product of the artist's employment, whether or not such exercise involves exhibition of the subject's motion pictures in connection with commercial advertising." When Autry lost at the lower level Judge Harrison ruled, with regard to the quality of the films aired on television, that Republic had the right "to cut, edit and otherwise revise and to license others (to do likewise) ... in any manner, to any length and for any purpose..." The appeals court approved that judgment, with minor modifications. Those prevented Republic from editing the movies to less than 53 minutes of running time, from presenting them as other than feature films, or from permitting them to be exhibited in connection with advertising in a manner which would suggest that Autry endorsed the product of the sponsors of the show. Generally, this decision established that studios had clear title to movies to present them on television in connection with advertising—in the absence of specific contractual clauses to the contrary—and that they had a very broad right to edit them in most any fashion they chose.[41]

When the U.S. Supreme Court declined to hear the appeal of either Roy Rogers or Gene Autry, in October 1954, it let the above rulings stand.[42]

Opposition to sales of movies to television was most vocal from the exhibitors. At a 1949 board meeting of the Theater Owners of America a report prepared by a committee from that organization studying the impact of television recommended, "All producing and distributing companies be counseled by this association in the strongest terms that a grave danger and injustice would be presented should television be provided with motion picture film designed and created for exhibition in motion picture theatres."[43]

When *Life* magazine wondered in a 1952 editorial why Hollywood was not selling its old movies to television it answered its question by saying that cinema owners were exerting a "deadening influence" on its behavior: "they have banded together and threatened any producing company that furnishes feature films—old or new—to TV."[44]

The Pacific Coast Conference of Independent Theatre Owners adopted the usual resolution opposing the release to television of any theatrical film product, regardless of age. Going a little further, they also urged producers to prevent their contract players from appearing too often on television programs.[45]

When Republic leased 104 movies to New York City station WCBS for a total of $200,000 for a number of runs, exhibitors called it a "stab in the back." Harry Brandt, who owned an area theater circuit, demanded that Republic lease movies to his chain on the same basis; that is, $2,000 per title. Brandt stated he resented Republic "for taking pictures away from the people who made it possible for the studio to make pictures." If Republic didn't get film rental revenue from cinemas where would it get the money to produce pictures and accumulate the backlog it was then selling to television, Brandt mused.[46]

When Republic began to offer and to sell large lots of films to television one cinema owner suddenly announced a boycott of Republic theatrical releases. Claiming several chains were going to join in, the unnamed theater chain head called it a coincidence. "If there were any concert in the action, the theatremen certainly weren't admitting it," reported one account. Any concerted boycott could open them to a conspiracy charge. Said the cinema owner: "I've ordered my buyers and bookers to keep hands off the product of companies that have been selling to television. I haven't talked to any other exhibs on the subject, but I've heard through the grapevine that a lot of others are doing the same thing. If we get charged with conspiracy, that will be too bad. But at least we'll be alive to defend ourselves. If we don't do anything there will be no charges against us because we won't even be in business. I think the time has come for action." Despite the brave talk, no boycott took place.[47]

Although exhibitors often thundered about the dire consequences that would befall any producer who released to television it was noted by observers that Republic didn't appear to have suffered to any extent from exhibitor retaliation in the wake of its decision to do business with television. Republic president Herbert Yates commented, "One or two (exhibs) complained but we pay no attention to these complaints at all." Such threats from exhibitors were only rhetoric. Hollywood's majors took 90-some percent of the U.S. box office receipts, leaving Republic and all the others to divide up the remainder. Cinema owners could not afford to actually boycott any of the majors, which would cut their own throats. Any sort of boycott would hurt both sides but the majors were richer and could hold out longer. Exhibitors could have launched a boycott against a small outfit like Republic (which was destined to go out of business in a few years) but it didn't even have the heart or the solidarity for that fight. Hollywood's majors liked, however, to use exhibitor pressure as one reason for not selling to television. It could be used to deflect any governmental suggestion it was conspiring to deny product.[48]

Just before the majors did execute their first sale to television in 1955 some exhibitors worried about other potential Hollywood involvement with the home screen. Said one exhibitor: "But aren't we hurt just as much if a Warner Bros. or a 20th–Fox comes along and creates some sort of 'super' show for a network? The ultimate effect, almost regardless what the studios decide to put on the air, is still going to be the same. The better the show, the more people will stay home… How can the majors play both sides against the middle?" Another exhibitor was philosophical: If the majors didn't get into series production for television somebody else would. At least if the majors did it, he hoped, they might use the big profits to make better theatrical movies.[49]

Although the majors released nothing to television until 1955 movies were a part of television programming from the beginning. Given the wholly commercial nature of American television ecomomic forces drove stations to longer and longer broadcast days. Without feature films to fill time slots that process would have been slowed considerably. The fact that movies were available meant that stations could and would move relatively quickly to 24-hour-a-day, 7-day-a-week programming. In that early period the only movies available to television consisted of westerns, B films produced by "Poverty Row" studios such as Republic and Monogram, a few A pictures from independents and some foreign fare, virtually all from the U.K.

In New York City in mid–1950 distributors charged a station anywhere from $200 to $800 to rent a feature for one run. The price depended on the age of the product, its stars, how it had been received in cinemas, how many times it had been shown on television, whether it was to be sponsored, the number of television sets in the area and, perhaps most importantly, "how much money the distributor can shake loose from the station." *Cheers for Miss Bishop*, which had opened theatrically at Radio City Music Hall in 1941 had shown up on New York television stations six times within the three years ending in 1950, commanding a fluctuating rental fee. On August 7, 1947, WABD had telecast it for $150; June 1, 1948, WNBT $400; August 20, 1948, WPIX $200; November 25, 1948, WJZ-TV $800; August 30, 1949, WABD $250; March 6, 1950, WCBS-TV $325. One of the more popular items on television were the Hopalong Cassidy western movies. One Los Angeles station rented one of the titles for $250. One year later the station repeated the movie for the fifth time, and had to pay $1,000. William Boyd (Hopalong) controlled the television rights to 54 of his old features which were being repeated again and again. The rights to several more would revert to him that year and into the future. Most of the independently produced films were released for cinemas through one of the majors. The contracts stipulated that after a certain amount of time (usually three years during which the distributor controlled all the film rights) the rights reverted to the producer. He was then free to market it himself, or through another distributor. Rights were time-defined in contracts because the majors felt that after three years from theatrical release, usually earlier, a feature simply had no value left in it. That was generally true, before television. With a fair amount of competition among film sellers, and a relatively small number of stations, price cutting could result in a movie being obtained for as little as $35, but not in a market the size of New York or Los Angeles. Some stations shopped on budget alone simply notifying a distributor that they needed, for example, "a $100 picture." At that time Newark, New Jersey, station WATV was on the air 77 hours a week with about 70 percent of that time used for feature films. Using 40 movies each week (15 of them westerns) meant WATV went through a total of 2,080 films per year. Hollywood was then producing well under 500 titles a year.[50]

Even if those TV movies were old and obscure ratings were said to be good. Plenty of advertisers came forward and commercial rates were increasing. CBS network's flagship station in New York City, WCBS (owned and operated by CBS) was running the *Late Show* from 11:15 P.M. until station closing, seven nights a week. It was a ratings leader with a total of 27 different ad spots sold per week. The non-movie program that had previously held the time period had never sold more than 13 ad spots per week. Movies programmed were a group of Eagle Lion releases, vintage 1946-1949. The show took pride that it had "ruled out the lengthy pitchman commercials usually associated with old films on TV, concentrating instead on short spots at the rate of not more than one every 20 minutes." It might be that WCBS would pay $2,500 per film for one run but a country-wide average, circa March 1951, would be $500 to $750 for one run on one station for good "first-run" product. A movie aired before, if brought back for a repeat showing, would cost $300 to $450. Western movies were the cheapest to obtain, commanding around $150 to $200.[51]

In one of the largest deals of the time Republic sold 175 features and serials to Los Angeles outlet KPTZ. Reportedly the package went for $225,000 giving KPTZ the right to show each of the films twice during a one year span. No Gene Autry or Roy Rogers movies were included in the deal, which worked out to $1,285 on average per title, $643 per run, edited to fit a one hour time slot.[52]

Columnist Jack Gould pointed out a growing trend to telecast more British films on U.S. television. Estimates were that English films accounted for at least 20 percent of feature-length films shown on some stations in the larger cities. Overall the U.S. figure was believed to be about ten percent. By contrast the percentage of British movies in cinemas "is barely measureable," something under one percent. Some of those U.K. films were of 1949 and 1950 vintage; there was even a sampling of 1951 productions—this in 1951 itself. Included was product from prominent U.K. producers such as J. Arthur Rank and Alexander Korda. For the better class of U.K. imports upwards of $20,000 could be realized in a year of sales to U.S. outlets, from the existing 107 stations. Ratings of even those imported films were consistently good, although they did poorly in the South and Southwest. That gave Hollywood something to worry about. It didn't want to see imported movies gain any kind of permanent foothold on American television.[53]

By mid–1952 nearly every station in America was telecasting movies, virtually all in the late night hours, starting around 11 P.M. Ratings continued high city-by-city across the country. WCBS was then paying as high as $4,000 per film in order to screen it three to four times over an eight-month span. In Los Angeles, outlets paid up to $6,000 while in Cincinnati stations paid up to $2,000. Ratings climbed rather than diminished during reruns. Regarding commercial rates WCBS was getting $400 per "interruption." Some stations were running spotlight ads in the daily papers to announce specific titles, and even bigger ads for blockbusters.[54]

Another large sale, at the end of 1952, saw WCBS pay Republic $200,000 for 104 movies (still no Autry or Rogers titles). By then the station was running three regular film shows, the *Early Show*, *Late Matinee* and *Late Show*. Under their programming setup WCBS rotated each movie through each of the different programs, putting off reruns in a specific time slot. That way the station hoped "to escape the mounting squawks from viewers about being forced to watch repeats of features." According to station film buyer David Savage the scarcity of available features for television was a problem and one that required consistent scrounging to get new material.[55]

When the Bank of America leased 30 films to the General Teleradio chain of stations in 1954 it marked the highest price ever paid for television features. The bank, which had gained control of the titles through various bankruptcy proceedings, leased the movies for four years for $1.25 million, an average of about $42,000 per title. Until then about 3,000 movies had been shown on television, almost all at prices of $20,000 or less, usually much less. Horrified by the amount of trashy movies on television, and the escalating prices, writer Hugh Garner commended, "We shudder to think what might be the result if Howard Hughes should sell a thousand old RKO movies to TV, but it will be worse still if MGM should ever unload its collection of Technicolored junk on the unsuspecting home viewer." Garner continued, "We warn the prospective sponsors of these old movies that we will never use their products again if such films appear on our television screens, even if it means riding a bicycle, brushing our teeth with baking soda and washing our neck with home-made soap."[56]

During one week in March 1955 New York City television stations telecast 91 movies. Pittsburgh's KDKA-TV ran films through the night. If there were any doubts within the television or film industries about the public's tolerance for repeats they were all put to rest by the practices of one New York outlet, WOR, with its *Million Dollar Movie* program. It showed the same movie 16 times each week, twice each evening in primetime, 7 days a week, with an afternoon airing added on Saturdays and Sundays. Over the course of one week more than 84 percent of New York's 4.5 million television households confessed that they had, during that week, caught one of the airings of the *Million Dollar Movie*. Assessing the quality of those features on television the magazine declared, "As a group, though, they run to the biggest lot of turkeys, American or British, to be found outside a barnyard... But whether station bosses counted on mass idiocy or a growing national fear of going to bed, they seemed to have no doubts that the pictures were being watched." One station film buyer was thinking of stopping the search for a good movie. He had decided it may have been a waste of money: "There'll always be somebody who hasn't seen a certain movie and doesn't care how bad it is. For free, people will sit though anything—more than once, too."[57]

Also in March 1955 Republic announced it was releasing to television 123 western movies originally produced at a total cost of $25 million. It was the largest block of films ever released to the new medium. Included were 56 titles starring Gene Autry and 67 with Roy Rogers. Distribution was handled by MCA-TV which grew, from its television activities, to the point years later where it would buy up Universal Studios. All those films had been reedited for hour-long programming. Television's hour was then about 53 minutes long. Republic's B pictures, as with all B movies, tended in theatrical release to range from 60 to 70 minutes.[58]

The amount of money films could realize from television sales was mounting dramatically. In 1955 Television Programs of America (TPA, an independent distributor) had a package of 27 features which had grossed $2,575,000 over the previous four years, $95,000 per title. Still grossing some $32,000 per month as a package, the average per title was expected to pass the $100,000 mark before year's end. When General Teleradio struck its well-publicized deal 18 months earlier, paying an average of $42,000 per title, "the trade scoffed," feeling the company would never recover its costs. Yet General Teleradio earned back its investment the first time around. TPA's package had by then played on 114 outlets (255 were on the air), with reruns in most. The package was then playing in 58 markets. Most of the 100 or so untouched markets were small ones. Television was then about 50 percent live, 50 percent taped, down from close to 100 percent live five years earlier.[59]

Chapter 2

Hollywood Launches Its Assets, 1940s–1955

> *[Movies on TV can] "easily set back the standards of TV five or ten years."*
> Frederic Ziv,
> Ziv Television, 1956.

> *[Pay-TV] "ultimately would mean the end of our American system of free television."*
> David Sarnoff,
> NBC, 1955

Although Hollywood was not selling any movies to television it was not ignoring the new medium. From early on it tried to buy into television station ownership, and to develop commercial alternatives to television, namely theater TV and subscription TV. Back in 1938 Paramount acquired a sizable interest in the Allen B. DuMont Laboratories to direct DuMont research and experimentation in the direction of theater TV. During the 1940s Paramount operated the first experimental station in Chicago and the first commercial station in Los Angeles. Following that studio's lead Warner, MGM and Fox all filed petitions with the FCC during the war years to own stations in the major markets.[1]

By 1945 Paramount had a financial stake in a couple of companies which manufactured television equipment as well as holding valuable patents covering the projection of large-sized TV images on theater screens. Its subsidiary,

Television Productions, Inc., then operated stations WGXYZ and WGXLA in Los Angeles. Pending with the FCC was Paramount's application for two nationwide experimental relay networks. If approved, the plan was to test the feasibility of a relay service that would bring major news and special events to cinema audiences as they happened. Fox had recently set up a TV department while its ownership application lay pending, and RKO had also just set up a TV department. Warner purchased a tract of land near Hollywood for the erection of a television studio and transmitter as it had received permission a few months earlier to erect a commercial television station. Pending applications with the FCC by MGM would have provided the studio with four TV stations, one each in Los Angeles, Chicago, Washington, and New York City, if the FCC approved.[2]

In the early years the majors declined to produce any material for television. A major reason was the problem of cost. One half-hour program made for television in 1949 by the independent producers cost from $5,000 to $8,000, a cost they were having trouble recovering in the TV market. By comparison, Hollywood's majors were geared up to production costs on the order of $1 million for 90 minutes worth of entertainment. One reporter observed that production of even a short feature for less than $50,000 "would manifestly call for extreme belt-tightening and even then would be out of present reach." And, of course, Hollywood first wanted to buy into television, or develop viable alternatives, before merely producing for the rival.[3]

By 1949 some of the majors were making more aggressive moves to try and buy into station control. The MGM studio was exploring a move into the Mutual television network while at the same time Fox was rumored to have reopened talks with ABC. Previous negotiations had collapsed with a major reason being that Fox couldn't get past the FCC in view of the antitrust overtones such a merger conjured up. If those deals had come to pass it was a foregone conclusion that the other majors would certainly follow suit. The potential MGM deal was seen as one that would solve Mutual's current programming dilemma—it couldn't find enough—by putting at the network's disposal the whole roster of MGM personalities, thus giving Mutual a cheaper source of name talent as MGM "would program the network."[4]

While the FCC had granted a few early ownership applications to the majors most of them were put on hold as the FCC decided it was best to await the resolution of the antitrust action then in progress against the majors. When the Supreme Court upheld the monopoly charges against the majors in 1948 the repercussions killed any chance the film industry ever had of moving into television broadcasting in any substantial way. The FCC imposed rules limiting ownership of stations to a maximum of five outlets. Forming a network was then impossible since most of the major cities needed to define a true national network had only three outlets—part of the FCC's allocation procedure—some had only two. Three networks were then functioning, ABC,

NBC, and CBS. Since the FCC's intent was clear the majors all withdrew their license applications by around 1950.⁵

As early as 1945 the majors had been ruled out of the game. Chairman of the FCC Paul Porter warned a meeting of executives from all the major movie companies that they "should not count on extensive ownership and control in the postwar television industry."⁶

The first commercial alternative to be explored was theater television. A type of large-screen TV, it would show original programs shot by a television camera on the outside then transmitted by coaxial cable or microwave relays to cinemas equipped with special television pickups. Through their ownership of first-run theaters (exploration of this option began before the court-ordered divestment) and theater television Hollywood hoped to appropriate television as a source of profits. At war's end there were in the neighborhood of 18,000 movie houses in America. Dreamers envisioned cinemas forming regional and national networks to present news, concerts, opera, Broadway plays, sports events such as major league baseball, and even educational programs for schools. Two major systems were experimented with, one by RCA and one by Paramount. At the start of 1949 *U.S. News & World Report* stated, when it detailed the hard times in Hollywood, "By 1952, most important theaters are expected to be equipped with television screens."⁷

One year later Harry Brandt, owner of 153 cinemas and president of the Independent Theatre Owners of America admitted television constituted "the worst opposition to movie theatres in history" and that it had substantially decreased the box office receipts. However, he predicted the new medium would become the greatest boon to the film industry since the coming of sound. Predicting a wedding between the two industries, Brandt said, "When television is able to present programs good enough to serve as added attractions in the theatre, we'll have the greatest boom in history." He predicted all cinemas would soon install coaxial cable so that such items as news and sports could be piped into cinemas "as a cost-free addition." At that time he felt, "There is nothing on TV at present that people will pay out pocket money to see."⁸

Equally optimistic about theater television's prospects was Samuel Goldwyn. He acknowledged its advent would likely mean the death of the B pictures in theaters. Several movie houses were then offering theater television to the public. The Brooklyn Fox had presented seven shows in nine weeks while New York's Paramount had screened over 75 events since installing television equipment 18 months earlier. For Goldwyn the key lay in having different events on theater television than were carried at home. One example he cited was the 1949 World Series whose exclusive, nationwide television rights had been sold for $200,000 to one of the TV networks. Goldwyn argued that 200 television-equipped movie houses could profitably meet that price ($1,000 each) while 1,000 cinemas could pay $1 million for the rights.

Baseball commissioner A. B. Chandler expressed a belief "that nothing can stop the development of World Series television on theatre screens." Goldwyn, however, understood the political ramifications of no free baseball on the tube might preclude that development.[9]

Seeing even greater possibilities was Fox president Spyros Skouras who declared in his April 1950 speech before a convention of the Society of Motion Picture and Television Engineers that, by linking fortunes the two industries would launch a "golden era for theatres unlike any they have ever known." He foresaw four or five competing theater television networks in New York, Chicago, Denver, Atlanta and Los Angeles to service from 500 to 1,000 cinemas in each circuit. Television material would be an extra, replacing the second film (Bs) in double features. "Through theatre television the finest productions of all the greatest talents on earth will be brought within the means of every citizen in every village and hamlet. The effects will be worldwide," enthused the mogul. Predicting cinema attendance would be tripled in a short time Skouras added "audiences will pay for professional big-league stuff even though they can see sandlot performances free of charge at home."[10]

Apparently optimism for theater television was limitless in 1950. Speaking for the Theatre Owners of America, consultant Nathan Halpern acclaimed theater television for its future potential. Suddenly the heady predictions started to worry Hollywood. Speaking for the majors, industry executive William Perlberg fretted that if theater television could mean so much to the box office then "exhibitors will be in a position to push us around... How can we get top rentals on our best product if theater TV holds that position?" Trying to soothe the situation Halpern responded: "Nobody knows how to turn out pictures as well as you. The quality of your pictures, consequently, will enable them to hold their position as the fundamental lure at the box office, with theater TV only as a supplement to the features." Like other theater television enthusiasts Halpern saw theater TV bringing to cinemas such events as Broadway plays, national sports events, special television productions "and other outstanding stuff."[11]

Late in 1950 at a session of the Theatre Owners of America most of the talk was about theater television. Approved was a resolution urging exhibitors to investigate television opportunities and to "participate in the development of television, wherever possible." Prompting all the hype was yet another cinema box office slump. During the long box office decline there were periods when the decline seemed to have stabilized, leading to hope among exhibitors that the worst was over, only to have attendance turn downward anew, leading to more panic. In pinning their hopes on theater television, exhibitors were ignoring a couple of main points. In television-mad New York the box office was off, but it was down equally in Honolulu, where there was no television at all. A comparison of television and non-television cities found the same general results; slumps were about equal. While there were some 17,000 cinemas in the country in late 1950 only 16 of them had spent the estimated $25,000 needed to install large-screen television equipment. As a box office draw theater television was doing poorly. In Chicago nobody stood in line for the special events that Balaban and Katz was showing on its circuit. Nobody had any real idea of what the programming should be to keep material on the theater television screen day-in, day-out.[12]

Although it was an idea that was dying, Fox went ahead in 1952 and acquired the U.S. rights to a Swiss system known as Eidophor, a large-screen color theater television. At a public demonstration of the experimental system Skouras stressed its potential "as a part of regular motion picture theatre entertainment."[13]

By 1952 the number of cinemas with theatre television, or definite plans to convert, reached, at most, 100. That was well under one percent of the existing movie houses. Afterward it disappeared. As a closed circuit system the public airwaves were not involved, so no FCC permission was needed to operate the system. However, transmission costs were higher than had been anticipated, which led to fewer cinemas signing up and less money with which to bid for sports events against the networks. One solution to transmission costs lay in allocating a part of the much-underutilized UHF spectrum known as the "movie band" to theater television. Film industry representatives petitioned the FCC in 1949 for ten to twelve channels. Hearings were held in 1952 and 1953, but once again the FCC denied the applications on the ground of the industry's past monopolistic practices. It hardly mattered since events had already rendered it obsolete. Theater television did not address the fact that people didn't go to the cinema nearly as often as they had in the past, and never would again. They didn't go due to changes in lifestyle, such as moving to suburbs, other entertainment alternatives, and so on, not just what was or was not playing at the cinema. More time and effort went into the other commercial alternative, known as toll television, or subscription television. Its focus was on the home. If people would not go to Hollywood's box office at the local movie house then Hollywood would take it to them by installing a box office in every home.[14]

Those subscription television experiments were all forerunners of what we know today as pay-per-view. Each system was designed to charge each household for each item it watched. And while various types of events were foreseen on the schedules they were to be dominated by, of course, Hollywood films. The first such system was the brainchild of the Zenith Radio Corporation, known as "Phonevision," which had filed with the FCC as early as 1949 for permission to test its system in Chicago. Meeting in Hollywood at the start of 1950 for a conference with film industry executives was Zenith president Eugene McDonald, who predicted that phonevision "will save the film industry financially unless somebody fumbles the ball." With signals transmitted over the phone lines McDonald explained that the necessary "black box" in the home would cost around $10. "You will call the central operator, give your phone number and your choice of pictures being shown that night. When you receive your phone bill it will include a charge of about $1 for the screening." A movie ticket then cost an average of 48.5¢ in America. Estimates by McDonald were that the film industry could draw more than $500 million a year from phonevision, roughly $10 million per week, versus $33 million a week from cinemas.[15]

Around that time the FCC issued a permit for a test of phonevision, slated to run for 90 days in Chicago starting on September 15, 1950. For the test a television set would be placed without charge in 300 homes of varied income levels in the Chicago area. Said households were to be selected by a television/film committee. A different film would be shown on each of the 90 consecutive nights, transmitted by Zenith station KS2XBS using television channel 2. Zenith claimed to have done its own survey of 25,000 phone subscribers in 25 large cities finding that four out of five phone subscribers expressed a willingness to pay $1 to see a first-run film at home. The company had signed a contract with Illinois Bell agreeing to pay them $70,000 for billing services and use of the phone lines for that 90-day experiment. Right after the announcement of the FCC green light the Allied States Association of Motion Picture Exhibitors Television Committee declared phonevision "the greatest threat to (theater) exhibition to date." On the other hand *Daily Variety* enthused that this "may provide the opening up of the hugest market for motion pictures in history." McDonald explained that 50 percent of the receipts would go to the film producer, 25 percent to the phone company and 25 percent to the television broadcaster. Many in Hollywood saw this type of development as opening up a whole new market of perhaps 40 to 50 million Americans who never went to the movies—"elderly, phobics, frail, obese, handicapped, those who live in isolated areas." However, cold water was thrown on the project when the trade publication *Film Daily* reported the majors would not make their films available to phonevision for two reasons; fear of antagonizing exhibitors, and the existence of a clause in the industry's basic agreement with the AFM prohibiting the use of films' sound tracks on television. In fact, McDonald's early efforts to obtain 90 "important" movies from Hollywood had been "coolly received." So cool in fact that McDonald abandoned long distance negotiations to travel directly to Hollywood. After that visit all he said was that, before the slated September 15 startup, Hollywood—"which really will benefit the most from all this"—will come through. Zenith's main interest was in the hardware end, selling those black boxes and, of course, more television sets.[16]

Around March 1, 1950, RKO became the first of the majors to formally decline to supply movies for Phonevision when it sent a letter to that effect to McDonald. In his reply letter he argued the demand for films via Phonevision would give Hollywood "at least three times the market they have ever been able to reach via theatres alone." He concluded: "Your industry had better try out the new lifeboat, Phonevision, before your ship sinks any further and leaves you floundering."[17]

It did no good as, some ten weeks later, McDonald was forced to announce his Phonevision test might be delayed because all the majors had refused to rent their films to him even though Zenith had offered to pay the same rate as a conventional cinema with a comparable audience. If enough "acceptable" pictures were not made available it would be impossible to demonstrate to the FCC that the operation of Phonevision would be in the public interest, and that people wanted it and were willing to pay a fee "to see high class television programs in their homes," lamented the executive. Acceptable movies meant, of course, product from the majors. McDonald had not even contacted any independent producers. If all eight majors declined to sign on, the project was dead.[18]

Citing the AFM contract as a reason not to supply movies to Phonevision was being relied on by the majors to meet any legal challenges McDonald might try and mount. Reportedly, during negotiations, he suggested the possibility of charging conspiracy in an antitrust proceeding if all the majors refused to let him have product.[19]

Further negotiations did take place with the result that Phonevision launched its test in Chicago on January 1, 1951, some 3½ months late. That experiment was made possible by the "cooperation of major Hollywood studios." Why Hollywood changed its mind went unrecorded but may have had something to do with the fact that Hollywood still had various applications pending with the FCC and didn't wish to antagonize that agency, or the Justice Department (where divestment plans still had to be approved). Three hundred families were involved with the charge being $1 per movie. Three films were shown each day, at 4 P.M., 7 P.M. and 9 P.M. On the second day the 4 P.M. film moved to 7 P.M., on the third day it went to 9 P.M., then disappeared the next day. Each day a new film was added in the 4 P.M. slot. On January 1 the three movies telecast, in time slot order, were: *April Showers* (a 1947 musical starring Jack Carson), *Welcome Stranger* (1948, Bing Crosby) and *Homecoming* (1948, Clark Gable and Lana Turner). All three were produced in the previous three years and had earned an aggregate of $12 million at the box office. More broadly, the Phonevision test was to determine if the public was willing to pay for premium entertainment in the home, first-run films, Broadway plays, sports events and other items for which "people are accustomed to pay an admission charge." One worry was that even the best movies, on a pay basis, would receive strong competition from the best free features on sponsored television. There were no commercials on Phonevision. There also weren't a lot of viewers. Technically the system was too complex with too many problems. Zenith had had too many difficulties in securing the few films it did get. Phonevision had dialed a wrong number.[20]

A second system was called Skiatron. It was developed by Matthew Fox, with the help of IBM. Skiatron developed a method called Subscribervision which was based on a punch card to be inserted into a top-of-the-television black box. A home viewer could consult a printed catalog of the film schedule, set a few dials to the appropriate numbers on the black box, then insert his card to be punched. Cards were mailed back to the company for subsequent billing, in exchange for the next month's listings and cards were mailed to the home viewers. This system never made it to the testing stage and disappeared after its fifteen minutes of notice, if not fame.[21]

Biggest of the systems by far was Telemeter. Developed by outside companies, Paramount bought a controlling 50 percent interest in the system for $350,000, around 1951. This system also featured a black box on top of the television. Coins were inserted into the box at the appropriate time, which unscrambled a signal allowing the home set to bring in the picture. At the end of the month the black boxes were collected (another one was left) containing the money and an electronic tape recording indicating what movies the home had watched. No phone lines were required but the system did need its own channel or the temporary use of an already established channel on a rental basis. As Paramount conducted research on the system, it came to think there might not be any reason why the same movies couldn't be used in both television and cinemas at the same time. Paramount was thinking of letting an exhibitor in each town be its franchise holder for the sale and servicing of Telemeter equipment—a move it thought might be helpful in holding down opposition.[22]

In the fall of 1953 Paramount announced the long-awaited Telemeter test of films running concurrently in cinemas and on television was slated for November 1, 1953, in the California desert community of Palm Springs. About 100 miles outside of Hollywood itself the community was a favorite winter spot for Hollywood stars. International Telemeter Corporation stated that 400 homes in the community had been wired to receive the closed-circuit telecasts. Paramount, of course, supplied all the movies. Additionally Telemeter was lining up sports events such as football games locally blacked out to commercial television. But the test was to find out one thing only, public acceptance, or lack thereof, for the concept of paying for movies screened at home. Cooperating in the venture was the Earle C. Strebe cinema circuit in Palm Springs—it owned all three of the city's theaters. Television showings of the films started fifteen minutes after they began screening at the cinema. That allowed the film to be "bicycled" reel-by-reel from the movie house to the television transmitter site.[23]

Telemeter's experiment began a little late, on November 28, 1953. However, it started with only 71 sets connected. By the end of February, 1954, 148 households were hooked up to the system, out of 614 homes there. Films were shown twice nightly at a price of $1 per movie—higher than at the theater. Earle Strebe claimed that so far there had been no appreciable effects on his business.[24]

As toll television got more publicity, exhibitors took stands against it that were more and more vocal. A "stop toll-television" fight was organized by the Theatre Owners of America (TOA) and the Allied States Association of Motion Picture Exhibitors, the two biggest national organizations. The Southern California Theatre Owners Association claimed box office television would give a "favored few" licensed broadcasters "absolute control of the media" and that those favored few would acquire a "national monopoly of the motion picture exhibition business." Paramount maintained a discreet silence. Eugene McDonald reappeared to chide the theater owners in a statement which read, in part, "It should be borne in mind that this astonishing defense of free TV is something new under the sun, since it comes from the same group that has fought TV all the way, even to the point of threatening to boycott producers who release films to television."[25]

At a TOA convention late in 1954 the exhibitors continued to demand the FCC put a stop to toll-television (the agency would have to approve the concept but had not then even indicated when it might take the matter up) arguing in favor of the public's "inalienable" right to have television entertainment "without cost." Their opposition, of course, was not to box office television per se, but to where the box office was located. They had not opposed in principle theater television, which left the box office where it was. Toll television promised to move it to the home.[26]

Telemeter shut down the Palm Springs experiment temporarily in the summer of 1954, supposedly because many of the residents moved away during the summer heat. When it didn't restart that fall Telemeter insisted again it was only "temporary" and denied toll television had failed in Palm Springs. The company claimed "subscription television is better than ever." Paul McNamara, Telemeter executive, explained the system had not restarted because of a "shortage of first-run movies." Paramount was the only studio to allow Telemeter to use its movies.[27]

Contributing to the downfall was the steep installation charge which ranged from $150 to $450 (depending on the home's location), a "wire charge" of $60 a year, a one-time fee of $21.75 for the Telemeter box and a minimum of $3 per month in movie buys. Although the downtown Palm Springs cinemas were part of the test, opposition soon arose from local drive-in owners who charged Paramount/Telemeter with violation of the then still-very-recent antitrust divestiture decree. Those exhibitors charged that Paramount "is in the position of making the pictures, distributing the pictures, and is also acting as an exhibitor in the guise of Telemeter Corporation—the very thing that the government fought for over ten years to prevent in the distribution of motion pictures." When the system closed, Telemeter claimed the trial had been a success, reaching 2,500 subscribers and generating revenue of $10 per household per month.[28]

The FCC did move to hold hearings on toll television, with the last day for filing submissions with them being in mid-1955, just around the time of the majors first films' sale to TV. Making it unanimous for the three commercial networks NBC board chair David Sarnoff strongly condemned what he called "no fee—no see" television. Free television would be endangered and that "ultimately would mean the end of our American system of free television." He added it would be tragic for the FCC to authorize "dollar video" which would "cripple this great democratic medium for the free dissemination of ideas, education and entertainment to all the people of America." Regarding the recent alliance between Hollywood majors and toll television (meaning Paramount and Telemeter), Sarnoff told the FCC it was worrisome: "We believe it would be fatal to the continued dynamic growth of television to enable Hollywood to dominate and control television programming." By this time there was so much public heat about fee television—most of it was against the concept—that it was temporarily buried by its proponents. The time was not right and there were technical problems. Toll television may have appeared dead by 1955, but it would resurrect.[29]

While Hollywood was refusing to sell its movies to television and while it was attempting to develop alternatives, it moved to embrace television in other ways, by allowing stars to appear on the new medium and by producing series. Helping to lead the way were actors from the Poverty Row studios. If anything the additional exposure from series work on television by western stars such as William Boyd (Hopalong Cassidy) boosted their careers at the theatrical box office. Western star Gene Autry was making a half-hour television series by 1950. A series of 22 episodes (27 minutes long) was made on a two-per-week shooting schedule with each one costing $17,500. Autry owned his television show, selling it directly to sponsors who then purchased air time. A total of twelve sponsors had bought in, including the Wrigley chewing gum company. "Viewers have already noticed the casual manner in which Autry will unwrap a stick of gum and put it in his mouth right in the middle of his pictures. The outlaws never seem to chew gum," observed one account. Unlike Boyd, Autry felt theatrical films had no place in television. Autry's actions in putting himself before the viewing public on a weekly basis stirred up resentment among some movie exhibitors who felt he was being unfair "by offering a free show on television." Defenders of Autry argued his television series might be looked upon as a trailer, whetting the viewer's appetite to go to the movie houses. As well, television was making Autry known to youngsters who never heard of him before, thus building more movie audiences.[30]

Also in 1950 the wall erected by the majors showed signs of crumbling when Paramount began an attempt at star buildup using the hitherto shunned medium. The studio arranged a string of television guest shots by Wendell Corey to publicize his film *Thelma Jordan*, opening in early 1950. Independent producer Stanley Kramer was hyping Marlon Brando (a then-legitimate actor breaking into films as a star of 1950's *The Men*) in the same fashion. Kramer filmed a 15-minute short, including scenes from *The Men*, to introduce Brando to set owners. That short was given free to any television station that cared to telecast it. Earlier Kramer used television successfully to publicize Kirk Douglas in *Champion* (1949). Douglas made many guest appearances. Those spots by Corey were a direct reversal of a studio ban against television appearances by its stars. Bob Hope, for example, was permitted to appear in a one-shot television program only on condition that the film of Hope be immediately destroyed after the one telecasting. Paramount publicity executive Max Youngstein claimed Corey was not making the customary series of casual shots but the agenda "is a deliberately planned one to sell tickets for *Jordan*."[31]

Columnist Jack Gould observed, in 1951, that Hollywood was increasingly making comedy actors available to television "but the studios have kept a tight rein on major dramatic players."[32]

Metro-Goldwyn-Mayer organized an arrangement with TV variety show host Ed Sullivan whereby the latter's show presented clips of upcoming movies and presented players to take a brief bow. That studio found itself soon frozen out, however, when Fox moved in and made a better deal with Sullivan. The MGM studio then moved to strike a deal with NBC for the appearance of MGM footage and players on the networks' television shows. The idea was to work the film stars into the shows' formats. While both sides agreed in principle they could not agree on the specifics around the proper integration of clips and stars into established NBC programs. According to one account television shows in general had "bombarded" studios with requests for movie footage for airing on their programs.[33]

In the summer of 1955 Jack Gould railed against plugs on television for upcoming theatrical films. He said he had watched one on TV the night before which lasted for 60 minutes, showing how the movie was made, featured members of the supporting cast doing a few numbers, plugged the producers, etc.: "It is time for both television and Hollywood to call a halt... It is also high time the TV networks recognized the dangers of their new liaison with the film capital." Ed Sullivan started "the routine of turning over his hour to a Hollywood studio, and for a time it had a novelty value," said Gould.[34]

Hollywood also turned to the production of series for television, becoming in time the dominant player in that arena. Rising fees for television programming, especially after the FCC lifted a four-year freeze in 1952 on the construction of new TV stations, was one of the reasons. The period of 1952 to 1956 has been called the golden age of television, particularly because of its live, anthology-style drama programs. By muscling in on TV series programming, Hollywood would be a principal reason why that format died. The increased appeal of filmed programming—Hollywood of course, wasn't equipped nor inclined to get into live production—in the mid–1950s resulted from different factors. One was the recognition of audience acceptance of telefilm reruns, another was the growing value of afternoon and late-night time slots on both independent and network-affiliated outlets. Arguments over the reuse of filmed product in television had been present since the advent of commercial TV. Frequent comparisons to theatrical movies suggested that few viewers would be interested in seeing even a popular program more than once; therefore the practical value of telefilms would be limited to a single telecast. *Sponsor* magazine warned in 1952 that estimates of the future value of telefilm product were exaggerated, arguing that consumers and dealers of advertised goods would object to reruns. It cited sponsor Blatz Beer's cancellation of *Amos 'n' Andy* reruns because of viewer protests. For the publication the issue of reruns was not just one of ratings "but of audience attitudes," pointing to an industry consensus that reruns were perceived as "unwelcome and unacceptable by audiences and might provoke a powerful if intangible negative response against the television advertiser." However, by 1954, *Sponsor* noted that summer rerun ratings could in fact exceed those of the originally aired episode. One year later a telefilm producer argued that a TV series could be reused endlessly in rerun cycles of three years. By the fall of 1955 the telefilm industry was consuming ten times the amount of raw film stock used by all the theatrical producers. One thing that did change the industry view on reruns were the many repeat airings of feature films on TV, and the usually resultant high ratings. This growing market for telefilms did not go unnoticed by the majors.[35]

First of the majors to move into television work in a serious way was Columbia which started out making TV commercials around 1950. Through its video subsidiary, Screen Gems, it moved into series production in 1952 when it announced it would make a series of 39 half-hour telefilms for the Ford Motor Company, NBC's *The Ford Television Theater*. This anthology-type series was telecast over NBC beginning October 1952 and running for five years. Columbia retained ownership of the series and thus was in a position to potentially sell it over and over. Ford got exclusive first-run rights to the series for telecasting over the 51-station NBC network. As well, Ford had the right to option the series for second-run showing, and agreed to pay 75 percent of the $25,000 per episode cost. Initially Columbia said it would use its contract players in the series, but later the studio declared emphatically that it had no intention of doing so and that only independent, or freelance, performers with no studio ties would be hired. Apparently the studio was anxious to head off possible complaints from cinema owners about using its contract people to help further the entertainment potential of the competing medium.[36]

In the mid–1950s, ABC was a distant third in the network rankings; it had only 84 affiliated stations, compared to 121 outlets with CBS and 104 with

NBC. At the time it had only a 58 percent live clearance rate (proportion of affiliated outlets airing a network-supplied program live) versus a 90 percent rate for both NBC and CBS. ABC's dependence on delayed broadcast by its affiliates made filmed programs more attractive because they required neither simultaneous clearances nor the use of visually degraded kinescope transcriptions (a live show was "taped" in those days by pointing a motion picture camera at a TV set airing the live program with the result known as kinescopes, or kinnies). ABC gained the financial resources to acquire new programming only through its merger with the United Paramount Theaters—the latter was a spin-off company as a result of Paramount having to divest its theaters. Network program strategy was not built upon network production but rather upon the licensing of independently produced programs by the network, instead of the sponsor. One source ABC turned to was the Disney studio. While Disney was not then a major—it would become one later—it was moving out of cartoon production as its staple product as it understood that ultimately TV would cause the elimination of items such as newsreels, cartoons and the double bill. Instead Disney would move into more feature film productions, live action as well as animated, and into the theme park business. Disney turned to TV as much for exploitation and promotion as for programming. ABC and Disney struck a deal for the 60-minute series *Disneyland*. Anywhere from a third to a fifth of those weekly shows were devoted to direct studio promotion. In part those promotional segments were designed to appease cinema owners by advertising current theatrical releases. As well they were used by Disney to promote its new amusement park, Disneyland.[37]

One *Disneyland* episode presented a 60-minute promotional film for the forthcoming 1954 theatrical feature *20,000 Leagues Under the Sea*. Many in the industry credited the television promotion with the box office success of the movie. As a primetime network series *Disneyland* was also unprecedented in the number of reruns it employed, with only 20 original episodes per season. The standard then was around 39 episodes per season. So successful was the venture that in 1955 ABC and Disney announced plans for *The Mickey Mouse Club* as the network's first afternoon show. In its initial season the hour-long program followed the *Disneyland* formula by telecasting 20 original episodes, 20 reruns and 12 reruns of reruns. Also, the *Club* featured heavy promotion of Disney movies, comic books and amusement park operations. Reporting on widespread objections to the show's large amount of ads per program, *Television* magazine warned of "overcommercialization in the program." Those two Disney series were responsible for making 1955 ABC's first profitable year as a network and as a station owner. Its deal with ABC stood as a model for the entrance of the majors into telefilm production for the networks.[38]

That concept of using programming as both product and promotion was too alluring for the other majors to ignore. After observing the success of *Disneyland* the majors began producing series with their names in the title such as *Warner Bros. Presents, The MGM Parade* and *20th Century–Fox Theatre.* Containing commercials for forthcoming movies, those series were not particularly popular. Format of the studio shows varied from TV spin-offs of existing studio properties (such as the rotating series of *Casablanca, King's Row* and *Cheyenne* from Warner) to extended "looks behind the scenes" at studio feature activities to direct recyclings of existing studio footage. *MGM Parade* was a 30-minute compilation and promotional program, produced directly by the studio's trailer department. All the new studio programs set aside from nine to fifteen minutes each week for straight promotion of forthcoming theatricals.[39]

Paramount signed up to provide a full hour of entertainment three Sundays every month on NBC *Colgate Comedy Hour.* The studio agreed to make available its roster of stars, upcoming players, properties, musical scores, and clips of movies in release and in the preview stage. Both Warner and Paramount announced that in their series they would have "10-minute studio exploitation inserts" in each 60 minutes.[40]

An MGM executive, Nicholas Schenck, declared his company was not overlooking the interests of cinema owners by entering TV because a portion of the program "will be devoted to information about the studio's forthcoming pictures to be played exclusively in motion picture theatres." By then Hollywood was also thinking TV could be a relatively cheap testing ground for ideas. If an idea worked on television, why not turn it into a feature film? One worry was what would happen if a studio was too successful on TV with series material, would it drain off its own audience by keeping people home?[41]

At the end of 1955 *Television* magazine attributed the rating weakness of most of the new studio series to the persistent overcommercialization, while *Sponsor* warned advertisers that the major studios often demanded promotional time above their production fee for telefilm programming. Major studios generally favored the 60-minute format not only because it permitted the extended theatrical promotions but also because the 60-minute length gave an advantage to the majors as telefilm producers over their independent competition; the studios were better able to handle the higher budgets of the longer programs.[42]

The proportion of live shows on primetime declined on all three networks during the 1950s; it declined dramatically after 1955 as the relationship between Hollywood and the commercial broadcasters was cemented. At the same time the networks ignored the opinions of influential television critics who championed dramatic anthology series based on a live theater model in favor of continuing-character series based on a motion picture model. For the networks telefilms also functioned as a means of maintaining their power base. Despite the prestige of the anthology drama—a programming staple during the early- to mid-1950s—that type of programming often contained controversial material and would not "clear" all the affiliates. By comparison the blandness and nontopicality of Hollywood telefilms made them acceptable to sponsors sensitive to offending any consumer taste. Telefilms also solved the time-zone problems. Perhaps the most important motivation for the networks' switch to telefilms was the opportunity to shift the risk of production to outside producers while retaining control over programming.[43]

Hollywood soon moved away from the directly promotional telefilms into the more conventional series. As it did so the fairly large number of independent producers quickly shrank as the majors took over. One of the larger independent outfits was Television Programs of America. In 1955 it was absorbed by Screen Gems. A few years later, in 1962, the reverse happened when independent television producer/distributor MCA bought Universal. By 1959 Warner alone was supplying one-third of ABC's primetime schedule. ABC had by then achieved ratings parity with CBS and NBC in markets where the networks had equal affiliation status.[44]

In 1948 the FCC imposed a freeze on the allocation of new TV licenses. There were then about 60 stations on the air. Another 60 or so licenses had been allocated. They were allowed to complete construction and go on the air. Although the freeze had been expected to last about six months it lasted for four years, not being lifted until 1952. The freeze was imposed to deal principally with the technical aspects of spectrum allocation but other issues revolved around the question of televisions station ownership concentration. When the freeze was lifted the number of operating stations increased dramatically meaning much more money was made available to purchase programming, another reason for Hollywood to get more involved. It was during this freeze period that the networks gained control of television broadcasting with other interests being frozen out. Early TV licenses were overwhelmingly held by the radio broadcasters. The freeze had the effect of transferring the affiliate structure of radio directly to TV. By the time the freeze was lifted new stations were forced to compete in a market that had already had its system of program supply determined; network broadcasting had started in 1948. Only VHF channels (2–13) were authorized by the FCC because UHF (14–83) was not then technically ready. During the freeze period some 17 million television receivers were sold, none equipped for UHF reception. UHF utilization would, theoretically, have meant a greater and more diverse supply of programming. However, the idea of FCC action in 1952 making all those sets obsolete was not politically popular. Thus it was already too late to conveniently switch to UHF and it was not until 1964 that the FCC required set manufacturers to produce receivers with UHF reception capabilities. The result was to limit the number of TV stations in most markets to the point where only three networks could hope to survive in any national sense. The FCC's allocation plan left about 70 of the top 100 American markets with three VHF channels each, and only about 15 of the top 100 with more than three. It all conveniently corresponded to the existing network structure of the time. Not surprisingly, DuMont, the fledgling fourth network of the era went out of business by 1955, largely because not enough stations in enough major markets were left to affiliate with it. That allocation plan was based on a set of assignment priorities with the two most important being the provision of television service to all parts of the USA and the allocation of at least one station to every community, of a certain size. Educational interests were assigned UHF frequencies although the FCC knew there were no UHF-equipped receivers generally being sold, nor would there be for a long time.[45]

Another situation dealt with by the FCC during the freeze period was the question of ownership. For a time the agency considered banning movie producers outright from owning TV stations. They considered some sort of ban on antitrust violators in an ownership position, a category which the Hollywood majors fell into. During its antitrust case against Hollywood, the Justice Department recommended to the FCC that the agency withhold licenses from the movie companies. In the end the FCC imposed a rule whereby a company or individual could own no more than five TV outlets, which applied as well to the networks. While the majors could have each bought up to five stations, there was no way that position would allow them to form any sort of network since the FCC allocation plan, in a de facto sense, limited to three the number of networks that could survive as national entities. Thus Hollywood lost interest in station ownership. However, the end of the freeze meant skyrocketing prices for programs and Hollywood entered, determined to control the software, if shut out of hardware control.[46]

In the mid-1950s ABC was clearly the weakest of the three networks. It turned to Hollywood for salvation but was turned away by the majors. When it couldn't get any movies for its network programming it turned to the U.K. buying the rights to 39 feature films made in the U.K. Some of them were from J. Arthur Rank; some had already played in American cinemas. They were slated for telecast in September 1955 in primetime from 7:30 to 9 PM on Sundays. At the time, ABC was a distant third in the Sunday night ratings, going up against *Toast of the Town* (Ed Sullivan) on CBS and the *Colgate Variety Hour* on NBC.[47]

General Teleradio (General Tire was the parent company) owned five television stations under the Mutual network banner. Company president Thomas O'Neil was interested in setting up an all-movie network of TV stations, and had been so for at least a couple of years. He had purchased a large block of English films and bank foreclosures and had just laid out $1.5 million for the Roy Rogers and Gene Autry westerns for "practically unlimited runs" over a two-year span. Anchor stations were to be KHJ in Los Angeles and WOR in New York (both Mutual-controlled) along with other stations unaffiliated with the other networks on an exclusive basis. While that movie network did not develop, it illustrated the tendency of stations to turn to movies for programming, particularly stations or networks in a weak ratings position. More pressure was put on Hollywood to sell its backlog, more money was offered. Generally throughout the 1950s, films were programmed outside primetime hours by network-affiliated stations and programmed at all hours by the independent stations.[48]

Another pressure on Hollywood to sell its backlog came from the development of color television broadcasting. Early in November 1953, NBC made the first coast-to-coast transmission of color TV. It was touted as being just around the corner with the volume production of color TV sets expected to be in as little as two years. Of course, none of that happened. Color TV didn't become standard in the home until the mid to late 1960s. However, the imminent arrival of color TV worried Hollywood in 1953 since most of its backlog was black and white. Would they lose value or be worthless if everybody had a color set and television broadcasting was mostly in color, wondered the majors.[49]

Another pressure on Hollywood to release its movies came from the Justice Department which launched an antitrust lawsuit in 1952 against 12 companies charging they had conspired to prevent the licensing of 16mm prints of past and current movies to television and with having restricted the exhibition of 16mm prints in such a manner as to constitute unlawful restraint of trade. Charged were Fox, Warner, Universal, Columbia, RKO, Republic, and the separate subsidiary companies each had established as their TV arm, such as Columbia's Screen Gems. The remaining majors were not party to the suit because they did not engage in 16mm business in the U.S. Additionally, the Theatre Owners of America lobby group was named as a co-conspirator in the suit although it wasn't listed as a defendant.[50]

A consent decree was signed in mid–September 1955, between Justice and Republic in which it was agreed that Republic would offer within 90 days for TV licensing 80 percent of its movies produced before August 1, 1948, and that it would undertake with SAG the negotiations necessary to making available to television films produced since the 1948 date. Within two years following successful negotiations with SAG, Republic agreed to license for television at least 25 percent of its feature films three years after they had received national theatrical showing; to offer for television licensing in each calendar year thereafter at least 25 percent of the movies released by the company three years earlier for U.S. theatrical distribution.[51]

Republic moved to reassure cinema owners that it didn't contemplate releasing to TV in the immediate future its backlog of post–48s. In the consent decree it had been given an indeterminate amount of time to negotiate with SAG. Republic President Herbert Yates issued a "clarifying" statement following an inquiry from the Theatre Owners of America about the studio's position. He said Republic had already released about 300 movies to television: "Actually, Republic has already released to TV 80 percent of its old products released prior to 1948. Consequently, Republic is not required to release any additional pictures to television at this time or in the immediate future."52

Meanwhile, the trial against the other defendants pushed ahead, also in September 1955. By taking itself out of the case it was thought Republic did not in any way weaken the position of the other defendants. While the government argued it was "concerted" action to deny films to TV, counsel for the defendants categorically denied any conspiracy contending that each company had separately concluded it was serving its own best interests by not leasing to television and that the mutuality of action was an unavoidable coincidence. One of the defense attorneys, Homer Mitchell, said the four-year FCC freeze on new station allocations limited TV's ability to pay for movies. Said Mitchell, "it would have been economic insanity for any of the defendants to have licensed their quality pictures to TV prior to 1952." He noted that between 1949 and 1954, advertising expenditures for television programs increased from $24 million to $209 million. Mitchell also argued the absence of conspiracy was demonstrated by the fact that "over 3,600" movies were made available to TV by 1954. While that was true, more or less, he didn't point out that not so much as a single movie had been released by the five defendant majors.53

When CBS-TV President J. L. Van Volkenburg testified, he recounted that CBS had not tried to obtain movies from the majors for about the last five years because he understood they were not available. He derived that impression from reading trade journals. CBS had approached Universal in 1948 in an effort to obtain a small number of films but no deal was struck because the network considered the price too high. Not long thereafter CBS opened negotiations with RKO with the intent of acquiring the studio's backlog. Once again no deal was reached. In 1948, television paid from $125 to $300 for six or seven airings of a film while in 1955, the same movie would cost TV an average of $7,500 for a smaller number of runs.54

When Ned Depinet, President of RKO until his 1952 retirement, took the stand, he denied any conspiracy. RKO never authorized the sale of any movies to TV because it "never" received an offer it considered to be "commensurate" with the potential value of the movies as theatrical re-issues. Asked if RKO withheld films from TV because it was afraid of reprisals by exhibitors, Depinet replied: "Oh no. I don't want to kill the goose that laid the golden eggs."55

Fox President Spyros Skouras testified the impact of television on cinemas was so severe that almost 6,500 had closed down within a three-year period. If studios had put their movies on television "for free home viewing" he believed the number of closures would have been much higher, from 8,000 to 10,000. Skouras explained he was "never approached by any important officer of any of the networks to negotiate seriously a proposition that could be given serious consideration." He denied NBC board chairman David Sarnoff had ever specifically negotiated with him for putting movies on TV. All he had discussed with Sarnoff was television in general. Acknowledging that Fox had received occasional offers from "insignificant sources" to put its movies on TV, Skouras added "they offered us off time, not primetime," and to make movies available under those circumstances "would dissipate very valuable corporate assets."[56]

Jack L. Warner testified that Warner then had no set policy about putting its features on television and "will entertain any offers for selling to television." However, he did admit that in 1948, his company had adopted a policy of not making any of its movies or scenes from them available to TV. That decision was made, explained Warner, to protect the company's business because exhibition on TV would "naturally keep a certain amount of people away from theatres." Warner executive Benjamin Kalmenson told the court he was "against the psychology of giving them (pictures) away one day and selling them the next. I am against the entire principle of entertainment for nothing."[57]

U.S. District Judge Leon Yankwich rendered a decision in December 1955, in which he ruled the government had failed to prove any of the violations it had alleged, dismissing the complaint. Although Yankwich found many of the restrictive practices complained of by the government did exist, he ruled the Sherman Antitrust Act condemned only "unreasonable restraints" on trade. The ruling superseded the consent decrees signed by Republic.[58]

Some three months later, Justice announced it would not appeal the dismissal of its antitrust suit, declaring that a substantial flow of movies from the majors to television had begun. In the weeks before this announcement by Justice, RKO, Columbia, Warner, Universal and Republic had licensed or sold some 1,800 movies to television. While the antitrust suit had failed, it was one more piece of pressure working on the majors, leading to the ultimate release to TV of its enormous backlog.[59]

That first move toward the majors releasing their films to television took place in July 1955 when General Teleradio, a subsidiary of General Tire and Rubber Company, announced it had purchased RKO from Howard Hughes for $25 million. Included in the sale was RKO's entire library of about 740 features. Financially weakest of the eight majors, RKO suffered further problems when it fell under the erratic leadership of Hughes, who purchased the studio in the 1940s. Producing more B films than the other majors, RKO was unable to successfully switch to A production; B films would soon disappear completely from cinema bills as the double-feature gave way to the single feature theater bill—one of the responses made by the majors to television inroads. Later in the 1950s RKO expired as a film producer. One of General Teleradio's five owned stations in the Mutual network was New York's WOR. With seven stations then operating in the city, three affiliated with the three major networks, WOR had a ratings problem. Starting in 1951, WOR decided to go with feature films, initiating its *Million Dollar Movie* series in 1954, which ran the same movie 16 times a week. Soon WOR became one of New York's most watched stations. However, General needed films, a lot of them. It had leased a batch of 30 movies held by the Bank of America, for $42,000 per film. Each title had returned $70,000, a profit of $28,000 per title, from rentals to 95 other television stations, in addition to running the titles on its own outlets. One allure of movies for stations was the fact it was possible for an individual outlet to make more money from telecasting a film than from carrying a network spectacular. That was because a station presenting a movie sold time on the basis of its local rates and kept all the income whereas when airing network fare the station had to split fees with the network. Secondly, the film permitted insertion of spot announcements more frequently than on most network offerings.[60]

That deal marked the first crack in the united front Hollywood had presented in refusing to sell its backlog. While RKO was one of Hollywood's oldest studios, it was also one of the weakest. Hughes had reduced the payroll from 2,000 to 300 people, and RKO lost its distribution contracts for Walt Disney and Samuel Goldwyn films. Through the first seven months of 1955, RKO had not shot a single foot of film. Thomas O'Neil, son of Akron's General Tire and Rubber president William O'Neil was head of the firm's General Teleradio, which had a 569-radio station network besides the five TV outlets. When O'Neil got control of Manhattan's WOR in 1951 he didn't have the money to compete with CBS or NBC so he turned to movie programming, calling the pickups from the Bank of America the *Million Dollar Movie* series. O'Neil was as surprised as anyone when programming a single film 16 times a week led WOR to the top of the ratings, and at the enormous profit his company turned by leasing those films to other stations.[61]

Things remained quiet until December 1955 when General Teleradio announced it had sold (not leased) the entire 740-feature RKO library for $15.2 million to C&C Super Corporation, which controlled various business enterprises unrelated to the film industry. While the films covered RKO's output for the previous 30 years, most of the films had been produced between 1935 and 1948. Included were classics such as *Citizen Kane* (1941), *Hunchback of Notre Dame* (1939), and eight musicals starring Fred Astaire and Ginger Rogers. RKO reserved the right not to release any movies to TV until they had been released to cinemas for three years, meaning a release delay for the handful of recent releases. General Teleradio retained the right to use all 740 titles on its owned television outlets as well as the right to rent 150 of the titles to a national advertiser for a one-time showing before they passed on to C&C. Still, C&C, expected a return of $43 million within five years.[62]

Setting up a new subsidiary called C&C Television Corporation, the company emphasized the films would be sold in an "orderly fashion" so as not to depress the market. Part of the payment by stations could be in the form of "spots" on which C&C would advertise its own products including Super Coola, other canned soft drinks, and hand power tools. One welcome aspect of the deal, for viewers, "will be to retire many of the old features that have been haunting television screens for years."[63]

At the very end of 1955 Columbia, through its Screen Gems subsidiary, announced it would lease, rather than sell, 104 of its old movies to TV. This would be the first time a movie producer would be marketing films to both cinemas and television. CBS retained all property rights to the titles. Until then, the independent producers who had channeled movies to TV had done so by selling them for fixed prices to television distribution companies. RKO had followed that practice. There was more than a little unease about the reaction of cinema owners to a major directly serving both types of customers. The hesitancy to sell outright was influenced by the fact the FCC had not yet ruled on pay-TV. The decision came down to selling to a separate television distribution company for fixed profits, or renting directly to gamble on inestimable income. In its announcement of the decision, Columbia stated its decision "takes cognizance of the changing character of our business, and the need for all companies to remain fluid and flexible." It added: "As a matter of good business judgment our management has decided that it wants to study at first hand the potential of the television market as it relates to feature pictures which have already been reissued theatrically and are now dormant in a so-called backlog." All of the 104 titles were made before August 1, 1948, meaning SAG did not need to be dealt with. For films made after that date, no television release could be implemented until some sort of agreement was made with SAG.[64]

That union had recently reached an agreement with Allied Artists (who was then distributing post–48 Monogram product) in which SAG got an extra payment of 12 to 15 percent of the original salaries for the actors involved. Those were low budget efforts with average actors' salaries in the range of $2,000 to $4,000.[65]

Other majors watched closely. Some feared C&C might wreck the market by a sudden unloading of RKO fare. However, by the end of 1955, there were about 458 stations on the air. C&C announced it would embark on a national advertising campaign to tell the public they could see these "new" films on TV. Called "Movietime USA," the campaign was built around the theme "See a Movie Tonight at Home." Matthew Fox, President of C&C Television said he hoped to lease the RKO films as an entire 740-title package to television stations, with the sweetener that they could telecast them as often as they wanted, forever. The practice of block booking, banned in cinemas as a result of the 1948 Supreme Court decision, was about to arrive in television. Matthew Fox's plan to lease forever never worked, perhaps because, as *Business Week* observed, "Then, too, there is the impression that many of the 740 films in Fox's package are elderly specimens of the same poor quality that most stations want to retire."[66]

Two months later, an even bigger deal took place when Warner announced it had sold outright for $21 million its entire backlog of 850 features and some 1,500 shorts and cartoons (made between 1912 and 1950) to a company that would market them to television.[67]

By October 1956, all of the Hollywood majors (except Paramount and Universal) had made its pre–48 movie backlog available to television outlets. The question was what would those features do to viewing habits? Network affiliates would run them only off-prime so just local competition was involved. However, every major market had one or more independent stations which would run features in prime, perhaps drawing audiences away from the networks. CBS programming executive Hubbell Robinson, Jr. thought that the more immediate and up-to-date network shows would prevail, adding, "if the nets were to throw feature films into good network viewing time, it would end TV's development as an entertainment medium." One report added, "And the nets would want to show a given film only once—for the sake of program variety and the development of their own live shows—whereas the small independent stations will sometimes run it as often as five times a week." ABC planned to continue its "Famous Film Festival" series on Sunday nights for the 1956-57 season, once again with English imports. CBS was running *The Wizard of Oz* (1939) in primetime but only as a one-time special. Other than that, the networks declined to run movies in primetime. Paramount continued to hold out releasing because it had the biggest stake in, and the biggest hopes for, pay-TV. However, the release of this huge pile of pre–48 movies to free television signaled the end of hope for most majors with regard to pay-TV. The time wasn't right; the technology wasn't right. It wouldn't work so the majors sold to commercial television. Pay-TV would have to wait.[68]

Throughout this early period in television, the increasing costs of live TV moved the medium closer and closer to production on film, which could be shown, saved, and rerun when a station wanted. Who better to do filmed production than Hollywood? As the number of stations increased, so did the cost to sponsors. When Ed Sullivan's *Toast of the Town*, a live show originating in New York,[69] made its debut over CBS on June 20, 1948, Sullivan had a budget of $500 weekly to hire talent, usually six or seven acts were booked each show. On that first show, Dean Martin and Jerry Lewis were paid $200, pianist Eugene List $75, singer Monica Lewis $50, dancer Kathryn Lee $50, boxing referee Ruby Goldstein $75, and a singing fireman was paid $25. The remaining $25 went to a man who planted celebrities in the audience, seating them within camera range. Less than four years later, the Sullivan program spent $15,000 a week for artists.[69]

Networks tripled their use of filmed material in the 1952-53 period.

During a typical week in July 1953, 22 percent of all programming on the networks was filmed, 78 percent live. By 1955, half or more of programming was filmed. By then, TV expected to use 3,068 hours of material annually while the majors produced perhaps 400 to 500 hours of theatrical films annually.[70]

When ABC still lacked regularly scheduled daytime television programming, in 1951, it announced a merger agreement with Paramount Theatres Inc. Television was then mostly all live. That was the first formal link between broadcasting and the motion picture industry. That merger was finally approved by the FCC in mid–1953. Within a year of that approval, the president of the newly merged ABC–Paramount produced a signed contract with Disney. That was soon followed by the ABC deal with Warner for a series for the 1955–56 season. Well underway then was the shift in production from live to filmed with the production center shifted from New York to Hollywood. As live gave way to taped, local programming yielded to networked fare. As media critic Erik Barnouw observed, "countless stations reduced staff, closed expensive studios, and took up round the clock film projection."[71]

Frederic Ziv, chairman of independent producer/distributor Ziv Television Programs, complained that the films moving from the majors' vaults to television can "easily set back the standards of TV five or ten years.... Only ten percent of them are first-rate pictures and another ten percent could be classed better than average."[72]

Chapter 3

TV Surrenders, 5,000 Times a Week, 1956–1961

> "We may be committing suicide."
> unnamed Hollywood executive, 1956.

> "Almost any time one can tune into programs offering films that were regarded as inferior even when they were first shown in theatres as long as twenty-five years ago."
> New York Times, 1956.

Then came the deluge. Within six months of the RKO sale to C&C, about 2,000 old movies came available to television, mostly from the majors, led by RKO with 740, Warner with 850 and Columbia with 104. Then MGM announced it would release through its own distribution arm 770 of its pictures and 900 short subjects and cartoons, produced from 1929 to 1949, to television. The only MGM movie from that era not made available to TV was *Gone with the Wind* (1939). Additionally, a number of features would be made available for presentation as spectaculars on the networks; those titles would be held back for national network showing then made available to local stations. Company executive Charles Barry emphasized: "we will only rent or lease our motion pictures for certain periods of time. We will not sell our films outright to television."[1]

According to a national survey conducted by Screen Gems in July, 1956, an estimated total of 5,212 hours of movies were being shown each week throughout the USA. From that *Variety* concluded that 73 million home hours in America were spent every week watching movies on TV. Another poll in New York City found that 90.1 percent of its respondents said they sometimes watched films on TV, while 31.8 percent said they watched them seven days a week. All of this was at a time before movies from the majors had arrived to a great extent on the screen. Regarding those films on television, reporter J. P. Shanley remarked: "Almost any time, one can tune into programs offering films that were regarded as inferior even when they were first shown in theatres as long as twenty-five years ago. Most of these products are painfully inept." Despite any quality deficiencies, those movies drew strong viewership. With the release from the majors, Shanley felt the quality of movies on the tube was improving.[2]

For an estimated $4–$5 million, MGM leased a block of 725 of its old movies to independent Los Angeles outlet KTTV in August 1956. The station, owned by the Times–Mirror company, got exclusive use of the films in the Los Angeles area for seven years, with unlimited runs. In a separate, but not unrelated deal, MGM paid a reported $1.6 million to KTTV for a 25 percent ownership position. Said Arthur Loew, president of MGM parent Loew's Inc., "we expect many more deals with similarly strategic outlets in other parts of the country."[3]

Within a couple of weeks, MGM had leased its block of 725 movies to television stations in 12 cities for a total of $20 million (including KTTV). One buyer was CBS for its five owned and operated outlets, except for its Los Angeles station. That transaction brought to over 1,000 the number of movies in the WCBS-TV (the network's New York City owned and operated station) library that had not been aired in New York. WCBS planned to telecast the material on *The Early Show*, *The Late Show* and *The Late Late Show*.[4]

Fox entered into a TV distribution deal for its pre–48s with National Telefilm Associates (NTA), to a maximum of 390 titles. That deal was to reach a minimum payment of around $30 million during a seven-year period with Fox receiving a minimum plus participation in gross profits beyond a specified but undisclosed sum. Movies were to be released to NTA in blocks. Simultaneously, Fox acquired a 50 percent interest in the NTA film network, a subsidiary of the company numbering over 100 stations. Fox also agreed to produce four new television series for NTA, starting no later than March 31, 1957. In its deal, Fox retained the approval of "cutting" in each case with the movies to be telecast full-length "wherever possible."[5]

As 1957 began, the sale of MGM's pre–48s stood at $30 million with the total then thought to not go much beyond $40 million. That was a disappointment for the studio which had hoped to reap $60–$70 million. MGM had been offered $50 million for an outright sale of its library but had declined, deciding to distribute them itself. Of the total, CBS had reportedly paid $11 million for the four of its five owned and operateds which were telecasting the library. Observers felt MGM had set its pricing too high, making it difficult for secondary markets to buy the package. Early sales strategies by the majors also showed an apparent belief that once a film had been sold to a market, any resales in the future would not be likely, or for very low amounts. Hence blocks were regularly offloaded for a seven-year period with unlimited runs during that time. Hollywood still wasn't sure it could sell the same movie over and over again in the same market, for large amounts each time, indefinitely.[6]

Giving a rosier picture was reporter Murray Horowitz who noted that in the 18 months since General Teleradio struck its deal with C&C films sold in the TV market had grossed about $150 million, mainly from the pre-48 product of the Hollywood majors. Those movies had been all written off on company books, carried as $1-nominal assets. Paramount and Universal were still holding out pre-48s while Columbia had released only about 200 of its backlog. Also, MGM, Warner, and Fox, each had many more markets to reach. Horowitz observed that some stations, such as WCBS, telecast its MGM library in early afternoon and late evening (after 11 PM) meaning many New Yorkers would have missed them entirely. Therefore, those movies would have significant value if sold in a second round to a New York independent station which could screen them in primetime. By then, MGM had grossed $42 million in 42 markets while Associated Artists Production, distributing Warner product, had grossed $20 million. Associated was selling the huge Warner library in blocks of 59 titles, predetermined by the seller; C&C had grossed $25 million on the RKO library, while Columbia and Fox had generated about $10 million each. Republic had picked up $11 million and United Artists about $3 million, on its package of 39 titles.[7]

Paramount ended its holdout when it sold outright all of its 750 pre-48 movies for $50 million to Music Corporation of America (MCA). That deal called for a $10 million cash down payment then a $24.5 million guarantee coming out of a 60/40 rental income split in Paramount's favor. After the $34.5 million plateau was reached, the same 60/40 rental split would continue until Paramount received a maximum return of $50 million, but there were no guarantees beyond the $35 million. In the wake of that agreement, Paramount President Barney Balaban declared his studio had committed itself to a policy of withholding its post-48s from television. Somewhat indirectly, he urged the other majors to also not unload their post-48s. It was, of course, all rhetoric to ease exhibitor anxieties. Exhibitors themselves had formed a loose group which had been seriously in the running to buy the Paramount backlog — to keep it off TV and presumably use it in theatrical reissue — but had walked away from a reported $40 million price tag. As well, just months earlier, Paramount was on the verge of selling the library to CBS, but the network got cold feet and backed away after becoming wary of possible antitrust repercussions.[8]

Independent producer David O. Selznick defended the majors' release of pre–48s to television as a "matter of survival." Some of the studios were facing financial disaster if they didn't sell, he explained. At the same time, he deplored the lack of a reissue market which, had it existed, might have kept a lot of movies from TV: "A way certainly could have been found to exploit old films, but no element in the industry gave any support."[9]

Within three years of the C&C/RKO deal, an estimated 3,700 features, virtually all pre–48s, had been sold by Hollywood's eight majors, (or those with the backlog rights) Warner, Fox, Columbia, Universal, MGM, RKO, UA, Paramount, and Republic for around $220 million. Sales by everyone else were perhaps $25 million in that 1955 to 1958 period. During that time, the average price per feature had risen from $10,000 to $75,000. Since those movies had been fully amortized, the receipts represented windfall profits for the studios. For those majors renting directly to television, everything above the distribution expense of 10–15 cents on the dollar was pure profit. However, a still increasing demand for movies had the majors worried they had undervalued and underpriced their libraries.[10]

As was to be expected from this huge release of product, movies came to hold an increasingly dominant position on station schedules. New York City's independent WATV followed the example of WOR and, beginning in October 1956, offered two showings of the same movie seven nights a week, at 7 and 10 PM, with extra telecasts at 2:30 PM on Saturdays and Sundays, a total of 16 airings per week. Reporter Jack Gould was amazed that the three networks had chosen to let the Hollywood backlog slip out of their hands into the control of the independent outlets.[11]

The question was where to slot all of these movies becoming available, most of which required at least a 90-minute time period. Not only were the networks unwilling to program movies in primetime, they were then maneuvering to extend primetime from 10:30 to 11 PM. In that they were successful. As early as 1956, *Variety* predicted that with so many films suddenly available to TV, the market would quickly become glutted with a resultant price crash.[12]

Variety reporter Murray Horowitz declared in the fall of 1956 that New York's WOR had the distinction of "being virtually the first all-grind house with 80 percent of its programming hours devoted to features." Utilizing the complete RKO library, WOR had revamped its line-up, eliminating some series to move to almost all movies. Remaining in the line-up was the *Million Dollar Movie*, with its 16 telecasts per week of the same film. Other movie series included *Love Story* which was broadcast Monday through Friday from 10 to 11:30 am with a different movie each week and *Theatre of Movie Classics* which broadcast on Sundays with four showings of the same film, three of them back to back.

Among stations with the MGM backlog, there was a tendency to hoard their MGM blockbusters by playing off only a few of the big A titles a month. They were not necessarily hoarding, but may not have been able to afford to play them all at once; that was because of the payment contract. A station paid up to 20 percent down, then 60 installments over a five-year term with a minimum per installment payment mandated. MGM's backlog was divided equally into five categories with each category having its own price. Categories were AAA, AA, A, B, and C. Say a station bought the MGM library for an average price of $1,000 per picture; an AAA title would be pegged at $3,000 with a C title at perhaps $300 (prices averaged out to $1,000 and were set after allowing for the down payment). Then the per run payment method kicked in which made things even more complicated. On the first telecast by a television station of any specific title the outlet had to pay 50 percent of the balance to MGM. Thus, for an AAA title pegged at $3,000 the station had to pay MGM $1,500 when it first ran the item. On the second run, 20 percent was due, on the third run ten percent, and on runs four through seven, five percent was due each time. If a station with this kind of contract were to schedule 20 AAA films per month, it would have to pay MGM $30,000 a month, almost as much as most or all of its other programming costs combined. The minimum monthly payment was based on the station's use of an equal number of films from each category. That scheme was said to serve to protect cinemas by preventing stations from airing too many blockbusters at once, thus minimizing the impact upon the theater box office. The effect of the formula was to space out the blockbusters to the public over an extended period of time. However, it also had other effects. By offloading huge blocks of movies on stations at a time they forced stations to take the bad with the good titles. Libraries of 700-plus titles were simply too big to absorb for outlets in medium or small markets, so majors marketed to them in groups of around 40 or so titles per block. Those packages were fixed by the majors and always contained a mix from desirable to atrocious. Complex payment methods also ensured that the turkeys would indeed get telecast. That was one of the points. If a station was screening, say, a Fox film, then it couldn't be telecasting somebody else's product.[14]

At one time when rumors circulated quite heavily that post–48s might be released to TV any day, MGM executive Ernie Emerling moved to kill those rumors, presumably to placate irritated exhibitors. Observing "the smart television boys aren't doing anything to prevent the misleading rumors," Emerling complained they announced the "best from MGM" and "the best from Warner Bros." etc., "but what they really mean but do not say is the best of old, old films—not any of the new ones." As part of his campaign to bury that rumor, Emerling was reportedly successful in inducing a number of newspapers to include the year of release of movies they listed as scheduled for TV showing on a particular night. He commented that the listing of the year represented a "service to the newspaper's readers."[15]

The station WCBS got strong ratings on *The Late Show* (which it started in 1951) and on *The Early Show* with most of the sponsor time slots sold out. Usually it led the city ratings for the late night time slot. It believed it would soon get its money back from the $8.4 million outlay for the Paramount backlog. With product from Fox, MGM, Universal, Warner, RKO, Columbia, United Artists, and Paramount, WCBS advertised itself as having "New York's Largest and Finest Library of Feature Films."[16]

Chicago's WBBM–TV, in 1959, was grinding out 1,100 movies per year, telecasting three per day, from a library containing only about 1,800 titles; reruns were slotted at different times of the day. Minneapolis had four commercial outlets, three network affiliates and one independent. WCCO–TV (CBS) used eight movies per week, WTCN (ABC) aired 13 films per week, KMPS–TV (independent) was big in film telecasting with airings at 7 and 10 PM nightly, a Friday night late show as well as five mornings per week. KMPS had gone big into films in November 1957 when it had been purchased by National Telefilm Associates, Fox's TV distributor and partner.[17]

Top price then paid for a big A title in New York was $15,000, around $10,000 in Los Angeles. WOR remained highly successful with its *Million Dollar Movie* format. In its fifth year advertising time remained completely sold out. WCBS had a stockpile of 2,150 titles and was telecasting features in 23 different time periods weekly. In Cincinnati WKRC–TV had been programming movies on week nights from 11:15 PM to 1 AM since 1950. At WLW–TV, an NBC Cincinnati affiliate, executive Robert Dunville explained his station was moving in the direction of airing more syndicated series material (both new and rerun), at the expense of movies, explaining: "At one time we had to go with features.... Features offer no choice—you must buy the whole package." Explaining his buying policy WKRC manager Roger Read commented: "We have found that large feature libraries from major distributors contain too high a percentage of old titles that are rejected by the public. By buying a wide variety of features from most major distributors rather than one large distributor we feel we can best maintain our dominance."[18]

Films shown on television were subject to various insults, from a complete banning due to content, to deletions due to content, to the more pervasive cut anything anywhere to make it fit a predetermined time slot, to a relentless onslaught of interruptions every few minutes for commercials. It was all carried out by the broadcasters and/or film producers. Back in January 1949 the Pennsylvania State Board of Censors ordered that no movie was to be shown on television unless it had first been approved by the Board. That ruling was opposed by broadcasters who launched a lawsuit. Losing every step of the way the U.S. Supreme Court in 1951 declined to review a lower court decision which ruled that states could not censor motion pictures shown on TV because Congress, by passing the Federal Communications Act, had occupied fully the field of television regulations. Thus, unlike in the field of theatrical films states had no power to censor those films when they made it to television. But there was no cause for alarm as many censorious types were willing to step into that void.[19]

Reporter Richard Shepard commented in 1956: "Often a televised movie has been merely a synopsis of the version that was seen by theatre audiences" with parts "hacked away by crude television surgery designed to fit the film into a niche in a crowded time schedule." Supposedly, that was starting to change. WATV (New York) instituted a policy of presenting "important" films in their entirety. WCBS was said to follow a similar no-cut policy on its two late night movie slots. Prime reason for making cuts was for scheduling to fit the time available in a slot, after allowing for ads, although Shepard cited evidence of some cuts made if the film were going to a family audience. "On rare occasions cuts may be made to avoid wounding the sensibilities of a sponsor. One film editor told of erasing a lurid auto crash involving a vehicle manufactured by a company that was contributing toward the evening's entertainment," he wrote. Station editors sometimes argued their cutting could actually help a film in that it "tightened" it up. On WOR's *Million Dollar Movie*, the staff cut 15–16 minutes from the average 90–minute feature.[20]

The MGM film *Cabin in the Sky* (1943)—starring Ethel Waters and a black cast—was barred from Miami outlet WCKT when it bought a half–MGM library, feeling a movie with a black cast might be too touchy for telecasting in the South. South Bend, Indiana's WNDU–TV banned Jean Harlow's *Red Dust* (1932) as too sexy, as well as other titles from MGM's pre–48 library. Features were banned on racial, sexual and good-taste grounds, as well as for political reasons. *Song of Russia* (1944) was released to television by MGM at the height of the Cold War. These titles all received the Motion Picture Association of America (MPAA) code seal (a sort of seal of approval). Also, none of these titles ever received a "Condemned" (or C) rating from the Catholic Legion of Decency. That group operated independently of the film industry and if a film received a C rating from them it could hurt the theatrical box office. The Legion of Decency had some influence on theatricals shown on TV. One station film buyer said, "I'd look twice before buying a feature with a 'C' rating." However, few features with a C were even shunted television's way. RKO Teleradio (as it was then called) implied it would never play a C film on its owned and operateds. Excessive violence was also cut from some movies in this period.[21]

The only blow struck against the practice was struck by foreigners, in a foreign land, in a foreign court. In London, England, the writing/producing team of Frank Launder and Sidney Gilliat sued British Lion Films and Shepperton Productions for breach of contract and libel; the nature of the libel being the alleged mutilation of their film *The Constant Husband* (1955) when it had its U.S. debut on television. The two companies sued agreed the men had a clause in their contract that provided for no cutting of the feature without their consent and Gilliat's personal supervision—which had not happened.

The men argued that when the movie was telecast "so many cuts had been made and it was interrupted at such frequent intervals by commercial advertisements that its humor, vitality and artistic quality were impaired." Since it still bore their names, people would suppose they were responsible for the "mutilated version" and their reputations would be impaired. An out-of-court settlement was reached with Launder and Gilliat receiving an undisclosed sum of money.[22]

As the Hollywood backlog flooded the TV market, NBC's David Sarnoff warned, in 1956, that "the true function of TV will have failed if the film programming snowballs as to become the dominant appeal." He didn't want television to become a motion picture circuit because it would "achieve nothing more than to give Hollywood just a new system of distribution." Believing the main thrust of television should be live programs, big spectaculars, public service shows, and so on, Sarnoff argued an extension of motion picture programming would explode all that. If NBC and CBS were forced into movie programming it would tend "to tear down" the entire medium. Later that same year, Sarnoff referred to the "film invasion" of television saying that the "flood of film" could change the character and scope of TV "if it is not thoughtfully assessed by broadcasters in long-range terms." By this time, he was referring to the release of the Hollywood backlog and to the mounting pile of filmed series made especially for the medium by Hollywood. Sarnoff called upon television not to surrender itself to Hollywood filmmakers but to place the emphasis on live programs of its own creation.[23]

As the 1956-57 TV season began, it was felt films on TV would attract their largest audience ever, with all the new releases. All the majors had released, except Paramount and Universal. So the dilemma was, where would that vast audience be—in cinemas watching new movies or at home viewing the majors' pre–48s? A survey by market research firm Sindlinger and Company on the TV versus theatre drawing power of *Dinner at Eight* (1933), one of MGM's all-star releases, clearly showed TV's edge. That survey indicated a "probable" cinema audience of 4,976,000 for *Dinner* if it was theatrically reissued without any publicity buildup. Under ideal conditions, the potential television audience was put at 22,414,000. The largest prospective TV viewership for *Dinner* was among people over 40 years of age—infrequent moviegoers. Sindlinger found that 85 percent of a week's box office gross came from the frequent moviegoers, who made up 25.8 percent of the total adult population. Also found by the survey was that if *Dinner* was sufficiently exploited through publicity and advertising for its television exhibition, the probable home audience could reach 45 million—35 million infrequent moviegoers and 10 million frequent attenders. MGM's full page ad in the TV section of the Sunday *New York Times* in September 1956 with 19 pictures of stars as they looked ten or more years earlier, projected from a TV-size screen, "sent cold shivers down many spines in the movie colony. It demonstrated that pictures are not going to be sneaked into television," observed a reporter. The seven outlets in Los Angeles then combined to present at least 17 hours a day of movies. Hollywood also worried about what would happen to the box office appeal of older stars when the younger generation of moviegoers suddenly realized how they looked ten or more years previously. Said one studio executive, "we may be committing suicide." With so many movies then on television, it meant the competition for the average citizen, thought a reporter, "will be consistent night after night rather than sporadic as in the former years."[24]

On a Friday night in October 1956, KTTV Los Angeles telecast the first of its 725 MGM features, *Thirty Seconds Over Tokyo* (1944) at 8 PM. Friday was a prime theatre night. That telecast gave KTTV a 600 percent rating increase over Friday nights for the previous month. Cinema business suffered an apparent 25 percent overall drop in Los Angeles that night as an estimated two million people watched the movie at home. KTTV planned to telecast a different MGM title every night, five days a week.[25]

Nationally, American television viewers were being offered 4,169 feature films per week on the tube, according to a 190-market study conducted by Screen Gems in the first week of April 1956. According to the study, movies had their greatest concentration, per outlet, in seven-station markets like New York and Los Angeles with the least concentration in the one-station markets. Features accounted for about 13 percent of the total programming of U.S. TV outlets. At the time the 412 operating stations averaged about 100 hours of air time weekly per outlet.[26]

As 1957 began, reporter Fred Hift commented that with the huge Hollywood release almost simultaneously, the quality of the live television shows had dropped appreciably. Hift worried "the medium has almost surrendered to Hollywood." An unidentified television network executive worried the growing interconnection between Hollywood and television would produce the same antitrust action as had previously befallen the film industry. He, and others, were concerned that "the true function of the television medium" was perhaps undermined, diluted and perhaps ultimately dissipated by the easier and quicker profit process that came by way of feature film programming; that "the horizons for solid network programming could be circumscribed as more and more feature film slottings are substituted."[27]

When rumors swirled around during the summer of 1957 that recent Hollywood films would be soon released to TV, the Sindlinger company prepared a research report purporting to show that 36 million potential cinema admissions were lost in America in July 1957, because of that misconception. Research showed that of all persons who said they had considered attending a cinema that month but didn't, 22 percent stayed away because they anticipated that the features in local theatres could be caught not too much later on their home screens—that translated into 36 million lost ticket sales.[28]

Another loss estimate was produced by Ernest Stellings, President of the

Theatre Owners of America. According to him, the film companies lost $60 million in rentals because of the sale of their backlog to TV. He based this on an estimated box office decrease of $130 million, minus $70 million gained in TV sales. Stellings revealed that Sindlinger had been retained by TOA "to verify its conclusions" that the sale of features to television is "detrimental to all segments of the industry." All of this came about as the release of recent Hollywood films to television seemed imminent.[29]

Sindlinger delivered his report to the TOA at a closed door meeting in Hollywood early in January 1958. In it, Sindlinger claimed that from October 1954 to September 1955 theatres had their best 12 months since 1948 because big movie stars stayed off TV and there were only a few old movies shown on television. However, with the beginning of the so-called "courtship of movies and TV" in 1955 signaled by the showing of film clips and film producers' programs on the air, significant changes began to appear. Cinema attendance was said to be off 17–20 percent in areas where the public had an opportunity to view such programs *as Warner Brothers Presents, Disneyland, MGM Parade,* and *The Ed Sullivan Show,* etc. In areas where the public could not watch those programs, attendance was reported to be up 3–7 percent over a comparable period of the previous year. Then with the "weddings of movies and television," which the report held began in October 1957 on the general release of the majors pre–48s, average weekly cinema attendance was said to be off 13.5 to 17.5 percent in the last six months of 1957, where it had been up 2.1 to 6.2 percent in the first six months, as compared to the same periods in 1956. Simultaneously the public's viewing time devoted to films on the tube rose from 86.5 million hours a week, pre–September to 426.2 million hours in December 1957. Sindlinger's report said the percentage of people who thought about going to the movies but didn't rose from 64.6 percent in the last quarter of 1956 to 76.5 percent in the last quarter of 1957. Putting a dollar value on that percentage of "lost admissions" Sindlinger held it was a potential $10 million per week. Factoring in the television revenues this report concluded the majors took a net loss of $5.3 million in 1957.[30]

While about 46 million cinema tickets were sold weekly in early 1958 — compared to 80-some million 11 years earlier — around 204 million people watched movies on TV each week. It was estimated people spent four times as many hours watching free movies on TV as they spent viewing new movies in the theatres. An unnamed movie company executive was cited as seeing TV "almost entirely responsible for the plight of our industry." He added, "When you take into consideration the fact that in New York City alone 175 films are available weekly on television, in addition to many other live television programs, principally between the hours of 7 PM and 10 PM, which is the best playing time for theatres, it is crystal clear that the competition the industry faces is of heart-breaking proportions." Many exhibitors blamed the Hollywood majors. One executive of a chain reduced from 43 to 14 theatres in the previous 11 years declared: "Many TV stations would have folded if the studios had not released their old films for TV. The very thing that saved TV is ruining the theatres."[31]

When researchers looked at the films on television, they found that 19 percent of the public thought the current theatrical movies on TV were "too old" and another 12 percent rated them as "inferior" to films in cinemas. However, 11 percent thought them equal in quality to the movies in theatres while another 11 percent rated them as "very good" to "excellent."[32]

Later in 1958 reporter Murray Horowitz wondered what would happen in two or three years when all the films were used up. Even a release of the post–48s wouldn't help much, he thought, since there were a limited number of them. He added, "Additionally, in many cases because of features, stations have increased their programming day, getting on the air earlier and signing off later." Horowitz believed there was a limit to the number of times a movie could be rerun on television.[33]

The major TV distributor NTA International conducted its own survey in mid-1959, finding that about 5,000 movies per week were telecast in the USA. This survey showed that independent TV outlets were telecasting an average of 21 movies per week (about 36 hours of time) while network affiliated stations averaged nine movies per week (15 hours). Generally, those films got high ratings, which allowed stations to charge premium prices for commercial time. In turn, of course, that put the outlets in the mood to do more feature programming. Three hundred stations were queried, some 45 percent of them devoted an average of 14 hours each week to movies and 40 percent aired an average of seven hours per week. In 10 representative markets about 20 percent of the total broadcasting hours were devoted to feature films.[34]

From the beginning of its dealings with television, Hollywood imposed the practice of block booking on television stations which bought its features. The practice involved selling features to buyers in blocks or packages with the producer having preselected the specific titles in a package. Each block contained some desirable product but also contained a lot of turkeys. Buyers who wished to assemble their own block of films from a major by picking their own films title by title were discouraged by pricing policies or simply denied that option by Hollywood. Block and blind booking were practices used for decades by Hollywood in its dealings with cinema exhibitors. Blind booking involved a demand that an exhibitor buy a film without having seen it. Traditionally, the industry had screening sites in various parts of the country where exhibitors could preview a film to help them determine if they wanted to book it. When the U.S. Supreme Court issued its divestment order against the majors in 1948, it also banned the practice of block and blind booking in the motion picture industry. Buying films in blocks, for theatres or for television, was not, and is not, an illegal practice per se. What was illegal was forcing a buyer to take title X as a condition of buying title Y, which was the only one the buyer really wanted. Selling in blocks allowed a major to control more screen time, or tube time, with his product, thus limiting time available for competitors. More importantly, it allowed the majors, when selling blocks to TV, to play with the numbers. Since the blocks were sold for a single total price, rather than a summed total of individually listed prices, the majors could allocate the proportion of the total going to a particular title in any way they wanted. This could have implications for any films in which somebody had a contract calling for a share of the profits. Thus a feature could have a much lower value assigned to it than its status within the block might warrant. For television station buyers purchasing in blocks was attractive because so much air time could be filled with relatively little time and effort. Much easier to buy a block of 100 movies from a single major rather than go through six or seven large catalogs and carefully select 100 movies title by title. In return for the convenience of buying a block, stations understood and accepted the fact that the block had been laced with its share of turkeys. But then there was always that 3 to 4:30 AM time slot, which could be filled with just about anything.

Phil Cooper, an executive with the independent movies-to-TV distributor Filmways Inc., came out strongly in 1956 against block booking in selling old movies to TV, a practice he acknowledged was then "widely" practiced. Trade publication *Variety* wrote, "Many distributors of pix-to-TV are following the practice of block booking, which was outlawed by the Government years ago when it separated theatres and film studios in the divorcement decree.... Indie pix-to-TV distributors in the main are similarly offering films packages wherein the stations must take all the pix and cannot choose individual product." Fox was then unloading its backlog in packs of 50 titles each. Columbia was selling a block of 104 movies. When the Warner and RKO backlogs were first offered to buyers, it was done on the basis of the buyer taking the library (over 700 titles in each) in its entirety or nothing. Because very few stations could afford that those backlogs were soon broken into smaller blocks. In all cases, the TV buyers (as in theatres in the past) had no choice but to buy inferior goods in order to get the outstanding titles. Al Flanagan, buyer for KCOP Los Angeles, explained that he wasn't allowed to select the films he wanted, but the distributors had a way of avoiding out-and-out dictation: "They offer me a package and I tell them there is one picture I would like to buy. They say it will cost me $17,000. But if I buy the package, I can have it for $6,000. So, of course, we wind up buying the package."[35]

Following the situation for some time had been the Justice Department which was considering whether the practice of block booking movies to TV violated the Sherman Antitrust Act. Victor Hansen, Assistant Attorney General in charge of the Antitrust Division, revealed he had been receiving complaints from television stations that they were compelled to purchase entire blocks of films to obtain those they wanted. When he testified in September 1956 before the Monopoly Subcommittee of the House of Representatives, Hansen said there was considerable similarity between what was going on in television and the practices outlawed by the Supreme Court in 1948.[36]

Justice filed suit in federal court in March 1957 asking for an injunction that would prevent MGM's parent Loew's Inc. from block booking movies to TV. Filed by the Department's Antitrust Division the suit charged Loew's with requiring stations to take large numbers of movies—"in many cases" more than 700—that were not desired in order to obtain the TV right to desired movies. Loew's issued a denial.[37]

A couple of weeks later, five more companies were named in the suit, Columbia subsidiary Screen Gems, United Artists, C&C Super Corporation, Associated Artists Productions (AAP), Fox partner company NTA. The president of NTA, Ely Landau, responded by saying "N.T.A. does not engage in compulsory block-booking. Its licenses do usually cover a number of films, but this is for the convenience of the television stations as well as N.T.A. and is not a requirement of N.T.A."[38]

Just about two weeks after charges were filed against it, MGM announced a new flexible selling arrangement on its 723-title library with each one being given a specific price. Supposedly, a television station would then buy from one movie on up with special discount arrangements for packs of 100, 350 and the full library. MGM executive Dick Harper declared the plan had been in the works for some time and it was just a coincidence it was publicly announced so soon after Justice filed suit. On individual titles, the MGM standard license was for one year, two runs although it said it would negotiate for periods up to seven years for an individual title, and up to an unlimited number of runs. Under its discount structure, stations buying the full MGM library got a 50 percent discount; for purchasers of a half-library (350 titles) the full price was divided by two and then discounted by 37.5 percent. For packs of 100, the total market price was divided by seven and then discounted by 25 percent. However, only three packs of 100 were then being offered, primarily, said MGM, because the prints were not ready. Buying a number of titles outside those ranges, say one, or 17, or 76 entitled the outlet to no discount. Nor could such a station expect exclusivity in its market since MGM would continue to try and sell half and full library packs to other stations in that market. When a station bought a preassembled block from a major, it got exclusivity in its market for the length of time contracted for. Harper insisted his company had carefully investigated all antitrust angles before ever commencing the sale of features to TV. He insisted that few stations had indicated any interest in packages less than the half-library size since they were deprived of exclusivity in their market, "along with the MGM identification" and the discount structure.[39]

The suit by Justice involved all the major distributors. Columbia, MGM, and UA did their own distributing while C&C licensed RKO, AAP did Warner, and NTA handled Fox. Paramount and Universal were later than the others in releasing pre–48s to television. They weren't named in the suit because they weren't releasing to television during the time span the suit alleged the block booking occurred. Also alleged was that none of the companies charged would license product on a film-by-film basis. Hansen argued the government suit was also to benefit the independent stations which relied heavily on movies to compete with the network affiliated outlets. Justice was seeking injunctive relief from enforced block booking only; stations would still be free to license blocks if they wished.[40]

United Artists was then in the process of buying a controlling interest in AAP while the latter was in the middle of mapping out a new sales strategy on the Warner product it handled. AAP pulled back 200 titles from the 750 Warner library, placing the remainder in groups of 52 to be released at intervals over the coming years. Previously, the titles had also been in packs of 52 but all blocks were on the market at the same time. Reportedly, all that was motivated by a fear of the antitrust action, especially since it was becoming tied up with UA. Hoping to forestall more charges of block booking, AAP argued that all the titles in the small bundles were good—and equal in quality—that is, stations were not getting stuck with any turkeys. No longer trying to sell the entire library in a block was evidence in AAP's mind that it could not be guilty of block booking. Unsaid was what AAP was going to do with the 200 titles it had withdrawn. Presumably, these were the turkeys, even in the eyes of their distributor.[41]

The CBS flagship outlet WCBS bought the entire 700 title Paramount library from MCA for $8.4 million. With Justice looking over its shoulder, MCA established a price list for each title, on a market-by-market basis with stations able to bid on one or more titles. That deal was done within 48 hours of the New York outlets receiving the MCA price list, which ranged from $2,400 up to $60,000 per title. WCBS had paid an average of $12,000 per movie. As well, WCBS had agreed to pay the residual fee to the American Federation of Musicians, which amounted to six percent of the gross, $504,000. WCBS also paid the print cost, $75 per negative.[42]

Another CBS owned and operated outlet, KNXT Los Angeles, bought the full Paramount library for $7 million in a deal giving them seven runs over seven years. The station then had its own backlog of 1,400 titles which had cost it $12 million and which it believed gave it enough first-run product to last for seven years. However, in that backlog, there were some rejects. KNXT eliminated any titles that didn't meet the requirements of the Television Code and CBS Continuity Acceptance (basically, the network's own censor). Other rejects included virtually all movies which originated prior to the early 1930s installation by Hollywood of the Hays Office (Hollywood's censor machinery), and a "good majority" of features made before 1935 were shelved because they were "dated." Examples were Park Avenue sophisticated drama or comedy made for escapism during the Depression and early gangster movies, then deemed "somewhat laughable." While KNXT couldn't estimate the number of films dropped for these reasons, a spokesman said "it comes to a considerable part of any major studio package."[43]

In 1960, Fox had about 300 pre–1935 movies still "uncommitted." Apparently because no buyer could be persuaded to take them. Rumors were then flying in the trade papers that when Fox finally released its post–48s, the studio "might try to package pix of recent vintage with the pre–'35 oldies." This doesn't seem to have happened.[44]

Early in December 1960, Judge Archie Dawson of New York's Southern District Federal Court ruled that block booking practices in selling movies to TV violated the Sherman Antitrust Act. He held that all six companies named in the suit had restrained interstate trade and commerce in the distribution of feature films and ruled that an injunction was needed such that a company could not condition the licensing of one television movie on the licensing of another television movie. Noting from the news the possible imminent release to TV of post–48s, Dawson stated, "Certainly, we would not want the defendants to follow certain of the procedures which they followed with reference to the pre–1948 films, which are found in this opinion to be violations of the antitrust laws."[45]

That decision did reject one of the remedy's sought by the Justice Department—the reopening of existing contracts between stations and distributors for renegotiation, if desired by stations. The suit had not alleged or charged any conspiracy to block book, simply that the defendants had all engaged in block booking. Dawson's decision also attempted to clarify the difference between illegal tie-in selling and acceptable package selling. Package selling was okay so long as there was no express or implied "conditioning" that put the sale of the pack on an all-or-nothing basis. Quantity discounts were acceptable if they had a reasonable relationship to the quality of the titles offered. Conditioning any sale to an owner of a group of stations on his purchasing the pack for the whole group of stations was merely another form of illegal package selling. However, it was ruled permissible for a distributor to refuse to sell a broken or part package to a television station if there was an "active possibility" of selling the whole package to a competitor.[46]

Justice found the decision too loose and appealed to the U.S. Supreme Court to have it tightened. Five of the six defendants found the decision too tight and appealed to the U.S. Supreme Court to have it loosened (NTA declined to join the appeal). If the decision stood, Justice declared, "anti-competitive practices" would be wielded against TV stations bidding for post–48s as well as pre–48s. What upset Justice was Dawson's ruling that block booking "on a temporary basis" was okay. That is, a distributor could refuse to sell individual titles to a station temporarily—while it shopped other stations in the same market to see if one would buy a package. The economic effects of block booking were the same, said Justice, whether or not the seller indicated he might sell the tied titles separately if they could not be sold as a package to anyone else in some market.[47]

On November 5, 1962, the U.S. Supreme Court upheld Dawson's decision as rendered, with some refinement in language. While this Court held the distributors, when putting movies on the market, should be required to list a price for each one separately and to sell them singly it also declared the price for a package could not be less than the total of the individual film prices, except to the extent that the distributor made actual cost savings. The principle of withholding single titles and/or broken packs from a ready-to-buy outlet on a "temporary" basis, or to "briefly defer," was upheld so long as a distributor had "a deal in negotiation" with a competitive station for a package. Since both parties had appealed and since the Supreme Court essentially left the decision unchanged, it was likely true that both sides were disappointed.[48]

Even as early as this period—only a few years into the release of pre–48s—Hollywood, and the television stations, were enthused by the profits in selling movies to TV, and by their durability. Since the release of the original group of Columbia features in January 1956 to television, the company returned to the market eight times in the following 3½ years with groups ranging from 20 to 112 features. Screen Gems then still had over 400 Columbia and Universal (for whom it was distributor) pre–48s unreleased to TV. Added Screen Gems executive Jermoe Hyams: "And, what's more, we're now back selling the reruns of features we originally released in 1956. In view of possible coming shortages, SG is taking a more conservative approach. Henceforth, it will release new pix only in such markets and such times as the stations demand it." MGM executive Richard Harper observed that feature films programmed on TV offered a number of built-in plus factors. One was that "they accommodate 12 or more one-minute commercials; four times as many as conventional half-hour programming" while a second one was that they have "tremendous residual playing value, picking up new audiences with every rerun." Over the eight years that WCBS had been running the *Late Show* it had telecast over 1,600 movies, aired an average of five times each, with about six months separating play dates. The station was then airing 24 hours of movies weekly with them consistently being the top rated shows in their time slots. More often than not, they were commercially sold out. WCBS general manager Frank Shakespeare, Jr. observed: "a library must be large enough to allow a sufficient resting period between play dates. It is a mistake to go into feature film programming with a limited schedule and a limited library."[49]

As early as 1957, some of the majors were trying to extract a premium price for their color films. MGM was leasing its pre–48 library to stations for black and white transmission with color telecasting left open for negotiations at a premium price. UA then had a post–48 pack of 39 titles in circulation,

12 of which were in color. Contracts with UA called for an extra 25 percent added to the bill for color telecasts, with UA footing the bill for the color negatives. Reportedly, UA had closed color "premium" deals with eight stations by then, with negotiations underway with another dozen outlets. Such efforts were generally unsuccessful at the time because few people had color sets.[50]

Joseph Vogel, president of MGM, announced in 1960 that 43 percent of the studio's net income came from television, 40 percent from theatrical films, with the remainder coming from other divisions. The bulk of the television income came from the sales of MGM's pre–48s. Yet, theatrical films accounted for 78 percent of the studio's gross income, with TV gross receipts being just ten percent of the total gross. It illustrated the high profit margins involved in selling old movies to TV. MGM declared it was in no hurry to sell its post–48s, citing Paramount's late release on its pre–48s, with a resultant even higher gain since prices paid by television stations had risen by the time Paramount joined in. By then, MGM had grossed $34 million in its sales of pre–48s, movies and short subjects, with another $24 million seen for the future.[51]

Just before it released its backlog, rumors circulated, in January 1957, that Paramount would be disinclined to dispose of its pre–48 library on any kind of straight leasing deal preferring instead arrangements whereby interests in additional television stations could be obtained. Paramount then owned 100 percent of Los Angeles outlet KTLA and, through its DuMont stock holdings, had interests in New York's WABD and WTTG in Washington, D.C. In fact, Paramount didn't add to its ownership position in outlets. While that had once been the hope and dream of the majors, the others had by then abandoned such plans, understanding that the rules constructed by the FCC and the structure of national networks precluded them from being a major player in either sphere. At best they could each hold a minor position in station ownership, but that was a far cry from the sort of control and domination the majors had envisioned. Paramount was just a little later than the others in giving up that dream.[52]

Screen Gems reached an agreement with Universal in 1957 whereby it would be the exclusive TV distributor for Universal's pre–48 backlog of 600 or so titles. The deal ran for 14 years with Universal guaranteed $20 million a year in each of the first seven years of the deal, against a complicated rental sharing formula. That led Justice to file a civil suit in April 1958 against Universal, Screen Gems, and the latter's parent company Columbia, charging them with being an unlawful combination in restraint of trade, with fixing prices and with reducing competition in distributing feature films to television stations. Justice cited the large part of the total broadcasting time of all television stations then devoted to feature films. Brought under the Sherman Antitrust Act, Justice hoped its action would foster more competition. What it wanted was for the deal to be voided, to be declared an "illegal conspiracy" under both the Sherman and the Clayton antitrust acts.[53]

However, in July 1960 Judge William Herlands of the U.S. District Court of Southern New York absolved the film companies of the antitrust charges. Herlands ruled the government had failed to prove the Sherman Act was violated. There was not enough evidence, he said, to prove that the agreement was made to fix prices "or in any way to affect the general market price of feature films or other television programming."[54]

Chapter 4

Television Defends Its Honor, 1956–1961

> "The public must be free to pick and pay in a competitive market."
> Barney Balaban,
> Paramount President,
> 1957.

> "If I had my way, we wouldn't sell to television ever."
> Alex Harrison,
> Fox Executive, 1958.

With pre–48s released, the majors continued to explore other ways of using TV. *MGM Parade* was discontinued in May 1956 after one disappointing season. Henceforth, the studio said it would produce programs especially for TV and acquire an interest in, or purchase, television stations. Asked if MGM planned to acquire the maximum of five outlets permitted by FCC rules, company executive Charles Barry replied, "If a major company enters this field, it eventually hopes to have the maximum number of stations a company can have."[1]

However, Hollywood moved into television in other ways, besides selling its old movies. Biggest by far was Screen Gems which, in 1957, had ten national series on the networks in primetime with 16 pilot deals for the next season. Fox had three series on the networks, Warner had two, with three new series set for the following season. MGM had one pilot with several other projects in process. Only Universal and Paramount were not then involved, excepting Paramount's small station ownership position.[2]

Just one year later, all the majors were involved in television series production, in one degree or another. Universal and Paramount were the last majors to get involved; they were also the last majors to release their pre–48s. RKO was inactive then, in everything, as it was in its death throes.[3]

It represented a major change in the way majors operated. At the time, TV producers turned out a half-hour series episode for around $35,000, whereas a Hollywood major spent $10,000 to $20,000 per single minute of feature film.[4]

Some observers believed the majors would have to soon go into the selling of their post–48s' backlog as the money stream from the pre–48s was expected to dry up soon. But the fact that all of them moved into telefilm production in a big way made that a weak economic argument. For 1959, Warner grossed about $30 million from its telefilm productions while it had sold its entire pre–48 library outright for $21 million. The latter, of course, was 100 percent profit while the former was not.[5]

Theater TV had died by this period as a hope and a dream for Hollywood as an alternative to TV. As a reality it still existed marginally and would sputter here and there with the odd program but, like RKO, it was in its death throes. What didn't exist in reality for Hollywood but which continued as a hope and a dream was pay-TV. When all the majors unloaded their pre-48s it seemed to most observers and to Hollywood itself, that that very action had severely wounded, if not destroyed, that dream. Yet it persisted. It did so because of the tremendous financial potential Hollywood knew it had and it was something the majors could likely control themselves, compared to theatre TV, which remained controlled by the exhibitors, and television itself, which had foreclosed a controlling interest to Hollywood.

Paramount was the only major actively working on pay–TV in this period. Its subsidiary company, the International Telemeter Corporation, gave a public demonstration in March 1957. Its system then had three component parts: a "pocket-sized" transmitting station where programs would originate, a wire distribution system to carry the movie signals, and a cash register which was hooked up to the TV set. When activated by a deposit of coins—denominations ranging from five to fifty cents were acceptable—the box would enable the user to make a selection from a minimum of three being offered by tuning to the designated channel where the signal had been unscrambled by the coin deposit. Since the programs would not be broadcast over the air, but transmitted closed-circuit by cables strung on utility poles, the system did not require FCC licensing. Being a versatile device, the coin box also posted the price of the program, registered the money as it was deposited, and established a credit if too much was inserted. As well, it also contained a tape recorded message of the available programs and starting times. Transmitting stations, which contained film and TV projectors, required an area of just 400 square feet. They could easily be installed in the lobby of most cinemas. Cost of a basic transmitting studio was said to be about $10,000 with the cost of wiring up individual homes ranging from $25 to $100 each. A profitable system could be established, claimed Telemeter, by servicing 2,000 to 2,500 homes in an area. Paramount President Barney Balaban expressed the hope that theatre owners would be the principal customers, but added, "first choice goes to the man who will pay the money, and that's all." Reportedly, operators of 1,000 cinemas all over America were making applications to city and state authorities (utility poles were involved) to obtain franchises.[6]

Telemeter and Fox West Coast Theatres Corp filed a joint application for a franchise for the City of Los Angeles to set up the system. Fox Theatres was a subsidiary of National Theatres Corporation, America's second largest cinema chain. Formerly, it had been part of the Fox empire but was sold off to satisfy the divestment order. Telemeter estimated the cost of "saturation coverage"—that is, 75 percent of the available sets—would come to $30–$50 million for the metro Los Angeles area, then containing an estimated 800,000 sets.[7]

At a stockholders' meeting, Balaban declared the potentials of TV beckoned even more invitingly but that toll TV was "inevitable." In an indirect rejection of flat-rate monthly pay–TV, the studio head said he was more convinced than ever that a "cash method" was the best method of collecting for pay–TV, and that's why Paramount had selected the Telemeter system, because "People like to buy their entertainment as their whim strikes them, and want to do it quickly and conveniently." Balaban argued the incentive for good programming would disappear if movies were sold to toll TV at a flat rate and that, "The public must be free to pick and pay in a competitive market." This system went nowhere. Partly that was because it wasn't technically feasible and partly because the whole concept of pay–TV was the focus of more and more public anger and subjected to political pressure.[8]

May 1957 was selected as the target date for a different experiment in Bartlesville, Oklahoma, a town of 35,000 with five theatres in operation (two being drive-ins). All were owned by Video Independent Theatres, which was also in the community antenna business (as cable was first called) when it was mostly used to rebroadcast television signals for communities that could not get a single TV channel clearly. Bartlesville could receive five TV channels, three of them very clearly. Video had wired up 4,000 homes to pipe movies directly to the homes of subscribers, using a channel not then in use. Charges were slated to be $9.50 per month, movies would run continuously and would be changed three times a week. As this was a closed system, it also did not require FCC approval. Asked what would happen if the experiment caught on and theatre attendance dropped, Video President Henry Griffing observed that attendance had fallen steadily in recent years so some would close with the rest offering the "kind of grand Hollywood fare, with scope and color, that home television can never equal." A problem was that Griffing needed new movie product for his system and, although he had no firm commitment from any major, he confidently declared they were showing interest.[9]

Launch of the system came on September 3, 1957 when Telemovie offered *The Pajama Game* (1957). One channel was used for first-run attractions while a second channel was used to show reruns of popular films of recent vintage. That night, *River Gambler* (1954; three years old) was telecast on the rerun channel. Customers received both channels for $9.50 a month. Bartlesville was chosen, said Griffing, because "we wanted to compete with television in an area where reception is good." The system carried no ads except announcements of coming attractions on the system. That absence of commercials, thought Griffing, was the greatest appeal of this kind of entertainment.[10]

Fox, Paramount, and MGM all refused to supply product to the system, only Warner and Columbia supplied some. When he argued his case before the majors, Griffing admitted "it fell on completely arid ground." One studio executive told him "What's the use of having a wonderful Telemovie setup in a town if it ruins all the theatres? We'd be right back where we started." Believing that people would not leave their homes, he decided to bring the movies to their homes, Griffing once remarked when asked about his contradictory position since he was also a big theatre owner. He said, "We are not doing this because we think we are exceedingly bright, but because we are exceedingly frightened." Reporter Fred Hift observed, "The backbone of any pay–TV system must be film."[11]

Hoping to attract 2,000 customers by the end of the first year, it had only about 340 by February 1958. A rate reduction that month down to $4.50 a month moved the customer base to 800 by May. However, it was not enough with the experiment canceled as of June 5, 1958, due to the poor response. Griffing blamed technical difficulties and the fact his system suffered because of the "hundreds of movies shown free on television." He felt that if the pay–TV concept was ever to succeed, it would have to be broadened to include other types of programs. Included in letters sent to subscribers telling them of the end of the system was a free pass to any movie house in Bartlesville.[12]

Opposition to any and all forms of pay–TV continued to mount. At a 1957 convention of the Theatre Owners of America (TOA), a unanimous resolution registered its opposition to all forms of pay–TV. Through its regional units, TOA planned to lobby the Senate, the House of Representatives and state and municipal authorities to pass legislation against toll TV. Free TV and pay could not co-exist, they said, because pay–TV would usurp all the popular programs; the U.S. public had invested in 45 million television sets with the expectation it would receive free programming. The "novelty of even seeing the poorest pictures on pay–TV systems would so damage theatre audiences that it would result in theatre closings which could almost completely eliminate the exhibition industry" argued the group, which also said the public, in both official and unofficial polls, had "overwhelmingly" opposed pay–TV. It was a warning to the majors that if they furnished movies in current release to toll, it would mean "the end of the motion picture theatres." Marcus Cohn, TOA counsel, pointed out that if toll TV came, it would be an "open invitation" for government regulation, the same as any utility with the result that prices would be set. That meant, declared Cohn, that rights now enjoyed by both the film and television industries such as "the right to charge what they want to theatre patrons and to advertisers" would disappear.[13]

At the same time the National Association of Radio and Television Broadcasters threw its support behind legislation that would outlaw pay–TV. Association President Harold Fellows said the issue was whether American people "are going to have to pay for the right to view programs on their home television sets." Senator Strom Thurmond (Dem. SC) and Representative Emanual Celler (Dem–NY) had introduced identical bills in Congress to prohibit pay–TV.[14]

An unusual alliance of exhibitors and TV broadcasters teamed up to oppose the concept under the name "Committee Against Pay to See TV." Marcus Cohn, also counsel of that group, said, "If the American public is ever told it will have to pay for its TV programs, the Boston Tea Party will fade into an insignificant skirmish." The campaign was fought under the themes of free speech and freedom of the airwaves, etc. Celler, chairman of the House Judiciary Committee warned the FCC to keep its hands off pay–TV and leave it to Congress to decide its fate. He also introduced a bill which would have imposed a five-year prison term or a fine of $10,000 or both, on anyone attempting to impose a fee on home television viewers. Hollywood producer/director Mervyn LeRoy was in favor of pay–TV, saying, "If anything justified the marriage of pay TV with the motion picture industry it is television's indiscriminate, wholesale appropriation of old movies."[15]

As the majors inevitably moved toward the release of post–48s to TV, Hollywood found its way blocked by the talent unions. Those unions had no intention of giving up their claim to a share of the income, as had happened with the pre–48s. While the American Federation of Musicians was a leader in militancy in the 1940s, it was basically not a player by the end of the 1950s. During the 1957–58 talks between the AFM and the film producers, negotiations over post–48 residuals broke down and, following the ensuing musicians' strike, the AFM lost jurisdiction over the studio musicians to the newly formed Musicians Guild of America. Thus, the AFM found itself in a somewhat peculiar position; in accordance with the 1946 agreement, film producers had to "negotiate" with AFM on any movie made between 1946 and 1958 but should a producer, in fact, refuse, AFM was powerless to do anything but sue. Since they no longer represented the studio musicians, an AFM strike would be meaningless.[16]

C&C Super Corporation reached an agreement in 1956 with SAG, and the Writers Guild of America (West) and the Screen Directors Guild for the TV release of 82 features made by RKO after August 1, 1948. Each union settled independently, for SAG the deal was for $615,000 plus another $100,000 after a certain gross was reached. Then in progress were negotiations between the guilds and the Association of Motion Picture Producers (the majors were the dominant force in that body). Those C&C deals did not necessarily establish a pattern for any future settlement.[17]

With no settlement coming easily, representatives of all the guilds met with exhibitors early in 1958 to discuss the possibilities of halting the sale of post–48s to TV. Openly expressed was a fear of "disaster" for the industry as a whole if sales to television were not halted. Exhibitor fear was, of course, over a further decline in box office while one worry for SAG was that with more sales to TV, Hollywood would turn more and more to that medium, with an overall reduction of work for actors. A problem for SAG was how to strike back considering such studios as RKO and Republic had by then ceased production. At the meeting, attention was drawn to a just concluded sale of Republic movies to NBC.[18]

Later that year, UA was offering a pack of 65 post–48 movies to stations; 45 were made offshore (20 from the U.K.'s J. Arthur Rank) and thus didn't come under the jurisdiction of American talent guilds. But 20 of them were U.S.–produced. However, since UA had no production arm (it was a distributor only), it could not be struck by SAG or the other guilds. UA was then arguing that movies which lost money in their theatrical release were not subject to talent guild demands for a share of TV residuals. Those guilds all continued negotiation, off and on. Reportedly, the position of the majors was to tell the guilds that films which failed to recoup costs theatrically should be exempt from residual payments. Fox President Spyros Skouras went further, maintaining that the motion picture industry would not meet union demands for a share of post–48 revenue regardless of whether a film lost money theatrically. By then, the situation was said to be nearing the critical stage with TV by then having "used up" from 8,000 to 9,000 movies with reruns being the order of the day by 1961. About 400 post–48s were making the rounds in mid–1958, 203 of them from Republic, 65 from UA.[19]

In 1959, SAG struck another deal when they reached agreement covering 17 post–48s distributed by UA calling for a flat payment of $40,000 to the guild for distribution to actors in those movies. The importance of that deal was that it covered seven films which had failed to recover their negative costs from cinema release. A second deal with American–International (TV distribution by NTA) covered five post–48 movies and called for payment to actors of 15 percent of their original salaries.[20]

Nevertheless, the MPAA had established and maintained as a "principle" non-participation with unions and guilds in revenue from post–48s sold to television. Through the Association of Motion Picture Producers, it maintained that principle in its negotiations with the guilds as the 1950s ended. All those guilds, of course, wanted participation. Following the MPAA's logic any sharing of revenue would be ruinous to the distributors and also the union groups. If handed out, percentages would eat up the major share of any income, making it virtually "senseless" to sell the items to television at all. Also, the majors needed the extra money from TV sales to plow back into their business and if they didn't get it, in the long run it would hurt labor as much as the producers. Existing contracts with the guilds, going back to the end of the 1940s, stated that a dispute existed on the question of television sales and that the union had the right to "blacklist" a producer who went ahead and sold post–48s to TV without satisfying the guilds. It was a foregone conclusion that if any producers did go ahead and sell post–48s, it would be struck by the guilds. The MPAA rejected the idea that the AFM contract represented a precedent, maintaining that the talents' part in a film ended when the movie was done.[21]

Skouras declared that if the writers, actors and directors guilds continued to demand post–48 residuals it would result in "a struggle to the death." Film producers, he continued, could not possibly comply because the reduced income would make it impossible for them to continue as move-making entities. Describing guild demands as "completely unreasonable" Skouras declared that if they continued in their demands "we will shut down our Hollywood studios."[22]

With such an impasse a strike seemed inevitable. Writers struck in January 1960, followed by SAG two months later. Reportedly, all issues had been settled except the post–48 revenue. *Variety* magazine thought that 15 percent of the gross revenue for the talent was a reasonable compromise. However, Association of Motion Picture Producers' spokesman Charles Boren continued taking a hard line stating it was "unreasonable and unrealistic" for the unions to ask that their members "be paid twice for doing one job." He added that if talent demands were met, "in effect, the producers would be precluded from licensing or selling theatrical motion pictures to television" and that a strike by actors "could permanently curtail studio employment."[23]

Struck were five of the majors plus Disney and Allied Artists. RKO no longer existed and, being a distributor only, UA could not be struck. The remaining major, Universal, broke ranks and settled early on in the writers' strike, and before SAG walked out. Under its deal with the Writers Guild of America, the guild got two percent of the gross, less 40 percent for distribution expenses, which worked out to about 1.2 percent of the total gross. Traditionally, residual payments had followed a three-to-one ratio, actors getting three times the amount that writers and directors got. Thus, actors were projected to get six percent (of the gross less 40 percent = 3.6 percent). It meant producers expected to end up paying ten percent in residuals, actually six percent of the gross, after the forty percent was deducted.[24]

Finally, in early March, SAG and the majors reached an agreement to end the strike. Somewhat surprisingly, SAG waived the right to share in any television income on movies made between 1948 and 1960. Trade-off for that was the producers agreeing to set up a pension plan and a health and welfare fund for the actors; none had been in place before. On movies begun after January 31, 1960, the producers agreed to pay six percent of television receipts, after deducting the 40 percent. That was the case where the producer assumed the distribution costs. In cases where the movie was sold outright to TV, the producer could deduct only ten percent before making the six percent payment. A special provision in the deal covered pay–TV, allowing for reopening of the contract if pay–TV became an important reality. It was then estimated that Hollywood had produced perhaps 4,000 movies between 1948 and 1960. Maybe 1,500 of them, one way or another, had already found their way to television but, noted an account, "Most of the post–48s already on the market are the indie low budget variety."[25]

Also functioning to prevent Hollywood from selling its post–48 backlog were the exhibitors, and sometimes others. At the end of 1957, the Screen Producers Guild went on record as opposing the release of movies to television. It urged specifically that post–48s be held back but concluded in general that it was a mistake to make films available to television at all, based on the idea that it was destroying cinema business.[26]

At a convention of theater owners at the close of 1956, the Allied States Association members adopted a resolution requesting that a study be made of the feasibility of establishing a legal clearance for cinemas over TV. That is, a specific period that had to pass before a movie could be released to the other medium. Although it was not specified in the resolution, Allied wanted a clause written into film contracts declaring that movies be withheld from video for at least five years. Group attorney Abram Myers declared in a speech that he was tired of seeing theaters absorb all of TV's punches without fighting back. He asserted that broadcasters' and sponsors' advertising of old features on TV was reaching the point that "theatres will have to strike back in self-defense." Film studios had discouraged such exhibitor efforts as they were "playing both sides of the street." Myers urged exhibitors to publicize their own facilities "where one new picture follows another and where they are presented in proper sequence without raucous and distracting commercials." In his speech, researcher Al Sindlinger described as "stupid" the policy of employing television advertising to see theatrical movies claiming that when *The Wizard of Oz* was shown on network television as a one-off special, it cost the nation's box offices a total gross loss of $2 million. Allied again went on record as opposing the introduction of pay–TV; it was an integral part of the Joint Committee Against Pay–TV then lobbying against the concept. However, Allied was interested in a form of pay–TV it could control, namely theater TV. It was still researching that concept which, of course, would originate, and keep, pay–TV in their theatres.[27]

4. Television Defends Its Honor, 1956–1961

Early in 1958, Allied stated that morale was very low in the exhibition business. Myers said confidence could be restored "if only the black beast television could be banished or its sharpest fangs drawn." Convinced Hollywood would continue to sell to television, Allied brought up its clearance theme again by suggesting "the very least they can do is to grant the theatres definite adequate clearances over TV which they can use in their advertising to offset the reckless and sometimes untrue advertising of the broadcasters."[28]

Julius Gordon, president of Allied States Association, urged studios to declare a three-year moratorium on the licensing to TV, that the showing of Hollywood films on the tube had "everybody (in the film business) bleeding to death." He thought that a moratorium would give the film industry a chance to recover. And even if it didn't, nothing would really be lost since at the end of the no-sales period, Hollywood's backlog would have increased substantially. Gordon, however, defended the distributors for their actions, noting they couldn't have foreseen the precarious position in which the trade was placed by the television sales.[29]

Through its organization COMPO (Council of Motion Picture Organizations of Texas), Texas exhibitors wrote a letter to MPAA requesting that it obtain permission from its member film studios for the exhibitors to state "this picture will not be shown on television for 10 years." COMPO was designing a special seal or insignia to indicate certain movies, if the studios agreed, would not be available to television for a decade. That insignia would be readily recognizable and would become an incorporated part of the feature itself, trailers, lobby displays, newspaper ads, etc.[30]

Fox announced at that time that it was maintaining the policy it had announced in November 1957: it stood ready to withhold its movies from television for at least five years after initial release. Company executive Alex Harrison declared he was in fact willing to extend that clearance period: "If I had my way, we wouldn't sell to television ever." Fox was the only major to take that stand. Justice said it would not intervene if other distributors followed that example and set up five-year clearances. Clearances were not illegal, per se, a position upheld by the U.S. Supreme Court in its 1948 decision which broke up the majors' monopoly. At that time, Justice wanted clearances (with regard to the first, second, third, etc. runs of movies in cinemas) banned. However, the court allowed clearances to stand, provided they were "reasonable."[31]

Walter Reade Jr., president of the Walter Reade Theatres chain, became the first exhibitor to declare his circuit would no longer book the films of any producer who released his movies to television. Asked if he had discussed this policy with other owners, Reade said no: "If we did, we might all end up in jail," he joked, referring to antitrust implications. Reade's actions were said to reflect the feeling among exhibitors that had they been more active in the past, the floodtide of old movies to television might have been stemmed. They then felt it was up to them through "legitimate" pressure to keep post–48s from TV. Another exhibitor, unnamed, commented, "The companies still are in business to serve the theatres. Any distributor who clearly understands that his theatrical business will suffer if he sells out to television may think twice before selling us down the river."[32]

Just eight months after his announcement, Reade said that, partly because of a lack of exhibitor unity, the studios would end up selling their post–48s to TV: "We exhibitors could have prevented the sale of the old films and we could still prevent the new libraries going to TV, but it's impractical. There just is no unity." When he launched his boycott campaign, he got no support from exhibitors. "The industry is a hopeless case," he lamented.[33]

When major studio heads met with Theatre Owners of America (TOA) officials in February 1958, the latter were said to have been encouraged that efforts would be made by Hollywood to withhold sale of the post–48s. Paramount President Barney Balaban issued a letter stating his company had "no plans to sell, nor do we anticipate the sale of, our post–1948 features to the free television screens of America, either currently or in the foreseeable future–and perhaps we may never sell them." That reference to "free" TV was open to interpretation. As already noted, Paramount was active then in its pay–TV ventures and had not then given up on the concept. TOA President Ernest Stellings remarked: "On the basis of discussions and conversations, we're sure that as far as management is concerned they are cognizant of the problems and realize what further sales to television would mean to the industry."[34]

As part of its campaign to keep post–48s off home screens, TOA sent a proposal to the majors regarding theatrical reissue of movies. Stellings proposed a two-month test during which each distributor would re-release two of their best older films each month. For its part, Stellings stressed that TOA and other exhibitor groups would urge cinemas to book the reissues. Also proposed by TOA was the establishment by exhibitors of a trust fund which would purchase the post–48s in order to keep them off television. Under the plan, exhibitors as a group would buy the movies with a small down payment. Bonds would be issued for the balance which would be amortized from box office receipts through an aggressive reissue program. None of this ever happened.[35]

The idea of theatrical reissues was often raised as a method of generating money for Hollywood from old movies, without selling them to television. However, it was rarely tried by the majors. Just once in a while and then usually only for spectaculars. It was all part of the Hollywood throwaway mentality; once a movie had made its way through the theatres in its first to third runs, it was finished, no other possibilities existed for it, at least prior to television. That was why when a major picked up an independent movie to distribute it took the rights for a limited period, almost never longer than three years. Only Disney had a reissue policy in which films were recycled back into cinemas every seven years or so, on the theory that a whole new crop of kids existed to see the studio's fare. The first time around, Disney's

Bambi (1942) took $1.2 million in 1942 in U.S. and Canadian rentals. Reissued in 1948, it took in $900,000. In its third time around, in 1957, it took in $2.7 million. Paramount's 1943 release *For Whom the Bell Tolls* picked up $800,000 in domestic rentals for its 1957 reissue. The best price from television for a movie was then $100,000 with very few commanding that figure. No one was sure what a more average Hollywood product might do in a theatrical reissue. However, it was generally agreed that the film capital had indeed "neglected" the reissue market.[36]

By the end of the 1950s exhibitor opposition was waning. They could achieve no unity in their efforts to halt the post–48 release. Even if they had attained unity, they lacked the necessary power. Slowly, they accepted the inevitable. Speaking at a TOA convention at the end of 1959, UA Vice President Max Youngstein was the first company executive in a high level position to state frankly that the sales of backlog movies to television "do serve a purpose." Youngstein was the first to state such an opinion in a public forum, although others had said so privately. Regarding the exhibitors' campaign to halt post–48 release he told them, "Don't put monkeys on our back." He explained that every dime UA got from selling films to television was poured back into theatrical productions, indicating that if the film industry did not supply movies to television some other source would fill the gap, or the television networks would make the movies themselves. Youngstein explained that this way, exhibitors would at least receive part of the benefit in the form of continued theatrical production.[37]

In the period after the pre–48 release and before the post–48 release, Hollywood and the three television networks engaged in sparring over whether or not those networks would program old movies in primetime. CBS did telecast *The Wizard of Oz* in late 1956 in primetime as a one-time special. It was such a ratings success that CBS would repeat *Oz* many times over the coming years, but always as a special. With the exception of ABC's experiments with primetime movies, the networks avoided the concept. One of the reasons for the networks' reluctance lay in the fact they had little faith in programming pre–48s in primetime as a regular concept. Also, the networks took the position that run-of-the-mill features had no place in network programming. There was a sincere conviction, at least in some quarters, that TV required a steady stream of imaginative, experimental entertainment suited to its own medium. Said NBC President Robert Sarnoff, "If there is any degradation of TV service it will come from film producers and the vaults of Hollywood." One New York advertising agency executive said that he "would hate to see TV turned over to the film industry." Yet stations running movies were reporting high ratings from those time slots. Boston's WBZ-TV tripled its ratings; the independent Los Angeles outlet KTTV, which programmed movies in primetime, on occasion outdrew the other six area stations combined. Early attempts to set up a film network among independent outlets had failed, due to scarcity of quality product, but the possibility of such a venture succeeding still worried the networks.[38]

David Sarnoff of NBC declared that feature films represented a "short road with a dead end" and warned of the television industry "surrendering" itself to Hollywood as features displaced network programming. Westinghouse Broadcasting President Donald McGannon reported in 1957 about pressure from Sarnoff on NBC affiliates to boycott movies. Besides the worry about the non-network distribution of films, the networks were often forced to bid for movie packages that tied less attractive titles to desirable ones. The process meant negotiating with a few major studios in a concentrated sellers' market, very different from the buyers' market for original series programs for television—at least in the early years. The biggest impact of feature films in 1950s television was not felt in network-controlled primetime, as one observer wrote, but in the affiliate-controlled afternoon and late-night fringe periods, "and the largest casualty was locally produced programs, especially children's programming."[39]

The ABC network did run its *Famous Film Festival* for two seasons in primetime, Sundays 7:30 to 9 PM and then Saturdays in the 1955–56 and 1956–57 seasons. Those films were from the U.K. and while there were a few strong titles, most were weak. NBC ran the U.K. production *Richard III* (1955) in primetime but, like CBS's treatment of *Oz*, it was a one-time special. Other than that, the three networks largely avoided programming movies. RKO, with its *Finest 52* package, along with MGM, had attempted to get network telecasting of its films but had failed. Conditions, though, were changing. The ratings potentials for theatricals were becoming better known as large and small outlets, affiliated and independent, on and off primetime, were tracked much better by the ratings agencies.[40]

The ABC flirtation with movies in primetime came precisely because it was the weakest of the three in the ratings race. As early as 1956, ABC and RKO began serious negotiations with the price then set by RKO at $50,000 per title, all releases to be pre–48s. When ABC signed an option deal with RKO in February 1957, the contract called for 52 movies to be screened in the 7:30 to 9 PM Sunday slot in the 1957-58 TV season. Price was then said to be slightly under $20,000 per title with some post–48s included in the pack. Those in the post–48 category had been made abroad and were thus exempt from residual payments to the talent guilds. With its *Famous Film Festival* series then dead and off the air, ABC hoped to fill the gap with what it hoped would be better-known and better-received titles from a Hollywood major. The deal was contingent on the network lining up enough advertising revenue, with the first title tentatively slated to air in April 1957. If no sponsors signed up there would be no deal. ABC did not exercise its option.[41]

Leonard Goldenson, president of ABC–Paramount (the cinema chain divested from Paramount studios) met with aluminum magnate Henry Kaiser in 1957, who wanted to sponsor a feature film from 8 to 10 PM on Sundays. Kaiser reasoned that since Goldenson owned so many theaters, if anyone could buy good movies to put on TV it would be him. Goldenson said, "Up to now, the motion picture industry hasn't been willing to do anything like that. But I'll try." He called all the major studios but was turned down by all. Going back to the industrialist the broadcaster told him the only movies available were "quite old and unsuitable."[42]

Fox struck a major deal with distributor National Telefilm Associates (NTA). In exchange for distribution rights, Fox received a 50 percent interest in NTA. Then NTA tried unsuccessfully to set up an ad-hoc network consisting of mostly independent television stations, on a barter basis. In exchange for a guaranteed 90 minutes of airtime a week to be sold by NTA to national advertisers, NTA would supply affiliates of the NTA Film Network with NTA's Fox features.[43]

Surprising most observers was a deal in principle reached early in 1957 by Paramount and CBS with the studio prepared to sell its entire library of pre–48s to CBS outright for $50 million. While directors for both the network and the studio had reportedly approved the deal, CBS later backed away due to worry over the reaction of Justice to the deal's antitrust possibilities.[44]

By the summer of 1960, little had changed. The majors had pitched themselves to the networks to program films in primetime but CBS and ABC both said no, while NBC had moved to a maybe. Having experienced *Oz* on their network, CBS executives didn't argue about the rating pull of *Oz* or the sponsor attraction for such a film but said *Oz* represented an almost unique attraction. As a network, CBS thought it might like to telecast the all time top ten movies as a series of specials, but "no more." On the other hand, CBS had made a huge investment in movies for its owned and operated stations and wondered why it should compete with similar product on those outlets. Despite its flirtations with movies in prime already, by 1960 ABC was officially opposed to movie programming on its network. They then wanted programming specifically made for television; borrowing programming from another medium for TV would add nothing to TV's creative capacity; interrupting regular network fare for movie specials would hurt the ratings of regular network programming. Traditionally, NBC had opposed movies on television, more strongly than the other two. However, at this time, their official position was that they had no blanket opposition to films on the tube.[45]

Paving the way for that next release was UA, which began selling a pack of 39 post–48s to television stations in the fall of 1956. It had been sold in some 85 markets in the first five months, although no arrangement had been reached with SAG or the other guilds. UA continued to sell but also continued to engage in talks with SAG to reach some settlement. Talent unions were in a weak position with regard to UA since they couldn't strike the distribution-only company.[46]

United Artists released another block of post–48s to TV, several months after the first, with most having been made in the 1950s. Most of the movies in both of those packs weren't subject to residuals as they had been made abroad. In the first block of 39 features only ten were subject to residual payments. By the time of the release of the second block UA had settled with SAG in that both accepted the "Monogram formula" for payment. UA granted SAG 12.5 percent of the original actor costs if the movie grossed up to $20,000 in the TV market, 15 percent if it grossed above that amount. That Monogram formula had been used for other releases of independent product to TV, and while SAG would have been happy to apply that formula to all the majors, Hollywood then was still stonewalling, insisting that any sharing of television revenue was economically prohibitive.[47]

When rumors surfaced in 1957 that recent Hollywood theatricals would soon show up on the home screen, MGM executive Ernie Emerline insisted that none of Hollywood's "important" movies made after 1948 had become available to free TV. All that was on the home screen, he said, were movies at least ten years old with most of them twice that "venerable age." Emerling argued that when post–48s were released they would still be years old: "Whatever happens, it is safe to say that the period before release of new films to free TV should be reckoned in terms of years and years—not weeks or months as some movie fans have been led to believe."[48]

Those post–48s were finally released to TV starting in the summer of 1960 when Warner struck a deal with distributor Creative Telefilm and Artists Ltd. Warner had made an outright sale of its pre–48s to Associated Artists Productions (AAP). In the fall of 1958, AAP assets, including non–Warner properties and Paramount's *Popeye* cartoons were purchased by UA Associated, a division of UA. Realizing how lucrative such backlogs could be, this time Warner retained ownership of its post–48s. The deal involved 110 movies with a cash payment of $100,000 per title ($11 million in total) plus 50 percent of the profits, after the costs of distribution were recovered. The majors were expected to release their post–48s in a gradual fashion, so as not to flood the market suddenly with product and perhaps depress prices. A second reason was the still-existing hope that pay–TV would become a pervasive reality. Its potential was enormous but the majors needed product they could feed it.[49]

At almost the same time, Fox began releasing some of its post–48s. Some of the majors hoped to withhold their blockbusters from the TV market, hoping for a network telecasting or even a theatrical reissue. However, if those big ones were needed to help move other recent movies to TV they would be. As one executive said, "Packages will be formed on a quality basis and if a big recent one is needed to make a group of 'Bs' palatable, the biggies of yesterday will be included."[50]

Pricing was sometimes difficult for the majors since they had little to guide them. With respect to post–48s bought by CBS for its five owned and operated television stations, Hollywood decided initially to ask for $68,000 to $75,000 per title. The highest price those stations had paid for pre–48s was an estimated $40,000 per movie for some from the Paramount library, a late releaser of pre–48s. In arriving at the asking price, the majors did their own estimating. All five outlets aired three movie series nightly, *The Late Show*, *The Late Late Show* and *The Early Show*. Each carried 11–14 one-minute spots and 4–7 10-second spots. One minute ads cost about $1,000 to buy. On just one showing of *The Late Show* all five outlets grossed about $50,000. Thus, with an average minimum of three exposures of each film on *The Late Show* (which was the primary—and most expensive—showcase of the three slots) CBS grossed nearly $150,000. Adding on repeats of a title on *The Early Show* would produce $30,000 more, while still more repeats of the title on *The Late Late Show* would generate at least another $10,000. Therefore, the majors assumed that a movie shown on all five of the outlets, rotated repeatedly through the various time slots would generate around $190,000 for CBS, against a fundamental outlay of $40,000 at most. For a $68,000 deal CBS would likely be buying the rights to 6–12 runs, but even if CBS took only 2–3 runs, Hollywood believed the network could afford the price.[51]

Columbia joined the group when Screen Gems made the biggest sale to date, in November 1960, of post–48s by selling a block of 275 movies to CBS's five outlets for a total of $12.5 million, an average of $45,450 for multiple runs extending for many years. That package contained 200 Columbia post–48s and 75 Universal pre–48 productions. Assuming the pre–48s were priced at the old maximum of $40,000 it meant the 200 more recent titles averaged out to $47,500, well below what the majors had hoped to attain.[52]

By November 1961, about 600 post–48s were available to television with Columbia, Warner, Fox, MGM, and UA all actively releasing. Among the majors, only Paramount and Universal were holdouts, as they had been with the pre–48s.[53]

Universal ended its holdout in July 1963 when it released 215 post–48s to the distributor Seven Arts Associated, under a 10-year TV leasing deal for $21.5 million plus profit participation after certain conditions were met. Seven Arts was also handling some Fox and some Warner post–48s. A difference between the release of pre–48 and post–48 product to TV was that in the earlier case a few of the majors had sold their backlogs outright. Financially, that had proved to be a major mistake. It didn't happen in the second release period. All of the majors retained their ownership rights in the post–48s.[54]

When the post–48s started to show up regularly on the home screen, exhibitors once again expressed anger and dismay, wanting more theatrical reissues, as an alternative to TV broadcasting. However, theater chains had failed to respond when given the chance. Reportedly, both Fox and UA having been approached on cinema reissue, were willing enough provided exhibitors would come up with a guarantee on minimum play dates. Fox President Spyros Skouras sought a base of 7,000 bookings for a group of features headed for TV but he only got half that number to firmly commit.[55]

Live television continued to wither away during this period. In addition to movies, running anytime on independent stations, and off primetime on the affiliated outlets, stations also then had the option of programming syndicated telefilms—rerun series. Many stations solved some of their problems by telecasting a greater number of hours per week but, as *Variety* observed, "most feature-oriented stations have given the heave-ho to local 'live' programming in many areas, rather than telefilms."[56]

Reporter Murray Horowitz argued in 1958 that, against the fading of live drama on TV, with fewer regular networked shows in that category year by year "is the compensatory rise in the quality of major studio features being telecast by the stations." It was an open question for him whether live dramas were getting worse, "but there is no question that the appetite for drama on TV is present and it's being fed by the better oldies out of the libraries of the majors and other cinematic sources." With a Hollywood movie being shown on TV having originally cost $1 million to produce, against a budget of about $50,000 for the live drama, Horowitz thought perhaps live networked drama shows just couldn't stand the competition: "There's hardly any comparison in terms of star and production values.... Almost in inverse proportion to the fewer networked drama shows has been the increasing pool of quality theatricals available to local stations." At the time, the networks programmed virtually no movies on TV, so they provided no head-to-head competition of live drama versus movies. However, every market of any size had two or more independent outlets. At least one of those in each market had turned heavily to movie programming, including in primetime. The 1959–60 television season was 70 percent telefilm.[57]

Ninety percent of U.S. households owned TV receivers as of June 1961. According to a survey done by Pulse, Inc., a total of 84 percent of New Yorkers were watching movies on the early, late and late late shows, up from 69 percent who watched features on TV three years earlier. Of those respondents who had watched movies on TV, 33.9 percent thought the films were "more enjoyable" than other TV programs while 50 percent thought they were just as enjoyable. Of little or no concern to the viewer was the age of the film being shown.[58]

In December 1960, NBC made a preliminary announcement of the following year's television season lineup, the September 1961 to April 1962 period. CBS then thoroughly dominated the Saturday night ratings. NBC announced it had tentatively slated movies at 9 PM on Saturdays. Speculation was that the network would have to pay about $200,000 per movie. It was a programming move that *Variety* called "nothing short of revolutionary." To make room in the schedule one hour's worth of public affairs programming, *The Nation's Future*, was axed.[59]

Chapter 5

Hollywood Goes Primetime on the Networks, 1961–1975

> *"We're not a transmission belt for Hollywood product."*
> unnamed TV executive, 1962.

> *"Your name is on it but it isn't the thing you did."*
> John Ford, 1962.

This period began with the first programming of Hollywood product on primetime network schedules, in serious fashion. It opened up another market for the majors as movies soon came to be a large component of network primetime. Hollywood could then sell to the networks first and then sell the same films to outlets individually and in small groups. Prices received by the majors for their product skyrocketed. As the period ended prices, while still high, had declined. A new creature, made-for-TV movies had emerged. The end of the period was marked by the launch of Home Box Office (HBO), the first satellite-delivered service. That was followed a few months later by the launch of TBS, the first of the so-called superstations. Thus the groundwork was laid for an even greater expansion for Hollywood movies.

Block booking continued to be a Hollywood practice in its sale of features to television. Otto Preminger and Carlyle Productions sued Columbia studios and Screen Gems in 1966 for monetary damages in an antitrust suit over Preminger's *Anatomy of a Murder*, (1959) charging the existence of block booking in the sale of that title to TV. Alleged was that Columbia used *Anatomy* to promote the television distribution of "inferior motion pictures and teleplays" resulting in allocating to *Anatomy* an "unreasonably and unfairly low share of the block license fee payable to Screen Gems" for that film. The major issue was that Carlyle did not receive a proper share of the sale because other features in the package were priced on a par with *Anatomy*. Under standard industry practice theatrical distributors did not split profits with producers until after costs were recovered. *Variety* observed that, "Several TV sources admit privately that a kind of 'block-booking' is indeed a factor in the sale of features to stations, claiming that programming necessitates serial exhibition of the films."[1]

Columbia had a glossy sales brochure, *Columbia Group II Post–1950; Feature Films for Television* which it used to promote its block of 60 movies, one of which was *Anatomy*. Two previous film promotion booklets, *Columbia Post '48s* and *Columbia Post '50s* had been used to hype two previous packs. According to the newest booklet those two previous movie packages were most influential in the transformation of movie programming from a fringe time into a primetime affair. All of the majors used expensive, glossy brochures to sell their packages. Columbia's newest issue first prominently hyped its "highlighters"—ten titles, one of them being *Anatomy*. Next, a group of 13 were outlined. Then the bottom 37 were listed separately, and last. The difference in comparative individual price between the first ten, the next 13, and the remaining 37 titles was partly the basis upon which Preminger based his ultimately unsuccessful block-booking complaint.[2]

As the stockpile of movies dwindled down in the middle 1960s NBC and CBS, nonetheless, remained cool to the idea of telecasting dubbed movies. ABC was considering the possibility, but without much enthusiasm. Under consideration by the network was one Italian film, then owned by former CBS-TV President Jim Aubrey. An unidentified network executive (not with ABC) explained his network would stay away from dubbed product as long as possible fearing that once a dubbed title was bought; "distributors would condition the sale of undubbed product on the purchase of dubbed product. I don't want to be caught in that trap."[3]

Prices paid by TV for motion pictures dramatically rose, for networking and for syndication. When CBS bought a Warner post–48 block of 25 titles in 1963 for its five owned and operated outlets, it paid about $100,000 per title. That meant the New York market (in which one of the five was located) then carried a price tag of about $35,000 per movie. Estimated for 1963 were that stations spent $100 million for filmed television product. About $65 million of that amount was spent in buying films with the remaining $35 million going to all other filmed product, mainly series. By then an estimated 8,000 pre–48s had been released to television with an average gross of $50,000, for a total gross of $400 million. An estimated 3,000 post–48s had been released averaging a gross of $125,000, for a total of $325 million. Thus, the total gross take from the sale of movies to TV, at the end of 1963, was estimated at $725 million with the vast bulk of that going to the majors.[4]

Hollywood producers (majors and independents) were grossing well over $400 million annually from television by 1965; that was more than the $315 million estimated as the 1964 gross rentals of movies at U.S. cinemas. For features alone, U.S. television was paying out $120 million yearly. Eighty-five percent of the 1965-66 primetime schedule was devoted to filmed material.[5]

A standard contract in the middle 1960s for a station buying a film was a contract for five runs over five years. The cost of buying a single title in all top 51 film markets on the basis of such a contract rose to $265,000 in June 1965, compared to $191,250 in October 1964—a time span of only ten months. Price in the top 25 markets was $222,400, up from $160,000. Top three markets were New York ($52,500, $35,000), Chicago, ($34,000, $25,000) and Los Angeles ($30,000, $25,000). At the low end of those top 51 markets were Scranton ($1,200, $800), Flint ($1,170, $700) and Birmingham ($1,100, $800). In the middle was Cincinnati($2,700, $1,800). Less than a decade earlier when outlets such as the five CBS owned and operateds were buying entire libraries such as 750 movies from Paramount, contracts ran to unlimited runs over seven years, or sometimes seven runs over seven years.[6]

Prices for films on networks rose from an average of $169,000 per title in 1962 to a range of $500,000 to $600,000 per title in 1966. Saturday night's film slot on NBC had 14 commercial minutes to sell over the two hours. Based on $46,000 per minute for original telecasts, $37,000 for spring repeats, $31,000 for summer repeats, NBC had yearly revenues of $30 million. Subtracted from that were agency commissions and station compensation to the affiliated outlets (networks paid affiliated stations for the time they took up). *Variety* estimated those costs at up to half of the income, leaving NBC with revenue of $15 million from its Saturday movie slot. Since the movies then telecast in the slot were acquired earlier, at a cost of perhaps $350,000 per title, NBC paid about $10.5 million to lease those motion pictures.[7]

Profits were indeed healthy. For 1967 profits before taxes in all top 50 television markets, except two, were above $1 million. Forty of those markets produced profits in excess of $2 million. New York was the top market. Its seven stations had $129.4 million in revenue (commissions subtracted), $85.3 million in expenses and $44 million in profit (before federal income taxes). Similar figures for Los Angeles (number two market with 11 stations) were, $92.6 million, $66 million, $26.6 million. Chicago (number three market with six outlets) $75.9 million, $51.8 million, $24.1 million. The eighth place market was Cleveland, with three stations. Its figures were, respectively, $30.8 million, $14.9 million, $15.9 million.[8]

In 1972, the three networks had pre-tax profits of $111 million (up 106 percent over 1971), in 1973 they had $185 million in pre-tax profits, up 66 percent. The 15 owned and operated television stations (five by each network) had 1973 pre-tax profits of $102 million. That same year the stations in the New York market had combined broadcast revenues of $173 million, $40.5 million in pre-tax profits while in Los Angeles the numbers were $134 million and $28.4 million. Tenth placed market Pittsburgh had total television broadcast revenue of $30.2 million, $9.5 million in pre-tax profits in 1973.[9]

Towards the end of 1963, there were an estimated 10,427 features in release for television use. Of those 2,997 were post–48s, 1,205 were available in color. Those movies were being shown on TV stations which were still increasing in number, but the rate of increase had slowed drastically. In the USA in 1953, there were 125 television stations on the air (119 VHF, 6 UHF); 1959, 509 outlets (432 VHF, 77 UHF), 1967, 608 stations (492 VHF, 116 UHF).[10]

A 1969 survey of the entire continental U.S. indicated that 692 movies were being telecast in primetime every week. The split was even with the independent outlets airing 355 while the network affiliates screened 337 a week. During a typical week in the fall of 1971 in New York City outlets telecast 258 hours of movies, the equivalent of 11 full days. For that same week in and around Los Angeles, a viewer was offered 233 hours of films. In a single night about 86 million people sat through a 4-hour telecast of *Ben-Hur* (1959) on the tube. A movie that could then attract 4.5 million customers into cinemas in the course of a year was usually pretty successful. As *Look* magazine joked: "The movies aren't dead. They're on television."[11]

In the 1960-61 period, Saturday night ratings were dominated by CBS with *Gunsmoke* and *Have Gun, Will Travel* while ABC countered with the popular *Lawrence Welk Show*. NBC was a distant third. On Saturday, September 23, 1961 Fox and NBC combined to present the first movie in the *Saturday Night at the Movies* series. That was the 1953 release *How to Marry a Millionaire*, with Marilyn Monroe, Lauren Bacall and Betty Grable. For that first season NBC obtained 31 post–50 movies from Fox, 15 of them in color. *Millionaire* was shot in color and Cinemascope. Ironically, it was shot in that format to draw viewers away from TV sets and back to theaters. During the first three years of *Saturday Night* it was so successful that *Gunsmoke* dropped down significantly in the ratings.[12]

As might have been expected, exhibitors howled in protest, specifically about the NBC series, and in general against the newer vintage of movies going into television release. On the four commercial outlets in the twin cities of Minneapolis/St. Paul 41 to 43 features were telecast weekly. Time–Life's independent outlet WTCN-TV (its ABC network affiliate status had recently been transferred to local rival KMSP-TV, owned by Fox) aired 25 while KMSP telecast nine to eleven each week. Minneapolis theater circuit owner Bennie Berger told his Allied States Association local unit, North Central Allied: "The film companies, of course, are responsible for this flood of feature films on TV that spells unbearable competition for our theatres, making a wreck of them and having a considerable number of them close to the end of the line." North Central Allied issued a warning to the majors that "unless they begin to see the light and come to their senses they'll be fought desperately from the word 'go.'"¹³

Exhibitors displayed a wave of anger that NBC's move would cut their Saturday night trade. When it did not, the protests eased within 2-3 months. Hollywood also worried about the broadcasting of movies on network primetime. They feared that movies would outdraw series; by then Hollywood's majors were becoming the chief producers of those series. If movies replaced many of the series the majors would see an income drop which, in turn, would force them to lease more movies to TV to get cash. That would lead to more competition for their series fare.¹⁴

Before the end of that first movie season NBC announced it would continue its Saturday movies in the 9 to 11 PM period for the 1962-63 season while ABC announced it would run a movie series of its own for that season, Sundays from 8 to 10 PM. In its deal with United Artists, ABC paid about $200,000 each for 30 titles. To the network that was a programming cost of $100,000 per hour which was, observed one account, "lower than the cost of virtually any hour vidfilm entry." That trend to more movies on network primetime upset some television stations. Network film purchases increased competition and put up the price for post–48s product in general. Independent outlets, many of which programmed movies in primetime were not happy with the head-to-head competition while the network affiliated outlets, which didn't program movies in primetime, wondered what creative programming role a network played in broadcasting old movies. For a long time those three networks had turned thumbs down on airing movies, arguing: "we're not a transmission belt for Hollywood product; we originate our own shows."¹⁵

Early in 1963 NBC found itself in ratings trouble on Monday nights with its two hour-long shows *It's a Man's World* and *Saints and Sinners* being boycotted by both viewers and advertisers. They went up against CBS giants Lucille Ball, Danny Thomas and Andy Griffith. NBC moved in a *Monday Night at the Movies* series. Ratings leapt immediately and the network announced that movies would continue on NBC on both Saturdays and Mondays for the 1963-64 TV season. Most of the films for 63-64 were of 1955–60 vintage, 30 from MGM, 30 from Fox. Price for a 1-minute spot ad on the Monday night movies was $16,000 with most of the 12 such spots available in each two-hour slot being sold out. Explained an ad agency executive: "Movies on TV have a name value. Sponsors who buy movies are buying numbers of heads and the movies deliver an incredible number of viewers. Advertisers couldn't care less about creative TV programs. They are looking for a vehicle that will get their advertising message into the home." Asked about the possibility of a third movie night each week NBC executive Walter Scott said: "No. There are not enough quality movies available. The success of the feature films on television depends upon getting good movies." At the same time ABC announced it would drop its Sunday night movies. Network spokesman Thomas Moore explained: "We think we ought to create our own product. Movies create very little viewer habits and it is difficult to maintain audience levels from week to week." Meanwhile New York's WCBS became the first New York station to operate 24 hours a day—it ran movies all through the night. Between 2:30 and 5:30 AM the audience ranged from 53,000 to 165,000 viewers. Noted station vice president Norman Walt: "In the first two months of the operation, we will make enough money to sustain the expense of the added hours for the remainder of the year. And even if we don't sell any more commercials." WCBS had a huge movie backlog. Reporter Val Adams observed, "It seems quite obvious that so long as Hollywood keeps making movies, TV is here to stay."[16]

A few months later in 1963 ABC reconfirmed that it had no plans for movies in primetime in the 1963-64 season, even though the series was sold out for 1962-63. That season would be the last for Sunday night movies. Network President Tom Moore explained; "We would rather create our own vitality."[17]

As the summer of 1963 came to an end NBC had two movie nights slated for the upcoming season, CBS and ABC none. Having to backtrack from its one-time "hard" policy that NBC "would never become a theater of the air," an unnamed executive with that network explained that features were "qualitative" TV fare which "we couldn't possibly afford, in programs sponsored by our own industry, the production values and the stars. When a movie is made it doesn't adhere to a seven-day shooting schedule; its script is not written hastily; it is not geared for one or two airings and then oblivion. Let's face it: movies are better entertainment than we can usually come up with." Taking a different view was CBS Vice President Michael Dann who declared, "Movies are not a form created specifically for television, and they are not interpretable as an event of public interest. If they are used in place of television-created programs, it distinctly means we are not filling out time well enough, and we're not doing our job well enough." Equally unhappy was ABC spokesman Stanley Chase who remarked, of his network's Sunday night films, "They're a stopgap. They don't represent a direction that is fruitful for us, and they don't give us consistent ratings either. Audience response varies according to the attractiveness of the pictures shown. And networks, when they purchase films, are forced to take them in blocks. It's like having to take two bottles of cheap gin along with every bottle of Scotch."[18]

A block of Paramount post–48s, many made between 1955 and 1960, were picked up by NBC to feed its Saturday and Wednesday (moved from Monday) film evenings. ABC's decision to forego movies lasted less than a year with Sunday nights opened up again for films. Each network spent about $8.4 million for a block of 30 movies (to be used over 52 weeks, 22 reruns) averaging out to $280,000 per title. Thus, $25 million was spent in a year for the three movie nights. A film sold to a network could also expect to earn another $140,000 in off-network, market-by-market syndication, after its network telecast. Without a network run the most a title could earn in straight syndication was around $250,000, for the best ones. It meant that a pack of 30 titles going to a network would gross $12.6 million, $8.4 million from the network and $4.2 million from syndication.[19]

As the 1965-66 television season started in September, all three networks were broadcasting movies in two-hour primetime slots. NBC ran them on Saturday and Tuesday, CBS on Thursday, and ABC on Sunday. In a deal for product, ABC paid MGM an average of $400,000 per title.[20]

From the time NBC telecast its first Saturday night movie until the spring of 1966, the three networks telecast 567 movies in primetime. In the 1965-66 season, the three networks aired a total of 116 movies. Illustrating the domination of the market by Hollywood's majors was the fact that 115 of those titles came from the majors, 112 of them from five studios. When CBS added a second film night for the 1966-67 season it meant there were five film nights. Movies accounted for 16 percent of NBC's primetime schedule, 16 percent on CBS and 8 percent on ABC. Assuming the average price paid was $350,000 per title, those 150 movies were estimated to cost the three networks $52.5 million.[21]

A new peak in network broadcasting of movies was reached in September 1966 when ABC aired the blockbuster *The Bridge on the River Kwai* (1957) from 8 to 11 PM. Drawing an estimated 60 million viewers in 25 million households, it was hugely successful, blowing away the competition and even reportedly reducing the attendance at cinemas. For many it was felt that event marked the death knoll for pay–TV. The Ford Motor Company paid about $1.2 million for the right to sponsor *Kwai* and $600,000 for air time on ABC. The network had an option for a second run of the title for which it wanted a sponsor to pay $800,000 plus air time rates.[22]

In the wake of that success, some of the largest transactions in the history of show business were completed. ABC made a $19.5 million deal with Fox for 17 titles. One of them was *Cleopatra* (1963) for which ABC paid $5 million for 2 showings. It would be released to ABC in 1971, over 4 years into the future. ABC was to make a series of regular installment payments, to be completed by October, 1970. Another ABC deal was with Paramount for 32 movies, for $20 million. Meanwhile, CBS closed a deal with MGM for 63 features, for $52.8 million. Thus Hollywood sold 112 movies for a total of $92.3 million. In the MGM deal, 45 of the titles were from the studio's library and 18 were new movies that the studio had not yet produced. They would get the usual theatrical release before going to TV. Also within that deal, CBS had the option of airing six to ten movies already telecast on NBC primetime which had by then reverted to MGM. That was the beginning of an arrangement whereby Hollywood could anticipate recurring income from broadcasting over more than one network. Until this time, no network would have considered telecasting in primetime a movie which had already been aired by another network. In other words, each network wanted only the "first run."[23]

Because of those deals, Richard Zanuck believed the minimum worth of any movie to TV was $500,000, an amount few producers could afford to ignore. He felt it was then self-evident that no studio could afford to make a black and white film, since the networks wanted nothing but color fare.[24]

When NBC made an announcement in December 1967 that it would run movies on Monday nights in the 1968–69 television season, starting in September 1968, it meant that movies were running in primetime on the networks seven nights a week. With one movie on each night, the networks avoided competing head-to-head with movies on any particular night of the week.[25]

A standard arrangement worked out between film companies and the networks for airing movies in the 1960s was for a network to lease a package of 30 films for a period of 1–3 years with a right to show each feature once, and 22 of them twice. That is, a one-year package. At the end of the period, those movies reverted to the studio which then syndicated them to independent television stations. Typically, by the end of the 1960s, TV distribution started 18 months after the end of the theatrical first run. In setting price levels with the networks for features the majors had greater power than they did for series programming. There was no real competition to Hollywood for movies. During the early 1960s a run-of-the-mill movie brought $150,000 from the network. That jumped to $400,000 in 1965. After *Kwai*, and in the wake of its huge success, the era of the blockbuster on TV was begun. By 1968, the average price for a regular movie in a package had moved to $800,000.[26]

Leonard Goldenson was president of ABC–Paramount during that period. He commented that a large number of color television sets did not start appearing in American homes until the early 1960s, with the result that both NBC and CBS moved quickly to color transmission and the addition of color programs to their lineups. ABC, being poorer, was slower in converting to color; the cost was around $50 million for a network. Advertisers quickly favored color programs as they believed their products looked so much better. Said Goldenson, "The motion picture industry had always withheld its best movies from network television. But the studios had gone through a decade of financial reverses, and now they saw an opportunity to recoup some of their losses by selling color films at greatly increased rates. NBC and CBS, anxious to fill their schedules with color were asked to pay as much as four times the previous license fee for movies." One of the reasons ABC's first movie night was less than a success may have been due to the fact that those films were black and white. "Once we had color, of course, we would have to add a second night of movies," continued Goldenson. "The Hollywood studios, who among themselves controlled virtually the entire supply, wanted $50 million for a three-year deal. And they wanted it in advance."[27]

Partly from the competition of made-for-TV movies, prices paid by the networks for theatrical movies declined somewhat in the early 1970s. It was back to around $600,000 per title. Another contributing factor to lower prices was the franker, more explicit content of the recent fare. A package of Fox titles, which included *M.A.S.H.* (1970) and *Butch Cassidy and the Sundance Kid* (1969), made the rounds but was rejected by both NBC and CBS for reasons of content. When less than three networks bid on a package, the price tended to drop.[28]

The versatility of movies as programming saviors was evident again in the early 1970s during the talk-show battles. CBS dumped its Merv Griffin show, which had never competed in the ratings against NBC's *Tonight* show or ABC's Dick Cavett. In its place, CBS networked a late night movie, Monday through Friday, starting at 11:30 PM. Under the confines of late night budgeting, CBS had to program on the cheap. With a talk/variety show then costing $100,00 a week, CBS planned to double that to go to the movies; that is, $40,000 per night per movie. Since the networks were paying $365,000 for primetime "theatrical soupbones," observers wondered what CBS could buy for $40,000. CBS struck a deal with MGM for 100 titles from the vaults, "pictures retired and 'rested' from local station use." Cost was $90,000 per title for three runs each, $30,000 per run.[29]

Midway through the 1960s, reporter Bill Greeley observed that in the past, the networks sheepishly admitted they would expand ad time to 14 commercial minutes in the two-hour time slot: "Nowadays, it is worse." During the first hour of its Thursday and Friday night movies (9 to 10 PM) CBS crammed in eight commercials, plus a local minute, plus three 20-second spots and a trailer for a coming attraction which ran nearly another minute. It was a primetime hour with almost 11 minutes of ads. New York station WNEW–TV squeezed in almost 12 minutes while ABC had 10½ minutes of ads in the 10–11 PM hour of its movies. All those numbers exceeded standards set by the National Association of Broadcasters, although WNEW didn't subscribe to that code. Those standards were voluntary with no penalty attached to noncompliance.[30]

Those ads were very lucrative. In the 1968-69 season, CBS charged $58,000 for one-minute on its Thursday or Friday night movies, NBC billed $56,000 for Monday, Tuesday or Saturday films while ABC charged $53,000 for Wednesday night and $56,000 for Sunday features. For 1973, the Television Bureau of Advertising calculated that national advertisers spent $3.5 billion for spot and network television ads that year, followed by $1.5 billion for magazines, $1.2 billion for newspapers and $450 million on radio ads. Thus, TV outdistanced the second, third and fourth place finishers combined.[31]

As the post–48s were beginning to make the television rounds the pre–48s were making the rounds for the second time. Their value the second time around was less if in the first round a title was sold on a seven–year unlimited run basis, as compared to a two-year deal with limitations on the number of runs. Pre–48 libraries of MGM, Paramount, Warner, Fox, Universal, Columbia, and RKO were thought to have grossed $270 million from TV, as of late 1961. For the second round, an estimated 40 percent of that product would have to be retired due to styles, outdated themes, and so on. Expecting a second round gross of 50 to 75 percent of the first round receipts, on the remaining films, led analysts to estimate the second round gross to be 25 percent of the first round, roughly $67.5 million.[32]

When stations booked the pre–48 material again it allowed many outlets to move toward extending their broadcast day, closing down later into the night, or not closing down at all. WCBS in New York had licensed MGM's entire pre–48 library, which WCBS had failed to renew. WNEW paid $1 million for a group of 125 MGM titles, an average of $8,000.[33]

During 1961 Los Angeles outlet KHJ-TV was on the air 18.5 hours a day, with 70 percent of the broadcast day devoted to old movies. In response to the station's observation that: "The loud cries of too many commercials on old pictures has long fallen on deaf ears at the stations," KHJ announced it would reduce the number of ads it ran, but increase its rates in order to generate the same amount of revenue. One national advertiser commented, "Well, at least now we're not smothered in a maze of commercials that leaves the viewers bewildered as to who is selling what."[34]

The WCBS network was running its movies with a policy of telecasting 200 first-run (on TV) features annually. Where possible, it still leased titles for seven years with unlimited runs, at prices that could go as high as $50,000 per title. The practice of the majors by the early 1960s was to offer titles to the networks, then to stations by way of syndication. Networks then paid around $175,000 per title, which included one rerun. In syndication, the same title could gross as much as another $150,000 to $175,000. Distribution costs when selling to a network were low, but relatively high when selling in syndication. Residual value of movies sold first in syndication were not nearly as high.[35]

When the seven commercial TV stations in Los Angeles were surveyed in the summer of 1964, it was found that 240 movies were telecast in one week. It was normal for the seven outlets to schedule 30 old movies on one night. KHJ paid up to $23,000 for unlimited runs of a title over seven years, down to a low of $1,200 for the same conditions. For a package of 50 "high grade" titles, the average paid worked out to $19,000, with unlimited runs over seven years. Many of the titles were given 20 runs over the seven years with station program director Wally Sherwin observing that three telecasts a year of a specific title was a "good average." Those seven stations were estimated to have spent a total of $50 million for their movie stockpile with KHJ and KNXT having spent the most, some $12 million each.[36]

By the middle of 1968, local TV stations found themselves to be running out of movies, both independent and network-affiliated outlets. With some titles having been shown up to 75 times each, different types of programs were, in some cases, being substituted for films. CBS's 200-plus affiliates were giving up 7.5 hours of local programming time per week, starting in 1969, to carry the *Merv Griffin Show*. Also, the *Joey Bishop Show* took 7.5 hours of weekly time away from ABC affiliates. According to one ABC executive that move reduced the need for movies by 260 per year. Individually, some stations made similar changes. Little Rock, Arkansas's KATV started a local talk-variety show, while WCBS in New York dropped its late afternoon movie slot in favor of *The Mike Douglas Show*. WOR's venerable *Million Dollar Movie* was dropped from primetime in September 1968 to make way for a syndicated talk show hosted by Steve Allen. One reason for the shortage had to do with the fact the networks were then running seven movie nights weekly, taking more and more features. Said Hal Hough, film buyer for all five CBS owned and operated: "Three or four years ago, we still got the good movies because they were being sold on local syndication. The problem isn't so much scarcity of movies to show. It's the scarcity of good films, the stuff we used to have. We're now offered movies after they've been shown two, three or even four times on the networks, along with stuff that can't make the networks at all." Old movies such as *Stagecoach* (1939), *Foreign Correspondent* (1940) and *The Long Voyage Home* (1940) had been sold to almost every station in New York and each had been telecast 75 times or more over the years. However, one television station buyer explained, "We feel that with each succeeding year, new people join our audience. So actually we're not re-showing it to the same people."[37]

With more movies on TV than ever before, the period 1961 to 1975 saw much more media attention paid to cuts and butchery performed on films. A couple of directors went so far at to engage in court action over the issue of artistic control. They would have no more success than the cowboy stars who launched similar action more than a decade earlier. CBS had penciled into its Thursday film series for the 1966-67 season a number of titles from Columbia. One was Otto Preminger's *Advise and Consent* (1962). Under the lease arrangement Preminger retained the right to withdraw the film if he disapproved of the editing down for TV. When Preminger viewed the newly cut version, he declared the movie had suffered too many cuts, objecting in particular to deletion of scenes dealing with the homosexuality of one of the principals. Defending its editing, CBS said the film "would have been televised next season in some areas of the Midwest at 8 PM." The network didn't believe that homosexuality was a suitable subject for family viewing during primetime. Unimpressed, Preminger withdrew his film.[38]

Preminger applied for a court injunction, in September 1965, to enjoin TV stations from showing his film *Anatomy of a Murder* as he was dissatisfied with the cuts. The New York State Supreme Court denied his petition while granting temporary permission for the movie to be shown. However, the court agreed that a later trial should consider whether Preminger had the right to prevent cuts by TV stations.[39]

In January 1966, Preminger lost his case to prevent any cutting or what he considered excessive commercial interruptions of his feature during its showing. State Supreme Court Justice Arthur Klein ruled that the court was inclined to view the right of the producer to final cutting and editing was limited to the original or theatrical production, not to TV showings. It was a case closely watched by Hollywood.[40]

Around the same time Preminger took legal action, film director George Stevens filed a $2 million suit against NBC and Paramount to prevent what he called the mutilation and dismemberment of his film *A Place in the Sun* (1952)—due to be shown on network television in the 1965-66 season. In filing his suit in Los Angeles Superior Court, Stevens denounced the networks for chopping up movies on TV and for allowing the insertion of dozens of commercials. Stevens made the feature for Liberty Films (later bought by Paramount) with a contract that specified the "right to edit, cut and score" would always remain with him. According to his complaint, Paramount licensed the title to NBC and gave permission to the network and its affiliates to cut the feature and to insert commercials. Stevens said he would probably agree to the showing of his feature on TV if it were shown in its entirety and divided into three parts, with ads inserted only within those two breaks.[41]

"A fine motion picture is a thing of value to both its creator and audience. Those who have seen it once, as well as those who have seen it many times hold something of value in their mutual recollection of the experience which viewing the film afforded them," explained Stevens. "Using a film as a means of lulling an audience into a receptive mood for a quick cut to the loud blast and hard sell of commercials is a destruction of that value and a mutilation of the film.... A motion picture should be respected as being more than a tool for selling soap, toothpaste, deodorant, used cars, beer and the whole gamut of products on television."[42]

Judge Ralph Nutter of Los Angeles Superior Court ruled in February 1966, that *Place* could not be televised if its artistic qualities were destroyed by the intrusion of commercials. It was slated to air on NBC on March 12. Stevens was granted a temporary injunction, valid until the case would come to trial a few months hence. Nutter noted he did not believe he could prohibit commercials entirely, but he added that the courts had a duty to protect artistic works from "emasculation."[43]

Columnist Jack Gould felt NBC might telecast the film as scheduled since it planned to air all 122 minutes of the feature. In general he commented, "The continuing massacre of films on TV, both on the networks, and, even worse, by independent stations, leaves the TV movie fan in the position of beginning with the promise of a full sirloin and finishing with a bunch of meat patties." Gould also noted one sneaky approach by TV programmers whereby a movie was started with relatively few interruptions. Then, as the movie unwound, the frequency of ads was stepped up on the assumption the audience was by then hooked.[44]

When NBC aired *Place* as scheduled, Stevens filed contempt proceedings against NBC. The network had, by Stevens' count, inserted 42 commercials and announcements. Los Angeles Superior Court Judge Richard Wells handed down a decision that NBC had not violated the earlier temporary court injunction preventing the network from emasculating *Place*. In his decision, Wells said the commercial interruptions did, in fact, "lessen, decrease, disturb, interrupt and weaken the mood, effect or continuity and the audience involvement, and therefore some of the artistry of the film." However, he continued, "I do not think they substantially or materially destroyed or distorted such elements." Wells also commented that "the average television viewer is thick-skinned about commercials." NBC attorney Richard Potter argued that a movie conveyed no "mood" that could be interrupted by commercials; TV audiences had been conditioned to "segmented programs." Stevens vowed to continue his original pending suit claiming his original contract left him with full authority over the work.[45]

That suit was settled in May 1967, when Judge Ben Koening found that the cutting of the movie was indeed a technical violation of the director's original contract. Koening viewed the film three times, in the original theatrical version, in the TV version with commercials, and in the TV version without commercials. The judge held those commercial interruptions did not substantially damage *A Place in the Sun* and that Steven's reputation for artistic achievement was not damaged by the telecast. Therefore, Koenig levied a token $1 judgment against NBC and Paramount. Stevens had sued for $2 million in damages.[46]

The only actor to be involved in similar action was William Holden who, in the summer of 1966, sued in court to stop *The Bridge on the River Kwai* from being aired that fall on ABC. His suit charged the movie's presentation on TV would hurt its future box office receipts. Holden was, of course, unsuccessful.[47]

Release of post–48 movies to TV created problems in terms of content. Films were becoming explicit. It was a problem that would get worse for stations. In the earlier periods, almost all the cuts to features were made to fit them into a specific period of time. Only occasionally was a cut necessary solely on the basis of content. Beginning in this period, more and more cuts would be made for reasons of content. Of course, cuts continued to be made for reasons of time. National Association of Broadcasters (NAB) executives met with representatives of the major film distributors in the spring of 1961 in what was described as an exploratory meeting. NAB wanted the right to screen "troublesome" post–48 items for its member stations. Those troubling movies were ones that might violate the group's TV code injunction against the broadcasting of "sex, violence, and horror." Taking the position that cinemas and TV were two different media, NAB argued that what was acceptable in a theater was not necessarily okay in the living-room, despite the fact that virtually all product from the majors carried the Motion Picture Production Code seal—in-house-awarded stamp of approval, decency and purity. Distributors told NAB that stations themselves should act as their own censors since each outlet was more familiar with the mores of its community. Hollywood quickly rejected NAB's idea.[48]

A few months later, in a speech to Michigan broadcasters, NAB Television Code Affairs director Edward Bronson admitted he had had "little success" in working with movie distributors to weed out blue material from post–48 product. He declared there was an "urgent need to edit carefully" those features before they were telecast. Recalling his days as a station manager in the pioneer days of TV, he felt obliged to carefully edit "an occasional Jean Harlow and Marie Dressler bit that would raise your eyebrows." Telling his audience the NAB had been working with distributors to try and winnow out the riskier bits, with no success, he said, "We are urging stations everywhere to keep a constant watch on this material and to let us know if, in your opinion, a particular film or a particular scene in a film seems to violate the code."[49]

Some 18 months later, *Variety* wondered what happened to the NAB idea of pre-screening those post–48s. The answer was—nothing. At the time the Roman Catholic National Legion of Decency was still handing out its "condemned" (C) rating to films it felt warranted such distinction. Attitudes of stations to those C movies varied enormously. Some stations would not play such a film, a few would, and "a larger group may try to cut objectionable scenes if the 'C' pic were bought."[50]

Indiscriminate TV deletions provoked the wrath of top directors in the early 1960s. "It makes me furious. I refuse to watch them on TV anymore," said John Ford, of his work. Of his own films, one of his favorites was *Young Mr. Lincoln* (1939) which originally ran for 100 minutes. But the station had slotted a 90-minute span for the telecast, including commercials. Ford added, "so they simply hacked it down to an hour and 15 minutes to make room for commercials. We had spent a lot of time building the character, showing a lot of humor, but they started right out with the trial scene on TV and it didn't make sense. It's a shame—your name's on it but it isn't the thing you did." With regard to *High Noon* (1952) on TV, director Fred Zinnemann said, "They butchered the thing. They cut large chunks out of it. I got so mad I turned it off." He then avoided watching his old movies on TV. After he watched Ford's *She Wore a Yellow Ribbon* (1949) he was so disturbed by the wholesale cuts that he called Ford to express his sympathy. Zinnemann hoped to get together with Ford, Frank Capra and a few others to see what could be done. Additionally, he said he planned to have a no-cut proviso inserted in all his future contracts: "I will see to it from now on that there is no butchery." Directors Guild of America President George Sidney called TV's cutting "an absolutely immoral practice." Sidney said the Guild had been talking with representatives of the FCC and the Better Business Bureau to see if there was not some misrepresentation of product involved when a movie was doctored with the viewers being none the wiser.[51]

In 1962, the American Cinema Editors complained to the FCC that "most movies being shown on television today have been wantonly divested of their carefully created mood and pace." It was a pitch for the FCC to take measures to eradicate the practice of wholesale re-editing. Three years later, the editors group said that "not one effectual step to our knowledge has been taken to correct the prevailing condition."[52]

Saul David, who had produced Fox's *Our Man Flint* (1965), watched the movie on TV one night. That galvanized him to write to his senator after he had seen his film "not so much re-edited as lobotomized into senselessness." In his letter to California Senator George Murphy he explained that ten to fifteen minutes had been deleted so that vital connective tissues were flagrantly destroyed. He asked Murphy, "Shouldn't people watching a televised film have the right to be cautioned that what they're getting is not what the theatre audience got—and by how much?" Before he became a film producer, David was an editorial director for Bantam Books at a time when abridged versions of literary works were commonly offered by publishers who wanted to save money by cutting down on the number of pages. Then the Federal Trade Commission (FTC) ruled the abridgments had to be prominently and clearly labeled as such. David complained that a reader had a choice but that TV viewers were not informed in any way that the televised film had been doctored from its theatrical version. David wondered: if the FTC held that abridged books had to be labeled, shouldn't the agency also hold the same for abridged movies?[53]

When the FTC conducted a survey of 164 movies broadcast on the three networks in the last six months of 1969, it found that in 84 percent of those films the public got less than a whole movie. Fifty-seven percent of the titles were cut by two minutes or more. That survey was undertaken by the FTC as part of a study to determine whether running a film at less than its full length without disclosing that fact to the public could be considered an unfair or deceptive trade practice. CBS called the investigation "absurd."[54]

The WCBS station ran so many films in its schedule in the early 1960s that five editing teams were kept busy cutting them up. Certain parts were cut to meet the station's standards of taste: "violence and vulgarity are the main targets. Cutting is also done to make the movies fit the allotted time."[55]

Speaking on behalf of Los Angeles station KHJ, with regard to cutting and ads, program director Wally Sherwin explained: "We employ nine editors who watch every foot of film and insert the commercials when they don't break in on a key scene. Of course, those long chases are trimmed but don't affect the play's continuity. You can't hold an audience with long, draggy scenes. Our viewers aren't captive as they are in theatres."[56]

When New York's WOR broadcast *The Pawnbroker* (1965), the station advertised the film as being "aired in its entirety." Yet reporter Jack Gould observed that a scene in which a black prostitute bared her breasts to star Rod Steiger had been cut. Gould also found the mood destroyed because the commercial breaks came with regularity at ten-minute intervals: "a viewer could tell time by the scheduling of the commericials."[57]

Good Neighbor Sam (1964) was a satire on Madison Avenue with a running gag throughout the movie which spoofed Hertz, the car rental company. When CBS telecast it, the item received a "merciless going over" with the cutters deleting all sequences kidding the Hertz "let us put you in the driver's seat" catch phrase. Also excised was a shot of an Allied Van Lines truck. CBS had scheduled a network telecast of Alfred Hitchcock's *Psycho* (1960) for September 1966. Then just four days before it was to screen the network announced it was postponed—some affiliate stations had expressed disapproval. A few weeks later, a network spokesman insisted it would be broadcast at a later date, he just wasn't sure when. Finally, in December, CBS disclosed it had made a "firm decision" never to show *Psycho*. Reportedly, the network had paid $800,000 to air the film twice.[58]

With *Lilies of the Field* (1963) slated for a CBS telecast in the spring of 1967, director Ralph Nelson asked and received permission to recut his work for television. He was resigned to the idea and felt if it had to be recut then he should do it. It was the first known case of a film director getting the okay to recut his movie for television. Talking about the "butchery" that was called TV editing, reporter Bill Greeley declared that, "None but the true hack could fail to be upset by the gutting of features for TV." One example cited was the CBS broadcast of Carl Foreman's *The Victors* (1963). In theatrical distribution the work ran three hours. CBS deleted some 70 minutes from the film rendering it difficult or impossible to follow or understand.[59]

By the time the 1970s arrived, the situation was even more difficult as theatrical movies became still more explicit and franker. Networks began to move beyond merely deleting or reducing cursing, sex, nudity, and violence for the tube version. However, such a fuss was made when *Three Into Two Won't Go* (1969) was given an extra character and a happy ending, and when a new scene was added to *Secret Ceremony* (1969), that networks began to hesitate to remodel plot structure. Standards were said to be loosening up a little here and there. At ABC, in 1971, it was all right for soldiers under stress to curse, as long as they didn't precede their "damns" with "Gods." It was permissible to shoot somebody, but not "senselessly" three or four times. To get *Some Like It Hot* (1959) on TV, ABC eliminated cleavage by cutting close to Marilyn Monroe's face. When American International Pictures filmed Bette Davis' *Bunny O'Hare* (1971), several different endings were shot. In one, Davis faced the audience and said "fuck you," while in another she said "Go to hell." One time a station took the quick and easy way to delete 30 minutes from a work to make room for ads: it simply omitted the first half-hour of the *Treasure of Sierra Madre* (1948). Director Delbert Mann recalled a version of his *Lover Come Back* (1961) in which the broadcaster dispensed with two reels (20 minutes) from the middle of the film. "It became sort of hard to follow," deadpanned Mann.[60]

Generally, all three networks refused to consider X-rated movies, even if the X scenes could be easily cut. For several years Warner offered *The Fox*, a 1968 X-rated film based on a D.H. Lawrence story in which the theme was lesbianism, with no takers. There was just one scene with frontal nudity. Said Warner executive Ed Bleier: "A 10-second cut would get the film a PG rating. But the networks won't touch it." When CBS tried an X a couple of years earlier with Visconti's *The Damned* (1969; a study of sexual and other corruption in pre–Hitler Germany) it was so heavily edited that, said Bleier, "it couldn't offend anyone except those who like the original." However, there was such an outcry from viewers when it was broadcast that CBS decided not to touch an X again. ABC was then taking even fewer chances refusing to consider R-rated movies in their original state. A producer who wanted to sell an R title to ABC first had to have it re-edited, then submit it to the MPAA for re-rating and then take it back to the network with a G or PG rating. Journalist William Johnson observed that, "Hardly any films reach the air untouched." At CBS, they could only think of one film in recent years which had been broadcast untouched—*Hello, Dolly* (1969). At NBC, nobody could think of a single title which had made it to the air untouched. Network spokesman Arnold Huberman said "We even made cuts in Disney's *20,000 Leagues Under the Sea* (1954)—there was some unnecessarily protracted fist fighting." Four words had to come out of *A Man for All Seasons* (1966)—"three goddamns and a Christ." Despite its vigilance NBC still got occasional complaints from viewers about an "unsuitable" film. Huberman remarked: "People won't accept the argument that they can always switch off. They look on television as a God-given right. We're expected to be the guardians of their family's morality." As to how decisions were made regarding what was unsuitable, and when was something unsuitable enough to be deleted broadcasters had the NAB code—which was vague—and each network had its own code (usually in Practices and Standards)—which was also vague. Huberman admitted that most of it was "subjective." All three networks agreed, however, in 1974, that the major problem areas in current films released to TV were "violence, profanity and nudity." Sam Peckinpah's *The Wild Bunch* (1969) had a climactic bloody scene running 7 minutes and 40 seconds. For its broadcast CBS trimmed it back to 3 minutes and 30 seconds. Johnson concluded: "All too often commercial television still treats movies as raw material to be carved and hammered into shape. Yet they already have a shape which writers, directors, and technicians have worked hard to achieve. It's high time the networks and stations recognized this fact and let us see more films without changes inflicted by 'editing' and—dare we hope?—without commercial interruptions."[61]

As to why the networks edited so much, reporter David Black explained: "First, they are in constant fear of offending the sensitivities of a small number of viewers whose dissatisfaction might be reflected in lowered Nielsen ratings. And second, they prefer to police themselves rather than have others do it for them—a state of affairs they fear might come to pass if raciness on the TV screen were ever to prompt a public outcry." ABC aired *Midnight Cowboy* (1969) in the fall of 1974. All scenes of homosexual encounters were deleted. *The Godfather* (1972) was telecast at the same time over NBC. One cut was in James Caan's death scene when a woman removed her dress. NBC Standards and Practices Vice President Herminio Traviesas said, of that scene, "We had to drop that scene even though it was not erotic." For *The Godfather* the executive remarked, "there were only 35 things we changed with Mr. Coppola." Director Francis Ford Coppola caught up with Caan in Europe where the actor did some new words himself for the TV version. Obscenities were changed to things like "you lousy rat." Actor John Marley was tracked down also to record some new words. The greatest piece of "ass" became "stuff." Traviesas observed that "In adapting movies for television, you must address yourself to language, sex and violence. When a supplier offers us a film, we look at the picture and make notes, explaining why certain scenes may not be acceptable. We then send the notes back to the supplier who has the responsibility for making changes."[62]

Tom Swafford, CBS vice president of program practices, said his department looked at 500 movies per year. For 1974 it rejected about 40 percent outright for reasons of sex, violence, nudity or language "which in our judgment would be uneditable or not worth editing." He added: "One of my worst mistakes was to think we could edit *The Damned*.... We edited 32 minutes out of it. It was difficult to understand in its original form. When we got done, it was incomprehensible." Swafford's toughest editing job was on *Who's Afraid of Virginia Woolf* (1966), which was laden with obscenities. New technology was a big help there, as journalist David Black explained: "The edited-for-TV version, in which many of the saltier words were either simply cut or replaced with less pungent ones plucked from elsewhere on the soundtrack, suffered accordingly." Looting of the audiotrack for safe words to replace unsuitable ones was also used by ABC on *Patton* (1970) broadcast in 1972. It was easier to use that technique when the character was not looking full face at the camera. To remove unwanted images, say, a naked breast, the film could be adjusted by blowing the picture up and cropping it. Some producers and directors were then exercising an option—recently won in negotiation by the Directors Guild—to be consulted during the editing of a movie for the tube.

Even that was mostly illusion. Director Robert Altman said: "You only have an option to make the cuts they want you to make. They won't let you really work on the editing for TV. The networks still have total control." In the film *Guess Who's Coming to Dinner* (1967) there's a scene where Spencer Tracy looks full face into the camera and says "I'll be a son-of-a-bitch." Swafford explained that he left it in because it seemed so right: "We left it in, and only got eighteen letters" of complaint.[63]

While the above examples relate to cuts of material deemed unsuitable, Robert Wise, then president of the Directors Guild, commented on the other, equally insidious cuts; "editing simply for length, cutting movies, often brutally, to fit a given time slot. Practically every theatrical movie shown on TV has anything from a few minutes to 30 or 40 minutes edited from it so it will fit into a 1½- or 2- or 2½-hour slot. This indiscriminate 'butchery' of our films is the most frustrating and maddening form of TV editing to every film director."[64]

Such butchery, of course, continued. When a New York station showed *The Good Earth* (1937) in the mid–1970s it simply left out the first 20 or 30 minutes of the movie. For the 1976 television premiere of the 1973 release *The Last Detail*, ABC hired the services of Jerry Ayres, a member of the new profession of expert in cleansing movies for television. *Detail* was so full of expletives that viewers would not likely accept a bleep every few minutes, or seconds. Ayres looted the soundtrack for safe words. Much of the work was easy if the character was off-camera, or had his back or side to the camera, or was in front view of a long-shot where the lip movements were not clearly visible. It was much harder to do with a character in close-up, facing the camera. Then the new word had to make sense and also had to come close to matching the character's lip movement.[65]

Concerned just as much with the insertion of ads into films on TV as with the cuts made to make room for them was an editorial in *Film Quarterly*. Editor Ernest Callenbach found it puzzling that Americans, who generally rejected the European practice of running commercials in movie theaters, had so placidly accepted the constant commercial interruption of films when they were televised. That interference "is brutal and unjustifiable as in any conceivable way beneficial to anybody except advertisers," he said. What was needed to put an end to it all, thought Callenbach, was a combination of massive public pressure, lawsuits based on the infringement of viewer and filmmaker interests, and challenges to the TV station licenses for outlets whose outrages in film treatment were particularly offensive—"But it is massive public pressure that is essential for real change." Callenbach concluded: "The practice is an abomination unto every viewer, and it becomes more, not less abominable when it is practiced by relatively 'benign' cutters— some of whom will go so far as to argue that films should be 'improved' by shortening them for TV and making interruption spots for commercials...."

The American public is being ripped off in a stupendous way by existing practice: not only are our minds being contaminated by commercials ... but our whole sense of pacing and structure is being perverted ... the dominant practice of inserting more and more frequent commercials toward the climax of a film is not only insulting but downright perverse—a kind of nationwide, nightly, weekly education in artistic coitus interruptus."[66]

What all the fuss was about, of course, were movies deemed unsuitable. TV stations did their own worrying, and when they didn't, others did. ABC-TV President Thomas Moore said, in 1965, "One-third of the feature pictures made in the last three or four years are not suitable for television." Because of that, he feared his network, and others, were running out of material to program: "I would say that we're only two or three years away from scraping bottom." Moore cited three titles as the type that had been rejected by ABC, but bought by other networks; *The Apartment* (1960), *I Want to Live* (1958), and *Elmer Gantry* (1960).[67]

The National Catholic Office for Motion Pictures, formerly the Catholic National Legion of Decency, while maintaining its policy of refusing to change the rating it had given a film once that film had had wide theatrical release, let it be known that it would take "a different attitude" toward the movie if it was re-edited. That was potentially a major benefit to distributors seeking to sell C-rated (condemned) titles to TV outlets which, observed Vincent Canby, "have until now generally regarded such films as untouchable." Embassy Pictures called the Catholic viewing group to see what might be done to fix *Boccaccio 70* (1962) before offering it to TV outlets. That title was an Italian film with three segments directed by Federico Fellini, Luchino Visconti and Vittorio De Sica. Embassy was told, if the picture was properly recut, the office's original objections obviously would not be valid. Msgr. Thomas Little, executive-secretary of the Catholic film office, confirmed this procedure but emphasized his office had no intention of publicizing its change in feeling toward pictures that had been re-edited. "We would also expect that distributors and television stations would let it be known that changes have been made in the films and thus they are no longer the films which had received the original classification." His point was that distributors should not seek to exploit a film's earlier notoriety.[68]

One suggestion made by some producers in the late 1960s was that all movies should be shot in two versions, one for cinemas, one for television. That was considered because of the dollar potential for a Hollywood film after its theatrical release. Estimates went as high as $1.750 million, based on $1 million for the first and second network runs, $500,000 for the third and fourth network runs and $250,000 in syndication.[69]

Congress made noises when Senator John McClennan (D-Ark) attacked "the flood of movies wallowing in sex, perversion and pornography" and implied that he might seek industry action or legislation to forbid the sale to

TV of movies not suitable for viewing by children. He sent queries to MPAA member studios, all TV stations and related trade groups asking whether they believed that the showing on TV of a film which had been classified as not suitable for minors "would be consistent with their responsibility to act in the public interest." As for cutting a movie for TV, he said that film classification was on the basis of overall impact and "the elimination of a few lines of dialog or the deletion of a few minutes of the film would not change the unsuitability of these films for showing on television." McClellan also supported the position of Senator John Pastore (D-RI) against sex and violence on TV in programs which were specifically made for that medium.[70]

At the end of 1969, Universal Vice-President Jennings Lang announced that henceforth his studio would shoot two versions of scenes for movies which it felt might not be acceptable under TV's much stricter censorship. Lang said: "We are redesigning motion pictures so that they will be acceptable to TV, just as pictures are carefully edited to conform when they are shown to censor boards or in foreign nations which have a different social structure." While many of those movies could be sold as is to TV with the stations deleting scenes Lang worried the movie's quality would suffer and might be "butchered" by such editing. "We are trying to anticipate censorship not just in TV, but all over the world. We send scripts of our pictures to a group of people aware of the different restrictions TV networks have from the theatres," explained Lang. "We are doing this on all of our pictures. Certain pix will never be seen on TV. If the basic theme is prohibited by the TV code, forget it."[71]

When CBS telecast Luchino Visconti's theatrically X-rated *The Damned*, in February 1972, about 30 CBS-affiliated stations defected from the normal network line-up of 171 outlets, refusing to air the film. Most of those outlets were in the South and Midwest. Thirty-six minutes had been deleted from the feature, 25 by Warner, 11 by CBS. Several weeks before the air date, a fundamentalist church paper in Tulsa, Oklahoma, *The Christian Weekly*, alerted its readers and urged them to write to CBS headquarters and local affiliated stations to protest. As well, they threatened an advertiser boycott. Hundreds of letters were received at the CBS main office. Everett Hughes, program director at Orlando, Florida's WDBO-TV, said it was against station policy to advertise or run X-rated titles, even when re-edited.[72]

At its annual assembly in 1972 the Southern Baptist Convention, the largest Protestant denomination in America, with 11.8 million members, described many contemporary motion pictures as "utterly degrading, lacking in redeeming social value" and vehicles for "gross moral depravity." Without dissent it adopted a proposal to oppose the showing of "offensive movies" in cinemas and on TV by letter writing, "selective" viewing, and so on. Also urged was that members make a "concerted" call to legislators to pass laws prohibiting the exhibition of obscenity either in cinemas or on TV. The Baptists criticized CBS for "breaking a critically important moral barrier" by telecasting for the first time an edited version of an X film, *The Damned*, which thus opened the way to the possible channeling of "morally offensive" pictures into American homes.[73]

Regardless of the suitability of Hollywood films for television, and despite the butchery performed in the editing process, those films garnered high ratings, which allowed stations to boost their advertising rates, which led to a desire to program even more movies. As the 1965-66 TV season got underway, the number of movie nights on the networks increased from three to four nights. The three networks were making movies serve a dual purpose by developing 30 and 60 minute series based on feature films. Fourteen of that year's programs were based on films, including *Mr. Roberts* (1955), *Gidget* (1959), *Tammy* (1957) and *The Long Hot Summer* (1958). At the start of the 1966-67 season, movies again led the way in the ratings. "So potent are the pix this year that they have stampeded the webs to new multi-million dollar purchases" of movies, observed reporter Les Brown.[74]

Writer Ronald Gold commented, "The webs have found that even a film which was a disaster at the box office, and even a rerun of a film shown on a network previously, will give it a better share of the audience than it can expect from many series." The networks also found that a feature in the blockbuster category, even if split up into two nights for telecasting, "can tear off the ratings roof." Observing all of this led Hollywood to dramatically raise their asking price.[75]

When movies were first introduced on TV, Les Brown felt they were a "crutch" but they had become "the ailment itself." By programming more movies the networks were, said Brown, "abdicating the very program role that justifies their existence—that of creating programs on a national scale that local stations with their limited artistic and financial resources, could not." It was a vicious circle with high ratings leading to more film buying, which drove up prices and reduced the stockpile even more quickly. Early in that 1966-67 season, all five network movie series made it into the top 16 positions in the Nielsen ratings, including three of the top four spots. That was in markets where all three networks were directly competitive. Equally important was the spillover effect as each network won the ratings for the entire night on its movie night.[76]

In the 1965-66 season, for the first time in Nielsen history, overall audience figures dropped slightly. But ratings for films on TV were up, while ratings for series overall were down, over the previous year.[77]

Marketing student Max Jarmoc of Loyola University in Chicago did a study of all movies shown on network primetime during the 1966-67 season. He found a correlation between box office success and Nielsen television ratings. About 26 percent of the viewers of those movies had seen the same film in a cinema before.[78]

On the basis of early returns, movies were a big ratings success again in the 1967-68 season, with features programmed six nights a week. Journalist Jack Gould commented that movies "have established themselves as the most stable form of TV programming. Studies have suggested, rather clearly, that many viewers will at least seek them out and hope for the best." One year later, CBS headed into the new season as the ratings winner from the previous year; yet, on the eve of the new season, wrote Les Brown, "it appears to be the underdog to NBC. The big reason is movies. First, NBC has added a third night of pictures ... Second, ABC is fielding much stronger movie titles this year than last." Which showed how important movies had become. ABC then ran movies on Wednesday and Sunday, CBS on Thursday and Friday, NBC on Monday, Tuesday, and Saturday.[79]

After five weeks and 35 individual nights of national Nielsen ratings returns at the beginning of the 1972-73 season, 19 of those nights had been won by a network that had a movie series scheduled on its winning night. NBC was running features on Saturday and Monday, CBS on Thursday and Tuesday (made-for-TV movies), ABC on Tuesday (made-fors), Wednesday (made-fors) and Sunday.[80]

In April 1975, NBC suspended the Monday night telecast of major league baseball games until June 2, replaced immediately with movies. That programming maneuver was widely described in the industry as an attempt by the network to build up ratings during a period where the A.C. Nielsen company and Arbitron were conducting their seasonal surveys of local stations. The practice of increasing audiences in that manner — known as "hypoing" — was technically illegal but the FCC had not been strict in enforcing the rules prohibiting it. All three networks engaged in hypoing to some degree. National TV ratings were charted daily but the stations in most areas of the country received local audience reports only three times a year, issued fall, winter and spring, containing the results of surveys — or sweeps — conducted over four-week periods overlapping October/November, February/March, and April/May. Sweep ratings were vital to local stations because they formed the data from which national advertisers made their buying decisions. Thus, when network programming was low in popularity during sweep periods, a local stations' revenues could be adversely affected. A baseball game normally drew more than 30 percent. NBC executive William Rubens explained the network suspended baseball "because we wanted to maintain a representative audience during the May rating period." During that spring sweep one account observed, "All of the networks will be offering the reruns of some of their most effective movies and specials...." NBC's airing of *The Godfather* in the fall of 1974 raised charges of hypoing by stations affiliated with other networks as it was scheduled during sweep week.

Then the movie ratings began to slip. During the 1974-75 season no movie period led its time slot in the ratings. None of those film slots had a better than 20 rating average; back in 1968-69 five of the six movie series averaged above a 20 rating. For the 1975-76 season each network cut back on its movie scheduling, a total cut of about six movie hours per week out of the primetime schedule.[82]

As the stockpile of films dwindled, and as the price escalated, the networks turned more and more to the rerunning of movies. Through the mid–1960s the pattern on network film series was to broadcast 30 features during the standard season, then repeat 22 of them in the summer. On NBC's Saturday movies advertisers paid $45,000 to $48,000 per commercial minute. The lowest rate was to sponsors who bought time in all originals, 30 per year. For Saturday repeats, the fee was $31,000 to $37,000 per minute, in 1966, depending on the season. On Tuesday repeats NBC charged $30,000 per minute. At that time the network announced its movie package for Saturdays in 1966-67 would contain three repeats (first aired in the 1965-66 season) within the 30-week season, but that full ad rates would be charged. NBC argued those were "special" features; *Stalag 17* (1953), *White Christmas* (1954), and *Bridges at Toko-Ri* (1954). Some advertisers were angry as they had already signed up thinking all the movies were to be originals. They had not been told in advance.[83]

Second runs of a movie on the networks were still considered a rarity in late 1967 but enough had been telecast to conclude that those repeats were drawing good ratings. The median rating for some 260 such titles was 18, good enough to make the top 30 in most Nielsen polls. Those successes often came only six to seven months after the first network run. It got the networks thinking about third, fourth and even fifth runs.[84]

When a particular package of films had finished at CBS distributor Screen Gems went ahead selling it in syndication, station by station, assuming it had no place else to go with the group. One buyer was the five ABC owned and operated outlets. When ABC President Tom Moore heard about the deal he tried to get those stations to relinquish the titles for ABC networking but the stations—in just as urgent need of features as the networks—said no. Moore's ardor to play movies previously aired on another network would not have set precedent but it would have moved the practice along. Precedent was set in the fall of 1966 when CBS acquired a block that included a few titles first networked by NBC.[85]

Over its three movie nights in the 1968-69 season, NBC sprinkled more than a dozen third run titles. All were from a UA block previously leased by ABC. From UA NBC had contracted for more than 50 third run movies, some 40 of them for a fourth run, and even a few for a fifth run. *The Miracle Worker* (1962) drew a 39 rating share for its first run, a 24 share for its second run and a 35 for its third run. *Birdman of Alcatraz* (1962) drew rating shares of 39, 21, and 29, respectively, for its three runs. Reporter Bill Greeley commented: "The numbers stamina of the pictures is interesting from an economic standpoint, for the third, fourth, fifth and beyond runs must be cheaper to the network while delivering virtually the same cost-per-thousand to the bankrollers. From a profit standpoint, TV features are getting better than ever."[86]

Reruns began earlier and earlier. For their January and February 1973 schedules CBS was into fourth run product, NBC into third run and ABC into second run. Some movies networked in that period had been telecast in the fall of 1972. Also, the networks were showing features originally shown on the other networks. In January, CBS broadcast *Vertigo* (1958) which had played NBC in 1965, 1966, and 1967, and on ABC in the early 1970s.[87]

Blocks offered in syndication increasingly had been exposed multiple times on the networks. An example was Paramount's block called Portfolio Six which was purchased by the five CBS owned and operateds in the spring of 1974. It contained 30 titles, nine of which had had two network runs, fourteen with three, and seven movies with four, five, six, or seven network plays. Despite the repeat history there was little or no effect on prices. Paramount's Portfolio Six was asking the highest price ever per title in the top 20 markets, more than $10,000 on average per title.[88]

During 1975 hearings when the FCC received comments on TV reruns it let it be known from the start it felt the government had no business in that area. Networks argued they couldn't afford to operate with less reruns. NBC declared that to reduce the rerun ratio for dramatic and sitcom series from 45 percent to 25 percent would cost, said NBC, in excess of another $70 million. Additionally the networks argued that reruns were in the public's interest since it gave people an opportunity to watch something missed the first time around.[89]

Chapter 6

A New Genre: The Made-for-TV Movie, 1961–1975

> "You simply cannot turn out anything good for $500,000 or $750,000—or maybe even $1 million."
> Richard Zanuck,
> Fox, 1966.

> "Something that can be summed up in one line in *TV Guide*."
> Unnamed Hollywood
> agent, 1972.

As the period began, each of the guilds had its own signed agreement with the majors for residual payments from TV sales on all movies made in 1960 and thereafter. Of the TV gross receipts, six percent went to SAG, two percent to the Directors Guild, two percent to the Writers Guild, 1.5 percent to the musicians and nine percent to other guilds. That 20 percent in total marked out for payment to the guilds was figured after 40 percent of receipts were taken off the top for distribution expenses. Thus the residuals amounted to 12.3 percent of the total gross television income.[1]

When SAG was negotiating to replace a contact expiring on July 31, 1965, it pushed for a larger share of the TV revenue arguing that the still increasing use of movies on TV was depriving them of work they would normally perform in turning out regular TV shows. SAG was then pushing for 10 percent. Union executive secretary John Dales said that as recently as 1960, it seemed unthinkable that movies would be shown on primetime network TV, yet for the 1965-66 season, those networks were devoting a total of 8–10 hours each week to movies. The telecasting of only one feature per week in network primetime, explained Dales, eliminated about 30 weeks of production of three or four TV series, representing more than 1,000 jobs for actors alone. Additionally, there had been a tremendous increase in the use of films in television syndication, which also cost jobs. Regarding the negotiations then underway, and SAG's demand for a greater share of television revenue, Dales declared, "We are ready to stake our economic lives on achieving a reasonable and substantial solution."[2]

An agreement was reached that summer in which SAG established a fee schedule setting a base dollar amount, depending on how long an actor had worked on a movie. From there a complicated formula kicked in, in which an actor received a percentage of the base amount, dependent on whether it was a film's first release to TV, whether it was on a network in primetime, total gross of the film from TV sales, and so forth.[3]

Motion Picture Association of America (MPAA) President Jack Valenti revealed in 1967 how much Hollywood then depended on TV film production to keep it in business. He said that members of the MPAA were making for TV the equivalent of over 500 features a year, but that only 190 features a year were being made for, and distributed in, cinemas. Film series from the majors filled 32 hours of weekly primetime on the networks, with movies in network prime accounting for another 12 hours per week. Thus Hollywood's majors took up 44 hours out of the 73.5 primetime hours available each week on the networks. Five years later their domination was unchanged as the majors had 34 hours weekly in primetime, plus movies, compared to just 18 hours from independent producers. As one account observed, "It's quite a turnabout from the early days of television, when indies were in the forefront."[4]

Journalist Les Brown wrote in 1968 that the influence of motion pictures on television was then so encompassing and profound "that the household medium cannot help but concede its dependency. The way things are going, nothing can stop primetime television from looking, a year from now, like yesterday's bijou. Ironic to think that only a dozen years ago video had threatened to buy the picture industry. But more ironic is that TV, which has all the endowments of a 'now' medium has chosen to abdicate the creative vanguard to motion pictures, the stage and recordings." Brown was unhappy not only with the amount of old movies being network telecast but also with the lifting of the plot elements from so many movies as the basis for network series, everything from *The Flying Nun* (born of *Mary Poppins* [1964] and *The Sound of Music* [1965]) to *Peyton Place* and *The Ghost and Mrs. Muir* among many others. While it was always easier to borrow a tried and proven story permise than to create a new one Brown thought "the big reason TV has taken to rewriting the movies is that they are easier to sell to advertisers. The situation is recognizable and usually is one that has already met with acceptance in the marketplace. Tell an advertiser you have a *Mary Poppins* kind of thing or a *To Sir with Love* (1967) kind of thing, and he knows what you're talking about, both in terms of story content and box office history."⁵

As that movie stockpile was exhausted, and as those prices climbed, the networks made two countering moves. One involved the birth of a new genre, the made-for-TV movies. The second was an attempt by some of the networks to become film producers themselves. When both CBS and ABC announced separately in the 1966-67 period that each planned to produce full-length features for showing in theaters it looked like a corporate struggle was shaping up between the majors and the networks. The majors, through the MPAA, protested to Justice about those plans fearing "ruination" if networks extended their economic power into movie production because of TV's ability to offer real or implied inducements for the television showing of those movies after their theater engagement. Justice declined to comment but admitted it had commissioned a long range study of network programming, including the production of films. That action by the majors encountered opposition from the National Association of Theater Owners (NATO). In a resolution adopted at its convention NATO applauded the entry of ABC and CBS into film-making—it promised to help overcome a shortage of available movies. NATO even chided specifically NBC's David Sarnoff for not yet joining television's challenge to Hollywood. Both networks were then in the process of setting up subsidiaries to make movies; ABC was then parent of, among others, 400 Paramount theaters. MPAA argued that the networks would have a monopolistic advantage over Hollywood. If the networks developed their own movie libraries then prices would decline. Hollywood had produced just 149 movies in 1966 whereas the three networks programmed films six nights a week and could use 156 titles per year (based on 26 a year for each series). Part of the appeal of showing movies in theaters before their airing on TV was, said a broadcasting executive, "the several years of advance publicity for a picture."⁶

Early in 1967 ABC got into movie production through two subsidiaries which soon merged into ABC Picture Corporation, while in May of the same year CBS got similarly involved through a division which came to be called Cinema Center Films. NBC did not join in. However, it was involved in made-for movies, which it also tried to sell to cinemas overseas. ABC executive Samuel Clark said, "Basically we make pictures that will be shown in theaters. But in addition to providing an increased number of features for theaters, there is the eventual residual value of helping to keep the prices of films for television showings down to a reasonable figure." With Justice showing at least some interest in the development, and worried about antitrust problems, both ABC and CBS decided not to distribute their own movies. Had they done so Justice may have gotten more interested. For example, ABC, with its cinema holdings, would be producing, distributing and exhibiting movies, a situation banned to Hollywood by the Supreme Court in 1948. On the other hand, neither network chose a Hollywood major to do their distributing. ABC picked Cinerama Releasing Corporation while CBS's Cinema Center selected National General Pictures, both independent firms.[7]

Seven film companies (MGM, Columbia, Paramount, UA, Universal, Warner and Avco Embassy) filed a complaint in federal court in New York in September 1970 to enjoin CBS, ABC and their affiliates from producing, distributing or having an interest in television entertainment programs other than exhibiting them. The suit also sought to prohibit the networks from any aspect of filmmaking other than the right to exhibit them on their network. Alleged by the majors was that the networks, through ownership of production and distribution companies, TV stations, large cinema chains and other facilities were tending toward a monopolistic control of these markets and were in violation of the Sherman Antitrust Act. Denying the charges CBS noted the majors supplied over 30 percent of the CBS primetime fare. ABC stated that it went into film production after the majors had reduced the number of features they produced thereby creating "an artificial shortage" which enabled them to command higher prices.[8]

Fox was the only major which abstained from joining the action. As that studio was then the theatrical distributor in many foreign territories of CBS made-for-TV movies Fox decided it might be unwise to sue.[9]

In retaliation ABC filed a countersuit against the majors seeking over $100 million while demanding the dissolution of the MPAA. Filed in federal court in New York the suit charged further that MPAA members "combined and conspired" to monopolize the production and distribution of feature films. Also, ABC's complaint charged that some of the majors engaged in block booking practices, compelling the network to buy all feature films and television series offered or get none.[10]

In 1972, after five years and some 37 movie releases, ABC shut down its filmmaking division with a loss reportedly upwards of $35 million.[11]

Two years later Columbia Pictures obtained U.S. theatrical distribution rights to 32 movies made by ABC in the 1967-72 period. Columbia already had the North American theatrical rights to the movies made by CBS's subsidiary—which had also shut down around the same time as ABC. Thus Columbia had marketing rights to over 60 movies made by the "instant majors." Ironically, Columbia's former management was one of the most hostile of the majors towards TV's entry into feature production. Columbia remained a plaintiff in the majors' suit against the networks, which was still pending. Both those distribution deals were, reportedly, contracted on a straight consignment basis with no up front money, guarantees, and so forth, with normal distribution terms prevailing on a "best efforts" basis. Neither network had licensed domestic TV rights for those films, due to the legal action of suits and countersuits. In any case the brief experiment of the networks was permanently over.[12]

Movies made especially for television were said to be the brainchild of Jennings Lang at Universal in 1962. Only ABC expressed any interest in the project but they then lacked the money to produce two-hour movies.[13]

A deal was made the next year between NBC and MCA following some two years of negotiations. Instigated by NBC, the deal had MCA subsidiary Universal studios agreeing to make a group of feature-length movies, each two hours long for initial release on the NBC network followed by theatrical release abroad. Also planned was a second-run in the U.S., in cinemas. Those films were slated to start being broadcast in the fall of 1964. Both parties insisted the films would be real A pictures, not Bs, but; "instead of shooting out for the lush extravagance of a *Cleopatra* or recruiting the talents of such old timers as a Cary Grant, Kirk Douglas or Burt Lancaster, it will emphasize the new stars coming up, particularly those with built-in TV audience appeal, as for example Dick Chamberlain."[14]

It was an ambitious undertaking that envisioned a full season of weekly films, 26 or more. However, it fell far short of expectations. Universal's first effort was *The Killers* (1964) which was turned down by NBC on the ground it was excessively violent. However, in the 1964-65 season NBC did air the other two Universal made-fors, *The Hanged Man* and *See How They Run*. Ratings were said to be okay but nothing special. Critical reviews were less than satisfactory. Both were slipped into NBC's Wednesday night film series with no notice to viewers they differed from the other theatrical Hollywood films in the lineup. *The Killers* was released not to TV, but directly to cinemas, with modest success.[15]

A deal for 21 films was made by ABC and MGM to be telecast in the 1966-67 season. Under the deal ABC received telecasting rights to 15 MGM theatrical movies plus the production of six made-fors. Those six items were to have a budget of at least $500,000 per picture. However, ABC was paying only $400,000 per movie, meaning Universal had to look to the foreign cinema box office and/or other sources, to turn a profit.[16] The trend toward made-fors aroused some fears in the film industry over this new type of movie. Produced on budgets of $500,000 to $1.5 million they were designed mainly for showing on television with their principal theatrical market being overseas. Networks put up roughly half the cost of the made-fors. At this time, early 1966, Hollywood movies continued to enjoy "extremely high ratings." Chief worry was that the alliance between Hollywood and TV would result in an outpouring of mediocre films that could destroy the extraordinary hold that movies exercised over the TV audience. Said Martin Ransohoff, chairman of the Independent Filmways Inc.: "Anything that might jeopardize the TV market for motion pictures would pose a severe threat to the economic well being of the movie industry. If we contaminate this market, we're in trouble."[17]

After a couple of years of sporadic experimentation in the field of made-fors Universal moved into production with a full slate of them in 1966. Three were being made with the studio planning to turn out 12 in total over the course of the year, for all three networks. While all the majors were active to some degree in the field, Universal was the most active. CBS predicted that the majors would soon be making 50 to 75 made-fors per year. Each of the made-fors was tailored for the "special requirements" of TV and the exigencies of the foreign market. Reflecting that strategy was a project called *The Four Winds*, which dealt with World War II. It was a theme deemed to have strong appeal both in the U.S. and abroad. Principal star, Doug McClure, was well known to the American TV audience but not abroad, so another actor, Ricardo Montalban, who was well known overseas, but not on U.S. television, was brought in to costar.[18]

Asked as to what type of product it could turn out on what for Hollywood was a meager budget some executives had reservation. MGM President Robert O'Brien said, "We can do good pictures, but not a strong feature with good box office names, directors and writers." Fox Vice President Richard Zanuck insisted his studio would have nothing to do with the production of made-fors because, "You simply cannot turn out anything good for $500,000 or $750,000—or maybe even $1 million. At least, the product wouldn't be good enough to compete with current attractions at the theater or with motion pictures already on television." Others, including many TV critics, were worried about what Charles Pemerantz, a public relations man involved in both media, called a "fear of lengthy anthologies neatly broken up for commercials." They were, in other words, fearful that made-fors were going to be made with climaxes neatly arranged for the convenience of advertisers. What was true then was that only movies with strong reputations had produced standout ratings but what was also true was that virtually any movie drew a solid portion of the available audience. Made-fors, thus, had the potential for relatively good coverage at low cost. For 1965, the seven Hollywood majors received $325 million in television revenue, some 33 percent of the year's total income. That figure was nearly triple their 1960 TV income. Misfires continued in the new genre. *The Plainsman* (1966) by Universal was rejected by CBS for unannounced reasons. It too, was then released directly to cinemas.[19]

Promising to be a critical year for made-fors was the 1966–67 season with several majors set to deliver six or so items each. It was believed they would be key in determining if the networks could sustain their then five film nights per week. If the made-fors were not successful many felt the networks could not sustain five movie nights—using 150 titles in total per year, a sum that equaled Hollywood's annual theatrical output. No commercial time sold as quickly, as easily, as profitably as the time available within the movie series. Almost all the minutes on all the showcases were sold out. For that season, MGM was slated to deliver six made-fors to ABC, Universal seven to NBC and

Warner six to CBS. Given the worry that the majors couldn't produce anything acceptable on such a small budget some of the networks, like CBS, had small made-for deals with independent producers. It was assumed that dropping six or seven made-fors into a given movie night would not dilute the overall rating value of that film night. When NBC had slipped those two Universal made-fors into its movie night a couple of years earlier that assumption was deemed to have held up. So powerful was the draw of movies then that ABC executive Len Goldberg predicted that whichever network had the strongest lineup of features would win the coming season's ratings war.[20]

Just a few months later the Warner deal with CBS was inactive and perhaps defunct. The parties clashed over what properties to develop, casting and other matters. Budgets proved higher than anticipated with the idea being to alter course, give the movies a theatrical release first, followed by CBS telecasting. CBS was to share in the theatrical revenue but no agreement was reached as to what percentage. The network turned then to independent producers to obtain a few made-fors.[21]

Instead of made-fors in the $500,000 to $1 million budget range Warner found itself with films in the $1 to $2 million range. Since that was too expensive for the CBS deal the studio decided the first title in that planned series had to be theatrically released. It was, said reporter Peter Bart, "an incredible disaster titled *The American Dream* (1966); released in the United States as *An American Dream*. That ended Warner's changed hope of continuing that series and turning it into a box office success. Bart thought that more and more Hollywood and the networks were coming to realize that mass produced "cheapies" would not fill the bill. That critical 1966-67 year for made-fors had gotten off to a disastrous start with an increasingly dim prospect. Then on November 26, 1966 NBC telecast Universal's made-for *Fame Is the Name of the Game* as the first in its season series of made-fors which were to be dropped into its Tuesday and Saturday night movie slots. Drawing a big audience, it was a huge ratings success. It would also lead to a series spin-off for the network. Suddenly things began to look better for the made-fors.[22]

A second made-for by Universal for NBC, *Doomsday Flight*, also scored excellent ratings, although, like *Fame*, both received poor press notices. Promotion of both items was heavy. Due to that, and less theatrical material available after major deals by ABC and CBS, NBC entered into a deal at the end of 1966 with Universal for theatrical features plus an unspecified number of two-hour made-fors. It represented a bigger move into the genre by the network. Budgets for the made-fors were to be $1 million or less with NBC paying $550,000 per title plus 20 percent, for studio overhead. Universal figured to recoup the remainder from domestic and foreign TV syndication, and possibly from theatrical distribution abroad. If those made-fors were successful they stood to cost NBC $200,000 less per title than paid recently by the other networks in their cinema movie deals.[23]

In reviewing the third round of made-fors (by Universal for NBC for the 1966-67 season) *Time* magazine wrote: "The casting in the three films shown so far is second-rate, the direction and pace third-rate and the scripts cut-rate. Noodling around the discarded film scraps from old adventure and spy movies, pasting the label 'camp' on anything that does not make sense, the producers are the flattest Pied Pipers ever to lead the television industry into its next phase." It was typical of the critical scorn heaped on those made-fors. In response Jennings Lang, vice president in charge of TV production at Universal argued that the quality of those movies "has been pretty good, compared to most movies and most of the programs on television." However, Lang admitted the made-fors' sights had been set, at least in the beginning, at a low level: "First we have to build a commercial appeal, then we will go on to other things."[24]

When marketing student Max Jarmoc of Chicago's Loyola University did a study of all movies shown on network primetime during the 1966-67 season he included made-fors. He found that no more than 25 percent of the viewers of made-fors were aware they were different from movies made for cinemas and then broadcast on TV. Less than five percent of the viewers surveyed could accurately describe a made-for movie as such. Jarmoc's results on made-fors suggested they did as well as they did in the ratings because viewers thought of them as just another movie. "The viewers are presently accepting these films because they are carefully being integrated into a lineup of Hollywood movies. But once these movies become abundant and awareness is increased, it is possible that a negative attitude may develop."[25]

MGM tried to straddle the line and produce cheap films, partly financed by a network, but released theatrically in the U.S. first, then telecast on the tube. In its older deal with ABC for six made-fors all were originally slated to go first to TV. However, that deal was renegotiated with the last three productions, *Day of the Evil Gun* (1968), *Hot Rods to Hell* (1967), and *Welcome to Hard Times* (1967) all being released to U.S. cinemas before being telecast. The first three items, *The Return of the Gunfighter*, *The Dangerous Days of Kiowa Jones*, and *The Scorpio Letters* played ABC as "premiere" offerings. As part of a larger deal with CBS in 1967 MGM agreed to produce six made-fors for the network. However, all were scheduled for theatrical release first with none to appear on TV until 1970 at the earliest.[26]

Late in 1967 Universal and CBS announced a long term deal in which the studio agreed to produce up to six two-hour made-fors for the network at a cost of between $1 million and $1.25 million. Those items were to be shown on TV first, then in U.S. theatres. Previously CBS had a similar deal with Warner. Part of that deal was that Universal's made-fors would serve on occasion as pilots of new television series. NBC's *Dragnet '67* and *Ironside* were introduced to the television audience as two-hour made-fors.[27]

As 1967 ended NBC announced it would move to three movie nights a week, starting in September 1968. That meant the 1968-69 season would have a total of seven primetime movie nights per week, one each day. NBC planned to interweave its made-fors on its movie nights. To meet the product demand NBC encouraged its house producers to do two-hour programs for TV that could play as a movie and spin-off into a series. If someone wanted to shoot a pilot to fill a two-hour slot and even if no series evolved at least a movie time slot was filled. Said an NBC source: "We know we wouldn't be working in our own interest to run features for features' sake. We want to use these showcases to develop for the medium, and to test our belief that long-form originals will work on TV. Eventually, two-hour specials will be the norm, and it'll be common practice for a new series to premiere in a two-hour episode just as *High Chaparral* did this year."[28]

In 1968 producer Roy Huggins got the idea to do a 90-minute made-for movie of the week series. When commercial time was factored out those made-fors would be just 70 minutes or so long. Huggins took the idea to NBC who rejected it. When he took it to CBS executive Mike Dann said, "Roy, that is the worst idea I've ever heard in my life." ABC bought the concept and was willing to parcel the whole series of 26 to Universal, who wanted too much money. Finally, ABC parceled the project out piece-meal to different majors and independent producers. The difference with this idea was that made-fors would not be interlaced with Hollywood theatricals within a film showcase but have an exclusive slot of their own, containing nothing but made-fors.[29]

Networks turned originally to made-fors to assure a steady supply of movies that was less expensive than the "used" Hollywood product and to recoup development costs by packaging series "pilots" into original movies. By the early 1970s the genre was well established with some movie slots showing nothing but made-fors over the entire season. A typical 90-minute made-for (74 minutes running time) was made in just 12 days; a 2-hour made-for (96–97 minutes) took 16 to 20 days to produce. Regarding script quality of the made-fors, director Steven Spielberg said, "Sixty-five percent of the stuff we get is 1950s sub-B." Networks imposed their own special demands. "The nets want a strong story premise and a promotable hook—something that can be summed up in one line in *TV Guide*," explained one Hollywood agent. Rarely did a made-for director graduate to doing theatricals. The stigma attached to the genre remained. It usually prevented name actors from stepping down to do them although that stigma was eroding, particularly after Richard Burton and Elizabeth Taylor signed up for two ABC made-fors for the 1973-74 season. The reason was exposure. As Universal actor Susan Clark explained: "You can beat your guts out doing a movie that two people see, but you can do dreck and 30 million see it."[30]

Putting it in perspective was *Saturday Evening Post* reporter Benjamin Stein who noted that an average made-for, with no special billing, or big stars, or advertising, would get 24 million viewers in one telecast. In 1973 only five movies shown in cinemas got over 20 million spectators. A made-for at a higher level, or simply publicized more, would draw 40 million viewers. In the entire history of theatrical movies there were no more than a couple dozen that had ever had audiences of that size.³¹

Meanwhile one idea that refused to die was pay–TV. By late in 1962 another experiment loomed, despite the fact that previous experiments in places such as Palm Springs, Chicago, Denver, Bartlesville and Etobicoke, Ontario were all failures. Home Entertainment Company of America was laying bold plans to wire 20,000 homes for pay–TV by September 1963. Like all systems before it Home hoped to make first-run movies its principal fare, intending to run nine movies per month on one of its three channels, an amount that would require virtually all of Hollywood's A product. With some exceptions the majors had not balked permanently at providing recent movies for those pay–TV tests. However, those titles had almost always had their theatrical run before being released to pay–TV. Still, the majors were attracted by the enormous potential, depending on the level of control they could attain in any such system. There were then some two billion paid admissions annually at the box offices of U.S. cinemas. Producers and distributors lived off their share of the $1.5 billion take. Studios considered such items as prints, which cost $250 to $200 each with perhaps 400 prints of a new feature being sent out. They dreamed of one print beamed in one night to 20 million television sets across the nation, attached to a single pay–TV network. Revenue from theatres could take up to 18 months to collect while pay–TV would return it in 30 to 60 days. With its test set for Santa Monica, California, Home had contracts with GE, General Telephone Company and RCA. As well, it had permits from the California Public Utilities Commission and the City of Santa Monica.³²

Close to a year behind schedule, Subscription Television Inc. got off to a start in Santa Monica on July 17, 1964 with three channels. The signals were carried over wires, not over the air. At start-up the company claimed 2,000 homes were connected, much less than hoped for. An electronic device connected to each set transmitted a signal to the company indicated which channels were tuning in. At the end of the month customers would be billed for the programs they had watched. Company President Sylvester Weaver predicted that one major problem—the refusal of Hollywood to lease new films to be broadcast over pay–TV—would be solved within the coming few months, but he gave no details.³³

Just one week later, but coming on the heels of many months of frustration, Subscription announced it had signed a one-year "experimental and exploratory" agreement with UA involving eight films, to be televised starting July 31. Weaver had charged the majors would not release new pictures to pay–TV because of the pressure from exhibitors. UA stressed the deal was experimental to explore the potential of pay–TV and how best the company could meet its responsibilities to exhibitors, movie producers and the public. Under the deal the movies would be made available to the system nine months after the end of their first run release in the Los Angeles area. Those movies would not be made available to commercial TV in the 12 months following release to pay–TV. Subscription planned to televise each title twice in one evening, repeating that every three months for a year. Films were telecast unedited and uninterrupted. Until then the system had been showing old foreign art-house titles—because no Hollywood product was available to it—which attracted few viewers. Those that did watch were charged $1 per film.[34]

A few weeks later Paramount signed a deal with Subscription for 20 of its titles. The new system had, however, still not succeeded in its goal of landing first-run product. Opposition to pay–TV formed up swiftly in the area, under the heading Citizens Committee for Free TV. It got enough signatures in a petition drive to put a referendum question on the November 1964 ballot—Proposition 15—to prohibit pay–TV. Financial support for the opposition forces came chiefly, as might be expected, from exhibitors and broadcasters, but also from others whose businesses were dependent on the public leaving home to obtain diversion, such as restaurant owners and parking lot operators. Subscription estimated that by election day it would have about $20 million invested in its system.[35]

Pay–TV was dealt a crushing blow with the state initiative to outlaw pay–TV being passed by a margin of more than two to one, a surprise all around since each side had expected a close vote. In part, size of the anti vote was attributed to the intensive advertising and publicity campaign by the nation's cinema owners. They claimed to have spent about $500,000 in opposition while Subscription estimated those exhibitors had really spent over $2 million. Pay–TV had planned to spend $1 million in campaigning but Weaver said those plans were canceled due to a "cash shortage." In the end, Subscription said it spent only $100,000 or less. In addition to support from broadcasting the anti forces were also buttressed by show business guilds, unions throughout the state, and by big name stars. Actors such as Dana Andrews, Charlton Heston, Henry Fonda and Walter Pidgeon all broadcast radio commercials denouncing pay–TV. Observers agreed the key reason for the outcome "was that a majority of the voters were convinced that they would eventually have to pay to watch the same TV shows that they now got free were Proposition 15 not approved."[36]

The Supreme Court of California ruled, in 1966, that the prohibition against pay–TV was unconstitutional. That decision opened the way for Subscription Television Inc. to resume the operations it had been forced to suspend back in 1964. However, by then the company had filed for bankruptcy. Weaver issued a statement that the company was not then able to resume operations in Santa Monica and San Francisco—to where it had expanded before the vote—but that his company hoped to resume operations "ultimately." At the time it closed the company claimed to have 6,000 customers. Later in 1966 the U.S. Supreme Court announced it would not review the California Supreme Court's ruling that a ban on pay–TV violated freedom of speech.[37]

Throughout the various pay–TV experiments the FCC and Congress had each held hearings on the issue, considered the matter, passed the issue to one another, and so forth, preferring, it seemed, to take no specific action. However, the Supreme Court decision made it clear that the concept could not be prohibited. So, in December 1968 the FCC authorized pay–TV on a national basis, a decision that was upheld in the latter part of 1969 by a Federal Appeals court. Under the FCC guidelines any such system that was set up (none then existed) would be allowed to show movies which were less than two years old, from the time of their theatrical release. With the majority of the theatergoers being under 30 years of age pay–TV was supposed to be able to recapture the vast, lost, older audience. Those FCC rules were designed to be a compromise to keep everybody happy. Exhibitors still got first-run product with no competition. Since it was felt a successful pay system would be able to outbid free, commercial TV for everything pay was not allowed to telecast any movies over two years old, leaving that field entirely to commercial TV. At the time it was not airing much that was less than two years old. Pay systems were left the window of bidding for titles finished their theatrical runs, but not yet two years old.[38]

One area where pay–TV did get a foothold was in hotels and motels. A test was conducted by a company called Computer Cinema at the Gateway Downtowner Motor Inn in Newark, New Jersey. As reporter Les Brown wrote: "The Newark motel is considered ideal for the test because the city is not one in which visiting businessmen (who else would go to Newark?) would be inclined to take an evening stroll." The hotel got 10 percent of the gross, the distributor 30–40 percent, with the rest going to Computer Cinema. Films on the system had had their theatrical first-run and would eventually play commercial TV. It was felt that even if a title played to one million hotel rooms it was still a small portion of the network audience so the TV sale price would not be affected. Estimates were that about three million hotel rooms in the U.S. were capable of carrying this type of system. Computer Cinema executive Paul Kein estimated that if 12 features were used, with one million rooms connected, each picture would earn $3.4 million, if 20 pictures were used each title could earn $2 million, based on an average cost of $2.50 charged per movie to the hotel room guest.[39]

When MPAA President Jack Valenti observed a demonstration of a second system, owned by Columbia Pictures subsidiary Trans-World Productions, he said the use of such systems offered a means of reaching an audience that eluded Hollywood. Valenti explained the median age of a person attending a cinema was just over 20 years while the median age of a hotel occupant was over 42 years. "Hotel room viewers are a nonmoviegoing audience," he added.[40]

Unhappy with hotel room pay–TV was the National Association of Theatre Owners (NATO). At its 1971 convention NATO was told by one of its speakers that motel films were "developed surreptitiously" under "unilateral processes" excluding exhibitors and that it was "a direct attack on our breadbasket." It was further charged that exhibitors provided the money which financed the new system.[41]

Computer Cinema ended its four-month Newark test late in 1971, utilizing 120 of the motor inn's 259 rooms. In that test two films were run at once at an average cost of $2.50 per title. According to Computer, because of its system, hotel occupancy increased from 50 to 65 percent. During the hours the system operated (5 PM to 2 AM) 65 percent of the occupied rooms watched TV, 37 percent tuned to the pay features. The second system, operated by Trans-World, began its four-month test in the 1,000 rooms of the Regency-Hyatt House in Atlanta. Said Columbia executive Jerome Hyams: "We're trying to get people back into the movie habit. We'll be playing to people who are not going to movie theaters—this is the lost audience." Eventually, of course, it was hoped such systems would be extended to apartments and homes. In the Trans-World system the hotels also received ten percent of the gross, with a "big chunk" going to the distributor. However, for the testing periods the distributors "have been abundantly generous." For Computer Cinema movies were provided at no charge by Fox, MGM and Paramount. Although cinema owners continued to view this development with dismay, some industry people, with stars in their eyes, believed the total revenue from movies telecast in hotel rooms could hit $50 million by the end of the 1970s.[42]

At the beginning of 1972, the FCC indicated there would be no obstacles to this concept when it declared there would be free and open competition in the delivery of movies for paid viewing in hotels and motels.[43]

Cable itself was a worrisome prospect to the broadcasters, back as early as 1966. The coming of what we now call basic cable—then called community television or CATV—was bothersome to broadcasters, because they feared CATV people would soon move to set up their own pay–TV system (that is, pay-per-view) outbidding the commercial broadcasters for the best programming. CATV systems first came into existence around the early 1950s to bring signals into remote areas that could not receive programs directly from a television station. Later, people in areas capable of receiving signals directly would sign up with cable to get better reception (to eliminate snow, ghosts, and so on) than their rooftop aerials could provide. In 1966 there were about 1,600 cable systems serving almost two million subscribing households. CATV permits had been issued in 800 communities and applied for in 1,200 other communities.[44]

By 1972, there were about 5.5 million cable users. As a result of new FCC rulings permitting pay–TV on CATV and over the air the potential of pay–TV and cable was seen as enormous. Estimates were that in the foreseeable future there would be 20 million cabled households, about one-third of the number of sets in the U.S.[45]

In 1972, pay–TV arrived on the scene to stay, in the private home market. One system was a standard pay-per-view arrangement. Columbia's hotel pay–TV subsidiary, Trans-World Communications, made its debut in 1973 as a new pay feature of an established Viacom cable system, Suffolk Cablevision on Long Island, New York. It was the first pay cable operation in the New York metropolitan area. The Trans-World connection added three new channels to the 30,000-subscriber Suffolk system. For the beginning period five to six different recent movies were offered each month over the two movie channels with each channel carrying a different title on an all-day grind. Films were changed every one or two weeks. Cost was $3 per film but the viewer had unlimited access to it on the day ordered, for the single charge. Each title was shown on average nine times a day in the 16-hour schedule, thus allowing families to watch in shifts, to have friends over to join in later, and so forth. The system's third channel carried kids' programs, "family-type" movies and cultural material, at various prices. As well, there was a separate channel supplied, at no charge, which advertised the programs on the other three — known in the business as a barker channel. In operation then some 19 months, Trans-World claimed it serviced 40,000 hotel rooms in America. This type of pay–TV never caught on the way it was hoped it would, and still hasn't to this day.[46]

What did catch on was what today we call premium cable—whereby a fixed monthly fee was paid, above the basic cable charge, for unlimited access to one or more channels. Sterling Manhattan Cable Television introduced pay–TV to its downtown Manhattan CATV system in the fall of 1973, through its subsidiary Home Box Office (HBO) as HBO was then already doing for several communities in Pennsylvania, where it started in late 1972. Sterling was then in the process of trying to sell HBO to Warner. It would later succeed. In Manhattan the pay system carried feature films and sports. Sterling then gave its basic cable customers home games of the New York Knicks basketball team and the New York Rangers hockey team. Although there was no FCC rule affecting a switch of games from CATV to pay–TV, as there was in the case of games which had been seen free on commercial TV, a Sterling executive admitted they were probably "protected by public opinion." In Pennsylvania, HBO was getting $6 a month, over and above the basic cable subscription fee.[47]

Early in 1974, NATO filed a petition with the FCC seeking to bar Warner from showing movies on its owned CATV systems. Warner owned more than 140 cable systems and, said NATO, had pay–TV channels on ten of them. In filing its petition NATO invoked the old Supreme Court decree which prohibited the majors from engaging in the film exhibition business. Pay–TV violated that edict, thought NATO. Also charged was that Warner's pay–TV venture was a violation of antitrust laws because the company got unreasonable leverage against theater owners and that the Warner venture would siphon features from cinemas, forcing their closing.[48]

By late in 1974, HBO had some 30,000 of the total of 100,000 pay subscribers in America. Programming consisted of 40 percent movies, 40 percent sports, and 20 percent for all other. According to company President Gerald Levin, it was in the interest of the majors to keep the new pay–TV system alive, for one reason: the price of features to commercial TV had virtually doubled since the advent of pay–TV. HBO was then a wholly owned subsidiary of Time, Inc. Later Time and Warner would merge.[49]

When the FCC declined NATO's petition to force Warner to stop renting movies to its pay–TV systems, in March 1975, it declared the authority to decide antitrust issues was outside its domain. It also stated that NATO lawyers had not cited any violations of FCC regulations by Warner.[50]

Home Box Office continued to grow, having about 100,000 customers, some 50 percent of the pay industry, by the spring of 1975. Observers were predicting it could have one million subscribers by the end of the decade. Exhibitors continued to worry. Cinema owner Harold deGraw stated: "If we in exhibition do not get our heads out of the sand and fight this threat to our very existence, we will probably deserve the fate we almost certainly will get." The networks also opposed pay–TV. Hollywood, of course, wanted to sell to everybody and thought it could extract big dollars from pay cable without harming either theaters or the networks. The problem lay in making sure that movies were out of theaters before they could play pay–cable, and off pay–TV before they aired on the networks. Neither cinema owners nor the broadcasters believed that was a realistic possibility. HBO would not air X-rated titles and those films with little commercial appeal that "simply aren't desired by the pay cable firms." Generally, the pay–TV revenue was split 40 percent to the producer and 60 percent to the pay system, such as HBO. That system charged cable providers $3.50 of the first $6 the cable system charged its subscribers, plus 50 percent of everything over $6. Given the number of titles telecast, it meant a film company received about 30¢ per movie per subscriber, per month. For Hollywood the dollar totals were not then impressive. For the year 1975, the motion picture industry grossed only about $5.4 million from pay cable, including hotel pay–TV operations. However, that income was mostly profit. One of the majors that year grossed around $720,000 from pay cable plus another $180,000 from its hotel systems, a total gross of $900,000. Expenses totaled $100,000 for administration and $20,000 for prints, the rest was profit. Producing a film-to-tape print of a movie for a network telecasting cost a film company $10,000 to $12,000.[51]

At the urging of the cable industry the Senate Antitrust subcommittee held hearings in May 1975 on the issue of network "warehousing" practices. Cable lashed out at the networks' strict exclusivity contracts for "emasculating" pay–TV in its infancy. Also on hand to testify were motion picture executives and broadcasters with the latter insisting that "siphoning" of movies by pay–TV was not in the public interest. Looking on with interest were exhibitors who claimed they would suffer the most with pay cable prosperity, and the FCC. That regulatory agency had initiated its own inquiry on the same subject. That week new FCC rules went into effect, which pleased no one. Cable claimed it would be strangled while film executives declared those rules disrupted an otherwise comfortable pipeline of movies through cinemas, pay–TV, networks and syndications. Miles Rubin, a cable executive, told the Senate panel that "the motion picture companies include in every one of our contracts a clause which allows them to yank a picture even after it has been sold to us, without notification." Because of their big spending on films (some $72 million in 1975) the networks could just about call their own shots at contract time. Hollywood executives conceded the network exclusivity contracts were indeed strangling the fledgling pay–TV industry but stopped short of recommending that such provisions be deleted from licensing agreements. It argued it was concerned to develop the pay–TV market because, while during the first quarter of 1975 the networks programmed 16½ hours of movies a week in primetime, it was scheduled to fall to 10 hours in the fall of 1975. Universal executive Herbert Stein told the hearing: "The problem is the power of the networks to make us write in the contract any amount of exclusivity they want. We have no place else to go to sell our products."[52]

Those FCC rules went back to 1970. The so-called "primetime access rule" took effect in the fall season of 1971. Stations in the top 50 markets were required to fill at least one of their four primetime hours (7–11 PM) with independently produced material. Those stations were not allowed to use network reruns or previously broadcast movies in their hour. Nearly 500 of the 621 television outlets were affiliated with a network. Affiliates use of non-network material in primetime then averaged four hours a week, although some of that was actually rerun network fare. Rules also banned the networks from buying secondary rights to programs they did not produce themselves. Also forbidden was network syndication of material—even their own—to local broadcasters in the U.S. Those top 50 markets served 40.6 million of the 58.4 million U.S. households with television sets. Those rules were designed to prevent the three commercial networks from gaining a stranglehold on the nation's dominant entertainment medium. Before the rules took effect an independent producer might take a series idea to a network. If the network proposed to buy the series, the producer might be placed under pressure to sell distribution, syndication or other rights to the network in return for getting a primetime slot on a network. These FCC rules curbed such powers, and indirectly strengthened the hand of Hollywood in dealing with those broadcasters.[53]

Also put in place in 1970, were FCC rules forbidding pay–TV from the airing of movies, or series, more than two years old, although a limited number of movies more than ten years old could be put on pay–TV, under various conditions. When those rules were reviewed, the MPAA asked the FCC to immediately suspend its rules restricting the showing of features and series on pay cable. In its filing the MPAA and its member firms declared, "the viewing public have suffered and are suffering irreparable injury to their First Amendment rights and development of a nationwide cable television system has been stifled." Those rules, said the MPAA, "are based on a protectionist philosophy" and they "contravene the antitrust laws by artificially protecting the oligopoly network structure from a new communications medium, by restricting the market from programming and by precluding program suppliers from selling and pay cable systems from buying in a competitive market."[54]

Those revised 1975 FCC rules liberalized the system by barring pay–TV from airing movies three to ten years old—a change from the old two to ten year rule. Pay cable was allowed to bid on titles three to ten years old, if they were not under exclusive contract. As well, pay was allowed to bid on movies over ten years old if not under contract and if they hadn't been telecast in the local market in the previous three years, or if those titles were under nonexclusive contract to a station, but hadn't aired recently.[55]

Through it all, NATO worried. At a pay cable symposium at its 1975 convention one speaker warned that once the per-program charge supplanted the monthly flat fee the large revenues would move pay–TV way and so would exclusive production. He urged exhibitors to buy into pay–TV themselves as the best strategy, viewing the day when an exhibitor would play day and date with his own pay–TV franchise, thereby tapping the widest market. MPAA President Jack Valenti assured the exhibitors of the theatrical primacy in the playoff of movies calling pay–TV not competitive with owners' interests, but complimentary. Valenti referred to pay–TV as "family choice" rather than the former term as it "offends my sensibilities." Outgoing NATO president Paul Roth observed: "I've been told that pay–TV was going to show opera, ballet, open heart surgery ... but all I see is movies, movies, movies." Trade journal *Variety* concluded that: "Exhibition fears being a marketing device to create the want-to-see for films that will achieve revenues for another medium."[56]

Even as early as 1975 there were clashes between the majors and the fledgling pay–TV industry. Beginning in spring 1975 HBO stopped telecasting Columbia movies, although it had once bragged that it had contracts with all the majors. Studio Vice President Allen Adler agreed Columbia had reached an impasse with HBO with the reasons including "a lack of sensitivity on their part in dealing with us and in handling product" plus "misinterpretation of contract." Columbia was still supplying features to other pay–TV companies. What it all boiled down to was money, Columbia wanted more. Adler explained, "We have been very supportive in getting pay-cable off the ground, but now they've got to pay." He added that the pay firms had to recognize they were middlemen with the right to take a profit in addition to expenses but that program suppliers were the risktakers who were entitled to take the bulk of the money. Producers, he observed, "nurtured the television networks. They couldn't have worked without us. Then they turned around and told us what prices they'd pay. We're not going to make that mistake with pay-cable." In his opinion consumers should pay about $12 a month for pay–TV service and that film producers should get a good chunk of it, instead of the 40 percent of the average charge of $6 per month. Adler also thought that pay-per-view was the fairest way of assessing viewers and accounting for dollars for program suppliers, as opposed to the flat monthly rate charged by HBO and most other pay cable systems.[57]

President Richard Nixon's Office of Telecommunications Policy released a report in 1973 called "Preliminary Analysis of the Causes and Effects of Rerun Programming and Related Issues in Primetime Network Television." It declared that network power and market power were "most plausibly" the cause of the increasing use of movies and reruns on TV. As a result of that power of the three networks "there exists a cycle of rivalry behavior which has the effect of driving down the quality of original programming in favor of the maintenance of high profits." The report said there were some circumstances of which "this may conceivably be one example" in which "rivalry among a few oligopolists may be even less desirable than outright monopoly. A similar degree of economic power is present but it is exercised more wastefully." It declared there was a serious long-term decline in television with several factors combining to reduce the output level of original Hollywood TV production including "reruns, longer programs, more theatrical motion pictures shown on TV." While network expenditure on primetime programming had increased 80 percent in the previous decade, original non-movie expenditure fell by 15 percent. Reruns and primetime movies accounted for the bulk of the difference. Increased reruns accounted for a decline in the previous decade of 343 hours per year of original programming on all three networks combined, in primetime. For CBS, reruns accounted for 30 percent of the decline in original programming over the decade, theatrical movies also accounted for 30 percent of the decline, various other factors contributed the other 40 percent, mainly the primetime access rule which decreased the amount of network primetime.[58]

Chapter 7

Cut, Colorized, Panned and Scanned, 1976–1998

"It was a disaster."
     Steven Spielberg, 1982.

"In the pursuit of a buck, the networks leave an art form defenseless."
     Warren Beatty, 1985.

This period saw commercial television become relatively less important to Hollywood as new delivery mechanisms came into play. HBO initiated the satellite era in 1975 and was soon followed by many competitors. In turn, that led to the multi-channel universe available to most American households, for a price. Movies dominated those satellite systems just as they had come to dominate commercial TV's primetime. The second delivery mechanism was the videocassette recorder (VCR) which, of course, also depended heavily on films produced by the majors. By 1981, there were 80 million TV households in the U.S.[1]

It had become a regular practice by the late 1970s for the networks to purchase broadcast rights to movies before their cinema showings, usually during the filming or editing stage. When the average price to TV of a theatrical movie rose from $100,000 for two network runs in 1961 to around $800,000 by the end of 1967, the number of hours of primetime features increased from two in 1961 to fourteen in 1968. Mean number of years elapsed between theatrical release and first network telecast was almost six years in 1972; in 1978 it was 3.74 years, with many features shown in less than two years. Researcher Barry Litman looked at four variables and their effect on the price of theatricals to the networks. He found movie length was positively correlated with contract price—each extra minute drove up the contract price by $3,847. Age was negatively correlated with contract price as each additional month of elapsed time between theatrical release and contract purchase drove down the price by $723. Box office receipts "were highly correlated with contract price" as each $1 million in adjusted rentals led to an additional $26,900 in the TV prices. Lastly, he found that critics' ratings of movies (four stars, and so on) were not significantly related to contract price. Forty percent of variation in price was explained by those four variables. Litman concluded: "This analysis has shown that television networks have the upper hand in bargaining with the producers of regularly scheduled programming" however, "such domination has eluded the networks in the market for theatrical movies of known quality. This market has always been very competitive, with frequent bidding wars for box office hits." Bidding for movies before their theater release, thought Litman, was a logical extension of the networks' activities and could be expected in the long run to adversely effect the negotiating power of the movie companies, given the high correlation between box office receipts and TV price. What Litman didn't take into account was Hollywood's response; while they did lease to TV before cinema release, they developed a floating contract price which depended on box office success.[2]

For the 1981-82 television season, the three networks started with only five movie nights in total—down from seven as ABC and NBC each dropped one night. However, in the summer of 1981, there were 11 movie nights on the schedule totaling 22 hours, almost one-third of total primetime programming—CBS had three movie slots, ABC and NBC four each. CBS was playing off much of its made-for backlog along with theatrical movies deemed a little soft for "regular season" exposure. One reason for so many movie nights was that the "summer replacement" show was no longer being made. No longer seen in summer were repeats of strong theatricals as those big hits were rested for another wintertime telecast, when the ratings numbers counted. Television's audience was at its lowest point from May to late August.[3]

If the average price paid for a film by the networks was declining, the blockbusters still commanded top dollar. Fox let all the networks know, in late 1981, that *Star Wars* and its sequel *The Empire Strikes Back* were available as a package for the right price, with Fox asking $20 million for one run of each title. Those two films were the two highest grossing of all time. The most money a network could receive from one telecast (over 2½ hours) was $7 million, based on 35 30-second spots at $200,000 per spot. Additionally, network affiliates as a group would gross an extra $1 million from each airing, from local spots. On the surface that may not have seemed to be a wise move for a network, but it could pay off. If a network telecast a blockbuster in one of the rating sweep periods it could drive up the audience figures substantially which, in turn, would allow the network and its affiliates to increase advertising rates, for all time periods.[4]

When NBC bought 17 titles from Paramount in 1983 for about $70 million, it was believed to be a record price. However, that figure could move to $80 million, or more, if a number of those titles exceeded a certain theatrical gross, triggering the percentage escalators written into the contract. Although 17 was a much smaller package than was bought in the past, it was a larger block than was usually bought by the early 1980s. Usually the network bought an average of two runs per title, good ones got three, bad ones one each, determined by the TV ratings of the first telecast. Those Paramount titles would not be available to NBC until the mid to late 1980s. One reason why networks bought smaller blocks was because so many titles were shopworn by the time they reached the networks, having been through pay–TV and videocassettes, even at that early stage in their development. More and more the networks tried to rely on made-fors, which were relatively cheap to make, could deal with topical subjects as the lead time was shorter, and could draw on television stars who had mass recognition among TV viewers but almost no marquee value to the cinema-going public.[5]

Lew Erlicht, ABC Entertainment president, declared in 1984 that the networks would buy fewer movies and pay less per title because the over-exposure of theatrical features through cassettes and pay–TV had diluted their value in the network market. Having begun that process itself some five years earlier, for the previous three years ABC had confined its film buys to a few titles it believed could deliver in the ratings. He said, "You will see a continued diminution of license fees being paid by the networks as well as a diminution of feature pictures on television. Why buy a feature when you can make a TV film for $2,500,000 which is first-run, with big TV stars, with a fresh concept? Why should you pay more for a movie not only released theatrically but seen perhaps 8–12 times on cable?" Erlicht added: "My solution would be that the networks would pay for features once again if they got big ratings. Let them (the studios) first sell to the networks, and then to cable and pay–TV."[6]

One example of that practice occurred later in 1984 when ABC bought at least three runs of *Ghostbusters* from Columbia for $15 million. However, the network couldn't get physical rights to the title before the 1987-88 season because Columbia had an option to theatrically re-release the title in the summer of 1985. Then HBO had an extended pay–TV window that could begin as early as Christmas 1985 or as late as the summer of 1986. HBO had a partnership interest with Columbia, having paid about $8 million to cover a quarter of the production costs of the title. That pay channel was paying a premium price due to escalator clauses in the contract, and for exclusivity rights. The HBO exclusivity made *Ghostbusters* more valuable because it would not have had any runs on other pay channels such as Showtime/TMC by the time it finally reached ABC.[7]

From September 1985 to April 1986 the three networks combined played only 54 theatricals in primetime, compared to 67 for the same period a year earlier. The average Nielsen ratings for them, following a steadily declining pattern since the late 1970s, slipped again, from a 14.3 share in 1984-85, to a 14.2 in 1985-86. On the other hand, 162 made-fors were telecast in 1985-86, up from 117 the previous year, with the ratings climbing to 17.2 from a 16.4 share. NBC-TV executive Jerry Jaffe said, "Theatrical movies have been robbed of almost all of their value to the networks by overexposure on videocassette and pay cable." Buying selectively, networks then paid on average about $3 million for a theatrical title, about half of what they paid four to six years earlier. Of course, studios more than made up the difference in sales to pay cable and videocassettes. Hollywood's majors were making more made-fors themselves with Paramount and Columbia each making 10 to 12 of them in the coming year. Networks then paid a license fee of about $2.6 million for a made-for, which the majors produced for around $3 million, allowing a solid profit in immediate foreign sales and future domestic syndication sales.[8]

When CBS announced it would add a third movie night to its schedule, in November 1986, it illustrated an important and reliable network strategy—when the regular series started to fail, it was time to go to the movies. The use of movies was still a standard tactic used by all three networks to boost the ratings upon which the advertising revenues depended. Each of the three networks had 20 to 25 percent of its primetime schedule devoted to movies. However, made-fors comprised a greater and greater proportion of those slots. President of CBS Entertainment Donald Grant said, "We're using made-for-television movies on Sunday, Tuesday and now on Saturday to improve circulation, to get higher ratings."[9]

As the 1990s began, Hollywood was heavily utilizing television to publicize its product, all for free, as part of regular programming. Both NBC's *Today* show and ABC's *Good Morning America* wooed stars to appear on their programs to publicize their films. Most actors eagerly worked the morning talk-show circuit. Barbara Walters did evening interview specials, while CBS's *Saturday Night with Connie Chung, Prime-Time Live* and *20/20*, as well as other newsmagazines regularly weighed in with star profiles plus visits to movie sets. Cable was also linked to Hollywood with 24-hour-a-day coverage of the movie industry. Its stars were a staple of Movietime (which later changed its name to E! Entertainment). Every weekday CNN aired a 30-minute program *Showbiz Today*. Major pay-TV networks regularly featured behind the scenes shows about current films. MTV had a weekly movie program called *The Big Picture*, while on VH-1 the film studios actually funded the production of half-hour documentaries about the making of a particular release. With the proliferation of channels, both broadcast and cable networks had space to fill in their schedules: movie hype programs could fill them. In Hollywood, the majors viewed TV exposure as essential. It produced larger theatrical audiences which allowed the majors to reap even greater financial rewards from the movie as it worked its way down the distribution pipeline. Said Jon Katz, former executive producer of CBS *This Morning*, "Television had become an integral part of Hollywood marketing." David Nuell, executive on the syndicated hit program *Entertainment Tonight* commented, "When we started in 1981, we had the field to ourselves... Now there literally might be hundreds of requests to go behind the scenes of a movie." Some worried about the trend. Jon Katz, then an associate professor of journalism at New York University remarked, "There's no other arena in journalism where the journalist sells products so enthusiastically. In television entertainment news, they shill the stuff to the sky. The line between advertising and journalism is totally lost." Often that line was crossed. A common practice was for a film studio to guarantee first, or exclusive, access to a major movie to a TV entertainment show—if that program agreed to devote several segments to the title. Fox used that technique at the end of 1989 with *War of the Roses* (1989) on *Good Morning America*, wherein that show ran interviews with each of the three main stars (Michael Douglas, Kathleen Turner, and Danny DeVito) over the course of a week. Then, on Friday, all the stars appeared together. It was all very valuable to the TV show and to Hollywood, although no one knew for certain if the exposure increased cinema audiences or decreased them if the movie looked like a bomb.[10]

In 1996, primetime was defined as 8 to 11 PM six nights a week, and 7 to 11 PM on Sundays, for a total of 22 hours. ABC aired movies on Thursday, Saturday and Sunday, CBS on Tuesday and Sunday, and NBC on Monday and Sundays. All those movie nights played two hours, from 9 to 11 PM and were a mix of theatricals and made-fors. Thus 14 hours out of 66 total primetime hours, 21 percent, were devoted to movies. Fourth network Fox telecast 14½ hours of primetime material, two hours being movies. Fledgling networks WB and UPN were barely underway broadcasting, respectively, just five hours and six hours of weekly primetime material.[11]

Blockbuster films still commanded huge prices from network television. In 1996 ABC bought *Mission: Impossible* (1996) for around $20 million, in a package. CBS paid about the same for *Twister* (1996) even though in both cases the titles came to network television after home video release, pay-per-view and pay cable windows. In contrast NBC paid $30 million for *Jurassic Park* (1993) (receiving at least 4 runs) getting the title before any cable window. Theatricals remained reliable lures for advertisers seeking young adult and male audiences that made-fors typically lacked and, said a studio executive: "They repeat well." As well, they served as big-event promotional platforms for other fare. NBC built a sweeps rating period promotion entirely around *Park* receiving up to $650,000 for 30-second commercial spots in the film.[12]

By the late summer of 1996 all that season's theatrical blockbusters had been booked by the networks. All the contracts tied the TV price to box office receipts resulting in a cost to the networks of anywhere from $10 to $22 million for each title. Networks were due to receive the titles 30 months after theatrical release, coming fourth in the distribution chain after, in order, home video, pay-per-view, and pay cable. Those networks were stockpiling on high-visibility programming for the three major sweeps rating months, February, May, and November. Station affiliates set their advertising rates, often for months into the future, based on the ratings racked up during the sweeps period. Said Paul Schulman, head of his own advertising agency, "Theatrical movies have proven time and again that they can get enormously high ratings." With most contracts giving the networks the right to air each title twice, they may not have gotten their money back but the spillover effect was important. Telecasting a blockbuster was an "event" rather than just another movie under the *Tuesday Night at the Movies* banner. For the film *Independence Day* (1996) the Fox network could charge advertisers as much as $500,000 for each 30-second spot, receiving $16 million plus from its first run, and maybe $10 million for the second airing. Because of the massive promotion already unleashed on behalf of a title for its theatrical run, the networks could spend less in marketing that blockbuster, freeing up money to publicize made-fors and series. While those made-fors, filled with TV series actors and using ripped-from-the-headlines plots, could still generate decent ratings, some of the appeal was waning. New World Distribution Vice President Phil Oldham remarked that "the old formulas are getting tired. How many times can you recycle women in jeopardy and the disease of the week?"[13]

The highest price paid by a network for a theatrical occurred in June 1997 when the Fox network paid some $80 million to Universal for *The Lost World: Jurassic Park* (1997). Fox got the title exclusively for 12 years with the first telecast scheduled during the November 1998 sweeps. Prices had so escalated for the handful of sought-after titles that some networks got involved in sharing arrangements. Warner sold 15 titles to a combination of CBS and TBS/TNT. For some of the titles TBS got first, and multiple runs, for three to six months followed by a 15-month window during which CBS got one telecast. After that, TBS got them back for further multiple runs over the remainder of the four-year run. For the other titles, CBS got the first run, within a 12-month window, then TBS got multiple runs over the remainder of the contract. Turner paid $60 million for the 15 titles, plus an unstated amount from CBS. Many movies had their TV destiny predetermined. Hits from Disney, and subsidiaries Touchstone and Hollywood Pictures, automatically went to the Disney-owned ABC. Fox theatrical blockbusters went directly to the Fox network. Universal movies went exclusively to the USA cable network, of which it owned 50 percent. It was then in the process of buying the other 50 percent from Viacom.[14]

Besides *Lost World* other 1997 blockbusters sold for big prices. *Titanic* (1997) went to NBC for $50 million for five runs over five years, *Men in Black* (1997) to NBC for $30 million for five runs over five years, ABC picked up *Liar, Liar* (1997) for three runs over four years for $25 million. In the case of *Lost World* Fox bought out the pay–TV window in order to get the title within 15 months of its theatrical run.[15]

By the mid–1990s, pay–TV networks such as HBO and Showtime paid the majors around $4.5 million for exclusive pay–TV rights to a title.[16]

At the start of the 1997-98 season, the amount of time devoted to films was lower than it had been for decades. ABC, CBS and NBC each had one movie night, all on Sundays. Thus each devoted just two hours of their 22 weekly primetime hours to movies. Fox also had just one movie night (Tuesday) with two hours of its 15 primetime hours going to films. Those slots contained a mix of made-fors and theatricals. Blockbusters were often slotted into their own time period. Much of the decline in movie hours was due to the excessive exposure most titles received before becoming available to television.[17]

Cuts and deletions, and sometimes additions, to theatricals telecast on TV continued to draw ire from industry workers, however, it was an issue that didn't seem to engage the mass audience. Universal's 1976 release *Two Minute Warning*, about a psychotic sniper who killed dozens of spectators at a pro football game, received a whole new plot before it appeared on television in 1979. At a cost of over $500,000 Universal shot an additional 63 minutes which made the sniper only a diversion to allow the theft of a valuable art collection from a nearby museum. NBC declined to buy the original because of the violence, which was mostly removed. Having done poorly at the box office, the studio hoped a TV sale would reduce some of the red ink. Around the same time Universal stretched several of its films into four-hour two-part titles for TV. Additional material of the hijackers was shot for *Airport '77* (1977) which aired in 2-part format on NBC in September 1978. A new subplot involving a young couple in an airplane was filmed for *Earthquake* (1974) while *MacArthur* (1977) released as *MacArthur, the Rebel General* was filmed both as a 132-minute theatrical issue and as a two-night two-hour TV release, running about 195 minutes. Since networks, of course, paid more for a four-hour movie than a two-hour film it would be in the financial interests of a studio to stretch out a film. At the time *Goldengirl* (1979), which was partly financed by NBC—about a female member of the 1980 Olympic U.S. track team—was being produced two ways: a cinema version of about 120 minutes and a TV version to be aired over four hours, running around 184 minutes.[18]

Robert Radnitz, producer of *Where the Lilies Bloom* (1974) complained about the butchery of his film on TV: "The creator is being misused. The public is hoodwinked. There is a public trust here, and television has got to be called to task about it." That caused critic John O'Connor to remark, in 1978, "Over the years, the movies have been snipped into differing specifications for a variety of programming needs. Today, many are almost unrecognizable, with not only whole scenes but whole sections deleted." The *New York Times'* TV listings of films "regularly downgrades presentations on a particular station because generally the films have been cut to the point of being meaningless. Such mutilation, of course, merely reflects a total contempt for content. And that attitude reaches up into network levels ... Just about everything is reduced to a 'property' to be tinkered with mindlessly by executives who are essentially salesmen. In the made-for-TV genre, the process usually begins in the formative stages. Good, serious books are acquired for dramatizing and are subsequently mangled by people who get paid for coming up with trite ideas." In competing with TV films, producers offered the public products that contained more explicit sex and language. But, a sale to TV could be profitable. As O'Connor observed, "The solution is devilishly simple. On major productions, two separate sound tracks are now regularly produced, one sprinkled with four-letter words for the sophisticates who stand in line for a hit, the other cleaned up for television. On top of this, particular scenes might be shot twice—sexy and more sexy (which are also used for European distribution.)"[19]

Movie writer Janet Maslin complained that a "censor made mincemeat" out of *Dirty Harry* (1971) for a late night showing on TV early in 1982. Outrageous overediting resulted in scenes being trimmed wholesale whether they needed it or not. The contents of a ransom note had been bleeped out, rendering the entire plot nearly unintelligible. The beginning of Harry's famous speech: "I know what you're thinking—did he fire five shots or did he fire six?", was deleted, losing the key point that the detective always knew how many bullets remained in his weapon. As well, "The action scenes had been doctored so artlessly that the mayhem seemed entirely random, and thus even more violent than it had been in the first place." Maslin wondered if free TV could afford to continue to engage in such practices in the face of competition from home video and pay cable which ran titles unedited and uninterrupted. Still, the alternatives were expensive, with a cassette of a movie then costing $50 to $80 to buy, or "rented for the price of two or three movie tickets and kept for several days."[20]

For its winter 1982 telecast of *The Wild Geese* (1978)—about British mercenaries sent to rescue an imprisoned African leader—NBC erased most of the violence but also cut twelve other minutes from the movie, thereby eliminating such "minor" plot details as the African leader's death. Network executives defended censoring because the image came into the home, because TV was a family medium and therefore had to be less explicit. Donn O'Brien, CBS executive, said, "Most adults enjoy seeing R-rated films in theaters, but they have a problem sitting down next to their children to watch the same unedited movie in their home." It was in the late 1960s with the crumbling of moral taboos that movies became more explicit, putting the networks in a bind. They found themselves constrained by the conservative standards of their local affiliates, dozens of which threatened to run alternative programming unless controversial titles were toned down. Examples from that period were *The Graduate* (1967) and *Easy Rider* (1969). NBC sliced away at *The Birds* (1963) so relentlessly that the audience was left with only very brief glimpses of the carnage but multitudes of grimacing reaction shots. As profanity became more prolific in films, by the mid–1970s, bleeping it out could not be relied on because it was too obvious and too obtrusive. Studios turned to the practice of having the actors redo certain words, long after the fact—looping, as it was called. A problem with that method was that the audience could often read lips and an actor may have been unavailable or deceased. When CBS licensed *Network* (1976) the profanity-spouting character played by Peter Finch could not be looped since the actor passed away. Trying to avoid such problems, the networks and studios worked out a deal in the latter part of the 1970s: before a network purchased a title, its broadcast standards department would draw up a list of changes deemed necessary to make the film acceptable to TV. With around 80 percent of theatricals purchased in the 1977 to 1980 period by the networks before a production got underway, changes were fairly easy to make in those prebuy situations. Producers were told exactly which scenes to reshoot. However, the prebuy method faded away in popularity because the networks ended up with too many flops on their hands.[21]

With networks paying $3–4 million per title in the early 1980s, many producers, even if their movie had not yet been purchased for TV, routinely shot two versions in anticipation of a TV sale. In the movie *10* (1979) Blake Edwards had a number of cast members put on bathing suits for a previously all-nude swimming pool party that was reshot with a network in mind. When Universal reshot *Two Minute Warning* (1976) director Larry Peerce refused to participate in the venture while the producer Edward Feldman was not even invited to. That TV version featured a completely new group of actors and 45 minutes of "cheaply shot" new scenes and reworked original—a psycho who they fretted might provoke imitative behavior—he seemed in the TV version to have been hired by thieves to divert police away from their museum robbery. All three networks refused to telecast intact 1978's Oscar winning Best Picture *The Deer Hunter* although it ran intact on several independent outlets. The stretching out of movies to fill anywhere from 2½ to 4 hours, instead of the standard two hours, was still popular. It was pioneered by Universal on its 1974 release *Earthquake* after NBC requested that it be drawn out for a three-hour time slot. Inserting outtakes, creating new special effects and calling in some cast members for extra shooting, Universal added 40 minutes to the title. Other titles inflated for television included *King Kong* (1976), *Midway* (1976), *The Deep* (1977), and *The Concorde–Airport '79* (1979). Most of those stretched items relied entirely on outtakes for the added time. ABC inserted 49 extra minutes to pad *Superman* (1978) into a four-hour broadcast over two nights while NBC did the same by adding 70 minutes to *Airport '77* using both outtakes and new footage to expand the original 113 minutes. Problems such as these were another reason why the networks used an increasing proportion of made-fors to fill their movie slots. Being controlled by the broadcasters from conception onward they posed many fewer problems for the censor.[22]

Another major problem for television was the aspect ratio. In the early days of movies, before television, films were almost always made in just one shape, a rectangle that was 1.33 times as wide as it was high. Television's screen was somewhat narrower at 1.23 to 1 but essentially little or nothing was lost to the viewer when any title made prior to the early 1950s was broadcast. The viewer saw virtually everything the cinema-goer saw. Trouble arrived when the industry developed the wide screen processes then, such as Cinemascope, to give the viewers an experience they couldn't get at home. That innovation doubled the width of the screen, moving the aspect ratio to 2.6 to 1. How to get that big image onto the small TV? One solution was to show only the center of the film, but much was left out—all the sides. That led to the technique called panning and scanning in which a technician isolated a portion of the wide screen action, however, in the process 20 to 60 percent of the original image could still be lost. In Steven Spielberg's *Close Encounters of the Third Kind* (1977) scientists stared in wonder at the first appearance of a little space creature. In the 1981 TV version they just stared: the space creature had been cut out of the picture. "It was a disaster," said Spielberg. Panning and scanning involved creative decisions that were not made by the movie's creators. Commented Fox executive Richard Wolfe: "My experience is that directors are not interested in the pan-and-scan transfer session." A simple alternative did exist which involved masking the top and bottom of the transmitted TV image with a black border at the top and bottom showing the film in what the industry called "the letterbox format." It allowed most of the side image to be transmitted and was a method that was "better, but still not perfect." said Stanley Kubrick. It was a technique that reasonably preserved the director's original composition. European television had been using the letterbox format for years. During network preparation for the showing of *Close Encounters,* Spielberg asked about the possibility of showing the film letterboxed but was told by ABC executives that it was impossible, that FCC rules did not permit it. The latter was not true. There was then virtually no letterbox presentations on the networks, pay cable, videocassettes, and so forth. The supposition was that viewers neither cared nor noticed. However, those viewers had never been presented with a choice.[13]

Film directors did win a round in 1985 when an arbitrator prohibited ABC from cutting 9 minutes out of *Reds* (1981) in which Warren Beatty was producer, director, co-writer and star. In response ABC, which would have paid $6.5 million for the title, canceled its contract. ABC Broadcast Group

President Anthony Thomopoulos declared: "We had a contract with Paramount which stated simply that we have the right to edit for time and for standards and practices. Now their contract with us is not valid." Under studio and network contracts with the Directors Guild of America all disputes over cutting rights were subject to arbitration. In this instance arbitrator Edward Mosk, an entertainment lawyer, ruled Beatty had an absolute right of final cut that could not be violated by the network, except for trimming of words and images to make a film suitable for showing on TV. Since Beatty had not given his right of final cut to Paramount, they could not give it to ABC. About 15 major directors had similar right of final cut on their movies, including Mike Nichols, Steven Spielberg, Milos Forman, Richard Attenborough, and Sydney Pollack. It was a decision the Directors Guild, which had filed for arbitration on behalf of Beatty, called "a landmark victory." *Reds* had a running time of 3 hours and 16 minutes. ABC wanted to cut those minutes so that it would end by 11 PM and not interfere with the 11 o'clock news. Stations affiliated with the networks made a considerable amount of money by selling ad time for the 30 minutes after network programming ended at 11 PM and were reluctant to interfere with that, although they sometimes did with sports events. Beatty, who won the director's Oscar for *Reds*, commented: "In the pursuit of a buck, the networks leave an art form defenseless. The wrecking of films with commercials is a fait accompli. Years ago George Stevens took that issue to court and lost. When you mutilate movies for mass media, you tamper with the hearts and minds of America."[24]

Three film directors told a National Association of TV Program Executives general session that if stations wanted to air edited versions of their work then the public had the right to know just who cut what. The preferred method of informing the viewers, agreed the directors, was via notices placed at the start of the film, at the end, and at the start of each commercial break. Beatty, Milos Forman and Mark Rydell also agreed that such notices should tell if the movie was uncut, trimmed with the director's input, or edited without the director's cooperation.[25]

When superstar Bette Davis reminisced in 1986 about her career she mentioned that the first time *All About Eve* (1950) was on TV, the network received thousands of letters saying: "'Why did you cut out such-and-such a line?' But there aren't many films so well-known that they would cause such a reaction." Davis thought things might have been different: "If the motion-picture companies had bought into the networks in the beginning, they could have owned television... The studios wouldn't have had their films mutilated through cutting if they had gone in and controlled television."[26]

Stand By Me (1986) contained a short, casual scene in which hot-rodding teens smashed a few roadside mailboxes with a baseball bat. At the end of ABC's broadcast of that title the following message appeared in large white letters: "Willful Damage to Mailboxes is a Federal Crime." ABC was making it clear it was disclaiming any responsibility should the film be seen as provoking imitative behavior. Many years earlier CBS's telecast of *The Wizard of Oz* (1939) was interrupted by reassuring celebrities advising children not to be frightened since it was only a movie. In the mid-1980s NBC aired *Little Darlings* (1980) a film about two girls at summer camp who made a bet over which of them could lose her virginity first. When that idea first came up on the network's version the camera suddenly cut to an unfocused part of the room and a voice never heard until then — and not in the theatrical version at all — said "I get it! They're betting about which of them will be the first to fall in love!" Later when one character declared victory once again the camera cut away. Again the mysterious voice emerged, proclaiming: "Look! She did it! She's in love!"[27]

Even though an advantage of made-fors was that there was less censoring and editing for time considerations, they could still run into problems. Among other titles, Nicholas Meyer directed the 1983 made-for *The Day After*. In its initial broadcast it gained the largest audience of any made-for movie. He decried the cutting and chopping of films in general and also noted the technique called compression whereby a film, transferred to video tape for telecasting, was run at a faster speed in order to squeeze more of the narrative into a limited amount of viewing time. Compression was said to be not discernible to viewers, usually. Meyer received a letter at the beginning of 1989 from ABC advising him it would rerun *Day* on January 23, 1989 with more than 23 minutes removed, and four more minutes "gained" through the use of compression. Originally running time was two hours and fifteen minutes. In the letter ABC proclaimed its concern for "the integrity of the director's version" but went on to "list in chilling detail enough cuts to render the film totally incomprehensible." Meyer noted the practice of the networks to solicit the collaboration of the filmmakers in the process of evisceration, holding out the prospect that they would do the job more efficiently than would the broadcasters. Of course, that was true. But it was also handy for the broadcasters since it presumably got a better job done for them at no cost. Refusing to do the cuts Meyer stated: "If the viewing public is being cheated — and I think they are — I don't care to be a part of it. And won't. I'd rather the network performed its butchery openly and clumsily, so that viewers know they are being gypped." He thought it was the audience that should be complaining; "As long as people don't give a damn what they eat, why not keep serving up swill?" Perhaps they were. By then, and continuing to the present, the three networks were losing audience share to cable, cassettes and so forth — where movies continued to be available uninterrupted and uncut.[28]

Concern over the butchery of movies for TV reached Congress in 1991 when a bill was introduced in the House of Representatives by Robert Mrazek (D-NY). The next year a companion bill was introduced in the Senate by Howard Metzenbaum (D-Ohio) and Alan Simpson (R-Wyo); the Film

Disclosure Act of 1992 was designed to require broadcasters, cable programmers and videocassette dealers to provide labels before presentation of film programs that had been altered or edited. Disclaimers would be necessary if a film was colorized, shortened in the editing process, time compressed or panned-and-scanned before telecasting. Following a press conference to announce the Senate bill Robert Peck, American Civil Liberties Union legislative counsel, condemned the bill as "an unjustifiable burden on speech... The idea that the government could put labels on works of art can lead to other infringements on artistic expression that would seriously undermine First Amendment freedoms."[29]

A heavy turnout of House Copyright Subcommittee members came to hear Martin Scorsese during a March 1982 hearing. A majority of those members said they were fans of Scorsese's films but not of the Film Disclosure Act legislation he was promoting. Representing the Directors Guild, Scorsese showed video clips of altered versions of classic movies including *The Graduate* (1967), *Ben Hur* (1959), *Casablanca* (1942) and *It's a Wonderful Life* (1946) to demonstrate how video post-production often destroyed the original content of the filmmakers. "We're not asking for much. All we want is a little truth in labeling," said Scorsese. Simpson added, "I think it is in the spirit of the free market for the consumer to be well informed." However, most subcommittee members agreed with National Association of Broadcasters Vice President Howard Sherman who argued that the public was not calling on Congress to act on the issue. Others objected to the bill on First Amendment grounds. Said Representative Mike Synar (D-Okla): "Can anyone guarantee me that this label would be the end of labels?" Also opposed was the U.S. Commerce Department which released a statement against the proposed legislation for being "inconsistent with the policy of the President to reduce and simplify the burden of government regulation on U.S. industry."[30]

Directors and writers had been fighting in vain for years to place a disclaimer on all altered films, something which would appear at the start and say, roughly, "This film is not the version originally released." Those alterations symbolized the powerlessness and frustrations of filmmakers who earned a great deal of money but had little control over their product. After stubbornly resisting any changes, the studios in 1993, led by Walt Disney studio chairman Jeffrey Katzenburg, announced a willingness to change. They declared they were ready to sit down and negotiate some form of labeling agreement. That came after arm twisting which included heavyweights such as Scorsese and Spielberg appearing before Congress to urge the enacting of legislation. With that announcement from the studios two influential lawmakers felt the dispute seemed to be over and therefore, legislation was not necessary. Representative William J. Huges (D-NJ), chair of the House Judiciary Committee panel dealing with the issue, said, "The motion picture industry has finally agreed that they will sit down and work out voluntary agreements on film labeling. Last year the industry was not willing to talk to the directors. I indicated, in the course of the hearings, that this disappointed me. It's a truth-in-filming issue as much as anything. Now the industry seems to have done a 180-degree turn. They're willing to talk to the directors. I don't see any need for legislation at this point." Similar views were expressed by Senator Dennis DeConcini (D-Ariz), chair of the Judiciary subcommittee looking into the question. Katzenburg remarked, "the position of the directors seemed perfectly legitimate. The consumers are entitled to know truthfully about the product they're viewing. The more I got into this, no one could explain why producers had stonewalled on this." He added: "I approached the Directors guild and said I'd like to resolve this amicably. They said I was too late. They said they wanted to resolve this through legislation." Directors Guild President Arthur Hill replied, "We will listen to them. It's not negotiation. It's not even necessarily a discussion. It's a presentation by them. We feel it's an issue that must go before Congress." For Katzenburg it was "a terrible precedent to seek legislation on the issue." However, that was exactly what directors promised they would continue to seek. Observed director Elliot Silverstein: "Films are being defaced, and there is a steady habit of defacement as a way of life. The question really is, since all these things are done in the name of administrative convenience or profit, one wonders when values will survive price."[31]

Later in 1993, a studio-sponsored labeling plan was unveiled by their trade group, the Motion Picture Association of America (MPAA). Under the plan, films that had been colorized or materially altered would carry consumer notification labels when aired on broadcast television and home video. MPAA President Jack Valenti said the four-second labels would be inserted on all applicable movies, beginning by the end of 1993. Companies agreeing to the labeling system included, beside the majors, Turner Broadcasting, New Line Cinema, Miramax, and Goldwyn, produced more than 90 percent of all American films. Three different labels were to be used. For films that had been panned and scanned the label would read: "This film has been modified from its original version. It has been formatted to fit your TV." In the case of features that had been panned and scanned, edited and time compressed or expanded the label would read: "This film has been modified from its original version. It has been formatted to fit your TV, and edited for content and to run in the time allotted." Added to colorized movies was a label to read: "This is a colorized version of the original black and white film." Valenti agreed the plan was embraced to ward off possible legislation. The Directors Guild of America said it was pleased with this "first step" but wanted "the MPAA to promulgate labels that allow for full and truthful disclosure and look forward to continuing our discussion to improve the label." What they wanted were labels that stated the specific changes made and would also list objections by the title's creators. That was also the position of Senator Metzenbaum and Representative Barney Ross

(D-Mass) who supported the filmmakers. Both said the MPAA plan was inadequate and that they would continue to press for legislation.[32]

Martin Scorsese made another pitch for legislation on Capitol Hill in March 1995. He appeared at a press conference to announce support for a bill reintroduced by Simpson and Frank that allowed film creators to state their objections to movies that had been altered for the after-market. Also on hand was Representative John Bryant (D-Tex) who offered separate "moral rights" legislation that would define the director, screenwriter and cinematographer as the "author" of a film. U.S. law recognized the producing movie studio as the legal author of the film. Bryant called it absurd that Sony corporation was considered the author of *The Bridge on the River Kwai* (1957). The Simpson/Frank bill was similar to legislation that had died in the two previous sessions of Congress. Remaining adamantly opposed was the MPAA whose past successful lobbying had throttled bills in committee. One studio source confidently predicted the Simpson/Frank and Bryant proposed bills would be "dead on arrival" in the Republican Congress because "The only bills moving through this Congress will be deregulatory." He was right. He added that Congress was "not likely to regulate on top of a voluntary labeling system that's already working."[33]

Some films underwent no alterations because they never made it to the airwaves. It was the recurring problem of unsuitable titles. A tabulation of theatrical films aired over Los Angeles stations in a nine-week period in 1976 revealed the average number of movies telecast weekly was about 165, a drop of some 15 percent form 10 to 15 years earlier. More than 67 percent of those titles were 25 to 50 years old with 10 percent of them produced in the 1970s. That drop in the number of theatricals acquired by TV began to accelerate in the early 1970s when sex and violence became more prominent in features.[34]

Writing in the *Christian Century* in 1976, James Wall agitated to keep *Two Minute Warning* (1976) off TV. When the communications commission of the National Council of Churches (NCC) learned that *Death Wish* (1974) had been scheduled for primetime TV it fired off telegrams of protest to local CBS affiliates. However, not a single outlet canceled the title because of the NCC request. That request urged stations to consider voluntarily replacing *Death Wish* with a less violent picture. Wall admitted, "This appeal to a sense of public responsibility was almost totally ignored: few stations even bothered to acknowledge receipt of the communiqué." Some outlets had already replaced the title, for reasons of their own.[35]

Evaluating a movie for television, networks were influenced by all sorts of factors other than cinema grosses, which remained important. Certain screen themes remained dubious, such as homosexual themes and heavily violent titles, and therefore were avoided as home screen fare, at least in the early 1980s. Said one TV insider: "There are odd factors which are important to television that have to be considered. For instance length has a certain value to the networks because it allows them to sell more advertising time per hour.

The networks are permitted to sell more advertising time per hour when a film runs than when they schedule regular programming so that length has value." CBS Vice President of program planning Herman Keld generally felt that Americans liked "things American" and tended to shy away from films shot on foreign locations or with foreign actors—James Bond titles being an exception. Keld cited the majority of Michael Caine's movies which, regardless of theatrical success, didn't have a strong TV track record, a fact Keld attributed partially to Caine's British accent. One television executive observed, "No one's saying there aren't a slew of exceptions, but over the course of time the networks have gotten cautious about buying either foreign films or films where the foreign factor is a major element." On the other hand, a network could grab a John Wayne feature which did only fair cinema business, because of Wayne's TV following.[36]

Made-for-TV movies played an increasingly prominent role in the air time that TV devoted to features. For the 1979-80 season CBS announced production of a record 50 made-fors—38 to be telecast that season—representing an investment of $60–$70 million. ABC was committed to 22, NBC to 30–35. When made-fors began years earlier they were in effect C movies, costing around $400,000. By this time they were all 2-hour projects, with more flexible budgets averaging around $1.3 million.[37]

During 1980, Hollywood's majors released 176 features while 137 made-fors were shown on the networks, costing close to $2 million each to produce. Those theatricals cost on average $16 million, $10 million to produce, $6 million to sell. More and more the home screen played a role in those theatricals. Said Judith Crist: "Almost without exception, theatrical films are being made with an eye to their television destination, many with financing from television interests." That eye frequently involved special filming, as in the case of *Coming Home* (1978) wherein substitute scenes for those involving sexual activity and nudity were shot.[38]

From 1964 to 1983 approximately 1,400 made-fors were commissioned with the three networks then producing 80–120 each year, collectively. Made-fors commissioned by pay cable had budgets averaging $3.5 million while made-fors produced for network TV cost an average of $2.1 million.[39]

By the mid-1980s the majors produced less of the made-fors than in the past. Of 236 original and repeat made-fors and miniseries telecast, only 64 were supplied by the majors. The remainder came from both large and small independents and in-house by the networks. One reason was the complaint by the majors that they didn't make enough money from made-fors. Hollywood focused more on TV series which could generate much more money in syndication—if the series became a hit—compared to the ancillary potential of made-fors. A problem with made-fors was that they had little value in reruns on TV, and little in videocassettes.[40]

On its two movie nights in the 1985-86 season, CBS used about 90 percent made-fors. It had almost stopped using theatricals because of low ratings, which it attributed to previous exposure of theatricals on cable TV and the growth of videocassette recorders.[41]

Toward the end of the 1980s, the three networks combined commissioned, on average, over 100 made-fors each year. Those made-fors occupied around 20 percent of network primetime. One former network vice president in charge of TV movies referred to made-fors as "hot concept" movies, already invested with "high promotability." To be marketable to a network in the first place a made-for had to be sensational, to depend on a high degree of responsiveness to whatever issues were currently in heavy cultural circulation, for its economic survival and effectiveness in commanding an audience. Made-for independent producer Frank von Zerneck said: "No matter how good or bad a movie is, for television, if you can't summarize it in a sentence that will appear in *TV Guide*, and if you can't describe it in a paragraph, then you'll have a great deal of difficulty selling the project." Sometimes a network conducted a random sample of viewers to survey whether they would watch a made-for on the basis of a brief plot summary like the one that would appear in *TV Guide*. In effect, networks decided whether or not a project got produced. Remarked von Zerneck: "They control the money and the network. They also have a point of view about what they want on their network, what kind of movie they want. So you're essentially writing it to order. The script is custom made for them." For the networks, he added, the bottom line was "is it going to be a movie they can exploit? Will it get an audience? Will it have footage that they'll be able to put into a trailer to entice people to watch it?" Network notions about where popular sensibilities could be monitored were summed up by a former network executive in charge of made-fors, who said: "I look at TV commercials to look for a trend. Or places where money is spent, not free stuff like television. What's on the covers of magazines? What are the advertisers using to sell soap? What are they saying about what's going on in the country?" Hot concepts for made-fors were mined from national magazine covers, or from TV's reality programming, talk show issues and tabloid TV scandals.[42]

Around the same time made-fors were reportedly running out of steam. Said NBC Vice President Preston Backman, "I remember in 1991, we had all but abandoned the idea of buying theatricals." Yet in the summer of 1996, all three networks bought packages from the majors. In all cases, the networks pre-bought with price tied to box office receipts. Each package featured one or more blockbuster titles. Made-fors were seen as having used up all the exploitable themes—spousal abuse, polygamists, babies switched at birth, so-called women's issues, and docudramas ripped from the tabloids such as the three Joey Buttafuoco sagas. Another reason made-fors were falling out of favor was due to the fact that they were seldom telecast more than once. However, theatricals, especially action movies and comedies, seemed to be popular every time they were shown. As examples, ABC Vice President Alan

Sternfeld cited *Lethal Weapon* (1987), *Pretty Woman* (1990), and *National Lampoon's Christmas Vacation* (1989). Beckman called such titles "roller coasters" because people seemed only too happy to climb aboard for another ride. Another advantage of theatricals was that they were heavily promoted in advance. Television networks had perhaps one week to tell viewers about their movies while the majors spent millions to create awareness for their titles. Network programmers were becoming less concerned about films getting too much early exposure. The major title in NBC's package was *Twister* and even though that title would have been seen in cinemas, on video and on cable by around 40 million people by the time NBC got it, Beckman pointed out that left more than 200 million who had not seen it. Some networks worried about what would happen to the market when all the studios that had their own networks started keeping the best titles for themselves. Sternfeld said that was already taking place. At Fox, "Rupert Murdoch has told people: 'You're not going to get any of our movies that gross over $100 million.'" They ended up on the Fox television network. Time Warner was then merging with Turner Broadcasting (which owned TNT and TBS). In the future it was felt that Warner might sell its titles to its own cable network, HBO, then to TNT/TBS, and then possibly to its fledgling TV network, WB, before they were offered to the other networks. Disney then owned the ABC network.[43]

In the fall of 1997, the average made-for cost $3.1 million to produce but got only $2.7 million in license fees from a network. That shortfall had to be made up from TV and video sales outside the U.S., "because the domestic market for TV movie reruns is almost nonexistent." Hollywood's majors had all stopped producing made-fors completely, except for Disney which planned 16 over the next year, because of the low profits. Instead, they focused on producing series, because a series hit could lead to hundreds of millions of dollars in syndication. For 1996-97, ABC commissioned 35 made-fors, CBS 60, NBC 38 and Fox 12. Fox mostly ran Fox theatricals. As the number of movie nights on TV dropped, the number of made-fors decreased.[44]

Block booking remained a selling tactic of the majors but became less prominent simply because TV bought smaller and smaller amounts of theatricals. In 1978, the U.S. Justice Department's antitrust division confirmed it had launched an investigation into television block booking practices and had begun contacts with some Los Angeles stations seeking documentation of allegations. Nothing came of that probe.[45]

With the change in buying patterns, the network did not buy the large blocks they once did. One insider recalled the *Gone with the Wind* (1939) package bought by NBC in 1977: "the network paid $5,000,000 for one run of *Gone with the Wind* and $500,000 each for eight films which the network thought were turkeys when they bought them... Additionally, MGM got a series commitment." That industry executive added that just three years later, in 1980, "you simply couldn't sell a package like that with so many weak films and so few hits. The networks wouldn't buy it. Today there's a more rigorous competitive situation among the networks and they won't buy that kind of thing." Block booking was important to the majors for many reasons. One being that it allowed the distributor to undervalue a specific title in the package and thus limit the money paid to any profit participants on a particular film. Avco Embassy sold a package of seven movies to CBS for a total of $7 million. One title was *The Graduate*, with Avco allocating $2 million to it. Unhappy profit participants sued, claiming the title was undervalued in that package. After a trial in Los Angeles District Court the jury decided that movie was worth $4 million in the block total. Profit participants believed distributors had an interest in earmarking more money to an unsuccessful film—allowing a studio to recoup its money—whereas too much of the money allocated to a box office hit with profit sharers went to the latter. Because the majors had more product to sell they had more leverage with the networks than did the independents. Sidney Finger, a partner in the accounting firm of Solomon, Finger and Newman, which specialized in film, said he doubted there were any releases from the majors which didn't get sold to television, while numerous independents couldn't license their movies to TV. It was because of that leverage and block booking.[46]

At the end of the 1980s MCA (Universal) began to play pay cable against the networks. Initially Universal had not committed any of its recent batch of theatricals to pay cable as it was saving them for a movie night on the proposed MCA/Paramount "fifth network." Later that network, UPN, would begin operations, but at the end of the 1980s, the plan went on hold for the foreseeable future. MCA was then checking out other alternatives before doing an output deal with either HBO or Showtime, or both. Wrote reporter John Dempsey, "Such output deals are par for the course when a major studio engineers a theatrical-movie deal with HBO or Showtime." Output was just another name for block booking. In exchange for allowing a network to pick only the titles it really wanted from the Universal inventory (called cherry-picking), MCA could demand a couple of guaranteed 13-episode series commitments. "That kind of horsetrading goes on all the time at the networks," said Dempsey. By threatening to bypass cable and go directly to the networks, Universal hoped to pressure the likes of HBO and Showtime, who were resisting high prices for movies, arguing the growth of home video and pay-per-view systems was eroding the value of titles by the time they got to pay cable, a year or so after their theatrical release.[47]

None of it affected the financial situation of television outlets. The typical U.S. television station earned 1981 pre-tax profits of $1,064,900 on total revenues of $5,066,300. Station profit margins were 21.02 percent in 1981 and 21.78 percent in 1980.[48]

Hollywood continued to move into television in many other ways than just selling films to its rival. The majors continued to be a prominent force in the production of series for television, although their dominance was challenged. For the 1979-80 season the majors produced 20 hours of primetime network programming, compared to 24 hours from independent producers. Of course, that excluded their movies on network primetime. While the number of movie nights had increased, the proportion of Hollywood theatricals in those slots, compared to made-fors, had declined.[49]

By the mid–1980s, Hollywood was busy trying to expand its hold over the exhibition outlets for its films and TV series by buying TV stations and cinemas. In 1985, Fox purchased six stations in major cities, the beginnings of what would become the fourth network, the Fox network. MCA (Universal) bought TV station WOR in New Jersey in 1986 for $387 million. WOR was a so-called superstation, transmitting from satellite and available throughout the U.S., to cable companies prepared to carry it. Both Columbia and MCA were buying movie theaters at this time. A growth in independent TV stations from 98 to 225 over an eight-year period ending in 1986 had created a huge demand for old television shows and movies. That growth was also one of the factors leading the Fox studio to believe the time was right to start a fourth network. With regard to the WOR purchase MCA President Sidney Sheinberg said, "From a strategic standpoint, we should have been interested in doing this 20 years ago." Besides being a lucrative business in themselves, TV outlets were also buyers of the studios' non-movie programming. Universal had grossed an estimated $200 million by selling rerun rights (syndication) to its detective series *Magnum P.I.* Fox's purchase of six stations gave them coverage of 22 percent of the U.S. population. Universal purchased a one-third interest in the 1,117-screen Cineplex Odeon chain while Columbia bought a 30 percent stake in the 11-theater Walter Reade chain in New York in 1982. Three years later it bought the rest. Neither Universal nor Columbia were subject to the 1948 Supreme Court decision with respect to theater ownership as they had been part of the so-called Little Three. Those three majors (UA was the other) owned no cinemas in the 1940s, when the breakup was ordered. Warner then owned 101 cable systems in 21 states with a total of 1.2 million subscribers. Disney had started a pay cable network in April 1983, the Disney Channel.[50]

Over the 1986-87 season there was a total of 54 hours of series primetime programming produced weekly for the three networks. Twenty-two and a half hours were from the majors, six of them were produced by the networks with the remaining 25.5 hours coming from independent producers.[51]

That re-entry of the networks into programming came about when the rules were eased. Prior to 1970, the networks produced many of their own programs, and sold the reruns. Because of this practice, the majors felt they were often denied spots on the schedules. Flexing their political muscles, the Hollywood studios helped persuade Justice to enact the financial interest and syndication rules in the 1970s, which basically barred the networks from producing their own shows. Lobbying against that was continued by the television industry for years. When the FCC tried to relax those rules in 1983, President Ronald Reagan—with encouragement from his former agent and friend, MCA chairman Lew Wasserman—sided with the studios, blocking any changes. However, change did come with the rules eased to allow each network to produce up to three hours of primetime each week in the 1986-87 season, rising to five hours in 1988-89. Warner then owned a piece of six TV stations, had a financial interest in cable networks MTV and Nickelodeon and was the nation's third largest cable system owner. Paramount owned a stake in the USA cable networks and some 470 cinemas.[52]

With the rules limiting networks to ownership of five hours of primetime programming due to expire near the end of 1990, MPAA President Jack Valenti lobbied vigorously to leave things as they were; to preserve the two-decades-old rules that largely kept the networks out of the $4 billion a year business of producing and syndicating primetime shows. Left untouched, he argued, should be rules that barred the networks from having a financial interest in most programs that they licensed for broadcast over the air and that prohibited network production arms from selling, distributing, or syndication their shows to non-network stations. Valenti maintained that those networks were still tyrants with the power to squeeze out Hollywood: "This battle is all about three giant companies and their total domination over television." Yet the three networks share of the primetime viewing audience had fallen from 91 percent in 1979 to 67 percent in 1989. Fox the producer had broken ranks with Hollywood, calling for revising the rules so that it could syndicate its programs from the fledgling Fox network. Less than a decade later, of the four networks (Fox by then having achieved that status), two were owned by Hollywood (Disney owned ABC). The two new beginning networks (WB, UPN), whose futures were uncertain, were owned by Hollywood. CBS and NBC both were seriously considering whether they could survive if they didn't form some sort of "partnership" with a Hollywood major.[53]

Besides the huge deal in the mid–1990s which saw Walt Disney buy Capital Cities/ABC another giant deal took place in which Time Warner (those two had merged in 1989) merged with Turner Broadcasting, by then a large company in its own right. A major stockholder in that new entity was cable system leader TCI (Tele-Communication Inc). Between them Warner and TCI serviced around 40 percent of all cable homes. As well, they owned major cable networks such as CNN and the Discovery Channel, three movie firms, and the WB television network, among other assets. All that power could make it more difficult for rivals to get their programs on TW and TCI systems, or costlier to buy programming from the two. TW's cable system in New York City, the world's largest, dropped The Box, a music channel featuring hard-edged rap and rock videos. When it was canceled two new channels appeared—the History Channel, partly owned by Disney, and CNNfn, owned by Turner. TW said the move was made because The Box flopped. However, Box President Les Garland disputed that contention blaming the demise of his channel on corporate favoritism: "This just speaks to the difficulty of little independents like us getting distribution." Viacom (which owned Paramount, Blockbuster Video and MTV among others) claimed its pay channel Showtime had also been victimized. It competed for movies with TW's HBO and TCI's Encore. In 1995, Showtime said it had a deal for movies from Turner's New Line Cinema, effective once the studio's contract with Encore ended. Just days before the TW/Turner merger was announced, New Line cooled to the Showtime deal. It informed the channel that Turner executives insisted it give Encore the pay–TV deal. Why? Turner wanted to solidify TCI support for the merger. New Line agreed it had had long talks with Showtime but denied it ever had a deal. Viacom had waged fierce antitrust legal battles with both TW and TCI. To get TCI support for its merger deal TW granted the former some side deals. Among them was a commitment to 20 years of discounted fees when Turner channels ran on TCI cable systems.[54]

Lobbying over items such as financial interest and syndication rules largely came to an end in 1996 when President Bill Clinton signed into law a bill deregulating the telecommunications industry. It was a move most felt would strengthen the giant firms which already dominated the industry. When schedules for the networks for the 1997-98 television season were finalized, the leading producer was Fox with 10½ hours of primetime each week, Paramount nine hours, Columbia nine hours. In fourth place was Warner with eight hours. NBC was sixth with seven hours, CBS produced six hours. The Fox network owned about 69 percent of its schedule while for ABC the figure was 50 percent.[55]

When beginning network hopeful UPN commissioned 36 original made-for science fiction movies for its proposed movie night starting in 1998 it placed orders for the films with four different producers, but most were with Paramount. Showtime was to get some of those titles first on pay–TV, then a quick shift to UPN to take advantage of Showtime's marketing and publicity. Paramount and Showtime were owned by Viacom. UPN was co-owned by Viacom and Chris-Craft.[56]

A flurry of deals toward the end of 1997 saw most of the remaining stand alone cable networks either merged or acquired. Just two of the top 50 cable networks were then in independent hands. One was the Nostalgia Network (owned by a company affiliated with the Moonies and in financial difficulties). The other was the Weather Channel (received in 60 million homes and prosperous). Most cable channels were owned by cable operators such as TCI, TW, Comcast Corporation, or by entertainment conglomerates such as the Walt Disney Company, Viacom, Inc., and News Corporation (the Fox parent). In the previous year TW acquired Turner, Fox bought the Family Channel's parent, CBS's parent, Westinghouse, bought Gaylord Entertainment's

Nashville Network and Country Music Television. The Classic Sports Network was purchased by Disney subsidiary ESPN. Most of those deals were driven by the growing cost of launching a channel onto cable systems and the difficulty of maintaining a healthy network as a stand alone given the competition from companies that owned clusters of networks. A limited channel capacity and too many contenders made getting onto cable systems the biggest challenge facing a new network. It was, wrote reporter Martin Peers, a struggle "requiring networks to bribe their way onto systems either by offering huge cash payments or equity stakes." News Corp chairman Rupert Murdoch had to do both to put his Fox News Channel onto cable systems. It was paying $10 per subscriber—to the cable operators—and gave cable giant TCI an option to buy 20 percent of the channel, as an inducement to become the first major operator to carry the channel, placed to rival CNN. Before it was sold, Classic Sports tried to broaden its distribution by approaching Cablevision Systems Corp but was told it would have to give up an equity stake to get carriage, it alleged in a complaint to the FCC. Lack of sibling channels to cross promote was a crucial weakness holding back a network's ability to raise awareness among consumers. Digital expansion would lead to an increase in the number of channels but most cable operators didn't expect more than 15 to 20 percent of their subscribers to pay for digital service. With then some 70 million cable households in America it meant a channel on a digital cable tier would have a maximum of perhaps 14 million households to draw from in an attempt to be viable during the startup. Investment in the Fox News Channel was estimated at $450 million over the first 18 months. News Corp had tried to buy the Weather Channel—but was refused.[57]

Later in 1997, Universal bought Viacom's half interest in the USA Network and the Sci-Fi channel.[58]

For a long time the majors had been interested in forming television networks of their own. Around the mid–1980s three of the majors, Warner, MGM/UA, and MCA were eager to put together an ad-hoc network for some of their recent theatrical releases. Each studio was pursuing the idea independently. According to Lev Pope, president of WPIX-TV, the Tribune-owned independent New York City station, those majors had been sounding out independent TV station groups. One reason for a renewed interest in the idea was the fact that the three networks were then buying theatricals in decreasing numbers, and very selectively, mainly because the films didn't perform in the ratings as well as they had in the 1960s and 1970s. Networks argued that was because of the growth of pay cable and cassettes which led to overexposure. Studios countered it was because blockbuster movies were usually run by the networks in sweeps periods where they ended up being scheduled against blockbuster programming on competing networks. Whatever the reason, theatricals were at an all-time low in ratings and audience share in network primetime. ABC research showed that all the theatricals which ran in primetime on all three networks from September 1983 until the end of the May 1984 sweeps period averaged only a 15.2 rating and 24 share whereas all of the TV movies (including miniseries) averaged a 17.9 rating and a 28 share. In searching for ad-hoc networks the majors were looking for a barter deal whereby each TV station would give up five minutes of each movie hour to the supplier, who would then sell that commercial time. Each TV outlet would keep about the same amount of time for itself. Those recent theatricals could be publicized as first runs on commercial television. Estimates were that a good theatrical could gross $800,000 that way—a far cry from the $3 million or so the networks used to pay them a few years earlier. However, the ad-hoc network tied up the film for only a limited two-week period, after which it could be sold to pay–TV, or put into a syndication package. If the ad-hoc network delivered a good rating the movie could become more valuable to a follow up syndication package because most stations were looking for a rating track record when they bought titles. Pay–TV didn't provide such a track record. Another way to create an ad-hoc network was for the majors to sell some of their theatricals to an advertiser such as ITT or Bristol-Myers or General Foods. Then the advertiser lined up the network by buying two-hour time blocks on TV outlets in the top 50 or top 75 markets. Mobil did it that way for its Mobil Showcase Network, using all the commercial time for its in-house products.[59]

As it tried to form its ad-hoc network MGM/UA (those two had by then merged) signed up eight stations in eight large cities by mid–1984, for an entity to be called Premiere Network. Each station was required to commit to double run 24 theatricals on a one-per-month basis for two years, beginning in October 1984. Said MGM executive Larry Gershman, "The three networks are just not buying pictures in groups anymore, so we've got to get that revenue from somewhere else." In this deal, MGM kept 10½ minutes in each two hours while the stations kept 11½ minutes to sell locally. After playing on Premiere those 24 titles would go to a one-year pay–TV window then, in the third stage, the titles went into syndication as part of a "standard" theatrical package—which would be joined by six other titles each of which had at least one network primetime play, to make a block of 30 titles. Those packs would be sold by MGM for cash only to stations for terms of around four years and six to eight runs per movie. Based on various assumptions, MGM thought it could gross $24 million in total from the ad-hoc network run, $12 million total from the pay–TV window and $1.2 million per title in the stage three syndication phase. As part of the deal, to be involved in the Premiere Network those local stations had to agree to schedule 75 on-air ad/promo spots for each of the 24 titles during the two-year barter run. The higher the rating the better the movie would play when it later became part of a 30-title syndication block, said journalist John Dempsey, "because good track records give them a familiarity with TV watchers that encourages repeat viewing."[60]

Another major which launched an ad-hoc theatrical film network for television syndication was MCA-TV, in 1984. With a September 1985 delivery date MCA had, by late 1984, presold a two-phase package of 33 titles in ten markets, including New York, Los Angeles, and Chicago, under the banner Universal Pictures Debut Network. Most of those titles had never been telecast on any of the three networks, although they had run on pay-TV. Like MGM, Universal's motivation was to try and make up for lost revenue from the networks, then preferring the cheaper made-fors. CBS that season used 40 to 45 made-fors to feed its Tuesday and Wednesday night slots while NBC used 40 for its Sunday and Monday lineups. In both cases the number of made-fors was about double that used the previous season. Commented reporter Jack Loftus, "So Hollywood has to unload these for the most part marginal theatricals somewhere... And the biggest target is the independent station with gobs of hours to fill." The first phase of the MCA system was a barter arrangement wherein each movie would be edited down to 95 minutes, including credits. Of the 22 minutes for commercials MCA got 10½ with the local outlets keeping 11½ minutes. The remaining three minutes were devoted to promotion spots for one thing or another.[61]

By early in the 1990s, both Paramount and Warner were each working separately to set up a full-fledged fifth television network. Paramount then owned some TV stations—three of those Paramount-owned outlets were Fox network affiliates. Why the rush to create a new network? An investment banker who advised entertainment companies explained: "You don't have to look any further than Fox to understand why Paramount and Warner are so eager to get in. The name of the game is having mass distribution for your product." Startup costs for such an undertaking were estimated at $2.5 billion. Conventional wisdom of the time held that there was only room for one more network because in more than 25 percent of the country all the viable stations were affiliated with the existing four networks.[62]

Back in 1987, Fox pulled more than 100 independent stations out of the movie-buying business to a considerable extent by turning them into affiliates feeding off the primetime series supplied by the fourth network successfully brought into being by Fox. Over the course of 1994, dozens of other independent stations had to reevaluate their film needs because they had signed on as affiliates with those new networks being created for launch in 1995 by Paramount and Warner. The syndication market was depressed. Columbia made a deal for 26 titles from its current output plus another 34 films from its library with TBS and eight ABC-owned stations. ABC owned and operated outlets joined together to buy their first major studio movie package in more than a dozen years, paying out $30 million for ten runs over five years. As well, ABC got an extra run of each title, exclusively, in the first year, with TBS sharing the titles equally in years two to five. If studios had taken movies like that into syndication in the past, independent TV stations groups like those owned by Tribune or Chris Craft/United would have leased them for scheduling in primetime where high advertising rates allowed the independents to pay higher prices to the studios than affiliated outlets, whose primetime slots were booked with network material. But by this time Tribune outlets were a part of the Warner group while Chris Craft was a partner in Paramount's new network and therefore unwilling to shell out big money for pictures that might not be usable in primetime. President of ABC-owned stations Larry Pollock commented, "We couldn't pay the price Columbia felt it needed to get for its movies. But when TBS came on board to share the cost, we agreed." Warner had struck a similar deal to share titles when it sold 28 of its recent releases to TBS and the pay cable network, Encore.[63]

Both of those new networks started modestly in 1995 with WB (Warner) running one night of programming initially (two hours) while UPN (Paramount) launched with two nights (two hours each night). Both hoped to add at least one more night within the coming two years. The real driving force spurring the upstarts was a changing regulatory environment that allowed the Big Three networks to produce and syndicate more of their own programming. Creating their own network was a way for Paramount and Warner to ensure that their product got a home. UPN reached 72 percent of the country with its primary affiliates and eight percent with secondary affiliates (stations that didn't necessarily run a program at the network scheduled time). Warner reached 55 percent of the U.S. (all were primary affiliates). However, one outlet was Chicago superstation WGN: when its satellite reach of 25 additional percent was factored in, the WB coverage rose to 80 percent. In the future as WB expanded its programming it planned to go to cable operators to create local channels for the service in markets where no stations were left with which to affiliate. Of course, Time Warner's extensive cable holdings were expected to play a large role in that situation. Primetime was then defined as 8–11 PM Monday through Saturday and 7–11 PM Sunday (22 hours in total). Fox programmed 8–10 PM Monday through Wednesday and Friday, 8–10:30 Thursday and 7–10 Sunday (13½ hours in total).[64]

More new channels devoted specifically to movies were in the works in the mid-1990s. Sitting on a library of more than 3,000 Columbia titles, parent Sony Pictures Entertainment had a movie channel on the drawing board. So did MCA, which controlled more than 4,000 films, including all the pre–48 titles from Paramount. Turner Broadcasting launched a new outlet, Turner Classic Movies (TCM), in 1994 as a platform for its huge library which included 1,151 MGM titles, 850 pre–48 Warner movies and 800 RKO features. Fox created new channel FXM: Movies from Fox as a 24-hour-a-day showcase for its 2,200 theatricals. John Malone's Liberty Media, which set up the Encore cable network in 1991, helped to manufacture six clones of the channel in 1994—each offering a specific film genre: western, action/adventure, mystery, love stories, drama, and true stories. Showtime gave birth to FLIX, also in 1994, an all-movie network. While a problem at the time was a lack of sufficient channel capacity, that was expected to be solved in the near future with a conversion to digital from analog. An executive with the cable operator Colony Communications, Jeff Wayne, noted that as channel capacity expanded cable companies would be seeking more movie channels because subscribers couldn't get enough movies. He said: "All of the research we've conducted shows that when we ask our customers to choose among, say, 20 different network-program concepts, movie networks always wind up at or near the top."[65]

Additionally, the majors exported those channels abroad. The Warner Channel (WBTV) was added in 1996 to Australian cable company Optus Vision, after being launched in Latin America and the Caribbean Basin in September 1995, then expanded to a Portugese version for Brazil, in 1996. It also launched in the U.K. on Rupert Murdoch's BSkyB network and in Germany in mid–1997. Also launched in Australia at this time was the Disney Channel. MGM Gold was starting up in Asia and awaiting a launch in Australia after MGM's product licensing rights in that country with other parties expired. One of the suppliers of films for Optus Vision was MGM, which had a financial interest in Australia's Seven Network, which in turn was a stockholder in Optus Vision.[66]

As the number of delivery mechanisms increased for movies—such as pay–TV and cassettes—the majors struggled to adjust their release patterns to keep everybody happy, and to maximize their revenues. That was made somewhat easier by the FCC. After years of considering the effects of contract exclusivity in the televised movie market, in 1977 the FCC dropped its inquiry and decided that the best regulation, at least in this case, was no regulation at all. Cable had long argued that those exclusive contracts were the most obdurate of the restrictions on pay–TV's growth. The National Cable Television Association threatened to take the agency to court over its do-nothing approach. That FCC decision came as a result of a court decision six months earlier suggesting the agency come to some definite conclusion on exclusivity within 180 days.[67]

Owner of Sacramento's UHF independent station KTXL-TV, Jack Matranga, was unhappy with the film package sales in syndication. He was convinced, in 1981, that all the major distributors were in varying degrees guilty of reneging on their promise to deliver the strongest titles in their packs after a specified number of network and pay–TV runs and by a definite date as spelled out in the contract. Latest to annoy Matranga was Universal, which informed him that *Smokey and the Bandit* (1977) and *Airport '77*, two of the key titles in the "Grand 50" block it sold to KTXL a number of years earlier, were bought by one of the networks for extra runs. Matranga explained those extra network sales would push back the availability of *Smokey* to his station from 1982 to 1985, with similar delays for *Airport*. Stations allowed distributors to give them extra runs of the titles after they became available, thus easing the pain of delayed delivery. Harry Pappas, owner of Fresno's KPMN-TV, bought Paramount's "Portfolio 8" pack, which included *The Longest Yard* (1974). That title was also delayed in syndication. When Paramount sold a block to ABC some years earlier one contract provision stated that two of the titles could be used as wild cards for extra telecasts. Obviously the network decided on the basis of Nielsen ratings—one wild card turned out to be *The Longest Yard*.[68]

When Paramount and Warner hit the syndication market in 1982 with new feature blocks and limited availability it was evidence that even at that early date the majors were looking more to pay–TV as their major source of ancillary revenue for theatricals. Paramount TV distribution executive Steve Goldman said, "Pay–TV controls the marketplace, so we've built in shorter license terms for our syndicated packages." Both majors were offering stations three-year deals, instead of six-year license terms typical of previous film package sales in syndication. WPIX-TV (New York) bought both bundles for identical six runs-over-three-years deals. Speculation was that WPIX paid about $90,000 per title for each movie in both blocks (20 titles in each) for a grand total of $3.6 million. In Los Angeles KCOP paid over $100,000 per title for the 20 movies in the Warner block. WPIX President Lev Pope remarked, "The usual pattern of our previous buys was to get 10 runs of every movie for a period of six years. But now we're getting a much shorter window in syndication because the studios want to get their pictures back to sell them to cable again." Although it was sold in 1982, Paramount's bundle included many delayed availability dates. The first title would not be available until September 1984, three would be delayed until 1988, two others until 1989 and *Star Trek the Motion Picture* (1979) would not be available until 1990. Warner's block of 20 included eight available in 1983, five for 1984, three for 1985 and four delivered in 1986.[69]

One unique release was tried in 1983 with producer Joseph Papp's $12 million movie *The Pirates of Penzance* (1982) based on his updated Broadway production. Universal simultaneously aired the movie on 17 pay-per-view systems and opened it at 91 cinemas around the U.S. It was the first ever such day-and-date film release. It was a total flop. Of a potential television audience of 1.2 million only about 130,000 (11 percent) opted to pay $10 to watch the film at home. The most successful pay-per-view event to that date was the 1982 heavyweight boxing match between Gerry Cooney and Larry Holmes, which achieved a 30 percent buy rate across the 30 million American cable homes. At the theater box offices *Pirates* grossed a meager $225,000 for its first weekend, as well as earning the enmity of exhibitors who resented Universal's undermining of their customary exclusivity on movie debuts.[70]

With the increase in delivery mechanisms it became easier for Hollywood to make money, even on bombs. When MGM/UA released *Still of the*

Night in December 1982 it flopped, grossing just $3 million at the box office. Considering that MGM had spent $17 million on production, advertising and prints, the outlook was not promising. Company executive Frank Rothman explained, "It this had happened 10 years ago, we would have had a very serious loss. Once you blew the theater market, there was nowhere else to go." However, because times had changed within six months Rothman had pulled in another $6 million by selling the film to pay–TV, home video, foreign distribution, one of the networks, and local syndication. What could have been a total disaster suddenly stood a chance of making money.[71]

Despite the continued exposure of titles, local stations still bid up the syndication prices. When Columbia sold a block of 26 features to KCOP in Los Angeles for $8 million, it exceeded the previous high which was in the $250,000 per title range. KCOP received the right to eight runs per title over four years. The outlet telecast one movie in primetime each day and battled for audience with three other VHF independent stations.[72]

In an attempt to lock up product HBO signed a 1987 agreement with Paramount for the pay–TV rights to the studio's films released after mid–1988. The deal, which included 85 movies, was expected to last at least five years. No price was disclosed but some insiders estimated it at no less than $500,000 per title. Generally, HBO, and other pay cable channels, bought films at prices based on their box office performance as well as the number of subscribers. Already HBO held exclusive rights to movies from Columbia and, through a complex agreement, effectively had exclusive rights to Warner titles. Showtime/TMC had an exclusive deal with Disney, but had lost its exclusive deal with Paramount, to HBO. As well, Paramount and HBO entered into an agreement through which they would jointly finance a number of original made-fors for pay–TV.[73]

That deal could actually have cost HBO as much as $700,000 per title. However, the deal included some kind of cap on box office success. A few years earlier, HBO paid something like $25 million for Columbia's *Ghostbusters* (1984) when that title went through the box office roof and the contract was uncapped. As a result, all pay–TV networks insisted on some kind of cap clause in prices tied to box office receipts to avoid such ruinous costs. TMC had wanted to continue its exclusive deal with Paramount but its failure to add to its customer base over the time of its exclusive Paramount deal killed those hopes. TMC explained that, in general, it still favored exclusive deals as a move towards station "differentiation." That deal between Paramount and HBO, covering 85 movies or five years, whichever came first, ended a feud between them. At the start of the 1980s, then-Paramount head Barry Diller became furious at what he considered HBO's arrogance in negotiations. His first response was to refuse to sell to the outlet for a year, and then to join in the ill-fated startup of a pay-per-view network.[74]

A study by *Variety* of theatrical release patterns for films produced by the majors, compared to independent productions, showed the domination exercised by the majors. Theatrical release was crucial for movies because it established their "legitimacy" and set the price the title would command in all the ancillary markets, including television. A theatrically released title commanded more money all the way through the distribution pipeline. More videos of those titles were rented and sold. Over the period 1983–87, the study found that about 37 percent of all independent production failed to achieve any form of domestic theatrical release while virtually all of the majors' titles were released domestically to cinemas. The bulk of each year's production was released within two years by majors' distributors, but the independents had a significantly slower release pace. The study included made-for-video features (but excluded made-for-TV titles) and it appeared that about 25 percent of unreleased features were direct-to-video films (deliberately, as opposed to by default). Taking those into account resulted in a steady pattern of about 25 percent of independent production failing to achieve any domestic exposure, theatrical or video.[75]

When, in 1988, *Variety* looked at the release patterns of features made in 1986 it found that 537 U.S.-made movies entered production that year. All 67 titles made in-house by the majors were released while 52 of the 53 films they acquired for distribution were also released—one was shelved. That left 470 independent productions with 196 of them, plus the 52 noted above, (248 in total) having received theatrical release. Thus, 53 percent of independent 1986 output had been released to cinemas by near the end of 1988. Of those 196 independent titles released by independent distributors, 133 were distributed by the same outfit that made them, leaving only 63 that successfully negotiated arms-length deals and made it to theaters. By contrast, of the remaining 222 titles, 106 still had no distribution deal, an additional 87 features already had been released direct-to-video, and 29 were shelved. Most of them were made for theatrical release but no deal was achieved, or the title was shelved, when a decision was made to forego the expense of a theater launch. Around 69 of those independent theatrical releases received only token or marginal bookings, sometimes for only one week within a single city and no exposure in New York. Deducting those marginal titles, only 180 of 470 independent production, less than 40 percent, received national theatrical release in the U.S. on a timely basis.[76]

Even when they got theatrical release, chances were they wouldn't make much money. At the 1987 box office, the 205 U.S.-made independent releases (that in total cost $630 million to produce) earned back about $165 million in domestic rentals, on 141 full-release bookings. Sixty-four of them (31 percent) received only a marginal release or test booking ahead of their ancillary use. For the 1986 release year, 161 U.S.-made independent releases (costing $516 million collectively) earned $152 million in domestic film rentals; in 1985 141 titles (costing $362 million) earned $162 million. Marginal releases totaled 37 of 141 in 1985 and 45 of 161 in 1986. Low budget independent movies (under $2 million in cost) numbered 82, cost a total of $82 million and took in $10 million, yet 40 percent of that $10 million was earned by just two titles. In the next grouping (titles costing $2–4 million to produce) 60 films costing $159 million brought in $21 million with 40 percent of that also accounted for by just two titles. For movies costing $4–6 million to produce 43 movies costing $194 million earned $100 million with almost 50 percent of that sum coming from two titles.[77]

When a film ended up with little or no hope of being theatrically released, the most it could be expected to recoup was, in 1990, about $1.5 million from ancillary markets; $500,000 from foreign home video/TV, $500,000 from domestic home video and $500,000 from U.S. pay–TV, network and/or syndication.[78]

In 1993, on three of its major box office hits, Paramount extended by 50 days the exclusive video window, moving it from the industry standard of 30 days to 80 days. Pay-per-view customers would thus have to wait a full 80 days to see the likes of *The Firm* (1993) and *Indecent Proposal* (1993). Remarked Rob Stengel, vice president at Continental Cablevision, third largest multisystem cable operator in the country, "Paramount has just punched me in the face." Cablevision Industries' head of programming Michael Egan said, "Paramount's strategy stinks. Our company won't carry the three movies because we feel they're no longer of any value to our subscribers." Paramount Home Video President Bob Klingensmith argued that his company had little choice but to risk the anger of cable operators: "The operators are not marketing pay-per-view. They're burying it in the highest numbers on the dial—the 40s, the 50s, even the 90s. Many cable systems are not using barker channels to promote the movies. And operators are not fighting piracy as hard as they should." Home video's gross annual take was then around $12 billion with the majors' share being about $5.5 billion of that—they got less than $100 million a year from pay-per-view. Blockbuster Entertainment executive Ron Castell commented, "Home video has become the biggest source of theatrical-movie revenue for the studios. By contrast, the pay-per-view business is a pittance." Castell acknowledged Blockbuster would buy more copies of the three Paramount titles as a quid pro quo for the 80-day window. Warner was involved in a more limited way, giving a 45-day video window on two titles, which had done poorly at the box office but had much video potential as star names were involved. Meanwhile cable operator giant TCI said that 115 of its cable systems "are poised to begin the most aggressive pay-per-view promotion in the company's history." That promotion began with the discounting of *Groundhog Day* (1993) to $1.99 for 1.4 million TCI subscribers throughout the film's entire pay-per-view run.[79]

Throughout the 1980s and into the 1990s a movie released direct-to-video (DTV) had a stigma attached to it. The phrase "direct to video" became a badge of shame for a title. Generally those films were low budget, horror, slasher, sex, etc. Director Jim Wynorski, who produced the *Sins of Desire* (1993) and *Victim of Desire* (1996) observed, "Breasts are the cheapest special effects in our business." DTVs were the drive-in movies of the 1990s. Some 300 of those low budget items were released DTV in 1995—many more than the number produced by the Hollywood majors—and they returned about $200 million in total to the producers. However, a single blockbuster title from a major, such as Disney's *Alladin* (1992) made more from home video than all those other 300 combined. For the majors releasing a title directly to video was still largely a demotion. New Line demoted *Theodore Rex* (1995), an awful comedy about future cop Whoopi Goldberg and her dinosaur partner, to a video release.[80]

Increasingly though, in the mid-1990s, the majors viewed DTV as an attractive alternative, a place to release franchise spin-offs, thereby saving much of the marketing costs. Universal's *Darkman: The Return of Durant* (1994; a sequel to 1990's *Darkman*) went straight to video in 1994. With a budget of $3.5 million the sequel was much cheaper, compared to *Darkman's* $20 million cost. Producers for the Universal sequel proudly called it the first "home feature." MCA Home Video President Louis Feola exclaimed, "On any given Friday or Saturday night, video is the fifth network." By then VCRs could be found in 81 percent of U.S. homes. Disney's *The Return of Jafar* (1993; a sequel to *Alladin*) went straight to video. While the studio expected *Jafar* to sell perhaps two million copies, in fact, it sold close to 11 million units (earning the producer $100 million) causing Disney to announce it would release three or four DTV features a year, including sequels to *The Lion King* (1994) and *Beauty and the Beast* (1991). Roger Corman, then running the DTV factory New Horizons, worried: "We're seeing a slippage over the past two years of about 25% in our total video rentals. Just as the majors once crowded the independent producers out of the theaters, now they're crowding us out of direct-to-video."[81]

As 1997 began, twelve Warner-owned films, including *Mars Attacks!* (1996), *Michael* (1996), and *Space Jam* (1996), bypassed the networks and instead premiered on the company's own in-house cable outlets, namely TBS and TNT, underscoring the conglomerate's ability to provide supply and demand. It remained the fourth window, after home video, pay-per-view and pay cable. Turner Broadcasting (by then a part of Warner) issued a challenge to the USA network to also buy out the broadcast window of theatrical features "to give a boost to cable ratings in general." In conclusion Turner remarked, "Like Rupert Murdoch's purchase of the rights to the NFL these movies will be a loss leader for our networks, which will use them as a promotional platform for other programs."[82]

Paramount and Universal each owned a 50 percent stake in the USA network. The first pay cable window typically kicked in about a year after a film was theatrically released, and normally extended for about six months. Then, after 18 months, there was a long period when a producer usually sold the title to a broadcast network—not a basic cable channel—for two runs during a license term that lasted three to four years on average. A second pay window opened up after the end of that broadcast window. Besides Warner, both Fox and Disney had studio/network affiliations.[83]

As deregulation of the communications industry loomed and became a reality in the mid–1990s a new buyer for Hollywood fare began to emerge—phone service providers. The seven Baby Bells were starting to look for movies to feed their own proposed program delivery systems in competition with cable operators across the country. Some estimated that deals could total in the billions of dollars. Bell Atlantic President Bob Townsend acknowledged he was negotiating with all of the Hollywood majors, and most of the cable networks, to fill the pipeline of a system his company was building in New Jersey. Most of those commercial developments were still in the planning stages and/or awaiting FCC approval. those seven Bells were Bell Atlantic, U.S. West, Nynes, Southwestern Bell, Pacific Telesis, Ameritech, and Bell South. Although Turner and other cable network owners were hungry to get their channels into packages put together by the Baby Bells, Townsend noted that, "movies will be the main beneficiary" in the new competitive landscape. Bell Atlantic got FCC approval in 1994 to start work on a cable system in Toms River, New Jersey. Besides a lineup of regular cable channels it planned to offer a video on demand service that would allow subscribers to call up a pay-per-view movie with the touch of a button on their remote controls. If their phone rang, subscribers could put the pay-per-view movie on pause while they picked up that call. That made the studios, once again, optimistic about a rosy future for the pay-per-view idea. Said Bob Klingensmith, president of Paramount's Home Video division, "This is a tremendously healthy development for the movie companies." Meanwhile, Bell South was planning its first video on demand test, in suburban Atlanta. According to the studios pay-per-view had languished because cable systems were not aggressive in the promotion and marketing of pay-per-view. Competition from video on demand by the phone companies, said Klingensmith, "would light a fire under" the cable operator and force him to "get behind" pay-per-view in a big way.[84]

One method used to try and extract more money from old movies originated in the 1980s. Colorization was a technique where a black and white film was changed into a color title, thanks to computer technology. The innovation was pushed by Ted Turner, beginning just after his March 1986 purchase of MGM Entertainment. Within a couple of months, he announced he would colorize a select batch of 24 pre–1950 theatricals in the MGM and Warner libraries he then owned. The idea was to market them over the following two years to television stations on a barter basis by Turner Broadcasting System and MGM-TV under the umbrella of Color Classic Network. TBS believed that national and local advertisers would be willing to pay a premium for familiar and long-used product that would be given a shiny, new showcase presentation.[85]

Soon after Turner's announcement, opponents surfaced who charged that colorization degraded important works of art, comparing it to putting lipstick on a Greek statue. A coalition of British directors had already protested what they called the "vulgarization" of classic films and several American directors were then considering a similar move. Advocates, however, saw the process as a potential gold mine which enabled them to recycle old films for maximum profits through new technology. Colorization was an expensive and time-consuming technique with the average cost ranging from $2,000 to $3,000 per minute of film, depending on the complexity of the footage. Thus, the price to colorize an average 90-minute movie would be $225,000, $300,000 for a 2-hour title. Two main firms were then doing the process: Toronto-based Colorization Inc. and Los Angeles-based Color Systems Technology. The latter firm was the one Turner was using to alter his titles. It was owned by Hal Roach studios, a company that also owned a library of old black and white features.[86]

Wilson Markle, president of Colorization, explained, "The reason we're doing it is monetary. People don't like black and white. They do like color, and when we color it, they buy it." Color Systems chairman Earl Glick commented, "People who buy the movies for distribution and sale—television stations, networks, cable television and so one—always classify the black-and-white movies as a lesser picture, and therefore don't pay as much as they would for a color picture. Every time we went to sell something to them, they'd say, 'Well, this is only worth so much, because it's black-and-white.' So we thought, well, if these pictures were in color, they'd command a much bigger price." Hal Roach executives cited an audience survey conducted for the company: "It showed that 85 percent of people would only watch something if it was in color." Glick observed, "In the age group under 20, nobody wants to watch anything in black and white." Roach had by then released seven colorized titles including *Topper* (1937), *It's a Wonderful Life* (1946) and Laurel and Hardy's *Way Out West* (1937). Color cassettes of *Life* were selling for $39.95 while black and white ones cost $9.95. In the first three months of its release, colorized versions of *Life* sold 25,000 copies. "We've sold more color cassettes of *Way Out West* in six months than the black and white has sold in 10 years—and at a higher price," added Glick. Frank Capra (who wrote, produced and directed *Life*) waged a bitter campaign against plans to colorize it until he was incapacitated by a stroke. In a 1984 letter he wrote to the Library of Congress Capra said: "I chose to shoot it in black-and-white film. The lighting, makeup for the actors and actresses, the camera and laboratory work, all were geared for black-and-white film, not color. I beseech you with all my heart and mind not to tamper with a classic in any form of the arts. Leave them alone. They are classics because they are superior. Do not help the quick-money makers who have delusions about taking possession of classics by smearing them with paint." Despite Capra's pleas the Library of Congress granted a copyright on the colored version of the film, which, as a black-and-white, was in the public domain. No one creatively involved on the feature had any recourse. Seven of the titles Roach had colorized were either owned by them or were in the public domain. Glick remarked, "Nobody has any rights except the owner of the film." American Film Institute founder George Stevens Jr. said: "If this process were to flourish, I think it would represent a vulgarization of some of the most important creative works of this country in this century. A generation from now, no young person would ever see the world in the way it was seen by John Ford, William Wyler, Alfred Hitchcock, Orson Welles or Charlie Chaplin." Director John Huston termed the colorization process "as great an impertinence as for someone to wash flesh tones on a da Vinci Drawing." Woody Allen called it "an ugly practice, totally venal, anti-artistic and against the integrity of every film maker. Without the director's consent it seems to me a criminal mutilation of his work." Turner Broadcasting System (then with plans to colorize 100 titles from its holdings) executive Gerry Hogan said, "The classic lives on. If you turn the color knob off, you'll see it in perfect black-and-white. The option is there for anyone who doesn't appreciate the color version to see it in black-and-white. But we are taking advantage of new technology to freshen these films. We're giving them a more contemporary look, which we think will appeal to a new generation of viewers." He insisted that black and white cassette copies would always be available.[87]

Film Quarterly magazine issued its own denunciation of colorizing when Michael Dempsey, writing with the endorsement of the editorial board, declared, "We are dealing with people who are unreachable by cultural, artistic, or social appeals because they don't care about anything except money. Therefore, let us hurt them in the way most painful to their shriveled sensibilities, by depriving them of every dollar that we can. If we do not, their bottomless avarice will deprive us and future generations of infinitely more."[88]

Charles Powell, a Color Systems executive, observed, "I have always viewed this as a marketing project. Colored films are not necessarily better, they're not necessarily worse, they're not necessarily anything, but worth more. As a marketing man you ask yourself, 'How can I take a library that has basically been grinding out the same bucks each year and make it hot, make it sexy?' You put a marketing coat of paint on it. That's how we view colorizing movies."[89]

Film industry personnel such as Woody Allen and Ginger Rogers appeared at a Congressional hearing in Washington in May 1987 to oppose the colorizing of black-and-white movies. In conjunction with that hearing Representative Richard Gephardt (D-Missouri) announced that he would introduce legislation to control colorization. However, off the record, it was conceded that such legislation has no chance of survival.⁹⁰

When that hearing of the House Subcommittee on Colorization dragged into June a bill was introduced by Gephardt that would give directors and screenwriters the right to prohibit the coloring of their films and deny copyright to altered pictures. Also under consideration was a proposal by Representative Robert Mrzaek (D-NY) for a national film commission that would designate classic movies; such films would then have to be retitled and labeled if they were colored. Director Arthur Hill argued that colorizing "desecrates" works of art. Turner Entertainment Company President Roger Mayer charged that critics were taking an "elitist" approach "telling people what is the proper and pure way" to see films. In the end no legislation prevented the practice, yet it did not catch on in any big way.⁹¹

Chapter 8

Movies from the Sky, or the Corner Store, 1976–1998

> "Repeats are part of our business. The television networks have commercials; we have repeats."
> Seth Abraham,
> HBO, 1989.

> Pay-per-view is "the biggest teat on the udder."
> Unnamed Hollywood
> executive, 1983.

A big change in delivery mechanisms came when satellites began to uplink signals from existing terrestrial stations (and new channels created specifically to be satellite delivered) and transmit them to cable systems, then directly to satellite dish owners. HBO was the first such satellite channel and was an example of a specially created outlet. In the first category were the so-called superstations. They were local TV outlets—ones without network affiliation—that, in effect, became national stations when their signals were picked up by satellite and distributed around the country. It was a concern to Hollywood majors who feared a loss of revenue from selling movies to a single station whose national coverage may have precluded the sale to other stations. The first superstation was an obscure Atlanta outlet WTCG (part of the Ted Turner empire, later rechristened WTBS) which became satellite delivered at the end of 1976. Within a few months it was received on 106 cable systems in 27 states. Thus, its potential audience expanded from the population of metro Atlanta to 787,000 additional subscribing households on those cable systems. Shortly thereafter more superstations were born, including Chicago's WGN and Los Angeles-based KTLA. All specialized in programming old movies and the live coverage of sporting events. Ultimately, each station would be able to charge higher rates for advertising because of increased audience size. FCC rules of the time permitted cable systems to carry up to three non-network-affiliated stations imported from distant cities. Over time those rules were relaxed to the point of permitting unlimited carriage. There were some 3,000 cable systems in the U.S. in 1977 with 12 million subscribers. At the time of the WTCG launch the MPAA unsuccessfully petitioned the FCC to adopt a new rule to restrict the growth of superstations. It argued it was making such a proposal to protect smaller independent stations in local communities to continue to make it possible for movies to be sold separately to each. WTCG gave itself away free to cable systems, charging them no fee. Those cable operators paid 10¢ per month per subscriber to the satellite system which provided carriage facilities.[1]

The birth of HBO took place in 1972 when 365 subscribers to Service Electric Cable TV in Wilkes-Barre, Pennsylvania agreed to pay $6 a month above the basic cable rate to receive films and sports not available on regular channels. On November 8, 1972 those 365 households got a live NHL hockey game from Madison Square Garden between the New York Rangers and the Vancouver Canucks, followed by the year-old film *Sometimes a Great Notion* (1971; starring Paul Newman and Henry Fonda). Cable operator Service Electric paid HBO $3.50 a month for each of the subscribers. Movies were not the mainstay of the early schedules as it had more events from Madison Square Garden on the air than it had features, although those movies were given more repeats and filled more broadcast hours. During its first two years of existence, its parent company, Time Inc., looked upon HBO as an experiment whose task was to validate a theory that consumers would pay for TV programming not available on regular television. During 1973 HBO reached a high of 14,000 subscribers, from 14 cable systems, then dropped to 8,000 by year's end. In response, company executives strengthened programming and marketing with the result that by the end of 1974, the channel had 57,000 subscribers—the goal had been 20,000. HBO reported its first profit at the end of 1977. Looking to expand, HBO first thought about a series of regional networks, but then in 1975 it contracted with RCA Americon to lease a transponder on its satellite, at a cost of over $6 million. It launched on September 30, 1975, with the boxing match from Manila between Muhammad Ali and Joe Frazier. Fifteen months later WTCG flew. Two and a half years after HBO, Showtime went into orbit becoming the second pay cable channel on satellite.[2]

Just one year after launch HBO was available in 200 communities in 32 states. It aired movies which had been theatrically released within the past year: those titles ran unedited and uninterrupted by commercials. In New York

City HBO charged $9 (basic cable was $10 a month) while movie admission prices there were $3.50 to $5 per ticket. One title broadcast on HBO that year was American International's *Wild Party* (1974; about the life of silent screen star Roscoe "Fatty" Arbuckle). Commented reporter Walter Spencer: "As for *Wild Party* it is common knowledge in the movie industry that American International Pictures was dissatisfied with the film and the audience reaction at numerous previews; the picture was extensively re-edited over the objections of its director James Ivory, and, finally, the company evidently decided to cut its losses by accepting any additional money it could make by selling the film to pay–TV." HBO head Jerry Levine said his channel was serving people who didn't go to the movies and was re-introducing them to movies and "providing an avenue of distribution for a lot of films that couldn't make it in the commercial market place. We're taking films to Laredo, Texas, or Jackson, Mississippi, that would never play in a theater there."[3]

The concept of a second pay window for features was in place by 1979 when HBO announced it would telecast about 36 movies a year which would run after network airing, but before the film went into syndication. The licensing agreement timing was short, usually one month, with the price paid for the title by HBO usually being a flat rate varying from $40,000 to $100,000. With the exception of Columbia all the majors were by then licensing product for that second pay window, although not without reservations. One worry was that allowing a second pay–TV window would depress the price of the title when it ultimately went into syndication. As well, some studio executives worried that HBO might be stockpiling product, thus reducing its need for newer films, or at least increasing their bargaining position. Hollywood's majors also preferred to sell their titles on a per subscriber basis, as compared to a flat rate. Said HBO executive Gregory Cascanti: "We view off-network films as filler product. On a flat fee basis, it's cost efficient. If it gets too expensive, the studios are pricing themselves out of the market." Acquiring those off-network (second pay window) titles could make pay–TV more able to reduce buying of low and middle-range theatrical product, the turkeys and bombs, in other words. With the three networks then all reducing their theatrical buys, Hollywood was upset.[4]

By mid–1982, the pay–TV industry was dominated by three channels, HBO with nine million subscribers, Showtime with three million and The Movie Channel (TMC) with two million subscribers. HBO was seen as a hard bargainer by film companies because in most deals it refused to pay for films on a per subscriber basis, as did the other two, although HBO's flat rate payment was far higher than that of its competitors. Distributors remained annoyed. Although HBO paid more gross dollars for product they felt it paid less per subscriber.[5]

By the beginning of 1983, HBO had 52 percent of the pay cable market (12 million subscribers), Cinemax 9 percent (also owned by Time, Inc.),

Showtime 18 percent, TMC 11 percent, all others 10 percent. Several companies, including Paramount and Warner had combined to form a joint venture to operate a merged Showtime/TMC—to compete more strenuously against HBO. Stock market analyst Allan Raphael said, "There's a war going on. The motion picture companies a decade ago let HBO get a monopolistic position, and they've rued it ever since." Another analyst remarked, "They're all ganging up on HBO." The majors hoped the new competition would force HBO to pay more for their movies. MCA Vice President Thomas Wertheimer said, "We've been less than satisfied with the prices paid by HBO." Studios were trying to insure that Hollywood, not HBO and its friends, controlled the movie business. During 1982, HBO paid an estimated $250 million in movie rental fees. It also produced original material and financed the production costs of independent producers, in return for exclusive cable rights. A year later, HBO announced a joint venture with Columbia and CBS to make movies under the Nova banner. It was a venture that failed.[6]

In a June 1985 announcement, HBO declared it would increase the number of titles it used during a month by 25 percent, beginning in July and continuing into the fall, under the heading *HBO All-Star Summer*—the theme of a marketing push for new subscribers and retention of old ones. Channel executive Seth Abraham noted dryly, "we get very few letters complaining that films aren't repeated often enough." In fact, he added, grumblings about repeats "is our number one" subject in the complaint file. Some of those extra titles were older. The revised schedule included an 8 AM *Breakfast Special* movie, a *Lunchtime Matinee* at noon, and so on. Abraham hoped the umbrella title would stick in viewers' minds, particularly because many of the individual titles were old and familiar to them.[7]

At first, HBO set up a second, companion service, which died a quick death, in 1979. It was a mini-service which broadcast only a few hours a day and was sold at a much lower price than other pay services. Then HBO created a second companion service, Cinemax, a full-service, full-price adjunct to the senior channel. Cinemax went on satellite in the summer of 1980. Originally it was offered in a package with HBO and positioned as different than, but "compatible" with HBO. As more services became available and people decided that three or four services were more than they needed, Cinemax began to lose ground. Time Inc. turned it around by spending 50 percent more on programming.[8]

Complaints about repeats continued to hound HBO. Late in 1989 Seth Abraham admitted that excessive re-airing "is our number one consumer and programming complaint." With HBO and Cinemax both on the air 24 hours a day, 365 days a year, between them there were 17,520 hours to fill. Abraham added: "Repeats are a part of our business. The television networks have commercials; we have repeats." However, he said the number of times a title was shown had dropped from eight runs (four or five in primetime) in 1984 to five times a year in 1989 (two or three in primetime). "But our subscribers will never think it's enough until everything only plays once," moaned the executive. Despite the number of repeats, there were still a lot of mediocre titles in the lineup. Reporter Stanley Young wrote: "You may find the occasional foreign film on HBO—it aired *Das Boot* (1981) last year—but the buck stops at art-house features such as *Babette's Feast* (1987). They simply won't play in Boise."[9]

Although the coming of more and more cable channels, pay-per-view and satellite delivery systems proved to be a boon to the majors, Hollywood, paradoxically, often argued against the changes. In Washington in 1976 before the House Communications Subcommittee to discuss specific cable TV problems (such as the importation of distant signals and movies and sports events on cable and pay-per-view), MPAA President Jack Valenti told Congress that an unbridled cable industry would spoil the program syndication business. "Without leapfrogging rules, without distant signal carriage and exclusivity regulations, and with the aid of low cost satellite distribution, local markets can be swamped by importations of programs from these large metropolitan areas. Local television broadcasting as well as local advertising would no longer be able to survive," he explained. However, Valenti also wanted the FCC to repeal the pay cable rules which regulated the movies which those channels could telecast, noting "even if someday pay cable amasses the power to pay more than networks for feature films, that would not lead to siphoning." His position was bitterly contested by exhibitors and broadcasters. By this time Valenti had dropped the euphemism "family choice cable" which he had been using in place of pay–TV. He felt there was room for an additional market between theatrical and network exhibition without the FCC's pay cable regulations. Cable executives who testified argued in favor of their industry being allowed unlimited importation of distant signals.[10]

On March 25, 1977, the U.S. Court of Appeals threw out the FCC's two-year-old antisiphoning rules for movies and sports on pay cable insisting the agency had no jurisdiction to impose restrictions on cable TV programming. And, in any case, it said those rules violated the First Amendment rights of the cable industry. It was a unanimous decision. Unless a stay were granted, pending an appeal, the decision meant the unfettered use of films and sports on pay–TV would be permitted as soon as a ruling was mandated. Among the regulations struck down were those that prohibited the use of features three to ten years old on pay cable. Wrote the court: "The purpose of the commission's pay cable rules is to prevent 'siphoning' of feature films and sports material from conventional broadcast television to pay cable. Although there is dispute over the effectiveness of the rules, it is clear that their thrust is to prevent any competition by pay cable entrepreneurs for film or sports material that either has been shown on conventional TV or is likely to be shown there. How such an effect furthers any legitimate goal of the Communications Act is not clear." The court took particular issue, along with the cable industry, with the FCC's concern that siphoning was real and not imagined. Arguing that nothing in the FCC's voluminous record supported that contention the court added: "The commission's lack of a clear picture is directly attributable to its own choice to regulate rather than allow a period of unregulated experimentation in which data could be generated that could form a predicate for informed agency action."[11]

After studying the court's decision the FCC decided not to appeal the movie portion of the decision. Previously, movies could be shown on pay cable if they had been released theatrically within the previous three years. Features older than ten years could also be shown on pay cable under certain conditions, but clearances were complex. Now all were ripe for pay cable. Availability terms for specific movies were unclear as they were often tied up in complicated, long-term contracts that varied from market to market. Since HBO, and increasingly other pay cable channels, were programming nationally, the confusing pattern of contract exclusivity protection was becoming a severe handicap.[12]

Finally, in July 1980, the FCC terminated its syndication exclusivity rule as well as the regulation limiting the number of distant television station signals a cable system could import. Formerly cable systems were restricted to bringing in two or three out-of-area stations. Essentially, the FCC had deregulated the cable TV industry.[13]

Back in August 1977 the MPAA asked the FCC to institute a rule-making to determine whether curbs should be placed on the transmission of broadcast signals to cable systems via satellites. Catalyst for that petition was the launch of Ted Turner's WTCG-TV. By June 1977, noted the MPAA's submission, 465 cable systems in 27 states were authorized to carry WTCG to over 800,000 subscribers while an additional 207 cable operators, representing over 370,000 more subscribers, had applied to carry the Atlanta superstation. Then pending before the FCC were applications from other outlets, such as Chicago's WGN, to become superstations, as well as an application from Southern Satellite Systems to expand WTCG to Canada, Puerto Rico and Alaska. All of these moves were opposed by the Hollywood majors' lobby group, which claimed WTCG "seeks to become the hub of a national cable network." The MPAA argued the development of such superstations was contrary to the FCC's basic policy of localism. The main thrust of its argument was that superstations would outbid local outlets for programming and national advertisers thereby threatening the survival of local outlets. It was, of course, a self-serving argument since the heart of the matter was that Hollywood worried about the potential loss of syndication money for itself. Said the MPAA petition: "The producers of high-cost TV programming must rely upon multiple outlets to recoup their production costs. If superstations are allowed to develop at the cost of local television outlets, the economic base necessary to support program production will shrink and ultimately fewer programs will be produced." When the FCC asked the MPAA if it had tried to calculate the money it would receive through satellite distribution versus the potential without it, one staff member of the latter group said it was working on it.[14]

Before the 1970s ended, cable systems had begun offering pay cable tiers that saw smaller, more obscure pay channels bundled into a small package containing one of the major pay networks—there were then just two of them, Time's HBO and Viacom's Showtime. It was then unusual for HBO and Showtime to be offered in the same cable package. As late as 1979, communities such as Houston and Oklahoma City were still neophyte cable areas. By the end of that year, HBO had around four million subscribers, Showtime had slightly more than one million. Each had started to make money after passing the 750,000 mark.[15]

When Arbitron Television Marketing studied pay cable in 1980, it concluded that movies were the big reason for subscribing to pay cable and that the programming had to include movies that had not appeared on commercial TV. Among the findings were that pay subscribers liked the uninterrupted nature of pay cable features but few would object to ads at the beginning or end. Surveyed were 9,100 households (2,759 non-cable homes, 3,769 basic cable homes without pay–TV, and 2,572 households with basic and pay cable). For those who subscribed to basic but not pay cable, cost was cited as the chief bar to the system. Some 70 percent of all respondents preferred paying a monthly fee rather than paying on a pay-per-view basis. Keys to pay's successful future were determined to be programming and packaging, declared the survey: "with particular emphasis on movies and convincing subscribers that the monthly charge delivered its money's worth."[16]

When those major pay channels, all dependent on features for much of their programming, expanded broadcast hours at the start of the 1980s, nobody benefited more than the Hollywood majors. Moving to 24-hour-a-day telecasting in the 1981-82 period were Warner Amex's The Movie Channel, Showtime, Cinemax and HBO. Chief programmer for HBO, Michael Fuchs, indicated the "movie dependency" of the 24 hour pay cable services was going to bend the very structure of syndication out of shape. He said that feature films, even the oldies, were the "treasure houses" for the 24-hour services. HBO President Jim Heyworth declared: "We recognize that expansion to 24 hours will result in a commitment to additional programs. We're not going to loop the service." He meant no repeats three times a day of the same films. Fuchs told of HBO experimenting with and achieving "enormously good results" from some of the older feature films: "There is an enormous treasure of movies out there. I think the pay services are going to be just that much more involved in licensing them."[17]

Gustave Hauser, chairman of Warner Amex Cable Communications (which owned TMC), proposed, in 1981, day and date theatrical/pay cable movie release. It was an idea which angered and distressed exhibitors to a large degree; it quickly died. Perhaps fueling that suggestion was the fact that TMC was a distant third in the pay cable race, behind HBO and Showtime. Hauser noted that, while for a time it was easy to sell second and third pay services to cable subscribers, many were then beginning to drop what they saw as redundant services. Redundant, he thought, because they all showed the same things. Actually, among the three, only TMC did that. Both HBO and Showtime were into production of other kinds of entertainment, at least a little, precisely to try and "differentiate" themselves.[18]

By the early part of 1983, about 29 million U.S. households had cable, 35 percent of all homes with television. Over half of those equipped with cable had at least one movie channel for which they usually paid an extra $10 a month. HBO had 11 million subscribers, Showtime four million and TMC 2.3 million. The cable industry had started to produce its own original movies by then with one motive being a sense of panic among many cable operators over the high rate of subscriber cancellations, called the "churn" rate in the industry. About one in four pay cable customers quit each year, often citing repetition of programs or the presence of too many bad movies as the reason. However, cable channels broadcast 24 hours a day and Hollywood had to sell its turkeys. So, as business reporter William MacDougall noted, "A common practice is to persuade a cable company to buy three stinkers along with one winner" in a package deal.[19]

A 1982 study done by A.C. Nielsen Co. found pay cable penetration dropped by almost 50 percent in VCR-owning households that frequently rented cassettes. Pay–TV penetration averaged 42 percent in homes with VCRs that did not rent cassettes regularly but it hit only 23.4 percent in households that were regular cassette renters.[20]

As pay channels became more important, their movie deals and relationships with Hollywood became more complex, and closer. Late in 1983 Paramount and Showtime/TMC (by then merged) announced a five-year deal with the studio agreeing to provide the pay service with features and any special events programming it might become involved in, on an exclusive basis for five years. It shut out HBO. Paramount was to provide at least 15 titles per year with the alliance expected to enrich distributor Paramount to the tune of $400–$700 million over the life of the deal. It was the studio's response after being rebuffed twice that year by the government in its attempts to get an equity position in pay–TV. The contract did not involve any pre-financing of movies by Showtime/TMC, unlike a similar exclusive deal just entered into by HBO and Columbia. Executives of Paramount were confident they would have no trouble with the Justice Department, which a few months earlier gave HBO the green light for its partnership with Columbia and CBS in producing company TriStar.[21]

According to figures from Paul Kagan Associates, HBO went from 16.95 million subscribers in 1988 to 17.25 million at the end of 1991, Showtime went from

8. Movies from the Sky, or the Corner Store, 1976–1998

6.695 million to 7.3 million, Cinemax from 5.975 million to 6.285 million, and TMC had 2.625 million in 1991, down slightly from 2.69 million in 1988.[22]

Multiplexing of pay channels began around 1992/1993 with some systems producing seven separate channels from the big three; three HBO's, two Showtimes and two Cinemaxes. Initially the extra four channels were just a rejigging of the monthly schedules of each network; no extra programming was involved, just a greater variety of start times. By 1994, some 200 cable systems were testing some form of pay cable multiplexing. One of the key findings was that the number of HBO subscribers in multiplexed systems grew by 7.8 percent in 1992, compared with only 1.1 percent among HBO subscribers in nonplexed systems. It was a trend that continued in 1993.[23]

New satellite channels launched, but not without problems. When Turner officially launched TCM (Turner Classic Movies) in 1994 only about 200,000 cable subscribers in the U.S. had access to the channel right away, plus another estimated 800,000 homes with their own satellite dishes. The problem was the limited availability of channels on most systems. At the time about 63 million households subscribed to cable, up from 17.6 million in 1980 and 10.7 in 1976. Since Turner already owned a huge library of Warner, MGM, and RKO features, the program costs were covered. Turner figured it would need only two to three million subscribers to break even, thanks to having program costs paid for, whereas most cable networks needed 25 million subscribers. As there was no advertising on the channel Turner's only revenue came from monthly fees paid by the cable systems. If a system managed to sell TCM to only 29 percent of its subscriber base or less, it paid Turner 35¢ per month, per subscriber. If it sold between 30 and 69 percent of its base, the fee dropped to 25¢. At a 70 percent or higher rate the lowest cost kicked in, 15¢.[24]

Around mid–1995, HBO had 19.2 million subscribers while second place Showtime counted 8.1 million. New entrants four-year-old Encore (which specialized in old movies) and Starz (new titles) had less than two million combined, counting subscribers to both cable systems and direct broadcast satellite (DBS) distributors. Encore and Starz were owned by John Malone's Tele-Communications Inc. (TCI), a huge cable system operator. All but a tiny handful of cable subscribers to Starz were on systems owned by TCI. Showtime had just signed an exclusive deal with Paramount covering 196 titles produced by the studio for the seven-year period beginning January 1, 1998. Showtime would end up paying Paramount about $1.2 billion over the life of the contract, an average of $5 million or so per title, although the price was closely tied to the film's box office performance. That deal came as no surprise as by then Showtime and Paramount were wholly owned divisions of Viacom Inc., which also owned Blockbuster Video. Showtime also announced it planned to commission as many as 52 original movies a year, as early as 1995, although cable executive Jerry McKenna said, "But it's the hit theatricals that drive the pay TV business." Even Showtime admitted as much. Viacom cable executive Kerry Brochage remarked, "No subscriber pays $8 to $12 a month for original programming." However, Showtime was positioning itself, explained executives, in case pay-per-view took off, decreasing the audience for movies on pay cable. At that point, Showtime's original features and series could end up as its main attraction with theatricals added as extras.[25]

Phone companies busily positioned themselves to take advantage of telecommunications deregulation and its potentials. In 1996 AT&T announced it would invest $137 million for 2.5 percent of leading DBS operator DirectTV with options to go as high as 30 percent (for $1.6 billion). Days later, AT&T's nearest long distance rival MCI Communications bid $682.5 million to win the rights to the final license for satellite service to all 50 states. Along with its partner, Rupert Murdoch's News Corp. (Fox), MCI planned to invest an additional $1 billion to launch satellites to start the service. In the 18 months since DirectTV and rival USSB launched, those DBS services had picked up about 1.3 million customers. DBS offered the same types of services found on cable but had a somewhat wider range of sports and pay-per-view films. The biggest cost was the $700 households had to spend for the receiving dish. Another difference was that dish owners lost local stations since they were terrestrially based and not on satellites. Cable companies all carried their local stations, a legacy of FCC "must-carry" regulations. Theoretically dish owners could still receive local stations through the use of a home aerial as in the old days, or simply by disengaging the dish reception.[26]

As of September 1996 pay cable subscribers totaled 36.4 million households with HBO having 25.6 million, Cinemax 12.9 million, Showtime 13.4 million, and TMC at 6.9 million.[27]

At the end of 1996, Encore Media Corp., owned by TCI, announced ambitious plans to soon have eleven separately programmed movie channels. What it had then were Encore and Starz, with the former having laid out an estimated $3.5 billion in exclusive film output deals with virtually every major Hollywood studio. When it started in 1991, Encore was the only pay channel programming a diet of movies from the 60s, 70s, and 80s. At this time, it was spending $40 million on a massive consumer-branding campaign geared toward making cable customers remember the networks' names. Encore then had 10,000 titles under contract with a window of some sort. However, it had only 10 million subscribers, many on TCI systems. Turner, with 8,000 titles in his holdings, had three networks which ran a great deal of nothing but old movies. TNT ran 200 different titles each month, TBS aired 250, and TCM broadcast over 400 every month.[28]

John Malone's Starz network announced it would spend a record $40 million in 1998 to promote the channel's exclusive windows for such titles as *Liar Liar* and *The English Patient* under the banner *Movies Too Big to Miss*. And for the first time, Malone would create a $20 million campaign for

Encore. Martin Sheen had signed to do the Encore voice-overs. Leonard Maltin was to be critic-at-large for Encore, providing on-air analysis and commentary.[29]

Meanwhile, Showtime scheduled a March 1998 launch of another 24-hour-a-day pay–TV channel to be called Showtime Extreme, to exclusively program action-adventure titles such as the James Bond series. It was another in the growing list of services getting an early jump in anticipation of cable's switch-over to digital delivery from analog, a move that would eventually expand channel capacity as much as six-fold. The new channel would bring the number of Showtime services to eight; Showtime, Showtime 2, Showtime 3, Showtime Extreme, The Movie Channel, The Movie Channel 2, FLIX, and Sundance. All eight carried separate East Coast and West Coast feeds, while Showtime and TMC had recently added Mountain Time feeds as well. That caused company executive Jeff Wade to comment, "That means our multiplex has 18 separate screens." Primarily those services were then available to those who subscribed to such DBS services at DirectTV, Primestar, and Echostar. Not priced or available to viewers alone, Showtime Extreme was offered as part of a prepackaged tier. Said Wade: "We did a lot of research where we asked people which film genre they enjoyed most. And action-adventure always came out No. 1. [Extreme] is the only first-window premium channel dedicated to action programming in the marketplace."[30]

An informal 1997 survey of cable operators revealed that systems in the U.S. paid out between 65 and 75 percent of their total programming costs in monthly per-subscriber license fees to just three firms: Time Warner (then including Turner), Disney/ABC, and Viacom.[31]

Through the 1990s, the number of specialty channels increased. Supposedly more narrowly focused, they all seemed to include a film component. Cable network Comedy Central (CC) increased its movie lineup from 95 plays in the first quarter of 1995 to 250 plays in the first quarter of 1996. When CC created a Thursday night movie slot late in 1996, its ratings shot up 26 percent, compared to the mix of series programming previously in that slot. Michelle Ganeless, vice president of programming at CC said, "Movies provide great lead-ins to original programming. ...And movies give us a two-hour promotional bed on which we can lay out promos for all of our series." When music video network VH-1 launched *Rock 'n' Roll Picture Show* in June 1996, its ratings went up 45 percent over the comparable period one year earlier. Sports network Speedvision created a weekly Saturday night movie showcase featuring race-car movies such as *Grand Prix* and *Winning*.[32]

In the early years of pay cable some channels paid almost nothing for some movies, a lot for others. In 1979, Showtime estimated its payments ranged from 2¢ per subscriber to 40¢. HBO declared it bought some titles for a "very low" flat rate, while all-time expensive to that point was *Jaws* (1975), which cost more than 50¢ per subscriber.[33]

Five years later, HBO was trying to revise its costly deal with Columbia due to slower than expected subscriber growth. The squabble allowed the terms of the contract to become public. Columbia verified that HBO paid 40 percent of a movie's theatrical rentals for exclusive pay licensing, 20 percent for non-exclusive (against a fixed guarantee), and made equity investments of 30 percent of the negative cost for all the studio's films. Both firms were partners in TriStar. One analyst described it as an "onerous contract for HBO." The deal was originally signed in 1981 when HBO paid Columbia $50 million. There was a worry then that Columbia was after an equity stake in HBO rival Showtime, so, said Columbia executive Francis Vincent Jr., "HBO made us a very special offer to keep us in their camp." Another part of the deal required HBO to take at least half of the Columbia titles on an exclusive basis. For 1983, HBO spent $301.5 million in film licensing fees for its two services—which had a combined subscriber count of 16.2 million.[34]

With a scarcity of product, coupled with airing 24 hours a day, pay cable quickly became a significant outlet for unreleased theatrical movies—those bombs and turkeys again. HBO executive Steve Scheffer explained: "75% of HBO's programming is movies, with successful theatricals driving our service. As an ancillary to the big titles, we look for less widely known pictures which are still good, solid movies." He observed those films needed more promotion in advertising, *TV Guide* listings, and between other HBO shows. They were often designated as *Sleepers of the Month* in their promotion. Scheffer added, in speaking about HBO made-fors, "We will have world premieres tailored for HBO which will require both in-house promotion and also advertising in other media. We expect to conquer the lack of recognition problem by basing some of these films on pre-sold works from other fields, casting name talent and using intriguing subject matter." Those made-fors were sometimes turned to instead of scraping the very bottom of the theatrical barrel, both released and unreleased titles.[35]

Although everyone complained about pay-TV back in the 1970s when it began—exhibitors, the National Association of Broadcasters, the Hollywood majors—all wanted to buy into it. As early as 1975-76, a grouping of Paramount, United Artists and Fox had had preliminary talks with some cable companies about supplying their own and other films directly to cable, eliminating the middleman, such as channels like HBO. The majors were then complaining loudly to the government about the cable industry practice of importing distant signals wholesale and piping them to their subscribers without paying. Jack Valenti was screaming for copyright protection. At the same time, Justice itself had joined in a suit with 7 major cable companies, including HBO, against the FCC arguing its cable rules were too harsh and restrictive on cable firms.[36]

A 1980 agreement had four majors, Columbia, MCA, Paramount, and Fox, form a partnership with the Getty Oil Company (which itself owned a cable service dedicated to sports). Their joint venture pay cable network, called Premiere, planned to begin offering first-run features January 2, 1981, to subscribers for a monthly fee estimated at $8. Justice stepped in to charge that the five firms were violating antitrust laws by agreeing to establish a pay–TV network that would limit the availability of features to other pay channels. The suit by Justice asked that the agreement by the companies be declared illegal and that while the suit was pending the four majors be temporarily restrained from licensing any movies to Premiere. Through this arrangement in Premiere the majors hoped to command a large piece of the pay–TV market. Executives at some film studios had felt that HBO in particular had been able to use its power in the marketplace to command films from the studios at "very modest prices." HBO itself had been charged by competitors with monopolistic practices and Justice had then been looking into the company for more than a year but had not taken any action. In its suit against Premiere, Justice argued the majors involved had agreed not to license their films to other pay–TV services for at least nine months after they were made available to Premiere. Both HBO and Showtime complained about Premiere. They, and the other pay networks such as TMC, relied heavily on features, especially blockbusters, to attract subscribers. According to the Justice brief, movies accounted for 77 percent of HBO programming in 1979, 85 percent of Showtime's, and 100 percent of TMC's. Premiere's four Hollywood partners had all petitioned Justice to take action against HBO and were displeased that so far it had not. HBO then had four million subscribers, Showtime one million and TMC 400,000.[37]

Premiere planned to show 12 to 15 new titles a month. It was estimated that 50 percent of the product would be from the four partners. The new venture was to receive $3.75 per month per subscriber from the cable operators' $8 charge, plus 50 percent of any charge over $8. All product was to be theatrical motion pictures which had had their cinema release. As well, Premiere would receive those titles exclusively with a nine-month window. Three movies would be offered each night Monday through Thursday and four per night the other three days, all in primetime. Each film would be shown an average of eight times per year.[38]

The antitrust suit filed by Justice charged Premiere was a conspiracy to fix prices for features at artificial and noncompetitive levels. Premiere claimed its service would add competition to a market which was 85 percent controlled by HBO and Showtime, although the four Hollywood partners agreed that the fees paid for any movie made available to Premiere would be determined in accordance with a pricing formula agreed to by them. For 1979, HBO licensed 70 moves from those four majors, representing about 34 percent of its product and 42 percent of its film expenditures. Similarly, Showtime licensed 99 titles from them, 44 percent of all its titles, 56 percent of its movie expenditures.[39]

On December 31, 1980 U.S. District Court Judge Gerard Goettel issued an injunction against Premiere preventing it from going into service, as planned, just two days later. He issued the injunction on the ground that there was a "reasonable likelihood" Premiere had violated antitrust statutes forbidding price fixing. Noting the short notice, and estimated $15 million loss to Premiere (self-assessed), Goettel commented: "Any hardship an injunction will cause the defendant is not as significant as the harm Premiere would probably cause the existing pay-television industry." It was a major victory for HBO. More than 30 state attorneys general filed briefs in support of the Justice Department. Executives of existing pay networks, including HBO, testified they would be crippled by Premiere's exclusivity clause. The four Hollywood majors involved had already withheld 30 of their movies from the pay–TV market, in anticipation of starting Premiere. However, that venture's recently released January schedule included only three features which had not already been telecast on pay–TV.[40]

Annoyance with HBO's "low fees" did not go away. In the summer of 1982, three majors, Paramount, MCA, and Warner announced a plan to become partners in TMC, then owned by Warner-Amex Satellite Entertainment, a joint venture between American Express and Warner Communications (the parent company of Warner Bros.). Under the new plan TMC would continue to offer their movies to other pay networks as well. By taking that position the new venture hoped to avoid antitrust action being taken against it. Hollywood worried that HBO, with 50 percent of all pay–TV subscribers and increasingly using its resources to buy exclusive pay–TV rights to titles, would use its dominance to squeeze out competitors and thus diminish the pay–TV revenues to be earned by the majors. HBO countered that in general exclusivity had become essential to any service seeking to differentiate itself in an increasingly crowded marketplace.[41]

That deal was superseded at the end of 1982 by a different proposal when Viacom International (which had earlier purchased 50 percent of Showtime from Group W cable) became the fifth in a joint venture which would now operate a merged Showtime and TMC. Those five partners declared they would continue to offer their movies to all pay–TV services on a nonexclusive basis.[42]

After a four-month investigation Justice announced it would file a civil antitrust suit to block the merger, believing it would stifle competition. Thanks to changes in the proposed deal, Justice announced a couple of months later that it would permit a merger of Showtime and TMC because the venture proposed no longer included three major distributors as co-owners; it was then down to one—Warner. Those two services merged in September 1983 with Viacom owning 50 percent, Warner Communications 31 percent, Warner Amex 19 percent. Each service was kept running as a separate entity.[43]

A proposed deal in 1983 in which ABC, Fox, and Columbia proposed to buy 75 percent of Showtime from Viacom fell through at the last minute. Those moves and attempts by the majors to buy into pay–TV were a reflection of changing market structure and unhappiness over income. In 1977, Hollywood had 80 percent of its revenues come from cinemas, the rest from TV. Just five years later, only 58.8 percent of revenue came from theaters—the rest came from television and video. Producers were used to something close to a 50/50 split of the box office dollar with exhibitors but they took a much smaller percentage in other markets. In pay–TV studios sometimes kept only about 20 percent. According to studio executives, when a cable operator charged a subscriber $9 for HBO, an operator such as Group W Cable of Cox Cable Communications kept about $5 with HBO keeping the other $4, out of which it spent $1.50 to $1.75 for movies. It led to the complaint that "HBO virtually dictates how much it will pay for a film." Producers were livid that on the above type of transactions they earned only 16 to 20 percent of the pay–TV exhibition revenues. MCA's Sidney Sheinberg angrily described HBO as "unfair" and "arrogant" and that HBO "has become so powerful that it determines whether or not a film will be made." The situation was summed up by Roland Betts, President of International Film Investors Inc., who said: "When you lose control of a film's ancillary rights, you're in trouble. Today that's the core of the movie business."[44]

Hollywood was achieving in Europe what had proved elusive in America (at least through the mid–1980s), ownership of new companies that charged the public to see its product. Both Premiere International and UIP were assembling pay–TV partnerships country by country and every Hollywood major was represented in one of the two organizations. Many in Hollywood were convinced the majors turned the three U.S. commercial television networks into giant moneymakers by licensing their libraries to them in the 1950s. In return, Hollywood bitterly thought it got token payment, a troublesome rival, and no piece of the action whatsoever. Similarly, when HBO came along in 1975, Hollywood again licensed its fare for a fee, not ownership. In the case of the two organizations operating in Europe each followed the same strategy: find a heavyweight, experienced local partner in each country who, for political reasons, got a 51 percent stake. Premiere linked Fox, Warner, Columbia, HBO and Showtime/TMC, while UIP joined Universal, Paramount, and MGM in various combinations.[45]

At a House Telecommunications subcommittee hearing in 1988 about cable industry problems, Jack Valenti of the MPAA charged there was monopoly control by cablers. Replied TCI head John Malone, "MPAA is the communication industry's answer to OPEC." Later he added, "I get a little nervous when Jack steps forward to protect the public interest."[46]

Basic cable became more important to Hollywood as time passed. As the 1990s began, some majors were bypassing independent syndication deals in favor of license terms of up to four years on basic cable, principally USA and Lifetime networks. Those basic cable outlets were paying more money by then, but also the residuals the studios had to pay out to the unions were considerably less. Reportedly the actors', directors', and writers' unions shared a one-time only ten percent of the gross revenue of the sale of a movie to a basic cable network. In the case of the recent $2 million-a-title Fox and Touchstone (Disney) deals with USA network, for example, the three unions would divide up $200,000 for each title whereas in market-by-market syndication most studios set aside at least 15 percent of the gross they received for residuals. Also there was much less expense involved in sales and marketing outlays comparing a one-invoice wide coverage deal with, say, USA, to station-by-station sales in syndication to independent outlets.[47]

Later in 1990, USA did other large deals with Paramount (19 titles) and Universal (24 titles). Of course, MCA and Paramount co-owned USA. Once again, the syndication market was cut off. However, there was a fall off in demand, as some formerly independent stations were then affiliated with the recently formed Fox network. It meant less outlets bidding in syndication in each market. USA paid around $2.1–$2.2 million per title. Some believed Universal's decision was based less on dollars than a desire to strengthen USA's growing power in the cable marketplace.[48]

In a different 1990 deal, MCA sold a total of 336 titles for a gross of $28 million to three basic cable networks, the Family Channel, Lifetime, and Arts & Entertainment (A&E). Said industry analyst Jack Fentress: "As an outlet for movies, syndication has shrunk drastically. Network affiliates hardly ever play movies anymore, even on the weekends. And independent stations that were fairly consistent buyers of movies before they became Fox affiliates have reduced their purchases by 50% or more."[49]

When Fox sold 26 theatricals to the USA network in December 1989 for $50 million, the studio, to forestall future lawsuits, laid off almost one-third of that amount to the five biggest grossers. The top five draws got an allocation of $3.3 million each whereas the four titles with the lowest box office receipts (all were flops) were allocated at $500,000 each. Journalist John Dempsey observed, "Because USA had to take all 26 movies in the deal (it couldn't just cherry-pick the five winners and discard the other 21), a profit participant in the box office winners could argue that any dollar figure allocated to the low-end movies is excessive because these pictures have negligible basic cable value of their own. In the past, some studios would have simply averaged the 26 titles to come up with a figure of a little more than $1.9 million a picture—a clear undervaluing of the higher-octane titles and a red flag to profit participants and their lawyers." Still, it took a while for the titles to make their way to USA network. Twelve months after theatrical release those 26 movies had their first pay cable window, with HBO for 15 months; then 25 of the 26 got a couple of primetime runs on the Fox television network in a window extending from 15 months for the lesser fare up to

24–30 months for the big hits. After that, each title got a second pay cable window for six months. Then, the exclusive five-year USA network window kicked in for each title as it finished its second pay run. The stretch was so long that USA would still be running seven of the Fox titles in the following century.[50]

Columbia took its latest film package straight to basic cable in 1996, in a multi-year deal with TBS and TNT for such recent theatrical hits as *Sleepless in Seattle* (1993) and *Philadelphia* (1993). It marked the first time Columbia had sold a new movie package exclusively to basic cable. Price was estimated at $40–$50 million for the 25 titles. After shopping the block around to major station groups Columbia determined the Turner offer exceeded what the package would command in syndication. Fledgling new commercial networks WB and UPN threatened to pull even more independent outlets out of the syndication process.[51]

Turner made a $25 million dollar deal in 1996 licensing 101 classic and contemporary films from Paramount over the coming 10 years (chiefly for the years 2000–2005) for its movie-hungry networks TNT and TBS. Remarked Turner Entertainment's Bob Levi: "The studios are finally starting to open up their libraries for deals beyond the year 2000. The problem for a long time was that every studio had this dream of signing onto cable with its own movie network. I think they've finally come to the conclusion that's not going to happen." Chief rival in bidding for that package was Disney whose Disney Channel had recently revamped primetime to a movie format as part of the channel's transition from pay to being an enhanced basic cable service.[52]

Late in 1997, TBS took a ratings drop just as Warner was trying to get cable operators to pay a license fee for the station (for the first time in the outlet's history) as the station transformed itself from a superstation to a basic cable network. It was counting on a 13-day primetime showcase of James Bond features in December of that year "to give it a Nielsen adrenaline shot."[53]

There was much concentrated ownership in the cable television industry. As of early in 1997 Westinghouse/CBS owned the Nashville Network (TNN) and Country Music TV (CMT). Time Warner owned, among others, TNT, TBS, HBO, CNN, Cartoon Network, CNN Headline News, Cinemax, and Turner Classic Movies (TCM). Additionally, it had interests in, among others, Comedy Central, Court TV, and Black Entertainment Television. Disney/ABC had among its holdings the Disney Channel, an 80 percent stake in ESPN and ESPN2, 50 percent of Lifetime, and 37.5 percent of both A&E and the History Channel. Viacom owned MTV, Nickelodeon/Nick at Nite, VH1, Showtime, TMC, Nick at Nite's TV Land, and MTV spin-off channel M2. As well, Viacom owned 50 percent of USA and the Sci-Fi Channel (Paramount and Universal each owned 50 percent). The largest cable operator in America, TCI, through its Liberty Media subsidiary, owned a minority stake in a large number of cable networks including all the Time Warner channels along with the Discovery Channel, the Learning Channel, the Family Channel, Court TV, Encore, and Starz.[54]

Pay-per-view (ppv) was a system that Hollywood, and cable operators, had great hopes for. At a 1982 cable TV convention, pay-per-view was a hot topic with all kinds of grandiose predictions of its huge future. Andrew Walk, Fox pay–TV president, declared in a speech that movies would be the bread and butter of pay-per-view, just as they had been for television and pay cable. However, he emphatically held that pay-per-view should not try to go into the first-run business. "The theatres will create hits for you," he told delegates. Walk asked the cablers how many of them would have recognized *The French Connection* (1971), or *Star Wars* (1977) as super-hits if they were only described in a sales brochure. "Few people," he said, "are willing to pay for a movie they have not heard about." Rick Kulis, of Don King Sports, predicted that in a few years the pay-per-view industry would be daring the Super Bowl, the World Series, and other sports events not to join the pay-per-view revolution. Reporter Morry Roth observed, "That statement is a far cry from a few years ago when pay cable was humbly vowing not to touch those American events if it was allowed to otherwise operate."[55]

One year later, one Hollywood executive said, regarding the potential of pay-per-view, it could become "the biggest teat on the udder." Many in Hollywood couldn't understand why Universal released *Pirates of Penzance* (1982) day and date with cinemas and pay-per-view, antagonizing theater owners. Columbia executive Marvin Antonowski commented, "You don't bite the hand that feeds you unless you can bite it off." Cablesystems Pacific of Portland, Oregon presented three or four pay-per-view features a month, drawing about five percent of its subscribers. It aggressively promoted those offerings in its weekly program guide and on its channels. Pay-per-view coordinator for the company, Jennifer Lambert, said, "it's impossible to premiere a movie on pay-per-view" because it's an unknown quantity. She insisted that pay-per-view customers weren't gamblers; they wanted their money's worth. In September 1982 Fox showed *Star Wars* on pay-per-view, the highest grossing film of all time, until *E.T.* (1982). It sold to 30 percent of the potential viewership, better than expected. Sixty-two percent of those viewers hadn't seen the movie before, lending credence to the idea that pay-per-view could open wallets cinemas hadn't been able to reach. The catch was, said journalist Michael Schrage, that *Star Wars* was "probably the most presold media commodity of this half century."[56]

While the cable industry regarded home video as an evil empire that caused subscribers to disconnect to cut back to basic service, it liked the new pay-per-view industry since the idea was that movies would go to pay-per-view day and date with home video. That meant, they hoped, that many customers would not be able to find the hot new titles at their video stores (all rented out) and would therefore shell out $4–$5 on pay-per-view to see the feature. Added to that pay-per-view draw was the hoped-for impulse buying, which they agreed depended on the industry having reliable, addressable systems which encouraged quick and easy customer buys. As of early 1986, there were about 7 million addressable (wired for pay-per-view) households in America. A couple of new services started that year, Request Television and People's Choice. The oldest was Viewer's Choice which was started around 1979 by Warner Amex—Showtime picked it up in June 1985. Although movies were then supposed to be issued to pay-per-view day and date with home video release, it didn't always happen. Soon thereafter, as home video clearly became the financially more important of the two, home video exclusively got the first window after theatrical release, followed by pay-per-view which got the second window exclusively. It remains so today.[57]

At the 1987 convention of the National Cable Television Association, the idea was touted that pay-per-view would eventually crush the competition of the video store. Barry Lemieux, president of American Cablesystems, made it clear that pay-per-view was cable's "necessary competitive response to videocassette rentals. The consumer wants it now and we better provide it or the consumer will go elsewhere for excitement." He added that pay-per-view could be competitive with home video if "we offer our customers choice on more than one channel." As well he called for the use of convenient ordering systems such as impulse buying to give "the consumer the control and convenience he demands." At that convention, the video store was the main enemy attacked. Lemieux commented that if pay-per-view was positioned properly it didn't cannibalize pay–TV sales, answering one of the frequently voiced objections by cable operators to pay-per-view. He argued that a single pay-per-view title selling at $3–$4 a shot "sure makes 60–80 titles a month on HBO or Showtime look like a great bargain." Competition among video stores had produced, in many cases and places, the 99¢ cassette rental. Richard Maul, of cabler Western Communications, agreed cable was overwhelmed on the pricing comparison but won "hands down" on convenience. Even on pricing, Maul believed that when the big retailers took hold of the video industry, reducing the number of small dealers, prices for cassette rentals inevitably would increase sharply. Maul pointed out it was difficult for a video store to compete with pay-per-view's quick delivery, no returns and no line-ups advantages. Lemieux summarized that pay-per-view wasn't merely a frill, but a "necessary competitive development" and that "pay-per-view does not cannibalize other cable services." Although, he offered no evidence for the latter claim. As of 1987 pay-per-view was still a relatively insignificant industry. Cherry Hill, New Jersey–based NYT Cable TV systems had 43,700 pay-per-view subscribers. For the first four months of 1987, it billed them a total of $437,000 for the rental of the addressable equipment at $2.50 per month per household. In that period just under 30,000 of those subscribers were billed an extra $692,546 for program purchases.[58]

When the Video Software Dealers' Association looked at film release patterns at the end of 1988 they found the vast majority of titles had a home video lead time of one month (the window) during which those movies were available in video stores (and nowhere else), before they became available to pay-per-view. They found a few day and date releases and windows ranging up to two months in length.[59]

Paramount Pictures Video division commissioned a 1989 Harvard Business School study of four U.S. pay-per-view systems across the country. That study found that regular pay-per-view users were generally heavy TV and home video users, too. Aside from owning multiple television sets, pay-per-view viewers tended to own more than one VCR. Only eight percent of active pay-per-view users did not have at least one VCR; about 35 percent had at least two VCRs. Also discovered by the survey was that frequent pay-per-view users rented 5–6 videos per month. Two-thirds of those surveyed said pay-per-view was a real value with 65 percent of those saying they'd pay up to 10 percent more than at present for a pay-per-view movie; half said they would pay up to 15 percent more and one quarter claimed they'd pay up to 20 percent extra. At that time, for Paramount, in terms of worldwide revenues, home video receipts were 55 percent larger than the theatrical box office.[60]

When Warner Bros. conducted a study of the top nine cable systems (in terms of pay-per-view buy rates) for the period August 1987 to June 1990, they concluded that hit theatrical films were chalking up a better buy rate on pay-per-view than almost all other live events such as boxing, wrestling, and pop music concerts. Compared in that study were the 64 non-movie live events that were aired against the Warner films on those systems—Warner did not have access to the buy rates for movies from the other majors. Results were that five of the top six telecasts were Warner titles. Prices for those titles on pay-per-view were $4 to $5 each while the other compared events charged amounts ranging from $14.95 to $49.95. Number one buy-rate event (at 12.7 percent) was the June 1988 Spinks/Tyson fight. Next five in the ratings were all Warner movies with buy rates ranging from 9.7 percent down to 8.4 percent. Around this time pay-per-view revenue was about equally divided between movies, and all others. Warner executive Edward Bleier believed that when a cable system did its job reasonably well movies would outperform all other events on pay-per-view. By reasonably well he meant a system had to have at least two channels earmarked for pay-per-view, an additional 24–hour barker channel listing that day's pay-per-view movies and events, saturation scheduling for seven days on at least one of the pay-per-view channels of the biggest box office movie available that week, and technology that made it easy for an impulse buyer to order a movie on the spur of the moment.[61]

Warner launched a new campaign in 1991 to persuade more cable subscribers to buy more movies on pay-per-view. Bleier delivered a pitch to most of the large multisystem cable operators based on the study of the cable systems that racked up the biggest receipts from pay-per-view. Among the common factors in those systems was that they devoted as many as four channels to pay-per-view so movie offerings could be made available more frequently and more conveniently. One or more continuous hits channels would run the same high grossing films 24 hours a day for at least one full week. Viewers needed to be able to order a film easily, preferably by just punching up a number on their phone, he explained. When the cable system forced the viewers to remember personal-access codes and multi-digit film numbers it encouraged them to bypass pay-per-view and rent newer theatricals from the local video store. He thought cable systems should offer pay-per-view to all subscribers, not just those who bought at least one pay cable channel, even if that strategy would result in a sizable investment in addressable (two-way) technology. The most aggressive of those cable systems were grossing monthly subscriber fees of $4.15 for pay-per-view movies and other events. However, Bleier thought $10 per month was attainable. Some cable systems had their own pay-per-view systems, stand alones dealing directly with film suppliers. However, the two biggest pay-per-view networks were middlemen, Viewer's Choice and Request Television.[62]

Pay-per-view got a big boost a year later when Fox and cable operator giant TCI got together to buy a controlling interest in Request Television, the biggest pay-per-view distributor.[63]

According to Paul Kagan Associates, movies on pay-per-view generated only $103 million in sales for all of 1990; cable viewers paid an average of $4.30 per viewing. By contrast, home video sales were almost $3 billion that year. Close to $100 million was generated by just two pay-per-view events in 1991, April's Evander Holyfield/George Foreman boxing match and June's Mike Tyson/Razor Ruddick fight. Neither Hollywood's majors not the cable operators were satisfied with the pay-per-view movie sales, each blaming the other for the underwhelming performances. Main sources of friction were revenue split, releasing pattern, and marketing of pay-per-view titles. Cable operators were not happy with the fact they had to split 90 percent of the revenue approximately equally with the studios, with the other 10 percent going to the middleman pay-per-view distributor such as Viewer's Choice and Request Television. Operators of cable systems wanted more money from Hollywood but the latter said they didn't deserve it, pointing to disappointingly low buy rates, hovering well below ten percent. Hollywood argued cablers needed to have dedicated barker channels which would boost buy rates. Those barker channels had long been used by hotel/motel pay-per-view providers with the idea being that a provocative pitch for a title could generate an impulse buy. Many systems did not have barker channels. Cablers contended the 30–60 day lag (or window) between the time a movie was released on home video and the date it was shown on pay-per-view was "crippling." Hollywood, however, feared a substantial reduction in the potential of cassette sales and rentals by moving pay-per-view to an earlier window, it was also concerned about piracy of pay-per-view offerings. Paramount home video division President Bob Klingensmith said the head start was not a handicap, suggesting pay-per-view "just isn't trying hard enough."[64]

Hollywood's majors continued to dream of a day in the future when a new film premiered on pay-per-view for one night only, generating $100 million in revenue. The following day that title would open in 2,000 cinemas nationwide, capitalizing on the studio marketing campaign and instant word of mouth created by the one-night stand on pay-per-view. First, though, a number of obstacles had to be overcome. Early in 1992, the pay-per-view universe was thought to be around 15 million households (the VCR universe was 70 million). That universe would have to at least double before a film debut on pay-per-view would be viable. Pay-per-view itself would need to be more user-friendly; many systems were constraining and confusing. Even though the buy rate for pay-per-view movies was low, eight percent of 30 million was still impressive. Then there was price hesitation: above a price of $4 to $5 serious resistance kicked in. Yet a one-time pay-per-view title would have to charge $20 or more to return what the majors regarded as significant revenue. Anti-copying technology was being tested but studio executives looked for assurances that such technology couldn't be bypassed with their titles being pirated. Other stumbling blocks included exhibitors and the home video industry. Both the National Association of Theatre Owners and the Video Software Dealers Association responded very negatively to Hollywood's dream. Would the financial gain from a pay-per-view debut be enough to offset the potential loss of theatrical revenue? If 2–4 million homes paid $20–$25 to see a debut, the pay-per-view revenue would be $40–$100 million, half of which would go back to the studios. That still left a sizable audience to turn out at cinemas in the following days, thus there would be minimal cannibalization. TCI pay-per-view President Fred de Prez said, "A single premiere showing would generate word of mouth. This is based on the current evaluation that pay-per-view currently spices additional interest in video rental—rather than eating into the business." Scott Kurnit, head of Showtime pay-per-view remarked, "There's one truism about movies. The better it does, the better it does." The extra promotion and word of mouth from a one-shot showing could snowball interest on the film that opens the next day, he said, just as a "successful theatrical run further ignites interest when a film is released on video, cable and pay-per-view today." Studios saw an average return of 26¢ on every consumer dollar spent on video; whereas with pay-per-view their take was closer to the 50/50 split they enjoyed from theatrical receipts.[65]

Opposition to pay-per-view, and jockeying for position within the industry, reached a peak in 1993. When TCI acquired a one-quarter financial interest in Carolco Pictures they stated their intention, in the near future, to release an "event" feature to pay-per-view day-and-date with cinema release. Immediately exhibition executives announced they would bar movies at their theaters that had appeared on the small screen. NATO adopted a resolution in which it unequivocally opposed "the release of theatrical motion pictures on pay-per-view or any other medium prior to their full and complete release in movie theatres." Loews Theaters co-chair Barrie Loeks said pay-per-view release prior to cinema issue eroded the shared experience of watching first-run films on the big screen in the theater. Landmark Theaters President Steve Gilula commented that pay-per-view was a market issue that challenged "a rational, consumer-driven pipeline for movies. In the long run, all theaters will be affected equally because it devalues the commodity. You have to have a period of relative exclusivity for theatrical exhibition to survive."[66]

In the wake of that, virtually every major studio in Hollywood declared it would not distribute films theatrically that had had pay-per-view premieres on TV. Warner spokesman Barry Reardon remarked: "We would absolutely not be interested in distributing any movie that's going to premiere on pay-per-view. It would just be sounding the death note for the theatrical business. Basically, they'd be playing second-run." That followed a statement by MGM co-CEO Alan Ladd Jr., who said his company didn't intend to distribute the proposed TCI/Carolco pay-per-view debuts even though it would have first crack at them when its new distribution deal with Carolco became effective the next year. TCI, the nation's largest cable operator, planned to invest $90 million over four years in Carolco in exchange for four pay-per-view movie previews. Echoing Ladd, executives from WB, Fox, Paramount, Disney, MCA, Orion, and TriStar made the same message clear: films should be seen on the big screen first. Most spoke passionately on the issue arguing a day and date release would destroy the traditional release pattern and exhibitors' very existence. Fox Vice President Tom Sherak stated: "The movie business is about sitting alone in the dark with 600 people. It's between you and the screen. I think there's something magical about that."[67]

By 1996 DirectTV and other distributors of programming via DBS were racking up record buy rates for theatricals, boosting the entire pay-per-view industry. Emboldened by this, Warner continued its maverick stance as the only major demanding up front guarantees for the titles it distributed to pay-per-view. Most cable operators, led by the two biggest pay-per-view distributors, Request TV and Viewer's Choice, had refused to go along with Warner's attempt to extract minimum guarantees. Those that did pay guarantees got titles an average of 15 days before they found their way to those cable systems which did not pay up. Many of those cable operators weren't overly enthusiastic about making pay-per-view a real revenue generator for cable: most systems had limited channel capacity, so they couldn't set aside more than 1 or 2 channels for pay-per-view. Such a limited set-aside meant inconvenient scheduling of programs with the result that the majority of subscribers to those cablers "have never rented a pay-per-view movie in their lives." Video stores were then grossing about $12 billion a year, while pay-per-view was worth only about $500 million annually to the studios. Warner executive Ed Bleier thought that forcing cable operators to put money up front would make them try harder to market those titles. He noted that cinemas gave studios minimum guarantees, video stores paid cash for tapes, TV networks paid a license fee, HBO and Showtime paid a fixed amount: "Why should cable operators expect to get movies on consignment, at no risk to them?" Warner asked for a bigger buy-rate guarantee for hits than for flops. For example, *Eraser* (1996) went to cablers for a 5 percent buy rate guarantee while the flop *Diabolique* (1996) went for 3 percent. For a cable operator with 100,000 pay-per-view subscribers picking up *Eraser*, it worked out to a guarantee of $9,500 to Warner (5,000 subscribers times the $1.90 that Warner received from each buy). For DBS distributors, the guarantees were much stiffer, climbing as high as 20 percent. It wasn't so difficult for a system such as DirectTV (no capacity problems) which made about 60 channels available to pay-per-view, and used those movies as loss leaders for their cable network and sports packages. DirectTV charged subscribers only $2.99 per film instead of the typical cable system charge of $3.95. Yet the studio still got the same $1.90 from DirectTV. Said Bleier; "DirectTV is pay-per-view heaven—it's one of the best things that's ever happened to the movie business."[68]

Reinforcing Bleier's opinion, a study by Paul Kagan Associates found satellite distributors such as DirectTV, Primestar, and others had developed into a revenue generating dream for the majors, who had received almost a ten-fold increase in pay-per-view movie buys from home dish owners in just two years. Those DBS companies, commented Bleier, "are giving the industry hard evidence that pay-per-view works when it's done correctly." According to that study, pay-per-view movie revenue in satellite-dish households moved from $21 million in 1994 to $202 million in 1996. By comparison, cable households increased their pay-per-view film buys from $157 million in 1994 to $215 million in 1996. All other pay-per-view events, boxing, wrestling, music concerts, and so on, brought in $412 million in 1996, from both cable and DBS systems. Kagan's projections for 2006 estimated that pay-per-view movies would be reaping $820 million from DBS homes, $1.4 billion from cable households, adult movies would generate $665 million, while all other pay-per-view events would produce $2.1 billion in revenue in 2006.[69]

An estimate for 1997 put the pay-per-view gross at $1.27 billion for the year with $603 million of that from films; adult movies generated $253 million. The number of addressable homes for pay-per-view grew 16 percent to 37 million households in 1997.[70]

Over the course of 1997, people rented 4.2 percent fewer tapes, according to the Video Software Dealers Association (VSDA), who blamed satellite dish owners for the downturn. Those dish owners could choose from up to 50 pay-per-view channels, plus an array of pay–TV networks and basic cable movie channels. DirectTV led the way with 3.8 million dish owners signed up. Many cable operators planned to expand their channel capacity to 100 or more, through digital technology, within a year or two. Still, in 1997 video generated $7.38 billion while pay-per-view revenue for moves (from both DBS and cable pay-per-view) was only $778 million. The majors had to strike a balance between helping the pay-per-view industry maximize its revenues yet not alienate the video rental business. One battleground was over the length of the window. Said Jeff Eves, president of VSDA, "through a well-orchestrated campaign" video store owners "put enough pressure on to get the studios to push out their windows from an average of about 38 days in the fourth quarter of 1996 to the current 53 day average." Eves wanted to see it longer, at least 60 days. DirectTV was trying to lower it by putting up guaranteed dollars in exchange for getting titles earlier than 53 days. Some DirectTV guarantees went as high as $1.5 million for a blockbuster. In return the studio would shave off as many as 12 days from the video store window. Cable operators hoped the move to digital might allow them to shun pay-per-view, allowing them, under the new technology with greatly expanded channel capacity, to concentrate on multiplexed pay channels and advertiser supported cable networks—this brought cablers a better financial return.[71]

By far the biggest boon for Hollywood in generating revenue from their movies came from the home video industry. In the autumn of 1976, Andre Blay, a Michigan-based distributor of video equipment, sent a "cold call letter" to the Hollywood majors inquiring about the right to market their movies on videocassettes. Only two of the majors bothered to respond—and one of those was not interested. Videocassettes were still a novelty, and studio executives were divided in their attitude toward them, running between panic and indifference. Universal's lawsuit against Sony was then underway. Sidney Sheinberg, Universal's president, felt so strongly about the threat of copyright infringement through home taping that he declined to be the co-chair of a benefit for the American Film Institute upon learning that Sony had contributed $300,000 to the same cause. "I cannot condone or support any institution which is oblivious to the interests of the Hollywood community," he explained. Blay's concept challenged the Hollywood principle of never parting with the title to a copy of a movie. Once it had been sold on cassette, how could a studio monitor the size of the audience; how could it keep people from making unauthorized copies, and what value would a film retain in the television and theatrical markets? Blay's letter made its way to Fox's Steve Roberts who ran a subsidiary called 20th Century–Fox Telecommunications. Roberts was preparing a similar experiment: "We were about to go into the business ourselves—to test the waters. We would use films that were already on commercial television, so I felt we were risking very little, since anyone who wanted them could tape them off the air as it was. But we were going to sell those films without the commercials and unedited." For a trial venture, he felt it was sensible to let somebody else invest the capital. They signed a contract in July 1977 calling for Blay to advance Fox $300,000 plus pay a minimum of $500,000 annually, against a royalty of $7.50 on each cassette sold. Blay received the nonexclusive right to choose 50 movies—all had previously been sold to network TV—from a list of 100 prepared by Fox. Basing his choices on *Variety*'s box office receipts estimates, his picks included *Hello Dolly* (1969), *M.A.S.H.* (1970), *Patton* (1970), *The French Connection* (1971), and *The King and I* (1956).[72]

Under a company called Magnetic Video, Blay was ready to start selling in October 1977. He began by taking out ads in trade publications that catered to record and appliance stores. Knowing that appliance stores were "ill-equipped" to sell cassettes, Blay considered them to be a bridge until a better type of outlet emerged. As well, he launched a direct-mail operation called the Video Club of America with a $65,000 advertising campaign in *TV Guide*. From a potential population of less than 200,000 VCR owners some 9,000 joined the club, paying a $10 membership fee which alone covered the cost of the *TV Guide* promotion. By March 1978, Magnetic had sold 40,000 tapes, most of them to retailers for $37.50 wholesale, many others were bought for $49.95 through the Video Club. By the end of 1978, Blay had sold 250,000 units with his factory going 24 hours a day producing 30,000 cassettes per week. Back in July 1977, "50 copies a week were a lot" for Magnetic to produce, said Blay.[73]

At the same time, George Atkinson ran a small, not-very-successful Los Angeles-based business called Home Theater Systems whereby people would pay $25 for the privilege of renting a Super-8 projector, a screen and an old movie, lugging it all home for one night. Mostly the company catered to home parties. He thought that people who went to that much trouble, and many other people, would surely pay a few dollars to rent a movie on videocassette. To test that theory, he ran an ad in the *Los Angeles Times*, receiving almost 1,000 replies. Then he bought one Beta format and one VHS format copy of all those 50 Fox titles, and opened for business. He took out another ad in the newspaper. He established a video rental club which charged $50 for an annual membership, $100 for a "life" membership. A member was entitled to rent titles for $10 a day. While a few of his early customers wanted to buy tapes rather than rent them, Atkinson had little hope for that side of the business, saying: "The studio executives said Americans are not a renting public—like the English who rent television sets. They said Americans are an acquisition people. They want to own. I said, 'Well, movies may be the exception.'" Not many agreed with him at the time. None of the appliance stores that carried Fox tapes were renting them. In fact, their contract with Magnetic stipulated that the cassettes were to be sold for home use only.

Suspecting Fox executives might not like his rental business, Atkinson made a few phone calls to authorities to try and determine if he was legal or not—to the FBI and MPAA, among others. Nobody could say for sure. Eventually, he connected with Roberts to discuss the issue. After a few months, he received a call from an outside Fox consultant who suggested he'd better not rent. Atkinson then retained a lawyer who studied the issue and declared: "You can't copy it, you can't publicly exhibit it—that's a violation of copyright. But you can rent it, you can eat it, you can destroy it. You bought it. It's your property." None of it made much sense to Roberts and other Fox executives, especially as the law gave them no way to compel retailers to give the studio a piece of any rental action. Fox and Magnetic decided, for the time being, that they would make their distributors and retailers promise not to rent; anybody who disobeyed would be cut off. If it sounded foolproof, Atkinson (who had been buying his tapes directly from Magnetic) soon discovered there was nothing to stop him from "getting my stuff from another retailer or a friendly distributor." Nevertheless, Fox made a lot of money and other studios slowly joined the cassette industry.[74]

Sales of VCRs slowly started to move beginning around 1978. In the previous year, there were perhaps 250,000 VCRs purchased. There were then still three major, competing, incompatible systems—Sony's Betamax, Matsushita's VHS system, and Quasar's VX-2000. Not much pre-recorded material was available so Sony was advertising its system's ability to tape programs directly off the air. In response to that, MCA/Universal had brought a copyright suit against Sony, challenging the right of VCR makers to sell that feature of their equipment. MCA argued Sony was encouraging the infringement of its copyright by advertising that its Betamax system could copy shows off of the TV screen.[75]

The MPAA President Jack Valenti indicated late in 1978 that the major U.S. film companies would not be "plunged into" the home video market. Expressing extreme caution about the nature and dimension of the home video market, he did concede that a revolution in home entertainment could be underway. Estimates called for 750,000 VCRs in homes by the end of 1978, 1.2 million in 1980 and 8 million units in 1985. A nagging problem remained incompatibility with several systems still competing. Valenti noted the motion picture industry was entrenched in its current "sequential marketing pattern" under which product generated revenue over a long period of time, sometimes running three or four decades for blockbusters. He said Hollywood was asking, "What effect will sales of prerecorded cassettes and disks have on the continued ability to license films over the long term?" Worried about the risk of piracy, he added, "unless we understand that the avalanche of piracy now feeding on this new field of tape must be halted, then we may well be discussing a new industry that will succumb to cradle death." Valenti said the majors would be making product available on a non-exclusive basis to home video. At the time, some 50 companies were marketing a total of 6,000 to 8,000 titles with most of those being in the public domain and what Valenti called "erotica"—hard core pornography. UA Vice President Gerald Phillips suggested that rental of product for videotape distribution might be, from a legal point of view, a far stronger deterrent to piracy than outright sales.[76]

Disney was a partner with MCA in its suit against the Sony Betamax system. Relief sought was an injunction to stop Sony from manufacturing and selling Betamax machines and tapes in the U.S. Federal Judge Warren Ferguson ruled in Los Angeles in 1979 against Hollywood when he held: "The court finds that home use recording from free television is not a copyright infringement and that, even if it were, corporate defendants are not liable and an injunction is not appropriate."[77]

That decision was overturned in 1981 by the Ninth Circuit Court of Appeals which held that home videotaping was a clear-cut violation of copyright law. With several million VCRs sold the court did not issue an injunction, nor did it try to turn back the clock. Rather it suggested a compromise might still be practical, with copyright holders possibly getting some kind of blanket royalties from home copying.[78]

In 1984, the U.S. Supreme Court ruled that the widespread practice of home videotaping was not a violation of copyright laws in a 5–4 decision that amounted to a crushing defeat for Hollywood. The court ruled that "time shifting" (as taping programs off the air for later viewing was called) was a fair use of video product protected by law. Similarly, it ruled that manufacturers of VCRs were not contributory infringers as program suppliers alleged. It meant that Hollywood was expected to lobby harder for royalty fees and for repeal of the First Sale doctrine, part of a subsection of copyright law which said the first sale of a product was the last one over which a manufacturer had control. Because of that doctrine home video retailers could rent out videos they had purchased from the majors, without their permission and without any further compensation to those majors.[79]

Paramount started test-marketing the sale of pre-recorded cassettes in Phoenix and Denver in 1979 and moved to a national sales operation later that year. The studio's growing commitment to the home video concept was echoed by representatives of Fox, Disney, and UA. All saw an ultimate release pattern of product that would bring the release of movies to the home video market prior to, or concurrent with, release to pay–TV. One issue of disagreement remained over marketing: whether to opt to sell cassettes or to rent them. Fox remained adamant in its sales-only program while Paramount was experimenting with alternative techniques. UA and Disney saw the rental market as the only marketing strategy. Fox had not yet made tapes available prior to pay–TV release, but said it might move that way. A question was how long a title could be made available for cassette rental and, if rental tape availability was simultaneous with pay–TV telecasting, how much would that affect the cassette market. Disney had still not entered the home video market but indicated that when it did, it would go rental. It felt rentals would not disturb its seven-year theatrical reissue cycle because it allowed Disney to move in and out of the home video market.[80]

In comments made in March 1980, MPAA President Jack Valenti said that a "sea of change" had taken place in the home video market over the previous 16 months with the number of titles produced by MPAA member companies available on cassette having increased significantly. Just 16 months earlier, only one MPAA member firm had movies available in the home video market—50 titles. At the time of Valenti's comments all nine MPAA member firms had films available on tape, a total of 477 titles, seven companies had 360 titles on videocassette, and four producers had 139 titles on videodisk (there was some overlap). Disks competed with tapes to a degree at the end of the 1970s and very early 1980s, but the technology was not successful then with disk systems losing out completely, and quickly, to cassettes. Valenti emphasized the need to keep a "delicate balance" in film release patterns.[81]

Around the same time, Fox Vice Chairman Alan Hirschfield outlined a plan before the International Tape Association in which he proposed day-and-date theatrical and home video release of movies. He also said his plan would safeguard against piracy. It was a trial balloon which, said reporter Will Tusher, "was shot down in tatters." Exhibitors were outraged, registered shock and dismay, putting an end to that proposal.[82]

Before the final decision was rendered by the courts in the issue of the legality of home taping, Hollywood had already launched its strategy in case it lost. By early in 1982, the MPAA had started the fight of its life on behalf of a royalty for videotaping, what reporter Tom Goldsmith described as "an effort surpassing any lobbying campaign it has ever mounted." Valenti called the effort "truly a life or death issue" for the motion picture industry and made it clear that the true enemy was time. With actor Charlton Heston at his side, the MPAA head made the rounds on Capitol Hill arm-twisting for the home-taping fee all the while stressing its urgency. At stake, argued the pair, was nothing less than the survival of the film production industry itself. Heston was a close friend of President Ronald Reagan. Some conceded that Valenti's efforts were hampered by a lack of demonstrated harm from the VCRs sold to that time. Valenti was talking about adding a $50 fee to the cost of each VCR plus $1 tacked on to the cost of each blank videotape, to compensate Hollywood's majors for supposed lost income due to people videotaping material at home. The closest MPAA got to evidence was a letter from the Frito-Lay Company, which Valenti produced at a Senate session. That letter said the corporation wouldn't pay ad rates based on ratings that included VCR use, because many of those machines had controls which allowed viewers to skip commercial blurbs with fast forward buttons.[83]

A 1982 analysis done by the A.C. Nielsen company confirmed findings by other studies which showed an overwhelming preference for videocassette rentals over purchases. According to Nielsen, 45 percent of VCR-owning homes had rented a cassette in the previous twelve months, while 25 percent did so in the prior four weeks. People who rented tended to do so very frequently, with 70 percent renting an average of 4.8 cassettes per week per household. Purchase figures were far lower, with only 3.6 percent of the households buying a cassette in the previous 4 weeks and only 16 percent saying they had ever bought a tape. By the end of 1983, the U.S. VCR population was close to ten million, almost double what it was in 1982. Owners of units who had had a VCR for periods of 1–3 years were heavily into recording with time shifting as the main use of the unit. By contrast, recent VCR buyers were drawn into a unit purchase by lowered prices for VCRs and a growing prerecorded videocassette market. Nielsen found an average rental fee of $2 a night. As for the kind of programming either rented or bought by VCR owners, "feature films totally dominated the market." Regarding programs taped off the air by VCR owners, it was found that soap operas were first in terms of hours recorded, with feature films a close second. However, in terms of number of different programs, recorded movies were a clear winner.[84]

In 1985, HBO launched a marketing program touting the compatibility of pay–TV and VCRs, including a brochure that directly addressed the previously taboo subject of using pay–TV and a VCR to build a video library. It was a campaign which drew Hollywood's ire. Said Paramount executive Bob Klingensmith: "Of course this is absolutely counter to our whole philosophy and what we're trying to do. Beyond that, I've never seen any legislation or judicial decision telling consumers they can tape off of pay–TV. As far as I'm concerned, taping off of pay–TV or cassette-to-cassette is still a form of piracy." A sentence in the HBO brochure pointed out: "the fun of developing your own video library by taping HBO... It's the convenient and economical alternative" to renting tapes. HBO's campaign concentrated on educating cable systems in ways to promote the VCR/pay–TV compatibility to their subscribers. It was left primarily to those cable systems to reach consumers with the campaign. Showtime/TMC had promoted some of its film festival series with the phrase "VCR friendly." Some argued the attraction of taping movies from TV served as a strong force to increase the base of VCR owners, which expanded the universe for all suppliers of prerecorded product. With respect to the HBO idea of building one's own video library Klingensmith remarked, "I think it is in bad taste, but perhaps it's a case of desperation marketing."[85]

An entrepreneur named John Leonard set up the Nickelodeon Video Showcase parlors in three communities in Pennsylvania: Lock Haven, State College, and Clarion. It was set up to allow customers to rent a movie, and a small viewing room containing a VCR to watch it on. Catered to were people who didn't yet own a VCR—still the vast majority then. Leonard's business prompted the MPAA member firms to launch a suit against him on the ground of copyright infringement. In his defense Leonard argued his parlors did not violate U.S. copyright law because the parlors were private and did not themselves show the films: the customers had complete control over the VCR placed there for their use. Over the next couple of years, both lower and appeal courts held that video stores could not rent private screening rooms to customers because the practice was unfair to movie studios. Those decisions further held that such video parlors infringed on the exclusive right of movie companies to authorize public screenings of their copyright films. Watching a videotape in a rented room ranging in size from a one-person booth to a large lounge constituted a public showing.[86]

Over the course of 1984, Americans went to the movies an average of five times each; in 1946, each American went to the movies an average of 29 times. Most VCR owners said they went to the cinema less since they bought their units but they still attended more than the general public; VCR owners went to the movies an average of nine times in 1984. Three of every five VCR owners rented cassettes within the previous month and, on average, they rented nine tapes a month.[87]

According to a survey by Alexander & Associates, in one week in March 1987 about 41 percent of VCR households in the U.S. rented at least one cassette, a percentage that moved to 47 percent the following week. That survey placed VCR penetration of U.S. television households at 51 percent (44.5 million), notably higher than the 40–44 percent range then generally cited. Average number of tapes rented by VCR owners who did rent was 3.0 and 3.7 for those two weeks. Using the whole universe of renter and non-renter VCR owners produced cassette rental rates of 1.2 and 1.7 units in the two weeks. Four or five of the Hollywood majors had retained Alexander & Associates to conduct the study. While they were not named, speculation was that two of them were Walt Disney Home Video and RCA/Columbia Home Video. In the first week of the survey, four percent of VCR owners purchased prerecorded material, in the second week that figure was six percent.[88]

According to a survey by the Video Software Dealers Association, in 1986 "A" theatricals (product from the majors) rented an average of 80 times, "B" titles 42 times, and "C" movies 31 times. Prerecorded tapes sold for an average of $29 each in 1986, compared to $37.23 in 1985. Price per rental in 1986 was $2.40, compared to $2.66 a year earlier. Rental and sale of foreign movies in that survey amounted to 1.0 to 1.4 percent of the total, just about the same as the foreign theatricals' take at box offices.[89]

By about 1987, just about all of Hollywood's output was available on videotape. They were then going after old series, vintage drama and sitcom segments, made-fors, and so forth, and releasing them on tape in the continuing effort to find more stuff to sell. Examples were episodes from television series such as *I Love Lucy*, *The Honeymooners*, and *Star Trek*. The fact that many of these series were still in syndication and seen in many parts of the U.S., and available for taping directly from the home screen, did not seem to hamper sales. Some in the industry argued it increased consumer awareness and led to increased sales. In the New York area *The Honeymooners* was on television six nights a week, yet Jaffer Ali of the cassette supplier MPI Video said 35 percent of unit sales took place there. Asked why that was so Ali replied: "Over 275 minutes have been chopped off *The Honeymooners* for syndication. The only place you can see a complete, uncut version is video." For fans of the series Ali added, "cutting out one precious Ed Norton line is like cutting out a passage of the Dead Sea Scrolls."[90]

For 1987 about 60 million cassettes were sold to dealers for sell-through while 62 million units were sold to dealers for rentals. It was the first year the figures had been almost even—units sold for rental use had always been much higher. Video revenues were estimated at $3.3 billion for the year. With the prices going up on the rental-aimed tapes and down on the sell-through directed cassettes, the sales of the latter were expected to soon surpass the former. However, rental units were expected to remain the economic backbone of the business. Rental tape revenue for 1987 was $2.4 billion; for sell-through it was $900,000. In tapes destined for rental, 85 percent of the units fell into the feature film category; they accounted for 95 percent of all the revenue from rental destined product. With respect to the sell-through tapes, 51 percent of them were feature films, accounting for 55 percent of the revenue.[91]

Paramount Home Video launched its most comprehensive and unprecedented home video campaign in 1988, called "Hits Blitz," a $10 million media push designed to send rental demand for Paramount videos surging, and then to sell significantly more videos to satisfy that demand. The company figured its low sell-through price for titles such as *Top Gun* (1986) and *Crocodile Dundee* (1986) earned it $10 million more than it could have with higher unit pricing, so Paramount had come up with a plan designed to bring in that missing $10 million while maintaining the higher pricing. That campaign blitz was aimed squarely at the industry's "depth-of-copy" problem, described by Paramount video division President Robert Klingensmith as a "cancer" in the industry. According to Hollywood criticism, the depth problem involved the fact that video stores didn't buy enough copies of hit films to satisfy rental demand. Not only did many customers never see those particular titles on video, grumbled Hollywood, but their growing dissatisfaction was driving them away from participation as video store customers at all. Aspects of the blitz, a nine-month campaign to back Paramount's next six main "A" title video releases, included early ads and announcements about availability, and a two-week booster campaign 4–6 weeks after initial release to keep rental demand rolling, at a time when it usually started to subside. Minimum sales goal was a 15–20 percent increase over what the six titles would normally have sold. During 1987 a top "A" title from Paramount sold an average of 225,000 units. Thus the $100 million campaign on 6 titles was hoped to generate total sales of 1.5 to 1.62 million units, bringing wholesale payments to Paramount of $88–$92 million. Paramount was hopeful of even more since it felt more than twice that 225,000 unit figure was necessary for the depth problem to be resolved. By its thinking, it felt there should be one high-priced rental copy of a hit movie on the market for every 100 VCR homes—it was then one copy for every 222 homes. By the conclusion of the campaign Paramount estimated that 82 percent of the adult population of the U.S. would have seen "Hits Blitz" advertising 5.2 times per title. Ads would include pitches on network, syndication, and cable TV, plus *USA Today* newspaper advertisments.[92]

For 1988 the home video industry broke the $10 billion barrier at the retail level with suppliers taking $3 billion in wholesale-level receipts, a 30 percent increase over 1987. Retail sales of rental-aimed product were $8.3 billion, sell-through about $2 billion. Some of that dramatic increase was attributed to large increases in the advertising and cross promotion of rental titles. If sales grew impressively more and more the receipts concentrated in the hands of those who controlled the "A" titles—Hollywood's majors. Over half of all tapes sold in 1988 carried an $89.95 suggested retail price, ground held mostly by "A" product destined for rental. And two-thirds of the remainder were in the $10–$30 range, dominated by sell-through "A" products. Suppliers of less than "A" product had a harder time that year mainly because the majors started making TV ad campaigns and cross-promotional pushes work for them in a big way. Pepsi and MCA teamed up to put $25 million worth of promotional spending behind *E.T. The Extra-Terrestrial* (1982). Disney, Coca-Cola, McDonald's and Crest joined forces to generate a $40 million campaign behind *Cinderella* (1950) and the other 34 titles in Disney's Christmas promotion—$25 million of that amount was spent on *Cinderella* alone. Paramount had its previously mentioned "Hits Blitz" while Touchstone (Disney) invested $6 million of its own to publicize the low-priced cassette release of *Good Morning, Vietnam* (1987). Seven figure promotional campaigns became almost standard procedure for "A" rental releases in 1988. Sometimes results were spectacular: *E.T.* sold about 14 million units, *Cinderella* 7 million copies, while Touchstone's *Three Men and a Baby* (1987) set a new high-priced title sales record of 550,000 units. Going into 1988 the industry was contending with a seemingly impenetrable barrier of 300,000 units sold for high-priced product; by the end of that year some 17 high-priced titles had beaten that mark. Also by the end of that year, after much prodding by retailers, suppliers were giving video a more advantageous window over pay-per-view than had earlier existed.[93]

As 1990 began, there were some 60 million U.S. households equipped with a VCR (10 million late in 1984), yet the rental of videos was reportedly starting to slip. Renters had either seen all the blockbusters they wanted to see, or couldn't find other titles they wanted, wrote journalist Peter Nichols, "because many stores do not stock anything but the big hits." The percentage of VCR households that purchased a tape in the fourth quarter of 1986 was 6.2 percent, 9 percent in 1987, 15.6 percent in 1988 and 16.4 percent in 1989 (Christmas sales, of course, made the numbers higher for that quarter). According to studies by A.C. Nielsen Media Research the high water mark for rentals was in late 1986 when an estimated 43.3 million households with VCRs took home 111.9 million cassettes per month, an average of 3.26 per household. By mid-1989, 59.5 million VCR households rented 142 million cassettes per month, an average of 2.38. That figure had fallen to an average of 2.07 movie rentals per month per VCR household a year later. According to estimates, 70 percent of the stock in video stores was made up of the newest and most highly publicized movies (virtually all from the majors) with the remaining 30 percent of the stock tailored to the local tastes in the retailer's area. Seven out of ten U.S. households then had a VCR. Paramount's Robert Klingensmith explained that the industry anticipated rental falloffs: "Our strategy for the 90's began in 1982. We realized that rentals would be flat by the end of the decade. So we decided to focus on the big titles — ones people would watch again and again — and started to sell them." Videos had always been sold but true mass market selling of movies began in 1987 when Paramount brought out *Top Gun* (1986) for $26.95 and sold 3.5 million units. A year later MCA's *E.T.* (1982) sold 14 million units at $24.98. Prices had dipped occasionally below $15 for some hits. From 1987 until the end of 1989, the number of cassettes sold each year had moved from about 115 million to more than 195 million units. Sales in 1989 amounted to $2.5 billion, or about 22 percent of the $11.5 billion retail video gross.[94]

Research by the A.C. Nielsen company carried out in November 1989 found that 65 percent of all home taping was spent on network-affiliated station offerings, followed by 15 percent for independent outlets, 8 percent on basic cable channels, 7 percent on pay-TV services and 5 percent on public television.[95]

Globally the home video business accounted for more than half of the majors' revenues from filmed entertainment. For 1995 it accounted for 53 percent of the majors' worldwide income, theatricals brought in 27 percent, and television accounted for 18 percent. MPAA companies harvested about $8.6 billion worldwide in 1995 from video revenue, double the $4.4 billion from theatrical rentals. For 1994 worldwide video take was $7.6 billion. The next major move would be to digital video disk, designed to render all VCRs and cassettes obsolete — as the CD player had done to the cassette tape in the music field. That was still just a dot on the horizon of home video in the mid-1990s but one that the majors were preparing to try and exploit, as soon as there was a viable market. Video on demand, whereby a customer could, through the magic of technology, order up almost any movie he wanted to see at whatever time he wanted to see it, was a specter that worried the home video industry at times. However, in early 1996, video on demand was not worrying the industry very much as the systems tested till then had limited options, with a choice of only 20 titles or so. Remarked Paul Miller, president of CIC Video (the Paramount/Universal overseas co-venture): "I don't see it hurting the rental business; it's years away from developing." He also dismissed full video on demand as "a dream, not a reality."[96]

Annoyed and angered by copyright's First Sale doctrine, which allowed video retailers to buy cassettes and then rent them repeatedly without permission or extra compensation, Hollywood tried various methods to try and claim a share of rental revenues. When Warner Home Video announced a plan in 1981 under which titles would be licensed (leased) from wholesaler to retailer, rather than sold, it was stung by a firestorm of retailer's criticism. Warner defended its attempt to recapture copyright control of its product as essential for the industry's future viability. Company executive Leon Knize explained: "We're trying to preserve this business for the consumer. We can't stand by and watch an ever-expanding universe in which rental revenues we do not participate in get larger and larger and continue to invest millions of dollars in films to fuel this market and not get any of it back." While holding to the underlying concept of the new plan—essentially to rent titles to video retailers—Warner did make significant alterations to try and gain broader dealer acceptance. Sale of some of the titles after the rental window had closed was no longer ruled out. When Warner first unveiled its plan it declared that "we will no longer sell our product to anyone and thus lose the protection of the copyright laws." A little later Knize said, "We never said we'd never go back to sale. We did say we intend to participate in rental avenues. If a title is not a rental kind of title, or if it doesn't rent any more, we might put it up for sale at some point in the future." Reporter Steve Knoll observed that if the pre-recorded cassette business had developed as the sale market that was expected, the need for the majors to recover control would not have arisen. With repeated rental transactions of the same cassette replacing a single sale as the marketplace norm, the majors were being forced into rental-only or rental-window plans as their only way of staking a claim to the lost revenues, thought Knoll. Knize added: "Our entire plan would not exist if it had not been for unauthorized rental. If there isn't a system that protects the owner of the property, he'll not put his property in that system." He suggested the problem first arose when retailers ignored the no-rental clauses then contained in their contracts with the software manufacturers. Rather than "coming to us and saying people want to rent" and getting together on a plan, the retailers went ahead by themselves. Warner opted for its new scheme after concluding, said Knize, that "if we shut our eyes to (unauthorized rental) it will hurt our other businesses too much." With a bigger and bigger video business expected, Warner felt it had to claim a share of the rental revenue or it would be left with no other recourse except to withhold titles from home video. When asked by Warner why it had not adopted the surcharge approach pioneered by Paramount Home Video (whereby the supplier added a fixed sum to the cost of a cassette), to account for rental revenue, Knize said it was not a viable solution because as the VCR population increased and the number of rentals grew, therefore the surcharge "would have to grow or the studio would feel cheated." He foresaw a cassette costing a retailer $300–$400. A high sale price would, moreover, lead to more piracy.[97]

In the face of Warner's announcement of its new plan, leading national video distributor Sound/Video Unlimited declared it would no longer handle Warner product because of that plan. Company President Noel Gimbel estimated the Warner plan would have retailers paying $7–$8 a week for each unit handled. Actually, the complicated Warner plan was based on a sliding scale under which it received 75 percent of rental revenues per cassette, or $8.25 the first week (whichever was greater). That royalty was progressively reduced to $4.40 (or 40 percent) a week, over six consecutive weeks. Under the "old way" retailers bought a tape for around $50 and rented it as often as they wanted, keeping all the proceeds. When rental demand was dead the dealer usually sold the now "pre-viewed" tape.[98]

The irritation of the majors at cassette rental could be seen in the background to the Warner plan. One day in 1980 Frank Weel and Ted Ashley, president and chairman of Warner Bros., respectively, unloaded their concerns on Morton Fink, president of the newly formed Warner Home Video. According to Fink, they were concerned about a species of small business—video software dealers—whose existence they had never contemplated, and that the market had shifted from sales to rentals. The typical Warner tape, at $79.95 retail, brought Warner around $10 but they were annoyed that that $50 wholesale tape was rented out 100 times or more at $5 a shot. They viewed their share as a pittance. Warner, Fink was told, "was giving away its crown jewels." As Fink perceived it the message was "Unless you come up with a business system that allows us to participate in all the rentals that take place, you won't get any more product." The result was the rental plan. Fink declared, "We will no longer sell our product to anyone."[99]

Shortly after Warner's pronouncement, Fox unveiled a rental plan of its own. It planned to license selected top-draw titles to dealers for a six-month period that would constitute the rental-only window. Only high-profile, blockbuster titles would be rented with other new titles added to the sale-only library. After the six-month lease period, explained Fox executive Steve Roberts, "we can either continue to rent it or put it into sale or withdraw it from distribution temporarily." If the latter course was chosen "we can re-release theatrically and then come back into the home video market."[100]

Later that year MGM/CBS Home Video became the latest major to institute a formal program to share in rental revenues. Their goal remained the same as it did for the others: to extract royalties out of a marketplace that had gone primarily rental. MGM planned to lease its rent-only titles for a four-month period at a cost to the retailers of $60 ($3.50 a week, or 50¢ per day). All titles in rent-only mode would have been exhibited theatrically within the prior 12 months. The for sale version of the title would be released the day after the rental-only tape went out of circulation. Other new titles would continue to be sale-only while still others could be offered first to pay–TV and then offered for sale in home video. Since the average rental fee a retailer charged was $5, said MGM, it was reasoned that 25 transactions over the four months would bring in a total of $125.[101]

These attempts by the majors caused dealer protest to galvanize. In the fall of 1981, video retailers were disorganized and unsophisticated. Warner's plan brought them to political life. Speaking on behalf of 300 stores, Atkinson called for a boycott of Warner product. Despite Warner's effort to modify the plan, the boycott spread. No matter how much the studio insisted they were trying to improve the business for everybody, it looked to dealers as though Hollywood wanted a bigger share of the take. By the summer of 1982, Warner's rental plan, and similar ones by MGM and Fox, were dead. Studios then re-directed their energy to lobbying Washington, winning the Reagan Administration's support for a bill that would make each rental a transaction requiring the copyright owner's approval. When a Senate subcommittee threatened to approve the studio's bill, in the spring of 1984, those committee members found full-page ads in their local newspapers, from the video dealers' lobby, that warned readers: "DO YOU WANT TO PAY MORE TO RENT MOVIES? IF NOT, CALL SENATOR _____ TODAY!" In the face of such opposition, the senators let the issue slide off the congressional calendar.[102]

That same year, 1981, the 3M company surveyed VCR owners finding that 40 percent of owners had either rented or purchased a prerecorded tape. Forty-five percent of those owners intended to rent in the coming 12 months; 14 percent indicated they would definitely buy a prerecorded tape in the coming year. The mean number of rentals per user per year was put at 20 per year. 3M's research determined the markets for rental and purchase were "entirely separate."[103]

None of those plans worked because dealers refused to participate. Nevertheless, Hollywood took another crack at gaining a share of the rental income in 1986. The majors then generally maintained a suggested price list of $79.95 for a tape ($50–$52 wholesale). Ron Berger, president of the 650–store National Video franchise chain, announced what was called a pay-per-transaction (ppt) plan. The test involved ten National outlets in the month of January and studied the feasibility of selected retailers handing over 50 percent of rental revenue on certain titles for the privilege of receiving those titles weeks before their competitors, and at a price far below what they normally paid. Three majors were involved but Berger was sworn to silence as to their names. Some 40 titles from the three studios were involved in the experiment. If successful Berger saw 5,000 first-tier retailers each buying 100 copies of a tape for $6 each (compared to the usual $50–$52 per tape) and renting each copy at least 30 times during a 45-day period at $5 per rental. According to Berger's calculations the supplier would generate $3 million on the initial sale, $37.5 million on its 50 percent rental income share and another $35 million when, 45 days later, the title was released for sale at a suggested list price of $19.95 ($14 wholesale). The last amount was based on a "10% take rate by VCR owners, or 2,500,000 copies." If those numbers were reliable a participating studio, according to Berger, would have to sell about 1,275,000 copies of a $79.95 title at current wholesale prices to equal its take. A top-seller like *Ghostbusters* (1984) sold about 425,000 units. Taking 100 copies of a title meant an average video store would have to generate 3,000 rental transactions for a single title.[104]

That plan went nowhere. Two years later, Orion Home Video introduced its ppt system. Under the Orion plan, video stores paid $8 for each tape they ordered. That initial payment gave the store the use of the tape for four months, a period during which it was obligated to return to the distributor 50 percent of all rental revenue with a minimum return of $1 per rental. At the end of the four months, the store could return the tape to Orion, where it would be destroyed, or buy it outright for $10.[105]

At the Video Software Dealers Association's 1988 convention, delegates were almost unanimously against ppt. Tom Burnett, vice president of supplier Virgin Vision, summed up that sentiment by warning that through ppt "the studios can be an unwanted partner for you ... Never once that I've seen has a studio wanted to share your risk." Dealers saw ppt as a plan that would turn control of their businesses over to Hollywood.[106]

A study commissioned by the Video Software Dealers Association lent credence to Hollywood complaints that video stores weren't buying enough copies of hit movies—the depth of copy issue. Research found it took the average video store customer 2.7 trips to the store to get the particular title he wanted. In that average visit, the customer left with his first choice 43 percent of the time, settled for a second choice 37 percent of the time, went elsewhere 10 percent of the time, and went home with no video at all 10 percent of the time.[107]

Rental income accounted for 81.1 percent of total video dollar volume in 1987, sales were at 18.9 percent of the total. The average video store had 2,832 titles, "A" titles rented 110.7 times on average, "B" titles 64.9 times, and "C" titles 39.4 times. Ultimately, none of the Hollywood plans to share in the rental income worked, mainly because video stores could ignore them due to the copyright's First Sale doctrine.[108]

In selling tapes to consumers, Hollywood's majors experimented broadly, in order to maximize its revenues, of course, but also to exert some type of control over the rental business by, for example, setting prices to discourage rentals and encourage purchases. Paramount Home Video priced *Star Trek: the Wrath of Khan* (1982) in 1982 at $39.95 retail; a significantly lower price at the time. It was a move designed to push dealers into selling tapes instead of renting them. Only blockbusters then sold over 25,000 copies and even then sales rarely broke the 30,000 or 40,000 mark. It worked to the extent that Paramount shipped 70,000 units in the first few months. By pricing the tape so low, and by highly publicizing the cut as much as it did, Paramount hoped the dealers would have no choice but to sell and not rent them. Tapes retailed then at $60 and up. Independent distributor Herb Fischer, president of Major Video concepts, thought even the lower price was too high. He felt the sales price should be $19.95 for the average title and $29.95 for the blockbusters, which could then turn the home video market into something approaching a 50/50 sales/rental mix. Fischer thought that if sales hit 50 percent of the total gross that would be as high as it could go.[109]

When VCR owners were studied by Media Statistics Inc. in 1982, it was found that just 24 percent had plans to buy a pre-recorded cassette in the coming year with 72 percent saying they would not make any purchases. Although buying was low, about half of the VCR population used pre-recorded material. While tape rental was an important factor in keeping people from putting out the money to buy tapes, it was not a key one, according to the study. The study found 48.4 percent of all VCR owners had never rented a cassette; 74.8 percent had recorded off-air or from cable. Those who rented tended to do so regularly with 55.1 percent renting six cassettes in the six months preceding the study; seven percent rented 40 or more. However, 67 percent owned no prerecorded cassettes whatsoever, 90 percent owned less than five. As well, 83.6 percent skipped or erased commercials during playback of recording material.[110]

When Paramount released *An Officer and a Gentleman* (1982) in 1983 on video at the then-low price of $39.95, it sold around 150,000 units for a take of $4 million wholesale, $6 million retail. Spurred on by that high sale, Paramount Home Video went on to release *Airplane II: The Sequel* (1982) at $29.95 retail. According to the studio, those low prices had doubled the potential penetration of a title in the marketplace from about one percent to two percent. That price for *Airplane II* marked the first time a major title had been released at such a low price. However, company executive Bob Klingensmith complained, "We're not quite getting the margin we'd like to have." Estimates were that Paramount's gross margin may have been slimmer but was still more than respectable, at around 27 percent, but quite a drop from the former 60 percent gross margins home video companies were earning on their cassettes priced at $59.95 and up. Low priced tapes had caused some controversy among the majors because many saw them as hurting the chances of any legislation that would repeal the First Sale doctrine. Because of that, there were some studios that had refused to join the low-priced cassette movement.[111]

Home video companies were then trying to attract more than just new customers with low prices. They were trying to hook a whole new kind of retailer as well—mass merchandisers, such as the big department store chains. Capturing those mass merchandisers was seen by the industry as key to increased sales. The problem lay in rental or not for those retailers. It was seen as too much work for department stores to undertake, while the rack jobbers were not able to do it either. Also, market penetration of VCRs was then thought to be too low to lure department stores into video in a big way. Hollywood looked jealously at the rack-jobbed mass merchandise record industry where 50 percent of sales were through giant department store chains. A few such retailers had already entered the video business. In the New York area both Bloomingdales and Alexanders had rental programs. In most of those programs, a consumer who rented a tape was initially charged for the full price of the tape. That sum, less the rental charge, was refunded when the consumer returned the tape. At Bloomingdales, the minimum rental term was a week, for a $15 fee. Other credit card plans had more usual formats with overnight fees of $4 or so. A K-Mart spokesman said, "The only kind of videocassettes we sell are blank." That firm had been selling them for only one year.[112]

A few years later, when Paramount released *Top Gun* (1986) at an even cheaper price, $26.95, its sales hit the 2.5 million mark, and beyond, earning the company wholesale revenues of over $40 million. That was more than any movie earned in domestic theatrical rentals in 1986, except for seven titles, and was roughly half the $82 million in rentals which *Top Gun* itself brought back to Paramount. Reasons for the title's success included the fact that 90 percent of video stores were supporting the *Top Gun* sell-through effort, rather than simply stocking it as a rental title. Video release of the title was preceded by much publicity along with a Pepsi-Paramount promotion campaign worth about $8 million. That tape also contained "the first U.S. commercial on such a title." Generally blockbuster titles took, at most, one-fifth to one-quarter of theatrical revenue—*Top Gun* had gone to one-half. For years Paramount had issued its hits at low prices, while every other competitor had released initially at a high price, to maximize revenue when the film's demand as a rental title was high. If *Top Gun* had been sold at $89.95, it would have had to sell 625,000 units to equal the income from three million units sold at $26.95. At the higher price, usual sales were about 350,000 units.[113]

Hollywood was releasing its titles in the late 1980s in two price groups, around $90, or about $30. The discrepancy lay in Hollywood trying to determine which movies VCR owners wanted to rent and which they wanted to buy. In the case of most titles, home video companies assumed that fans would be satisfied with a one-time rental. Therefore, companies set a high tape price, assuming most copies would only be bought by retailers, who would rent them out. That higher price was typically reduced eight or nine months later, after initial video release. Paramount and Disney had pioneered prices of under $30 for titles deemed to be collectible.[114]

Ads began to appear on tapes beginning with the Pepsi ad on *Top Gun*. That was followed by a Nestle's spot on *Dirty Dancing* (1987) and a Lee Iacocca "tribute" to Chrysler's Jeep vehicles on *Platoon* (1986).[115]

More ads came in 1989 with Paramount Home Video including Pepsi ads on four of its video releases that year: MGM/UA Home Video placed an ad on *Moonstruck* (1987). Cy Leslie, a former head of MGM/UA Home Entertainment said, "Consumers will continue to accept these commercials with total equanimity so long as the film is strong and the advertisements are new, tasteful and in keeping with the mood and tenor of the motion picture."[116]

The ad on the *Top Gun* video was a Diet Pepsi parody of the film with a Tom Cruise look-alike. Cruise was so outraged about that ad that in his contract for *Rain Man* (1988) he demanded, and received, a say in the marketing of the video. Subsequently, *Rain Man* co-star Dustin Hoffman had the same clause added to his contract. A worry among advertising executives was that viewers would fast forward through those commercials. Yet Nielsen company research claimed to show that most people actually watched those ads, rather than fast forwarding. Video industry consultant Saul Melnick noted that making the product discernible even during fast forwarding was an essential "subliminal message."[117]

When Pepsi placed its spot on *Top Gun*, many in the ad industry called it the dawn of a new ad medium that could rival television. Yet just a few years later, by the end of 1991, such commercials were the exception rather than the rule. Bruce Aper, editor of the trade journal *Video Business* remarked, "The use of home video as a marketing tool has fizzled." When Pepsi placed an ad on *Home Alone* (1990) there was much less hoopla. According to one survey, of the more than 7,000 titles in video only about 60 contained commercials. Mainly they appeared on "event movies" like *Home Alone* as part of a broader multi-million-dollar promotional campaign for both the tape and the advertiser's product. Other ads included a Burger King spot on *Teenage Mutant Ninja Turtles II: The Secret of the Ooze* (1991), and one for Del Monte vegetables on the 50th anniversary re-release of *Citizen Kane* (1941). A commercial on a tape cost the advertiser about $1.50 to $2 a tape. For *Home Alone*, Fox Video added to the beginning of the tape a 30-second Pepsi ad and a 10-second spot for American Airlines. The deal also involved a $25 million campaign for both Pepsi and Fox. Pepsi said it had increased its sales by $16.7 million in the first month of its *Home Alone* promotion. The title then had 11 million tapes distributed, at a suggested retail price of $24.98. Saatchi & Saatchi ad agency executive Erica Gruen explained, "there aren't enough titles advertisers are interested in." Also, air time on TV had become less expensive making tapes less attractive. Christine Alvarez, director of advertising at Columbia Tristar Home Video said advertisers had been slow to respond to proposals for promotional tie-ins to her company's videos: "Like any new media, it takes time to wean people to it. The bigger packaged-goods companies see it as event marketing, and the agencies are frustrated because they can't track the numbers on it."[118]

Those entertainment conglomerates continued to get bigger. The top nine international entertainment companies, ranked by 1996–97 revenues were Time Warner $20.9 billion, Walt Disney $18.7 billion, Bertlesmann (German) $12.3 billion, Viacom (Paramount) $12 billion, News Corp. (Fox) $11.2 billion, Sony Entertainment (Columbia) $8.4 billion, Havas (France) $8.2 billion, Tele-Communications Inc. $8 billion, Universal Studios $6.5 billion. Six of Hollywood's majors could be found on that list.[119]

Notes

Chapter 1

1. "Paradise lost." *Time* 51 (January 19, 1948): 87–88, 90.
2. "Television: movies' friend or foe?" *U.S. News and World Report* 26 (January 7, 1949): 24; "Television: boon to movies." *U.S. News and World Report* 27 (October 14, 1949): 21.
3. "Films downtrend data—'45–'52." *Variety* 190 (April 22, 1953): 3; William Lafferty. "Feature films on prime-time television." In, Tino Balio, ed. *Hollywood in the Age of Television*. Boston: Unwin Hyman, 1990, p. 237.
4. Sidney Lohman. "Radio and TV news." *New York Times*, March 13, 1949, sec. 2, p. 11.
5. Samuel Goldwyn. "Hollywood in the television age." *New York Times Magazine*, February 13, 1949, p. 15; Jack Gould. "Television, in big strides, advances." *New York Times*, April 24, 1949, sec. 10, p. 1.
6. "11,748,400 TV sets in US." *Variety* 182 (March 28, 1951): 26.
7. Michele Hilmes. "Film industry alternatives to the networks: subscription television, 1949–1962." *Quarterly Review of Film Studies* 10 (n. 3, 1985): 221.
8. "Radio and television." *New York Times*, November 10, 1948, p. 58.
9. Samuel Goldwyn. "Hollywood in..." pp. 44, 47
10. Thomas M. Pryor. "'B' pictures facing new hurdle?" *New York Times*, March 27, 1949, sec. 2, p. 5.
11. "Radio decline seen with television rise." *New York Times*, April 6, 1949, p. 58; Samuel Goldwyn. "Hollywood in..." p. 44.
12. "Television: movies' friend or foe?" op. cit., pp. 24–55.
13. "Television: boon to movies." op. cit.
14. Samuel Goldwyn. "Is Hollywood through?" *Colliers* 128 (September 29, 1951): 18-19.

15. "Movies come out of the dog house." *Business Week*, November 10, 1951, pp. 140–142.

16. Thomas M. Pryor, "TV impact on films believed at peak." *New York Times*, July 26, 1951, p. 17.

17. Abel Green. "Sarnoff sees special pix for TV taking a fall out of H'wood backlog." *Variety* 185 (February 20,1952):1, 20.

18. Ken Aulette. *Three Blind Mice*. New York: Random, 1991, p. 76; Thomas Brady. "Television blocks coast movie deal." *New York Times*, April 28, 1950, p. 26.

19. Bette Davis. "Whatever happened to Hollywood?" *U.S. News & World Report* 101 (December 8, 1986): 76.

20. William Brody. *Fifties Television*. Urbana: University of Illinois Press, 1990, p. 135.

21. "Probe Hollywood's video ban." *Variety* 182 (April 4, 1951): 3, 18.

22. Jack Gould. "FCC bids Hollywood end feud with television or face video bar." *New York Times*, March 30, 1951, pp. 1, 27.

23. "TV films." *New York Times*, April 3, 1951, pp. 26.

24. Jack Gould. "Hollywood and TV." *New York Times*, April 8, 1951, sec. 2, p. 11.

25. Thomas M. Pryor. "Nassers sue U.A. over video clause." *New York Times*, December 15, 1951, p. 11.

26. "Schary sees pix made for TV when sponsors pay $1,000,000 per film." *Variety* 190 (May 13, 1953): 1.

27. "Speed of switch to Cinemascope will key 20th's pix flow to video." *Variety* 190 (April 15, 1953): 3, 24.

28. "Pix-to-TV dam." *Variety* 190 (April 15, 1953): 3, 25.

29. Jack Hellman. "Old pix never die." *Variety* 195 (August 18, 1954): 23, 26.

30. William Lafferty, op. cit., pp. 234, 237.

31. Thomas Brady. "TV in Hollywood." *New York Times*, June 4, 1950, sec. 2, p. 9.

32. Thomas F. Brady. "Lippert, Petrillo in accord on video." *New York Times*, April 24, 1951, p. 35.

33. Thomas F. Brady. "Cuddling up to TV." *New York Times*, June 10, 1951, sec. 2, p. 3.

34. J.D. Spiro. "Hollywood and TV." *New York Times*, July 1, 1951, sec. 2, p. 3.

35. Thomas M. Pryor. "Film actors guild cancels contract." *New York Times*, September 6, 1951, p. 39.

36. "4 film firms yield on TV release pay." *New York Times*, June 18, 1952, p. 37.

37. "Roy Rogers in suit to bar films on TV." *New York Times*, June 24, 1951, p. 36; J.D. Spiro, op. cit.

38. "Two groups plan films in this city." *New York Times*, June 26, 1951, p. 25.
39. "Roy Rogers ruling bars film sale to TV." *New York Times*, October 19, 1951, p. 24; "Autry sues studio over films for TV." *New York Times*, October 31, 1951, p. 32.
40. Thomas M. Pryor. "TV-movie ties remain confused." *New York Times*, May 15, 1952, p. 39.
41. Thomas M. Pryor. "Hollywood edict." *New York Times*, June 13, 1954, sec. 2, p. 5.
42. "Actors lost TV case." *New York Times*, October 19, 1954, p. 34.
43. Thomas M. Pryor. "By way of report." *New York Times*, February 6, 1949, sec. 2, p. 5.
44. "Hollywood and TV." *Life* 32 (February 25, 1952): 20.
45. Thomas M. Pryor. "By way of report." *New York Times*, July 29, 1951, sec. 2, p. 3.
46. "Exhibs rear up at Republic for 200G leasing to CBS Video." *Variety* 189 (December 24, 1952): 3, 34.
47. "Exhibs burn at pix sales to TV." *Variety* 185 (March 5, 1952): 1, 8.
48. "Pix-to-TV dam." *Variety* 190 (April 15, 1953): 25.
49. Fred Hift. "Exhibs plead: Don't T(V)KO us." *Variety* 198 (April 6, 1955): 1, 54.
50. Val Adams. "Where old TV films come from." *New York Times*, June 11, 1950, sec. 2, p. 9.
51. "Feature film oldies reaping TV spot biz harvest, high rating." *Variety* 182 (March 28, 1951): 26, 34.
52. Thomas M. Pryor. "Movies for video produced quickly." *New York Times*, August 21, 1951, p. 23.
53. Jack Gould. "Radio and television." *New York Times*, September 26, 1951, p. 43.
54. "Video's 'movie-mad' audience." *Variety* 186 (April 30, 1952): 25, 30.
55. "200G Rep deal releasing 104 pix for TV seen breaking log jam." *Variety* 189 (December 17, 1952): 1, 63.
56. Hugh Garner. "Seen any bad movies lately?" *Saturday Night* 69 (May 1, 1954): 17–18.
57. "Movies that never die." *Newsweek* 45 (March 7, 1955): 56.
58. "TV gets 123 westerns." *New York Times*, March 23, 1955, p. 39.
59. Bob Chandler. "The economics of features on TV." *Variety* 198 (May 11, 1955): 39.

Chapter 2

1. Tino Balio, ed. *Hollywood in the Age of Television*. Boston: Unwin Hyman, 1990, pp. 20–21.

2. "Hollywood digs in." *Business Week,* March 24, 1945, pp. 92, 95.
3. Gladwin Hill. "Hollywood is wary of TV." *New York Times,* April 24, 1949, sec. 10, p. 18.
4. George Rosen. "Pix-networks alliance in '50." *Variety* 177 (December 28, 1949): 1, 46.
5. Tino Balio, op. cit., p. 21.
6. Michele Hilmes. "Film industry alternatives to the networks: subscription television, 1949–1962." *Quarterly Review of Film Studies* 10 (no. 3, 1985): 219.
7. "Television: movies' friend or foe?" *U.S. News & World Report* 26 (January 7, 1949): 25.
8. "Video will aid films, theatre owner says." *New York Times,* March 19, 1959, p. 82.
9. Samuel Goldwyn. "Television's challenge to the movies." *New York Times Magazine,* March 26, 1950, p. 17.
10. "TV and films seen linking fortunes." *New York Times,* April 25, 1950, p. 26.
11. "Too wary of theatre tele." *Variety* 179 (August 2, 1950): 1, 6.
12. "Movies: new sick industry." *Business Week,* November 25, 1950, p. 26.
13. "Fox displays Eidophone." *New York Times,* June 26, 1952, p. 24.
14. Tino Balio, op. cit., p. 22.
15. "And now 'Phonevision.'" *New York Times,* January 2, 1950, p. 26.
16. Phil Koury. "Phonevision issue." *New York Times,* February 19, 1950, sec. 2, p. 5.
17. "Phonevision block." *New York Times,* March 5, 1950, p. 4.
18. "Zenith Radio sees Phonevision fight." *New York Times,* May 26, 1950, p. 35.
19. "Phonevision dials wrong no." *Variety* 177 (February 22, 1950): 3, 18.
20. "Movies on home TV at $1 fee started." *New York Times,* January 2, 1951, p. 28.
21. Michele Hilmes, op. cit., p. 214.
22. "Hollywood learns how to live with TV." *Business Week,* August 9, 1952, p. 48.
23. Thomas M. Pryor. "Hollywood ready for test with TV." *New York Times,* September 14, 1953, p. 24.
24. Thomas M. Pryor. "Films on home TV earning $10 a set." *New York Times,* February 20, 1954, p. 9.
25. Thomas M. Pryor. "Coast theatres fight toll video." *New York Times,* October 30, 1954, p. 14.
26. Thomas M. Pryor "Hollywood report." *New York Times,* November 7, 1954, sec. 2, p. 5.
27. "TV experiment held up." *New York Times,* November 10, 1954, p. 48.

28. Michele Hilmes, op. cit., pp. 214–215.
29. "Sarnoff doesn't mince words as he lashes at toll-TV system." *Variety* 199 (June 8, 1955): 29–30.
30. Val Adams. "Give a horse a man who can ride." *New York Times*, October 8, 1950, sec. 2, p. 11.
31. "Paramount in all-out buildup of pix via use of stars on TV." *Variety* 177 (January 18, 1950): 2.
32. Jack Gould. "FCC bids Hollywood end feud with television or face video bar." *New York Times*, March 30, 1951, p. 27.
33. "Metro, NBC huddling on deal for pix stars to be worked in TV formats." *Variety* 191 (August 26, 1953): 3, 61.
34. Jack Gould. "TV: one long plus." *New York Times*, July 25, 1955, p. 41.
35. William Brody. *Fifties Television*. Urbana: University of Illinois Press, 1990, pp. 141, 143.
36. Thomas M. Pryor. "Columbia plans 39 movies for TV." *New York Times*, June 10, 1952, p. 23; Thomas. M. Pryor. "Hollywood canvas." *New York Times*, June 15, 1952, sec. 2, p. 5; "Hollywood learns..." op. cit., p. 47.
37. William Brody, op. cit., pp. 143, 145–147.
38. Ibid., p. 147.
39. Ibid., pp. 147–48.
40. "Par's TV marriage vows." *Variety* 198 (March 30, 1955): 1; George Rosen. "Pix get second TV chance." *Variety* 198 (April 20, 1955): 35.
41. Val Adams. "Metro to offer weekly TV show." *New York Times*, June 22, 1955, p. 59.
42. William Brody, op. cit., p. 148.
43. Tino Balio, op. cit., pp. 32–33.
44. William Brody, op. cit., p. 148.
45. Robert Vianello. "The rise of the telefilm and the networks' hegemony over the motion picture industry." *Quarterly Review of Film Studies* 9 (no. 3, Summer 1984): 207.
46. "TV-movie policy." *Business Week*, July 1, 1950, p. 21.
47. Val Adams. "ABC-TV obtains 39 British films." *New York Times*, July 25, 1955, p. 41.
48. "O'Neil envisions TV film circuit in RKO buy." *Variety* 199 (July 20, 1955): 20.
49. Thomas M. Pryor. "Hollywood test." *New York Times*, November 8, 1953, sec. 2, p. 5.
50. Thomas M. Pryor. "Hollywood trial." *New York Times*, September 18, 1955, sec. 2, p. 7.
51. "Movies ordered released for TV." *New York Times*, September 13, 1955, p. 63.
52. Thomas M. Pryor. "Yates reassures theaters on TV." *New York Times*, September 15, 1955, p. 39.

53. Thomas M. Pryor. "5 film companies deny conspiracy." *New York Times,* September 23, 1955, p. 49.

54. "TV official cites high cost of film." *New York Times,* October 5, 1955, p. 71.

55. "Film suit hears ex-head of RKO." *New York Times,* October 22, 1955, p. 24.

56. Thomas M. Pryor. "Skouras is heard at trial on coast." *New York Times,* October 27, 1955, p. 67.

57. "Warner is heard in antitrust suit." *New York Times,* November 1, 1955, p. 63.

58. Thomas M. Pryor. "Movie companies upheld on TV ban." *New York Times,* December 6, 1955, p. 45.

59. "U.S. drops suit against movies." *New York Times,* March 7, 1956, p. 38.

60. Jack Gould. "TV: $25,000,000 bargain." *New York Times,* July 21, 1955, p. 47.

61. "Free movies every night." *Time* 66 (August 1, 1955): 54–55.

62. Val Adams. "All RKO movies sold for TV use." *New York Times,* December 27, 1955, pp. 1, 47.

63. "TV pays $2-million for RKO film library." *Business Week,* December 31, 1955, p. 45.

64. Thomas. M. Pryor. "Film studio to lease 104 movies to video." *New York Times,* December 31, 1955, pp. 1, 17.

65. Thomas M. Pryor. "Hollywood sale." *New York Times,* January 1, 1956, sec. 2, p. 5.

66. "Hollywood finally sells to TV." *Business Week,* January 28, 1956, p. 54.

67. Bosley Crowther. "Sale of birthrights." *New York Times,* March 11, 1956, sec. 2, p. 1.

68. "Billion-dollar season for TV." *Business Week,* October 13, 1956, pp. 32, 34.

69. Jack Gould. "Video in Hollywood." *New York Times,* March 23, 1952, sec. 2, p. 11.

70. "TV and film: marriage of necessity." *Business Week,* August 15, 1953, p. 108; Jack Gould. "TV films boom Hollywood into its greatest prosperity." *New York Times,* July 3, 1955, p. 1.

71. Richard Bunce. *Television in the Corporate Interest.* New York: Praeger, 1976, p. 77.

72. Oscar Godbout. "Film fare held harmful to TV." *New York Times,* March 31, 1956, p. 29.

Chapter 3

1. Milton Esterow. "Metro planning wide TV activity." *New York Times*, June 21, 1956, p. 35.
2. J.P. Shanley. "Movies on video." *New York Times*, July 15, 1956, sec. 2, p. 9.
3. "725 MGM movies leased for video." *New York Times*, August 15, 1956, p. 59.
4. J.P. Shanley. "725 MGM movies leased for video." *New York Times*, August 25, 1956, p. 31.
5. "More Fox films sold for TV use." *New York Times*, November 2, 1956, p. 54.
6. "Leo's TV roar now a grunt." *Variety* 205 (January 16, 1957): 33.
7. Murray Horowitz. "TV's $150,000,000 for old pix." *Variety* 206 (May 1, 1957): 1, 50.
8. Gene Arneel. "Par pledges no post–1948 sell." *Variety* 209 (February 12, 1958): 3, 22.
9. "Pre–1948 selloff was 'must'—Selznick." *Variety* 209 (January 15, 1958): 3.
10. Tino Balio, ed. *Hollywood in the Age of Television*. Boston: Unwin Hyman 1990, p. 32; Murray Horowitz. "Pre–48's $200,000,000 jackpot." *Variety* 212 (October 1, 1958): 25.
11. Jack Gould. "Superior movies." *New York Times*, September 2, 1956, sec. 2, p. 13.
12. George Rosen. "TV readies a time bomb." *Variety* 202 (March 7, 1956): 23, 26.
13. Murray Horowitz. "WOR: TV's all-grind house." *Variety* 203 (August 22, 1956): 31, 40.
14. "Hoarding the blockbusters." *Variety* 205 (February 13, 1957): 67.
15. "Wait for it on television." *Variety* 208 (October 23, 1957): 3–4.
16. "WCBS–TV posts billion-viewer mark for 7 years of late show." *Variety* 210 (May 28, 1958): 52.
17. "A market-by-market telefilm appraisal." *Variety* 215 (July 8, 1959): 40, 42.
18. Murray Horowitz. "Market-by-market report on '58–'59 vidpix ascent." *Variety* 213 (January 14, 1959): 51.
19. "TV film ruling stands." *New York Times*, February 27, 1951, p. 22.
20. Richard Shepard. "Movies on TV—the unkindest cuts of all." *New York Times*, October 7, 1956, sec. 2, p. 11.
21. Murray Horowitz. "TV sugar-'codes' old features." *Variety* 306 (April 17, 1957): 1, 15.
22. Stephen Watts. "British screen scene." *New York Times*, June 23, 1959, sec. 2, p. 5.

Notes—Chapter 3

23. Abel Green. "Gen. Sarnoff deplores trend turning TV into 'motion picture circuit.'" *Variety* 201 (February 22, 1956): 63; "Educational TV stations." *New York Times*, December 14, 1956, pp. 1, 59.

24. Thomas M. Pryor. "Hollywood dilemma." *New York Times*, September 23, 1956, sec. 2, p. 7.

25. Thomas M. Pryor. "Movies on TV cut theatre business." *New York Times*, October 15, 1956, p. 28.

26. Murray Horowitz. "TV's 73,000,000-hour pic grind." *Variety* 203 (July 4, 1956): 1, 40.

27. Fred Hift. "Adjustment to TV is biggest issue." *Variety* 205 (January 9, 1957): 7; "Wedding of H'wood–TV inviting bigger 'n' ever monopoly hazard." *Variety* 206 (March 13, 1957): 1, 18.

28. "'See it soon on TV' misconception is murder for B.O." *Variety* 208 (November 6, 1957): 1, 79.

29. "TV-bird-in-hand lost $60-mil?" *Variety* 209 (Dec. 18, 1957): 5, 18.

30. Bosley Crowther. "Old movies on TV peril Hollywood." *New York Times*, January 27, 1958, p. 55.

31. "What TV is doing to the movie industry." *U.S. News & World Report*, February 7, 1958, p. 88.

32. "How old is too old?" *Variety* 209 (January 22, 1958): 11.

33. Murray Horowitz. "TV feature famine dilemma." *Variety* 212 (September 17, 1958): 29.

34. Harold Goldman. "5,000 feature exposures a week." *Variety* 215 (July 8, 1959): 31.

35. "Block booking of old features assailed." *Variety* 202 (April 25, 1956): 31, 35.

36. "Justice Dept. ruling seen imminent." *Variety* 206 (March 27, 1957): 22.

37. "Loew's sales to TV cited in trust suit." *New York Times*, April 19, 1957, p. 63.

38. Val Adams. "Slezak will star in fall TV series." *New York Times*, April 19, 1957, p. 43.

39. "M-G's new flexible sales plan on features." *Variety* 206 (April 10, 1957): 35, 38.

40. "Long drawn-out legal hassle seen." *Variety* 206 (April 24, 1957): 22, 38.

41. "AAP's 'VIP' sales pattern." *Variety* 209 (January 15, 1958): 31.

42. "WCBS-TV pays record $8,400,000 for Par's library of 700 pix." *Variety* 210 (May 14, 1958): 21.

43. "KNXT's enviable status: 7 years of first-run product still on tap." *Variety* 212 (October 1, 1958): 25, 45.

44. "20th–Fox still has 300 pre '35s, but are they marketable?" *Variety* 219 (July 20, 1960): 27.

45. "U.S. wins decision in TV-movies suit." *New York Times*, December 3, 1960, p. 47.
46. "Movie block-booking hit again." *Business Week*, December 10, 1960, p. 38.
47. "Justice Dept. asking for reversal of ruling on vidpix block-booking." *Variety* 224 (November 22, 1961): 24.
48. Anthony Lewis. "TV block booking of movies barred." *New York Times*, November 6, 1962, pp. 1, 14.
49. "The future of features on TV." *Variety* 215 (July 8, 1959): 30.
50. "Most stations don't go for extra premium on color-casting of pix." *Variety* 205 (February 13, 1957): 67.
51. "Why do H'wood studios sell off pix oldies?" *Variety* 219 (July 13, 1960): 25.
52. "Video rises on Par's horizon." *Variety* 205 (January 2, 1957): 5, 63.
53. Russell Porter. "3 companies sued as TV film trust." *New York Times*, April 11, 1958, pp. 1, 22.
54. "U.S. to appeal TV film ruling." *Business Week*, August 13, 1960, pp. 53–54.

Chapter 4

1. Milton Esterow. "Metro planning wide TV activity." *New York Times*, June 21, 1956, p. 35.
2. "Majors' race for TV dollar." *Variety* 205 (February 27, 1957): 27, 34.
3. "All majors now active." *Variety* 209 (February 19, 1958): 24.
4. "Though comparison lopsized cheapies made for television influence Paramount's ideas." *Variety* 212 (October 8, 1958): 5
5. Murray Horowitz. "Don't pin hopes on post-48s." *Variety* 215 (July 29, 1959): 25, 95.
6. "Movie-in-home TV is shown on coast." *New York Times*, March 22, 1957, p. 47.
7. Thomas M. Pryor. "Film groups seek pay-TV franchise." *New York Times*, July 20, 1957, p. 33.
8. "Video can't pay for itself." *Variety* 207 (June 5, 1957): 3, 10.
9. "Electronic home theatre." *Variety* 205 (December 12, 1956): 3, 20.
10. "New film is piped into homes." *New York Times*, September 4, 1957, p. 67.
11. Fred Hift. "Coming to grips with pay-TV." *Variety* 208 (September 11, 1957): 5, 22.
12. "Meter TV films to end on June 6." *New York Times*, May 23, 1958, p. 46.

13. Hy Hollinger. "Theatre owners condemn any/all 'toll.'" *Variety* 208 (November 27, 1957): 31.
14. "Trade unit hits toll TV." *New York Times,* June 17, 1957, p. 47.
15. Mervyn LeRoy. "Motion pictures and pay TV." *Atlantic Monthly* 200 (December, 1957): 84–86.
16. "Oddity of AFM status re TV strike." *Variety* 217 (December 30, 1959): 3.
17. "TV plan approved by actors group." *New York Times,* December 19, 1956, p. 62.
18. "Hollywood: they shall not sell *U.S. News and World Report* down TV syndicators river." *Variety* 209 (January 22, 1958): 3, 11.
19. Murray Horowitz. "Despite all the 'hold the line' talk." *Variety* 210 (May 28, 1958): 26, 52.
20. "Residual deals on 17 more post–48s negotiated by SAG." *Variety* 215 (July 15, 1959): 39.
21. "Ours alone to sell position by majors presages TV-residuals showdown." *Variety* 217 (December 2, 1959): 3.
22. Vincent Canby. "Skouras-eye view of strike." *Variety* 217 (December 30, 1959): 2, 48.
23. "Talent guilds' $30-mil stake-out based on post–48 films $190–$250-mil value." *Variety* 217 (January 20, 1960): 1, 4; Murray Schumach. "Producers group hits film unions." *New York Times,* February 1, 1960, p. 22.
24. Bob Chandler. "U's TV terms to actors: 3.6%" *Variety* 218 (March 2, 1960): 3.
25. "Accord reached in movie strike." *New York Times,* April 9, 1960, p. 21; "SAG-majors peace pipe not figured to unleash post–'48s in a hurry." *Variety* 218 (April 6, 1960): 33, 54.
26. Thomas M. Pryor. "Movie producers oppose TV sales." *New York Times,* December 4, 1957, p. 52.
27. "Television as theatre rival dominates Dallas meet." *Variety* 205 (December 5, 1956): 31.
28. "Draw fangs of the television beast." *Variety* 209 (January 1, 1958): 17.
29. "Gordon to firms: don't sell any to TV for next 3 yrs." *Variety* 209 (January 15, 1958); 3, 22.
30. "Texas exhibs design 'no-television' seal." *Variety* 209 (January 1, 1958): 17.
31. "20th's clearance pledge okay–D. of J." *Variety* 209 (January 22, 1958): 11.
32. "Pressure majors on post–'48s." *Variety* 209 (February 5, 1958): 27.
33. "Post-48s 'sure' for TV; Reade blames exhibs." *Variety* 212 (September 17, 1958): 1, 22.
34. "Hedged 'promises' on post–'48." *Variety* 209 (February 26, 1958): 7.

35. "Feed the kitty or video will." *Variety* 210 (May 7, 1958): 7.
36. Murray Horowitz. "Theatre reissue $ mocks TV." *Variety* 209 (January 1, 1958): 5.
37. "Suppose we selloff to TV." *Variety* 216 (November 18, 1959): 3.
38. "Will feature films reshape TV?" *Business Week*, November 24, 1956, pp. 132, 134.
39. William Brody. *Fifties Television*. Urbana: University of Illinois Press, 1990, pp. 137, 139.
40. "Networks may open up prime time." *Variety* 205 (January 16, 1957): 33, 44.
41. "ABC-TV options 52 RKO features to compete with Sullivan, Allen." *Variety* 205 (February 13, 1957): 31.
42. Leonard Goldenson. *Beating the Odds*. New York: Scribners, 1991, pp. 153–154.
43. William Lafferty. "Feature films on prime time television." In Tino Balio, ed. *Hollywood in the Age of Television*. Boston: Unwin Hyman, 1990, p. 241.
44. Gene Arneel. "$50,000,000 CBS-Par pix deal." *Variety* 205 (February 27, 1957): 1, 15.
45. Murray Horowitz. "Post–'48s in webs' future?" *Variety* 219 (August 17, 1960): 25.
46. "$2,200,000 sales in UA's bundle of post–48 features." *Variety* 205 (February 13, 1957): 31, 52.
47. "UA in unique status on post–'48 features." *Variety* 206 (March 20, 1957): 31, 52.
48. "Wait for it on television." *Variety* 208 (October 23, 1957): 3–4.
49. Jack Gould. "Movies for TV." *New York Times*, July 24, 1960, sec. 2, p. 11.
50. Murray Horowitz. "20th–Fox unloading post–'48s." *Variety* 219 (July 20, 1960): 27.
51. Art Woodstone. "TV features' sound economy." *Variety* 220 (August 31, 1960): 25, 37.
52. "$12,500,000 post–'48 pix sale." *Variety* 221 (November 30, 1960): 27.
53. "Majors release 600 post–'48s." *Variety* 224 (November 15, 1961): 25.
54. "7 Arts in $21,500,000 U buy." *Variety* 231 (July 17, 1963): 49.
55. "Post–1950 films on TV in doses, and exhibs fret." *Variety* 229 (December 12, 1962): 1, 60.
56. "Good reruns better 'n ever." *Variety* 205 (February 13, 1957): 31.
57. Murray Horowitz. "Features vs. live drama." *Variety* 209 (February 26, 1958): 23, 26; Murray Horowitz. "'60–'61 on webs: mostly film." *Variety* 217 (February 17, 1960): 23.
58. Peter Bart. "Advertising: business is brisk for TV time." *New York*

Times, August 8, 1961, p. 44; Val Adams. "News of TV and radio." *New York Times,* August 13, 1961, sec. 2, p. 13.

59. "NBC-TV: Sat nite movie night." *Variety* 221 (December 21, 1960): 19.

Chapter 5

1. "Wanna TV-sale watchdog?" *Variety* 241 (February 9, 1966): 7.
2. "Screen Gems brochure an issue." *Variety* 241 (February 9, 1966): 7.
3. "Networks cool to dubbed pix." *Variety* 242 (May 4, 1966): 175.
4. Murray Horowitz. "Syndication's peak pix prices." *Variety* 231 (August 7, 1963): 39; "$100,000,000 syndie gross." *Variety* 233 (January 1, 1964): 25; Murray Horowitz. "11,000 pix on TV – $725 mil." *Variety* 233 (February 5, 1964): 1, 42.
5. Murray Horowitz. "Films' $400,000,000 from TV." *Variety* 238 (April 14, 1965): 1, 68.
6. "What they paid for features." *Variety* 241 (February 2, 1966): 32.
7. "See end of pix spiral era." *Variety* 243 (April 10, 1966): 35, 47.
8. "1967 financial markets—top 50 U.S. TV markets." *Variety* 252 (October 9, 1968): 32.
9. Larry Michie. "Television's 1973 'operation moneybag.'" *Variety* 276 (September 4, 1974): 39.
10. "TV's 10,427 features." *Variety* 232 (October 30, 1963): 31; "Comm'l TV station count." *Variety* 252 (September 11, 1968): 35.
11. Bill Greeley. "692 movies 'prime' local TV." *Variety* 255 (May 28, 1969): 1, 79; "Every night at the movies." *Look* 35 (September 7, 1971): 62.
12. William Lafferty. "Feature films on prime time television." In, Tino Balio, ed. *Hollywood in the Age of Television.* Boston: Unwin Hyman, 1990, p. 245.
13. "41 not-so-old pix every week in competition." *Variety* 224 (November 1, 1961): 3, 21.
14. Murray Schumach. "Movie men wary about TV deals." *New York Times,* December 26, 1961, p. 28.
15. Murray Horowitz. "TV's battle for cinematics." *Variety* 227 (April 18, 1962): 27, 45.
16. Val Adams. "Formula: more movies." *New York Times,* April 7, 1963, sec. 2, p. 23.
17. "ABC-TV's Tom Moore pledges affils, 'no features in 1963–64 prime time.'" *Variety* 231 (June 26, 1963): 29.
18. Hollis Alpert. "Now the earlier, earlier show." *New York Times Magazine* August 11, 1963, pp. 22–23.
19. Val Adams. "NBC-TV acquires post-1948 movies." *New York Times,* February 12, 1964, p. 67; Murray Horowitz. "It's open season on pix-to-TV." *Variety* 234 (March 4, 1964): 35.

Notes—Chapter 5   213

20. Jack Gould. "Fade-out on old movies." *New York Times*, September 5, 1965, sec. 2, p. 11.

21. "Col, WB Metro top TV pix ratings." *Variety* 243 (April 10, 1966): 35; Murray Horowitz. "TV's $52-mil pix 'insurance.'" *Variety* 244 (August 21, 1966): 1, 62.

22. Jack Gould. "TV review." *New York Times*, September 26, 1966, p. 83.

23. Jack Gould. "Two networks invest $92.3-million on TV films." *New York Times*, September 28, 1966, p. 95.

24. Charles Champlin. "The American motion picture: 1966." *Saturday Review* 49 (December 24, 1966): 12–13.

25. Les Brown. "Set 7th night of TV movies." *Variety* 249 (December 27, 1967): 1, 34.

26. Tino Balio, ed. *Hollywood in the Age of Television*. Boston: Unwin, Hyman, 1990, p. 38.

27. Leonard Goldenson. *Beating the Odds*. New York: Scribners, 1991, pp. 251–252.

28. "TV webs paying less for pix." *Variety* 264 (November 10, 1971): 1, 39.

29. "CBS late features budgeted at 40G." *Variety* 245 (November 23, 1966): 31, 46.

30. Bill Greeley. "Movies: TV's 50-minute hour." *Variety* 245 (November 23, 1966): 31, 46.

31. "Webs '69–'70 feature rates." *Variety* 254 (April 30, 1969): 35; "TV's $3½-billion '73." *Variety* 276 (September 4, 1974): 39.

32. "Pre-48s: '67,500,000 untapped." *Variety* 233 (November 15, 1961): 25.

33. "TV cinematics' brisk biz." *Variety* 233 (December 11, 1963): 27.

34. "'Movie station' (KHJ-TV) sprinkled with culture: parlay pays off." *Variety* 224 (November 22, 1961): 25.

35. Paul Gardner. "Late late show addiction." *New York Times*, November 3, 1963, sec. 2, p. 15; Murray Horowitz. "Economics of TV cinematics." *Variety* 228 (October 31, 1962): 31, 38.

36. Jack Hellman. "L.A.'s features-to-TV stockpile: $50,000,000." *Variety* 235 (July 29, 1964): 37.

37. Robert Dallos. "Local TV stations are running out of movies." *New York Times*, August 13, 1968, p. 79.

38. George Gent. "Preminger stops film's sale to TV." *New York Times*, May 10, 1965, p. 67.

39. Peter Bart. "NBC–TV is sued by film director." *New York Times*, October 27, 1965, p. 39.

40. "Preminger loses case on film cuts." *New York Times*, January 20, 1966, p. 71.

41. Peter Bart. "NBC–TV is sued..." op. cit.

42. "Stevens sues NBC and Par." *Variety* 240 (October 27, 1965): 1, 24.

43. Peter Bart. "'Place in the Sun' is spared scissors." *New York Times*, February 14, 1966, p. 33.

44. Jack Gould. "The unkindest cut of all." *New York Times*, February 27, 1966, sec. 2, p. 23.

45. Peter Bart. "NBC is upheld on commercials." *New York Times*, June 4, 1966, p. 18.

46. "Stevens loses suit over his film on TV." *New York Times*, May 24, 1967, p. 95.

47. "Holden sues to bar TV 'Kwai.'" *New York Times*, July 19, 1966, p. 33.

48. Murray Horowitz. "NAB post–48 censor threat." *Variety* 222 (May 10, 1961): 31, 68.

49. "NAB's new caution on post–'48s." *Variety* 224 (September 20, 1961): 25.

50. "Whatever happened to that NAB screening of post–'48s?" *Variety* 228 (October 31, 1962): 31.

51. Larry Glenn. "Hollywood cloud." *New York Times*, December 2, 1962, sec. 2, p. 9.

52. "Everybody's rights trampled upon when TV stations mutilate." *Variety* 241 (December 8, 1965): 5.

53. Robert Lewis Shayon. "David and the network Goliaths." *Saturday Review* 52 (November 1, 1969): 52.

54. "TV films trimmed, F.T.C. survey finds." *New York Times*, July 9, 1970, p 75.

55. Hollis Alpert. "Now the earlier, earlier show." *New York Times Magazine*, August 11, 1963, p. 38.

56. Jack Hellman. "L.A.'s features-to-TV stockpile: $50,000,000." *Variety* 235 (July 29, 1964): 37.

57. Jack Gould. "We interrupt this commercial for a movie." *New York Times*, December 3, 1967, sec. 2, p. 21.

58. "Although it Hertz." *Variety* 244 (September 28, 1966): 49; Val Adams. "Psycho gets the ax." *New York Times*, December 18, 1966, sec. 2, p. 21.

59. Bill Greeley. "Butchery in TV's grindhouse." *Variety* 244 (October 19, 1966): 1, 36.

60. "Every night at the movies." *Look* 35 (September 7, 1981): 62–63.

61. William Johnson. "Hold it! Where's that great scene with..." *New York Times*, May 26, 1974, sec. 2, p. 13.

62. David Black. "How the gosh-darn networks edit the heck out of movies." *New York Times*, January 26, 1975, sec. 2, pp. 1, 33.

63. Ibid.

64. "Letters." *New York Times*, February 9, 1975, p. 27.

65. "Bowdlerizing 'The Last Detail.'" *New York Times*, February 22, 1976 sec. 2, p. 29.
66. Ernest Callenbach. "Television 'version.'" *Film Quarterly* 29 (Winter, 1975): 1–2.
67. "33% of recent pix tabu for TV." *Variety* 238 (April 21, 1965): 29.
68. Vincent Canby. "Catholic film office is easing policy." *New York Times*, April 9, 1966, p. 11.
69. Murray Horowitz. "New blood line of pix & TV." *Variety* 245 (January 4, 1967): 83, 98.
70. "Adult films-to-TV problem." *Variety* 256 (September 24, 1969): 1, 38.
71. Dave Kaufman. "Universal to prepare alternative scenes for TV of too-rough footage." *Variety* 256 (October 8, 1969): 35, 49.
72. Frank Beerman. "Estimate 30 CBS stations dropouts for X-rated pix." *Variety* 266 (March 8, 1972): 1, 71.
73. George Dugan. "Baptists say films are lacking in social values." *New York Times*, June 8, 1972, p. 50.
74. "Reel attraction." *Newsweek* 66 (November 15, 1965): 116, 118; Les Brown. "'66–67: season without salt." *Variety* 244 (September 28, 1966): 49.
75. Ronald Gold. "New era of film security." *Variety* 244 (October 12, 1966): 1, 30.
76. Les Brown. "Pix on TV." *Variety* 244 (October 12, 1966): 35.
77. Murray Horowitz. "New mix for networks pix." *Variety* 244 (December 28, 1966): 23.
78. "Rating RV pix on theatre B.O." *Variety* 248 (September 6, 1967): 38.
79. Jack Gould. "The movie revolution." *New York Times*, October 8, 1967, sec. 2, p. 27; Les Brown. "Movie gang-up, CBS hang up." *Variety* 252 (September 18, 1968): 33, 52.
80. Bob Knight. "TV nights are 'made' by movies." *Variety* 268 (October 25, 1972): 1, 59.
81. Les Brown. "NBC will pinch hit for baseball." *New York Times*, April 24, 1975, p. 70.
82. Bob Knight. "Fed up with reel life, webs nix pix." *Variety* 278 (May 7, 1975): 327, 335.
83. Murray Horowitz. "NBC-TV skeds 3 pic repeats at 1st run prices." *Variety* 242 (May 11, 1966): 33.
84. "Pix payoff in 2d playoff." *Variety* 248 (October 11, 1967): 71.
85. "ABC web wanted off-CBS features its O&Os bought." *Variety* 245 (December 14, 1966): 25, 42.
86. Bill Greeley. "Lotsa juice in NBC 3d-runs." *Variety* 254 (February 26, 1969): 43.
87. Bill Greeley. "Short season for new pix." *Variety* 270 (January 17, 1973): 35.

88. Bill Greeley. "Great off-web movie grinder." *Variety* 275 (June 5, 1974): 1, 70.

89. "Rerun issue grinds away." *Variety* 277 (February 5, 1975): 45, 62.

Chapter 6

1. "That post–'60 residual pie." *Variety* 234 (February 26, 1964): 39.

2. Peter Bart. "Actors alarmed by movies on TV." *New York Times*, July 7, 1965, p. 25.

3. Peter Bart. "'Hawaii' changes directors twice." *New York Times*, August 4, 1965, p. 22.

4. Val Adams. "TV primes Hollywood." *New York Times*, January 19, 1967, p. 71; "Majors' 34 hours vs. indies' 18 on webs for '72–'73." *Variety* 267 (May 31, 1972): 34.

5. Les Brown. "TV '69–'70: yesterday's bijou." *Variety* 252 (August 28, 1968): 33, 42.

6. Jack Gould. "TV faces a fight on movie-making." *New York Times*, October 23, 1967, pp. 1, 90.

7. Leonard Sloane. "TV movies now major factor in filmdom." *New York Times*, March 13, 1970, pp. 53, 56.

8. A.H. Weiler. "7 movie companies sue A.B.C., C.B.S. over programming." *New York Times*, September 30, 1970, p. 39.

9. "Pix biz sues TV: 'monopoly.'" *Variety* 260 (Sept. 30, 1970): 1, 25.

10. Arnold Lubasch. "ABC counters film trust suit." *New York Times*, April 15, 1971, p. 86.

11. Lee Beaupre. "ABC pix: post-mortem 'audit.'" *Variety* 271 (May 30, 1973): 5, 22.

12. "Once fought ABC films, now got them." *Variety* 276 (October 30, 1974): 5.

13. Leonard Goldenson. *Beating the Odds*. New York: Scribners, 1991, p. 254.

14. George Rosen. "New H'wood pix preem on TV." *Variety* 231 (June 12, 1963): 1, 44.

15. "TV and Hollywood sing a new duet." *Business Week*, April 16, 1966, p. 108.

16. "ABC-TV in whopping deal for features." *Variety* 240 (August 25, 1965): 25; "Metro at 'bridge pic' crossing." *Variety* 240 (August 25, 1965): 25.

17. Peter Bart. "TV-film accords arousing doubts." *New York Times*, March 10, 1966, p. 26.

18. Peter Bart. "TV moviemaking begins in earnest." *New York Times*, Januart 7, 1966, p. 26.

19. "TV and Hollywood sing a new duet." *Business Week*, April 16, 1966, p. 108.

Notes—Chapter 6 217

    20. Murray Horowitz. "A season to reason on pix." *Variety* 242 (May 4, 1966): 175; "Can 'made for TV' features equal the audience pull of theatricals?" *Variety* 242 (May 4, 1966): 175.
    21. "CBS taps indies for feature pix." *Variety* 243 (August 17, 1966): 19.
    22. Peter Bart. "The gold rush is on." *New York Times,* October 30, 1966, sec. 2, p. 11; Val Adams. "Are TV movies better than ever?" *New York Times,* November 27, 1966, sec. 2, p. 21.
    23. Les Brown. "NBC comes in from the cold." *Variety* 245 (December 14, 1966): 25, 42.
    24. "Non-movie movies." *Time* 89 (January 13, 1967): 42.
    25. "Rating TV pix on theatre B.O." *Variety* 248 (September 6, 1967): 38.
    26. "CBS pays Metro $700,000 apiece." *Variety* 248 (October 4, 1967): 3.
    27. George Gent. "C.B.S. to produce feature movies." *New York Times,* December 6, 1967, p. 95.
    28. Les Brown. "Set 7th night of TV movies." *Variety* 249 (December 27, 1967): 34.
    29. Leonard Goldenson. op. cit., p. 255.
    30. "Movies on the tube." *Newsweek* 79 (April 10, 1972): 87–88.
    31. Benjamin Stein. "Hooked on television movies." *Saturday Evening Post* 246 (May, 1974): 30–33, 144.
    32. Larry Glenn. "Testing Hollywood." *New York Times,* Dec. 9, 1962, p. 11.
    33. "California gets pay television with programs on 3 channels." *New York Times,* July 18, 1964, p. 47.
    34. "Pay–TV acquires first-run films." *New York Times,* July 23, 1964, p. 54.
    35. "Paramount films will go on pay–TV." *New York Times,* August 7, 1964, p. 55; "Pay–TV vote drive to cost $2 million." *New York Times,* August 17, 1964, pp. 1, 51.
    36. Peter Bart. "California votes to bar pay–TV." *New York Times,* November 5, 1964, p. 91.
    37. Val Adams. "Pay–TV stalled by money needs." *New York Times,* March 4, 1966, p. 67; "Supreme Court rules California cannot prohibit pay television." *New York Times,* October 11, 1966, p. 95.
    38. Joseph Wright. "Subscription TV may recapture lost audience for motion pictures." *Variety* 257 (January 7, 1970): 68.
    39. Les Brown. "New film box office: hotels." *Variety* 263 (June 30, 1971): 62.
    40. Jack Gould. "Pay–TV for apartments is proposed." *New York Times,* October 8, 1971, p. 86.
    41. Robert Landry. "Exhibs fear 'motel movies.'" *Variety* 264 (October 27, 1971): 3.
    42. Leonard Sloane. "Pay-as-you-view movies for hotels." *New York Times,* November 14, 1971, sec. 3, p. 5.

43. Larry Michie. "FCC: 'open door' for hotel pix." *Variety* 269 (January 24, 1972): 1, 62.
44. Val Adams. "CATV is debated by broadcasters." *New York Times,* January 20, 1966, p. 71.
45. "Cable pay-see big ticket for pix." *Variety* 266 (March 1, 1972): 34.
46. "TWC-Viacom pay-cable bow." *Variety* 271 (July 19, 1973): 26.
47. Frank Beerman. "Sterling project for N.Y. pay–TV." *Variety* 271 (July 18, 1973): 24.
48. "NATO asks FCC to ban pay–TV pix on Warner's cable systems." *Variety* 273 (January 16, 1974): 51.
49. "Feature pix are backbone of pay–TV." *Variety* 276 (September 25, 1974): 35, 42.
50. "Warners' use of films on CATV not 'alternative theatre' to FCC." *Variety* 278 (March 19, 1975): 16.
51. Larry Michie. "New film B.O. horizons on cable TV." *Variety* 279 (May 21, 1975): 1, 78.
52. Paul Harris. "Web pix exclusivity bedevils pay–C." *Variety* 279 (May 28, 1975): 57, 70.
53. Christopher Lydon. "F.C.C. puts limit on networks' TV." *New York Times,* May 8, 1970, pp. 1, 63.
54. "MPAA bids FCC suspend rules curbing pix, series on pay cable." *Variety* 275 (July 31, 1974): 37.
55. "NAB asks FCC to kayo movie and sports rules for pay cable." *Variety* 279 (May 14, 1975): 133.
56. "Exhib fret: for whom cable tolls." *Variety* 280 (October 8, 1975): 7, 36.
57. Larry Michie. "Pay cable payoff on pix too pallid now: Columbia." *Variety* 280 (October 1, 1975): 84, 104.
58. Steve Toy. "OTP draft blames network rivalry." *Variety* 269 (January 31, 1973): 33, 42.

Chapter 7

1. "TV homes at 80-mil." *Variety* 303 (June 3, 1981): 1.
2. Barry R. Litman. "The economics of the television market for theatrical movies." *Journal of Communication* 29 (n.4, 1979): 28–33.
3. Bob Knight. "Network film paradox: cutting back in winter but 22 hours airing now." *Variety* 303 (June 24, 1981): 40, 70.
4. John Dempsey. "Offer 'Empire,' 'Star Wars' to TV." *Variety* 304 (October 21, 1981): 1, 80.
5. "NBC coughs up $70 mil for Par pix." *Variety* 311 (July 27, 1983): 43, 57.

6. Dave Kaufman. "ABC topper sez teevee pix deals hurting H'wood." *Variety* 314 (March 7, 1984): 377, 385.
7. "ABC gobbles up 'Ghostbusters' for $15-million after HBO play." *Variety* 316 (September 19, 1984): 47.
8. John Dempsey. "As webs close doors on theatricals, majors use other TV windows." *Variety* 324 (August 13, 1986): 33, 48.
9. Thomas Morgan. "Networks raise ratings by showing more films." *New York Times*, October 23, 1986, p. C26.
10. Howard Polskin. "TV's love affair with the movies." *TV Guide* 38 (May 26, 1990): 16–18.
11. "Midseason primetime schedule 1995–1996." *Variety* 360 (January 8, 1996): 63.
12. Gary Levin. "Hit films form pricey platforms." *Variety* 363 (June 3, 1996): 25–26.
13. John Dempsey. "Big four b'casters line up around the blockbusters." *Variety*, September 2, 1996, pp. 23, 26.
14. John Dempsey. "Webs go extra mile to pack pix." *Variety*, June 9, 1997, pp. 21, 23.
15. "Nets bet bucks on pix appeal." *Variety*, January 12, 1998, pp. 79, 84.
16. John Dempsey. "Showtime sees silver lining in cloud around original pix." *Variety* 360 (November 6, 1995): 40.
17. "Primetime schedule." *Vancouver Sun TVtimes*, Sept. 5–11, 1997, p. 11.
18. Aljean Harmetz. "Movies are revised for TV showings." *New York Times*, December 3, 1978, p. 101.
19. John T. O'Connor. "When films go under the knife." *New York Times*, July 16, 1978, sec. 2, p. 25.
20. Janet Maslin. "Cable TV, home video and chopping of movies." *New York Times*, March 25, 1982, p. C19.
21. Lawrence Linderman. "Son of a buck, Godfather: what have they done to you?" *TV Guide* 30 (July 17, 1982): 4–6.
22. Ibid., pp. 6–8.
23. Jay Cocks. "The shape of things that were." *Time* 120 (August 30, 1982): 78.
24. Aljean Harmetz. "ABC cancels 'Reds' after prohibition on editing." *New York Times*, April 17, 1985, p. C26.
25. Bill Daniels. "Directors seek TV disclaimer on edited films." *Variety* 321 (January 22, 1986): 32.
26. Bette Davis. "What ever happened to Hollywood?" *U.S. News & World Report* 101 (December 8, 1986): 76.
27. Hy Bender. "Dogmatic disclaimers." *American Film* 14 (May, 1989): 12–13.
28. Nicholas Meyer. "Are the networks trimming more than just film." *New York Times*, January 22, 1989, sec. 2, p. 27.

29. "Hill seeks final cut on edited films." *Broadcasting* 122 (March 2, 1992): 29.

30. "DGA pans altered states of movies." *Broadcasting* 122 (March 9, 1992): 14.

31. Bernard Weinraub. "Warning: this movie is harmful to directors." *New York Times*, March 9, 1993, pp. C13–C14.

32. Dennis Wharton. "MPAA members say they'll 'fess up' to altered states." *Variety* 353 (November 8, 1993): 17.

33. Dennis Wharton. "Scorsese plugs for artists' rights on Hill." *Variety* 358 (March 20, 1995): 20.

34. Don Carle Gillette. "With sex and gore pix off-limits TV faces famine of new films." *Variety* 282 (February 25, 1976): 1, 76.

35. James M. Wall. "Pornographic violence and public outrage." *Christian Century* 93 (December 15, 1976): 1115–1116.

36. Geri Fabrikant. "B.O. smash pic can be home-tube no-no." *Variety* 299 (July 9, 1980): 7, 30.

37. Kirk Honeycutt. "Made for TV movies." *New York Times*, August 19, 1979, sec. 2, pp. 1, 27.

38. Judith Crist. "TV movies in disguise." *Saturday Review* 8 (March, 1981): 86–87.

39. Lawrence Cohn. "Made-for ancillary pics burgeoning." *Variety* 311 (July 6, 1983): 3, 35.

40. John Dempsey. "Majors pass up telepics & minis." *Variety* 316 (October 17, 1984): 1, 147.

41. "Made-fors fill CBS movie nights as web stops buying theatricals." *Variety* 319 (May 22, 1985): 47.

42. Laurie Schulze. "The made-for-TV movies." In Tino Balio, ed. *Hollywood in the Age of Television*. Boston: Unwin Hyman, 1990, pp. 358, 362–363.

43. Bill Carter. "Media." *New York Times*, July 15, 1996, p. D9.

44. John Dempsey. "Mickey's mad for made-fors." *Variety* 368 (September 1, 1997): 87.

45. Dave Kaufman. "Feds probe TV block booking by syndicators." *Variety* 291 (August 2, 1978): 58.

46. Geri Fabrikant. "Box office smash pic can be home-tube no-no." *Variety* 299 (July 9, 1980): 7, 30.

47. John Dempsey. "MCA may shut pay cable window for hit Universal pictures." *Variety* 337 (November 8, 1989): 1–2.

48. "Typical TV station profits top $1-mil." *Variety* 307 (June 9, 1982): 43.

49. Dave Kaufman. "Majors now minors on web skeds." *Variety* 296 (August 22, 1979): 1, 69.

50. Aljean Harmetz. "Hollywood seeks control of outlets." *New York Times*, March 3, 1986, pp. D1, D5.

51. "Primetime studio scorecard." *Variety* 323 (May 21, 1986): 61, 87.
52. Ken Auletta. *Three Blind Mice*. New York: Random, 1991, pp. 198–200.
53. Mark Lewyn. "The networks vs. Hollywood: it's prime time for a truce." *Business Week*, April 9, 1990, p. 26.
54. "The friendly giant." *Newsweek* 127 (February 19, 1996): 49.
55. Jenny Hontz. "Warners top supplier ... but can't crack WB." *Variety*, June 2, 1997, p. 24.
56. John Dempsey. "UPN beams Sci-fi flicks Thursdays." *Variety* 368 (September 1, 1997): 21–22.
57. Martin Peers. "Giants chow down indies." *Variety* 368 (September 29, 1997): 31, 37.
58. John Dempsey. "U pix may be USA capital." *Variety* 368 (September 29, 1997): 31, 37.
59. John Dempsey. "H'wood majors eye ad-hoc TV networks." *Variety* 315 (June 13, 1984): 41, 70.
60. John Dempsey. "MGM/UA building barter film web." *Variety* 315 (June 13, 1984): 1, 82.
61. Jack Loftus. "H'wood starts indie films webs." *Variety* 317 (December 19, 1984): 1, 94.
62. Jim Benson. "Par takes the fifth." *Variety* 353 (November 8, 1993): 17, 21, 51.
63. John Dempsey. "New movie game for majors." *Variety* 356 (October 3, 1994): 30.
64. Joe Flint. "WB, Par weblets square off." *Variety* 357 (January 2, 1995): 37.
65. John Dempsey. "Future stock: movie libraries dictate next cable net battle." *Variety* 359 (May 29, 1995): 21, 25.
66. Mark Woods. "Warner signing on in Oz." *Variety*, September 2, 1996, p. 32.
67. Robert Engelman. "FCC, perhaps miffed at court turns down pay cable demands to life movie exclusivity pacts." *Variety* 288 (September 28, 1977): 45, 52.
68. John Dempsey. "Film-buying TV stations riled over title diddles." *Variety* 303 (June 3, 1981): 50.
69. John Dempsey. "Studios now looking to pay–TV as a major source of ancillary coin, abbreviated syndie playoff." *Variety* 309 (December 29, 1982): 1, 34.
70. "Double-edged disappointment." *Time* 121 (March 7, 1983): 69.
71. Stephen Taub. "Sunny skies ahead for the old dream machine." *Financial World* 152 (July 15, 1983): 46.
72. "L.A. indie gobbles up 26-title Columbia pic package for $8-mil." *Variety* 317 (January 2, 1985): 25, 124.

73. Geraldine Fabrikant. "HBO buying rights to Paramount films." *New York Times*, July 15, 1987, p. D1.
74. Frank Beerman. "S-TMC slump gives HBO Par pics pack." *Variety* 327 (July 22, 1987): 50.
75. "Major distribs picking up more indie productions." *Variety* 330 (February 24, 1988): 66.
76. Lawrence Cohn. "Half of indie pix denied release." *Variety* 332 (October 19, 1988): 1, 509.
77. Lawrence Cohn. "Ancillary market saves indies." *Variety* 330 (February 24, 1988): 1, 295.
78. John Dempsey. "Shelved theatricals find TV life after death." *Variety* 340 (August 8, 1990): 1, 70.
79. John Dempsey. "Pay-per-view peeved at Par's longer video window." *Variety* 352 (November 27, 1993): 25, 30.
80. Richard Corliss. "There's gold in that there schlock." *Time* 148 (August 26, 1996): 55.
81. Ibid., p. 56; M. Faust. "Straight to tape." *Video* 18 (December, 1994): 64–66.
82. John Dempsey. "TW 12-pack of pix synergize Ted's nets." *Variety*, January 20, 1997, p. 35.
83. John Dempsey. "Ted's pic pact busts theatrical window." *Variety*, January 27, 1997, pp. 25, 28.
84. John Dempsey. "Baby Bells begin movie buying binge." *Variety* 355 (July 25, 1994): 1, 72.
85. "Turner's 1st major move at MGM; colorizing 24 pics for syndie." *Variety* 323 (May 28, 1986): 48, 58.
86. Leslie Bennetts. "Colorizing film classics; a boon or a bane?" *New York Times*, August 5, 1986, p. A1.
87. Ibid., pp. A1, C4.
88. Michael Dempsey. "Colorization." *Film Quarterly* 40 (no. 2, 1986/1987): 2–3.
89. Susan Linfield. "The color of money." *American Film* 12 (January/February 1987): 29–32.
90. "Fighting color in old movies." *New York Times*, November 29, 1987, p. 72.
91. Andrew L. Yarrow. "Debate heats up on coloring films." *New York Times*, June 22, 1988, p. C26.

Chapter 8

1. Les Brown. "Combination of cable TV and satellites created national 'super stations.'" *New York Times*, November 28, 1977, p. 60.

2. Frank Beerman. "HBO celebrates 10th Anni; it's the cat's meow now turning out new material." *Variety* 309 (November 17, 1982): 56.

3. Walter Troy Spencer. "Pay TV is giving filmmakers reason to pause." *New York Times*, November 7, 1976, p. 27.

4. Geri Fabrikant. "Home B.O. skeds 36 a year, price, timing, stockpiling, TV curbs upset distribs." *Variety* 296 (September 26, 1979): 4, 31.

5. Frank Beerman. "Three H'wood majors, Wasec mull movie channel combine, HBO dominance main target." *Variety* 308 (August 11, 1982): 47, 66.

6. Sandra Salmans. "Hollywood takes on HBO." *New York Times*, February 3, 1983, pp. D1, D4.

7. "Something new, some old in HBO's marketing push." *Variety* 319 (June 26, 1985): 68.

8. "Cinemax lowers its churn with drive for hip adults." *Variety* 320 (September 4, 1985): 54, 62.

9. Stanley Young. "Cable TV's 'Porky's' syndrome." *Los Angeles Magazine* 34 (November, 1989): 246, 248.

10. Paul Harris. "FCC the villain at cable hearings." *Variety* 283 (July 28, 1976): 39, 48.

11. Paul Harris. "Court upsets FCC's pay cable rules." *Variety* 286 (March 30, 1977): 1, 93.

12. Larry Michie. "Old films to ride pay cable cycle." *Variety* 287 (May 25, 1977): 37, 54.

13. John Dempsey. "New cable regs rile U.S. syndies." *Variety* 300 (August 20, 1980): 1, 79.

14. Paul Harris. "TV-to-cable via satellite blasted hard by MPAA." *Variety* 288 (August 31, 1977): 45.

15. Larry Michie. "Now pay cable is breaking out in tiers." *Variety* 296 (August 29, 1979): 61, 72.

16. "Features are biggest lure for pay cable." *Variety* 300 (August 20, 1980): 1, 86.

17. Morrie Gelman. "Pay cable webs; 24-hour plans seen as a bonanza for majors." *Variety* 303 (June 3, 1981): 1, 65.

18. Frank Beerman. "Joint cable–cinema releases?" *Variety* 304 (October 7, 1981): 165, 184.

19. William MacDougall. "Stampede to cash in on cable's new film market." *U.S. News & World Report* 94 (March 7, 1983): 49–50.

20. "Video rentals dilute pay cable, new owners drawn by prices." *Variety* 311 (July 20, 1983): 34.

21. Tom Girard. "Showtime anthem: 'Oh Par can you see.'" *Variety* 313 (December 21, 1983): 43, 61.

22. John Dempsey. "Pay cable & pics still mix." *Variety* 348 (July 27, 1992): 19, 23.

23. John Dempsey. "Plexing paying off for cables." *Variety* 353 (January 10, 1994): 45, 51.

24. John Dempsey. "Tough climate for TCM." *Variety* 354 (April 18, 1994): 25, 30.

25. John Dempsey. "Pay cable warriors bloody studio pic battleground." *Variety* 359 (May 22, 1995): 35, 40.

26. Martin Peers. "Satellite terror in cable sky." *Variety* 360 (January 29, 1996): 27–28.

27. John Dempsey. "Satellite TV boosts paybox subscribers." *Variety*, October 28, 1996, pp. 37, 39.

28. Ray Richmond. "Encore pours pix into mix." *Variety*, December 23, 1996, pp. 31, 36.

29. "Starz offers moon for big pix." *Variety*, February 16, 1998, p. 38.

30. "Showtime takes action with extreme plan." *Variety*, December 22, 1997, p. 28.

31. John Dempsey. "Cable ops caught in nets." *Variety*, February 17, 1997, pp. 1, 84.

32. John Dempsey. "Cable film frenzy fuels attack of the killer B's." *Variety*, April 8, 1997, pp. 49, 55.

33. "Pay cable finances & Showtime pre-buys." *Variety* 296 (August 29, 1979): 61.

34. Tom Girard. "Candid Col gives details of the HBO pact." *Variety* 317 (November 7, 1984): 59, 80.

35. Larry Cohn. "Pay cable taking unrelated pics, but deals vary." *Variety* 307 (July 21, 1982): 1, 68.

36. Larry Michie. "Stake claims to cable Klondike." *Variety* 282 (February 18, 1976): 1, 124.

37. Tony Schwartz. "U.S. says 5 companies broke law in plan to limit movies on pay TV." *New York Times*, August 5, 1980, pp. 1, D15.

38. "Getty's feevee web plans to air 150 new features yearly, 50% from pards." *Variety* 299 (May 21, 1980): 39, 59.

39. Paul Harris. "Trust busters nix Getty-feevee combo." *Variety* 300 (August 6, 1980): 43, 63.

40. Tony Schwartz. "Court halts pay-TV networks." *New York Times*, January 1, 1981, pp. 27, 35.

41. Tony Schwartz. "3 top movie studios are expected to join pay-TV film project." *New York Times*, August 8, 1982, pp. 1, 28.

42. Sally Bedell. "5 companies in venture to run 2 pay-TV units." *New York Times*, January 8, 1983, pp. 29, 32.

43. Sally Bedell Smith. "U.S. will fight pay-TV merger by film studios." *New York Times*, June 11, 1983, pp. 1, 21; "Pay-TV link accepted by U.S. after changes." *New York Times*, August 13, 1983, pp. 29, 32; Sandra Salmans. "2 pay-TV services merge." *New York Times*, September 7, 1983, p. D15.

44. "How TV is revolutionizing Hollywood." *Business Week*, February 21, 1983, pp. 78–79, 89.
45. Larry Michie. "Shut out of U.S. pay–TV, Hollywood takes Europe for piece of the action." *Variety* 317 (January 9, 1985): 77.
46. Paul Harris. "Cable, b'cast supply chiefs match wits at House hearing." *Variety* 337 (January 3, 1990): 34.
47. John Dempsey. "Execs fret as cable nets grab cream of new film crop." *Variety* 337 (January 3, 1990): 34.
48. John Dempsey. "MCA & cable nets in four-way foreplay." *Variety* 341 (October 22, 1990): 1, 91.
49. John Dempsey. "MCA & cable nets in four-way foreplay." *Variety* 341 (October 22, 1990): 1, 91.
50. John Dempsey. "Memo: Fox ducks legal eagles by linking cable fees to box office" *Variety* 342 (April 8, 1991): 23, 28.
51. Cynthia Littleton. "Big ticket C-deal." *Broadcasting & Cable* 126 (April 15, 1996): 67.
52. Ray Richmond. "Race on for 21st Century pix." *Variety*, August 12, 1996, p. 21.
53. "Basic cable advance continues." *Variety*, December 1, 1997, p. 38.
54. John Dempsey. "Cable ops caught in nets." *Variety*, February 17, 1997, pp. 1, 84.
55. Morry Roth. "Pay-per-view: on the cutting edge of TV." *Variety* 307 (July 28, 1982): 43, 62.
56. Michael Schrage. "The perils of pay-per-view." *American Film* 8 (April, 1983): 17–19.
57. Larry Michie. "Pay-per-view as home video foe." *Variety* 322 (March 19, 1986): 1, 36.
58. Morrie Gelman. "Pay-per-view sounds war cry against its homevid competition." *Variety* 327 (May 27, 1987): 54.
59. Tom Bierbaum. "Pay-per-view window closing, sez report." *Variety* 334 (January 18, 1989): 35.
60. Morrie Gelman. "Pay-per-view fans use VCR heavily, survey says." *Variety* 337 (December 20, 1989): 35.
61. John Dempsey. "WB study: hit pix fare best on pay-per-view." *Variety* 340 (September 10, 1990): 26.
62. John Dempsey. "Pay-per-view for the masses." *Variety* 342 (February 18, 1991): 37.
63. John Dempsey. "Fox, TCI, pay-per mates." *Variety* 346 (April 6, 1992): 1, 190.
64. Morrie Gelman. "Movies still looking for big break." *Variety* 344 (July 22, 1991): 49.
65. Richard Natale. "The pay-per chase for film & B'way preems." *Variety* 346 (February 24, 1992): 1, 271.

66. John Evan Frook. "Exhib bigs on pay-per-view pix: not in my theater." *Variety* 351 (May 10, 19930: 26.

67. Susan Ayscough. "Studios join in chorus of disapproval on pay-per-view." *Variety* 351 (May 24, 1993): 5, 18.

68. John Dempsey. "Satcasters help Warners guarantee pay-per-view success." *Variety,* October 7, 1996, pp. 37, 41.

69. John Dempsey. "Satellite pay-per-view buy rates skyrocketing." *Variety* 368 (August 18, 1997): 24.

70. "Pix, punches power up pay-per-view." *Variety,* November 24, 1997, p. 43; "Boxing fuels the box; pay-per-view up 16%." *Variety* , January 19, 1998, p. 64.

71. John Dempsey. "DBS slicing a bigger share of ancillary pie." *Variety,* February 16, 1998, pp. 37, 42.

72. James Lardner. "Romancing the cassette." *Video* 12 (October, 1988): 60–62.

73. Ibid., p. 62.

74. Ibid., pp. 62–64.

75. Herm Schoenfeld. "Home video systems spring up into likely billion dollar industry." *Variety* 289 (January 4, 1978): 118.

76. Herm Schoenfeld. "MPAA just now doubts 'home show biz.'" *Variety* 292 (October 25, 1978): 3, 40.

77. Jim Harwood. "Sony defeats majors on copying." *Variety* 296 (October 3, 1979): 1, 95.

78. Jim Harwood. "Federal court nixes in-home videotaping, Sony plans appeal." *Variety* 304 (October 21, 1981): 1, 96.

79. Paul Harris. "Supreme Court ok's home taping." *Variety* 313 (January 18, 1984): 1, 109.

80. Geri Fabrikant. "Cassettes in look-ahead; rentals vs. sales." *Variety* 296 (October 31, 1979): 71, 80.

81. Morrie Gelman. "Majors increase home vid titles 854% in 16 mos." *Variety* 298 (March 5, 1980): 1, 94.

82. Will Tusher. "Exhibs reject Hirschfield disk plan." *Variety* 298 (March 12, 1980): 7, 36.

83. Tom Goldsmith. "It's 'high noon' for home taping." *Variety* 306 (April 28, 1982): 1, 46.

84. "Video rentals dilute pay cable, new owners drawn by prices." *Variety* 311 (July 20, 1983): 34.

85. "H'wood unhappy with HBO pitch for VCR taping. *Variety* 321 (December 25, 1985): 1, 60.

86. "Ban upheld on stores' renting screening rooms." *New York Times,* September 8, 1986, p. C18.

87. Joe Schwartz. "Americans go to the movies." *American Demographics* 8 (September, 1986): 60.

88. James Melanson. "Vid survey sez 41% rent tape in March week." *Variety* 326 (March 25, 1987): 1, 180.
89. "'APRIL' titles turn over 80 times in '86; retailer results better." *Variety* 327 (June 17, 1987): 45.
90. Charles Kipps. "Home video now after TV oldies." *Variety* 328 (October 7, 1987): 1, 116.
91. Tom Bierbaum. "Sell through, not rentals, central to future growth, CBS/Fox sez." *Variety* 329 (November 25, 1987): 39–40.
92. Tom Bierbaum. "Video wades into depth of copy bog." *Variety* 330 (February 3, 1988): 35–36.
93. Tom Beirbaum. "Year of growth for homevid; eyed $10-bil in retail biz." *Variety* 333 (January 11, 1989): 89.
94. Peter M. Nichols. "Movie rentals fade, forcing an industry to change its focus." *New York Times*, May 6, 1990, pp. 1, 34.
95. "Networks dominate home taping." *Variety* 339 (April 11, 1990): 39.
96. Don Groves. "Global vidiots' delight." *Variety*, April 15, 1996, pp. 1, 43.
97. Steve Knoll. "Warners revises homevid policy." *Variety* 305 (November 11, 1981): 1, 81.
98. "Citing 'confusion,' Sound Video drops Warner Homevid product." *Variety* 305 (November 18, 1981): 39.
99. James Lardner, op. cit., pp. 64–65.
100. Steve Knoll. "Mag video launches cassette rent plan." *Variety* 305 (November 18, 1981): 39.
101. Steve Knoll. "MGM/CBS hops on rent-only bandwagon." *Variety* 305 (December 9, 1981): 29, 31.
102. James Lardner, op. cit., p. 65.
103. "Home video poll says 45% want feature rentals." *Variety* 305 (November 18, 1981): 1, 82.
104. James Melanson. "Majors to share video rentals." *Variety* 321 (January 8, 1986): 1, 68, 70.
105. "Orion homevid provides P.P.T. to qualifying distribs and stores." *Variety* 331 June 15, 1988): 30.
106. "P.P.T. raises ire of store owners." *Variety* 332 (August 10, 1988): 33.
107. "Study reinforces depth-of-copy gripes and profitability of P.P.T." *Variety* 332 (August 10, 1988): 33.
108. "VSDA report sales up 43%." *Variety* 332 (August 10, 1988): 33.
109. Tony Seideman. "Star Trek II: sales vs. rental fulcrum." *Variety* 308 (October 6, 1982): 31–32.
110. "Majors face uphill fight to boost software sales, survey sez." *Variety* 309 ID 22, 1982): 26.
111. "Par sets 'Airplane II' home video market debut at lowball $29.95." *Variety* 310 (March 9, 1983): 34.

112. Tony Seideman. "Low-priced vidtapes as lure for big retail chains." *Variety* 310 (March 9, 1983): 34, 122.

113. Tom Beirbaum. "Paramount's 'Gun' soars to revenue/sales marks." *Variety* 326 (March 25, 1987): 41–42.

114. Richard Zoglin. "Shopping for Hollywood's hits." *Time* 131 (March 4, 1988): 83.

115. Ibid.

116. Cy Leslie. "Doomsayers of yore, note: people are buying cassettes." *Variety* 383 (January 11, 1989): 89.

117. Stuart Miller. "Vid ad to head 'Home.'" *Variety* 342 (March 25, 1991): 24, 100.

118. "Commercials on video gain only a few fans." *New York Times*, December 2, 1991, p. D7.

119. "*Variety's* global 50." *Variety* 368 (August 25, 1997): 33, supplement.

Bibliography

"'A' titles turn over 80 times in '86, retailer results better." *Variety* 327 (June 17, 1987): 45.
"AAP's 'VIP' sales pattern." *Variety* 209 (January 15, 1958): 31.
"ABC gobbles up 'Ghostbusters' for $15-million after HBO play." *Variety* 316 (September 19, 1984): 47.
"ABC web wanted off-CBS features its O&Os bought." *Variety* 245 (December 14, 1966): 25, 42.
"ABC-TV in whopping Metro deal for features." *Variety* 240 (August 25, 1965): 25.
"ABC-TV options 52 RKO features to compete with Sullivan, Allen." *Variety* 205 (February 13, 1957): 31.
"ABC-TV's Tom Moore pledges affils, 'no features in 1963–64 prime time." *Variety* 231 (June 26, 1963): 29
"Accord reached in movie strike." *New York Times*, April 9, 1960, p. 21.
"Actors lose TV case." *New York Times*, October 19, 1954, p. 34.
Adams, Val. "ABC-TV obtains 30 British films." *New York Times*, July 25, 1955, p. 41.
———. "All RKO movies sold for TV use." *New York Times*, December 7, 1955, pp. 1, 47.
———. "Are TV movies better than ever?" *New York Times*, November 27, 1966, sec. 2, p. 21.
———. "CATV is debated by broadcasters." *New York Times*, January 20, 1966, p. 71.
———. "Formula: more movies." *New York Times*, April 7, 1963, sec. 2, p. 23.
———. "Give a horse a man who can ride." *New York Times*, October 8, 1950, sec. 2, p. 11.
———. "Metro to offer weekly TV show." *New York Times*, June 22, 1955, p. 59.

———. "NBC-TV acquires post-1948 movies." *New York Times*, February 12, 1964, p. 67.

———. "News of TV and radio." *New York Times*, August 13, 1961, sec. 2, p. 13.

———. "Pay-TV stalled by money needs." *New York Times*, March 4, 1966, p. 67.

———. "Psycho gets the axe." *New York Times*, December 18, 1966, sec. 2, p. 21.

———. "Slezak will star in fall TV series." *New York Times*, April 19, 1957, p. 43.

———. "TV primes Hollywood." *New York Times*, January 19, 1967, p. 71.

———. "Where old TV films come from." *New York Times*, June 11, 1950. Sec. 2, p. 9.

"Adult films-to-TV problem." *Variety* 256 (September 24, 1969): 1, 38.

"All majors now acting." *Variety* 209 (February 19, 1958): 24.

Alpert, Hollis, "Now the earlier, earlier show." *New York Times Magazine*, "August 11, 1963, pp. 22–23, 38.

"Although it Hertz." *Variety* 244 (September 28, 1966): 49.

"And now 'Phonevision.'" *New York Times*, January 2, 1950, p. 26.

Arneel, Gene. "Par pledges no post–1948 sell." *Variety* 209 (February 12, 1958): 3, 22.

Auletta, Ken. *Three Blind Mice*. New York: Random, 1991.

"Autry sues studio over films for TV." *New York Times*, October 31, 1951, p. 32.

Ayscough, Suzan. "Studios join in chorus of disapproval on pay-per-view." *Variety* 351 (May 24, 1993): 5, 18.

Balio, Tino, ed. *Hollywood in the Age of Television*. Boston: Unwin, Hyman, 1990.

"Ban upheld on stores' renting screening rooms." *New York Times*, September 8, 1986, p. C18.

Bart, Peter. "Actors alarmed by movies on TV." *New York Times*, July 7, 1965, p. 25.

———. "Advertising: business is brisk for TV time." *New York Times*, August 8, 1961, p. 44.

———. "California votes to bar pay-TV." *New York Times*, November 5, 1964, p. 91.

———. "'Hawaii' changes directors twice." *New York Times*, August 4, 1965, p. 22.

———. "NBC is upheld on commercials." *New York Times*, June 4, 1966, p. 18.

———. "NBC-TV is sued by film director." *New York Times*, October 27, 1965, p. 39.

———. "'Place in the Sun' is spared scissors." *New York Times*, February 14, 1966, p. 33.

———. "The gold rush is on." *New York Times*, October 30, 1966, sec. 2, p. 11.

Bart, Peter. "TV-film accords arousing doubts." *New York Times*, January 7, 1966, p. 19.
_____. "TV movie-making begins in earnest." *New York Times*, March 10, 1966, p. 26.
"Basic cable advance continues." *Variety*, December 1, 1997, p. 38.
Beaupre, Lee. "ABC pix: post-mortem 'audit.'" *Variety* 271 (May 30, 1973): 5, 22.
Bedell, Sally. "5 companies in venture to run 2 pay TV units." *New York Times*, January 8, 1983, pp. 29, 32.
Beerman, Frank. "Estimate 30 CBS stations dropouts for X-rated pix." *Variety* 266 (March 8, 1972): 1, 71.
_____. "HBO celebrates 10th anni; it's the cat's meow now turning out new material." *Variety* 309 (November 17, 1982): 56.
_____. "Joint cable-cinema releases?" *Variety* 304 (October 7, 1981): 165, 184.
_____. "Sterling project for N.Y. pay-TV." *Variety* 271 (July 18, 1973): 24.
_____. "S-TMC slump gives HBO Par pics back." *Variety* 327 (July 22, 1987): 50.
_____. "Three H'wood majors, Wasec mull movie channel combine; HBO dominance main target." *Variety* 308 (August 11, 1982): 47, 66.
Bender, Hy. "Dogmatic disclaimers." *American Film* 14 (May, 1989): 12–13.
Bennetts, Leslie. "Colorizing film classics: a boon or a bane?" *New York Times*, August 5, 1986, pp. A1, C14.
Benson, Jim. "Par takes the fifth." *Variety* 363 (November 8, 1993): 17, 21, 51.
Bierbaum, Tom. "Paramount's 'Gun' soars to revenue/sales marks." *Variety* 326 (March 25, 1987): 41–42.
_____. "Pay-per-view window closing, sez report." *Variety* 334 (January 18, 1989): 43.
_____. "Sell through, not rentals, central to future growth, CBS/Fox sez." *Variety* 329 (November 25, 1987): 39–40.
_____. "Video wades into depth of copy bog." *Variety* 330 (February 3, 1988): 35–36.
_____. "Year of growth for homevid; eyed $10-bil in retail biz." *Variety* 333 (January 11, 1989): 89.
"Billion-dollar season for TV." *Business Week*, October 13, 1956, pp. 32, 34.
Black, David. "How the gosh-darn networks edit the heck out of movies." *New York Times*, January 26, 1995, sec. 2, pp. 1, 33.
"Block booking of old features assailed." *Variety* 202 (April 25, 1956): 31, 35.
"Bowdlerizing 'The Last Detail.'" *New York Times*, February 22, 1976, sec. 2, p. 29.
"Boxing fuels the box: pay-per-view up 16%." *Variety*, January 19, 1998, p. 64.
Brady, Thomas F. "Cuddling up to TV." *New York Times*, June 10, 1981, sec. 2, p. 3.
_____. "Lippert, Petrillo in accord on video." *New York Times*, April 24, 1951, p. 35.

Brady, Thomas F. "Television blocks coast movie deal." *New York Times*, April 28, 1950, p. 26.
_____. "TV in Hollywood." *New York Times*, June 4, 1950, sec. 2, p. 9.
Brody, William. *Fifties Television*. Urbana: University of Illinois Press, 1990.
Brown, Les. "Combination of cable TV and satellites creates national 'super stations.'" *New York Times*, November 28, 1977, p. 60.
_____. "Movie gang-up, CBS hang up." *Variety* 252 (September 18, 1968): 33, 52.
_____. "NBC comes in from the cold." *Variety* 245 (December 14, 1966): 25, 42.
_____. "NBC will pinch-hit for baseball." *New York Times*, April 24, 1975, p. 70.
_____. "New film box office: hotels." *Variety* 263 (June 30, 1971): 1, 62.
_____. "Pix on TV." *Variety* 244 (October 12, 1966): 35.
_____. "Set 7th night of TV movies." *Variety* 249 (December 27, 1967): 1, 34.
_____. "'66–'67" season without salt." *Variety* 244 (September 28, 1966): 49.
_____. "TV '69–'70: yesterday's bijou." *Variety* 252 (August 28, 1968): 33, 42.
Brown, Stanley. "Hollywood rides again." *Fortune* 74 (November, 1966): 181–182+.
Bunce, Richard. *Television in the Corporate Interest*. New York: Praeger, 1976.
"Cable pay-see big ticket for pix." *Variety* 266 (March 1, 1972): 34.
"California gets pay television with programs on 3 channels." *New York Times*, July 18, 1964, p. 47.
Callenbach, Ernest. "Television 'version.'" *Film Quarterly* 29 (Winter, 1975): 1–2.
"Can 'made for TV' features equal the audience pull of theatricals?" *Variety* 242 (May 4, 1966): 175.
Canby, Vincent. "Catholic film office is easing policy." *New York Times*, April 9, 1966, p. 11.
_____. "Skouras–eye view of strike." *Variety* 217 (December 30, 1959): 3, 48.
Carter, Bill. "Media." *New York Times*, July 15, 1996. P. D9.
"CBS late features budgeted at 40G." *Variety* 265 (December 8, 1971): 25.
"CBS pays Metro $700,000 apiece." *Variety* 248 (October 4, 1967): 3.
"CBS taps indies for feature pix." *Variety* 243 (August 17, 1966): 19.
Champlin, Charles. "The American motion picture: 1966." *Saturday Review* 49 (December 24, 1966): 11–13.
Chandler, Bob. "The economies of features on TV." *Variety* 198 (May 11, 1955): 39.
_____. "U's TV terms to actors; 3.6%" *Variety* 218 (March 2, 1960): 3.
"Cinemax lowers its churn with drive for hip adults." *Variety* 320 (September 4, 1988): 54, 62.
"Citing 'confusion,' Sound Video drops Warner homevid product." *Variety* 305 (November 18, 1981): 39.

Cocks, Jay. "The shape of things that were." *Time* 120 (August 30, 1982): 78.
Cohn, Lawrence. "Ancillary market saves indies." *Variety* 330 (February 24, 1988): 295.
_____. "Half of indie pix denied release." *Variety* 332 (October 19, 1988): 295.
_____. "Made-for ancillary pics burgeoning." *Variety* 311 (July 6, 1983): 3, 35.
_____. "Pay cable taking unreleased pics, but deals vary." *Variety* 307 (July 21, 1982): 1, 6.
"Col, WB, Metro top TV pix ratings." *Variety* 243 (April 10, 1966): 35. "Commercials on video gain only a few fans." *New York Times*, December 2, 1991, p. D7.
"Comm'l TV station count." *Variety* 252 (September 11, 1968): 35.
Corliss, Richard. "There's gold in that there schlock." *Time* 148 (August 26, 1996): 55–56.
Crist, Judith. "TV movies in disguise." *Saturday Review* 8 (March 8, 1981): 86–87.
Crowther, Bosley. "Old movies on TV peril Hollywood." *New York Times*, January 27, 1958, pp. 1, 23.
_____. "Sale of birthrights." *New York Times*, March 11, 1956, sec. 2, p. 1.
Dallos, Robert. "Local TV stations are running out of movies." *New York Times*, August 13, 1968, p. 79.
Daniels, Bill. "Directors seek TV disclaimer on edited films." *Variety* 321 (January 22, 1986): 76.
Dempsey, John. "As webs close doors on theatricals, majors use other TV windows." *Variety* 324 (August 13, 1986): 33, 48.
_____. "Baby Bells begin movie buying binge." *Variety* 355 (July 25, 1994): 1, 72.
_____. "Big four b'casters line up around the blockbusters." *Variety* September 2, 1996, pp. 23, 26.
_____. "Cable film frenzy fuels attack of the killer B's." *Variety*, April 8, 1997, pp. 49, 55.
_____. "Cable ops caught in nets." *Variety*, February 17, 1997, pp. 1, 84.
_____. "DBS slicing a bigger share of ancillary pie." *Variety*, February 16, 1998, pp. 37, 42.
_____. "Execs fret as cable nets grab cream of new film crop." *Variety* 337 (January 3, 1990): 34.
_____. "Film-buying TV stations riled over title diddles." *Variety* 303 (June 3, 1981): 50.
_____. "Fox, TCI pay-per mates." *Variety* 346 (April 6, 1992): 1, 190.
_____. "Future stock: movie libraries dictate next cable net battle." *Variety* 359 (May 29, 1995): 21, 25.
_____. "H'wood majors eye ad-hoc TV networks." *Variety* 315 (June 13, 1984): 41, 70.
_____. "Indies buy Worldvision movies." *Variety* 343 (Sept. 15, 1990): 43–44.

———. "Majors pass up telepics & minis." *Variety* 316 (Oct. 17, 1984): 1, 147.
———. "MCA & cable nets in four-way foreplay." *Variety* 341 (October 22, 1990): 1, 91.
———. "MCA may shut pay cable window for hit Universal pictures." *Variety* 337 (November 8, 1989): 1–2.
———. "Memo: Fox ducks legal eagles by linking cable fees to B.O." *Variety* 342 (April 8, 1991): 23, 28.
———. "MGM/UA building barter film web." *Variety* 315 (July 25, 1984): 1, 82.
———. "Mickey's mad for made-fors." *Variety* 368 (September 1, 1997): 1, 87.
———. "New cable regs rile U.S. syndies." *Variety* 300 (August 20, 1980): 1, 79.
———. "New movie game for majors." *Variety* 356 (October 3, 1994): 30.
———. "Offer *Empire, Star Wars* to TV." *Variety* 304 (October 21, 1981): 1, 80.
———. "Pay cable & pics still mix." *Variety* 348 (July 27, 1992): 19, 23.
———. "Pay cable warriors bloody studio pic battleground." *Variety* 359 (May 22, 1995): 35, 40.
———. "Pay-per-view for the masses." *Variety* 342 (February 18, 1991): 37.
———. "Plexing paying off for cablers." *Variety* 353 (January 10, 1994): 45, 51.
———. "Pay-per-view peeved at Par's longer video window." *Variety* 352 (November 27, 1993): 25, 30.
———. "Satcasters help Warners guarantee pay-per-view success." *Variety*, October 7, 1996, pp. 37, 41.
———. "Satellite pay-per-view buy rates skyrocketing." *Variety* 368 (August 8, 1990): 1, 70.
———. "Satellite TV boosts paybox subscribers." *Variety*, October 28, 1996, pp. 37, 39.
———. "Shelved theatricals find TV life after death." *Variety* 340 (August 8, 1990): 1, 70.
———. "Showtime sees silver lining in cloud around original pix." *Variety* 360 (November 6, 1995): 33, 40.
———. "Studios now looking to pay–TV as a major source of ancillary coin; abbreviated syndie playoff." *Variety* 309 (December 29, 1982): 1, 34.
———. "Ted's pic pact busts theatrical window." *Variety*, January 27, 1997, p. 35.
———. "U pix may be USA capital." *Variety* 368 (September 1, 1997): 21–22.
———. "WB study: hit pix fare best on pay-per-view." *Variety* 3440 (September 10, 1990): 26.
———. "Webs go extra mile to pack pix." *Variety*, June 9, 1997, pp. 21, 23.
Dempsey, Michael. "Colorization." *Film Quarterly* 40 (n.2 1986–1987; 2–3.
"DGA moans altered states of movies." *Broadcasting* 122 (March 9, 1992): 14.
"Double-edged disappointment." *Time* 121 (March 7, 1983): 69.
"Draw fangs of the television beast." *Variety* 209 (January 1, 1958): 17.

Dugan, George. "Baptists say films are lacking in social value." *New York Times*, June 8, 1972, p. 50.

"Educational TV stations." *New York Times*, December 14, 1956, pp. 1, 59.

"Electronic home theatre." *Variety* 205 (December 12, 1956): 3, 20.

"22,748,400 TV sets in U.S." *Variety* 182 (March 28, 1951): 26.

Engelman, Robert. "FCC, perhaps miffed at court turns down pay cable demands to lift movie exclusivity pacts." *Variety* 288 (September 28, 1988): 45, 52.

Esteron, Milton. "Metro planning wide TV activity." *New York Times*, June 21, 1956, p. 35.

"Every night at the movies." *Look* 35 (September 7, 1971): 62–63.

"Everybody's right trampled upon when TV stations mutilate." *Variety* 241 (December 8, 1965): 5.

"Exhib fret: for whom cable tolls." *Variety* 280 (October 8, 1975): 7, 36.

"Exhibs burn at pix sale to TV." *Variety* 185 (March 5, 1952): 1, 78.

"Exhibs rear up at Republic for 200G leasing to CBS video." *Variety* 189 (December 24, 1952): 3, 34.

Fabrikant, Geri. "Box office smash pic can be home-tube no-no." *Variety* 299 (July 9, 1980): 7, 30.

_____. "Cassettes in look-ahead; rentals vs. Sales issue." *Variety* 296 (October 31, 1979): 71, 80.

_____. "HBO buying rights to Paramount films." *New York Times*, July 15, 1987, p. D1.

_____. "Home Box Office skeds 36 a year, price, timing, stockpiling, TV curbs upset distribs." *Variety* 296 (September 26, 1979): 4, 31.

Faust, M. "Straight to tape." *Video* 18 (December, 1994): 64–66.

"Feature films oldies reaping TV spot biz harvest, high ratings." *Variety* 182 (March 28, 1951): 26, 34.

"Feature pix are backbone of pay–TV." *Variety* 276 (September 25, 1974): 35, 42.

"Features are biggest lure for pay cable." *Variety* 300 (August 20, 1980): 1, 86.

"Feed the kitty or video will." *Variety* 210 (May 7, 1958): 7.

"Fighting color in old movies." *New York Times*, November 29, 1987, p. 72.

"Film suit hears ex-head of RKO" *New York Times*, October 22, 1955, p. 24.

"Films downtrend data—'46–'52." *Variety* 190 (April 22, 1953): 3.

Flint, Joe. "WB, Par weblets square off." *Variety* 357 (January 2, 1995): 37, 40.

"4 film firms yield on TV-release pay." *New York Times*, June 18, 1952, p. 37.

"41 not-so-old pix every week as competition." *Variety* 224 (November 1, 1961): 3, 21.

"Fox displays Eidophone." *New York Times*, June 26, 1952, p. 24.

"Free movies every night." *Time* 66 (August 1, 1955): 54–55.

"The friendly giant." *Newsweek* 127 (February 19, 1996): 49.

Frook, John Evan. "Exhib bigs on pay-per-view pix: not in my theater." *Variety* 351 (May 10, 1993): 26.

"The future of features on TV." *Variety* 215 (July 8, 1959): 30.

Gardner, Paul. "Late late show addiction." *New York Times*, November 3, 1963, sec. 2, p. 15.

Garner, Hugh. "See any bad movies lately?" *Saturday Night* 69 (May 1, 1954): 17–18.

Gelman, Morrie. "Majors increase home vid titles 854% in 16 mos." *Variety* 298 (March 5, 1980): 1, 94.

———. "Movies still looking for big break." *Variety* 344 (July 22, 1991): 49.

———. "Pay cable webs' 24-hour plans seen as a bonanza for majors." *Variety* 303 (June 3, 1981): 1, 65.

———. "Pay-per-view sounds war cry against its home video competition." *Variety* 327 (May 27, 1987): 54.

———. "Pay-per-view fans use VCR heavily, survey says." *Variety* 337 (December 20, 1989): 35.

Gent, George. "CBS to produce feature movies." *New York Times*, December 6, 1967, p. 95.

———. "Preminger stops film's sale to TV." *New York Times*, May 10, 1965, p. 67.

"Getty's feevee web plans to air 150 new features yearly, 50% from pards." *Variety* 299 (May 21, 1980): 39, 59.

Gillette, Don Carle. "With sex and gore pix off-limits TV faces famine of new films." *Variety* 282 (February 25, 1976): 1, 76.

Girard, Tom. "Candid Col gives details of HBO pact." *Variety* 317 (November 7, 1984): 59, 80.

———. "Showtime anthem: "Oh Par can you see?"" *Variety* 313 (December 2, 1983): 42, 61.

Glenn, Larry. "Hollywood cloud." *New York Times*, December 2, 1962, sec. 2, p. 9.

———. "Testing Hollywood." *New York Times*, December 9, 1962, sec. 2, p. 11.

Godbout, Oscar. "Film fare held harmful to TV." *New York Times*, March 31, 1956, p. 29.

Gold, Ronald. "New era of film security." *Variety* 244 (October 12, 1966): 1, 30.

Goldenson, Leonard H. *Beating the Odds*. New York: Scribners, 1991.

Goldman, Harold. "5,000 feature exposures a week." *Variety* 215 (July 8, 1959): 31.

Goldsmith, Tom. "It's 'high noon' for home taping." *Variety* 306 (April 28, 1982): 1, 46.

Goldwyn, Samuel. "Hollywood in the television age." *New York Times Magazine*, February 13, 1949, pp. 15, 44, 47.

Goldwyn, Samuel. "Is Hollywood through?" *Colliers* 128 (September 29, 1951): 18–19, 92–93.

———. "Television's challenge to the movies." *New York Times Magazine*, March 26, 1950, pp. 17+.

"Good reruns better 'n ever." *Variety* 205 (February 13, 1957): 31.
"Gordon to firms: don't sell any to TV for next 3 yrs." *Variety* 209 (January 15, 1958): 3, 22.
Gould, Jack. "Fade-out on old movies." *New York Times*, September 5, 1965, sec. 2, p. 11.
_____. "FCC bids Hollywood end feud with television or face video bar." *New York Times*, March 30, 1951, pp. 1, 27.
_____. "Pay–TV for apartments is proposed." *New York Times*, October 8, 1971, p. 86.
_____. "Pay–TV vote drive to cost $2 million." *New York Times*, August 17, 1964, pp. 1, 51.
_____. "Radio and television." *New York Times*, September 26, 1951, p. 43.
_____. "Superior movies." *New York Times*, September 9, 1956, sec. 2, p. 13.
_____. "Television, in big strides, advances." *New York Times*, April 24, 1949, sec. 10, p. 1.
_____. "The movie revolution." *New York Times*, October 8, 1967, sec. 2, p. 27.
_____. "The unkindest cuts of all." *New York Times*, February 27, 1966, sec. 2, p. 23.
_____. "TV faces a fight on movie-making." *New York Times*, October 23, 1967, pp. 1, 90.
_____. "TV films boom Hollywood into its greatest prosperity." *New York Times*, July 3, 1955, pp. 1, 26.
_____. "TV: one long plug." *New York Times*, July 25, 1955, p. 41.
_____. "TV review." *New York Times*, September 26, 1966, p. 83.
_____. "TV: $25,000,000 bargain." *New York Times*, July 21, 1955, p. 47.
_____. "Two networks invest $92.3-million on TV films." *New York Times*, September 28, 1966, p. 95.
_____. "Video in Hollywood." *New York Times*, March 23, 1952, sec. 2, p. 11.
_____. "We interrupt this commercial for a movie." *New York Times*, December 3, 1967, sec. 2, p. 21.
Greeley, Bill. "Butchery in TVs grind-house." *Variety* 244 (October 19, 1966): 1, 36.
_____. "Great off-web movie grinder." *Variety* 275 (June 5, 1974): 1, 70.
_____. "Lotsa juice in NBC 30-runs." *Variety* 254 (February 26, 1969): 43.
_____. "Movies: TV's 50-minute hour." *Variety* 245 (November 23, 1966): 31, 46.
_____. "Short season for new pix." *Variety* 270 (January 17, 1973): 35.
_____. "692 movies 'prime' local TV." *Variety* 255 (May 28, 1969): 1, 79.
Green, Abel. "Gen. Sarnoff deplores trend turning TV into 'motion-picture circuit.'" *Variety* 201 (February 22, 1956): 1, 63.
_____. "Sarnoff sees special pix for TV taking a fall out of H'wood backlog." *Variety* 185 (February 20, 1952): 1, 20.

Groves, Don. "Global vidiots' delight." *Variety*, April 15, 1996, pp. 1, 43.
Harmetz, Aljean. "ABC cancels 'Reds' after prohibition on editing." *New York Times*, April 17, 1985, p. Cohn, Lawrence. 26.
———. "Hollywood seeks control of outlets." *New York Times*, March 3, 1986, pp. D1, D5.
———. "Movies are revised for TV showings." *New York Times*, December 3, 1978, p. 101.
Harris, Paul. "Cable, b'cast, supply chiefs match wits at House hearing." *Variety* 331 (May 18, 1988): 130.
———. "FCC the villain at cable hearings." *Variety* 283 (July 28, 1976): 39, 48.
———. "Supreme Court O.K.'s home taping." *Variety* 313 (January 18, 1984): 1, 109.
———. "Trust busters nix Getty-feevee combo." *Variety* 300 (August 6, 1980): 43, 63.
———. "TV-to-cable pix satellite blasted hard by MPAA." *Variety* 288 (August 31, 1977): 45.
———. "Web pix exclusivity bedevils pay-C." *Variety* 279 (May 28, 1975): 57, 70.
Hardwood, Jim. "Federal court nixes in-home video-taping; Sony plans appeal." *Variety* 304 (October 21, 1981): 1, 96.
———. "Sony defeats majors on copying." *Variety* 296 (October 3, 1979): 1, 95.
"Hedged 'promises' on post-'48." *Variety* 209 (February 26, 1958): 7.
Hellman, Jack. "L.A.'s features-to-TV stockpile: $50,000,000." *Variety* 235 (July 29, 1964): 37.
———. "Old pix never die." *Variety* 195 (August 18, 1954): 23, 26.
Hift, Fred. "Adjustment to TV is biggest issue." *Variety* 205 (January 9, 1957): 7, 66.
———. "Coming to grips with pay–TV." *Variety* 208 (September 11, 1957): 5, 22.
———. "Exhibs plead: don't T(V)KO us." *Variety* 198 (April 6, 1955): 1, 54.
Hill, Gladwin. "Hollywood is wary of TV." *New York Times*, April 24, 1949, sec. 10, p. 18.
"Hill seeks final cut on edited films." *Broadcasting* 122 (March 2, 1992): 29.
Hilmes, Michelle. "Film industry alternatives to the networks: subscription television, 1949–1962." *Quarterly Review of Film Studies* 10 (no. 3, 1985): 213–223.
"Hoarding the blockbusters." *Variety* 205 (February 13, 1957): 67.
"Holden sues to bar TV 'Kwai.'" *New York Times*, July 19, 1966, p. 33.
Hollinger, Hy. "Theatre owners condemn any/all 'toll.'" *Variety* 208 (November 27, 1957): 31.
"Hollywood and TV." *Life* 32 (February 25, 1952): 20.
"Hollywood digs in." *Business Week*, March 24, 1945, pp. 92, 95.

"Hollywood finally sells to TV." *Business Week*, January 28, 1956, p. 54.
"Hollywood learns to live with TV." *Business Week*, August 9, 1952, pp. 46–48.
"Hollywood: they shall not sell us down TV syndicators river." *Variety* 209 (January 22, 1958): 3, 11.
"Home video poll says 45% want feature rentals." *Variety* 305 (November 18, 1981): 1, 82.
Honeycutt, Kirk. "Made for TV moves." *New York Times*, August 19, 1979, sec. 2, pp. 1, 27.
Hontz, Jenny. "Warners top supplier ... but can't crack WB." *Variety*, June 2, 1997, p. 24.
Horowitz, Murray. "A season to reason on pix." *Variety* 242 (May 4, 1966): 175.
_____. "Despite all the 'hold the line' talk." *Variety* 210 (May 28, 1958): 26, 52.
_____. "Don't pin hopes on post-'48s." *Variety* 215 (July 29, 1959): 25, 95.
_____. "Economies of TV cinematics." *Variety* 228 (October 31, 1962): 31, 38.
_____. "11,000 pix on TV—$715 mil." *Variety* 233 (February 5, 1964): 1, 42.
_____. "Features vs. live drama." *Variety* 209 (February 26, 1958): 23, 26.
_____. "Films' $400,000,000 from TV." *Variety* 238 (April 14, 1965): 1, 68.
_____. "It's open season on pix-to-TV." *Variety* 234 (March 4, 1964): 35.
_____. "Market-by-market report on '58–'59 vidpix ascent." *Variety* 213 (January 14, 1959): 51.
_____. "NAB post-'48 censor threat." *Variety* 222 (May 10, 1961): 31, 68.
_____. "NBC-TV skeds 3 pic repeats at 1st run prices." *Variety* 242 (May 11, 1966): 33.
_____. "New blood line of pix & TV." *Variety* 245 (January 4, 1967): 83, 98.
_____. "new mix for networks pix." *Variety* 244 (December 28, 1966): 23, 42.
_____. "Pre-'48's $200,000,000 jackpot." *Variety* 212 (October 1, 1958): 25.
_____. "Post-'48s in webs' future?" *Variety* 219 (August 17, 1960): 25.
_____. "'60–'61 on webs: mostly film." *Variety* 217 (February 17, 1960): 23.
_____. "Syndication's peak pix prices." *Variety* 231 (August 7, 1963): 39.
_____. "Theatre reissue $ mocks TV." *Variety* 209 (January 1, 1958): 5.
_____. "TV feature famine dilemma." *Variety* 212 (September 17, 1958): 29.
_____. "TV sugar-'codes' old features." *Variety* 206 (April 17, 1957): 1, 15.
_____. "TV's battle for cinematics." *Variety* 227 (April 18, 1962): 27, 45.
_____. "TV's $150,000,000 for old pix." *Variety* 206 (May 1, 1957): 1, 50.
_____. "TVs $52-mil pix 'insurance.'" *Variety* 244 (August 31, 1966): 1, 62.
_____. "TV's 73,000,000-hour pic grind." *Variety* 203 (July 4, 1956): 1, 40.
_____. "20th–Fox unloading post-'48s." *Variety* 219 (July 20, 1960): 27.
Horowitz, Murray. "WOR: TV's all-grind house." *Variety* 203 (August 22, 1956): 31, 40.
"How old is too old?" *Variety* 209 (January 22, 1958): 11.
"How TV is revolutionizing Hollywood." *Business Week*, February 21, 1983, pp. 78–81, 84, 89.

"H'wood unhappy with HBO pitch for VCR taping." *Variety* 321 (December 25, 1985): 1, 60.

Johnson, William. "Hold it! Where's that great scene with..." *New York Times*, May 26, 1974, sec. 2, p. 13.

"Justice Dept. Asking for reversal of ruling on vidpix block-booking." *Variety* 224 (November 22, 1961): 24.

"Justice Dept. ruling seen imminent." *Variety* 206 (March 27, 1957): 22.

Kaufman, Dave. "ABC topper sex feevee pix deals hurting H'wood." *Variety* 314 (March 7, 1984): 377, 385.

_____. "Feds probe TV block-booking by syndicators." *Variety* 291 (August 2, 1978): 1, 58.

_____. "Majors now minors on web skeds." *Variety* 296 (August 22, 1979): 1, 69.

_____. "Universal to prepare alternative scenes for TV of too-rough pic footage." *Variety* 256 (October 8, 1969): 35, 49.

Kipps, Charles. "Home video now after TV oldies." *Variety* 328 (October 7, 1987): 1, 116.

Klain, Stephen. "H'wood pix on home tape at $50 per." *Variety* 298 (December 7, 1977): 1, 90.

Knight, Bob. "Fed up with reel life, webs nix pix." *Variety* 278 (May 7, 1975): 327, 335.

_____. "Network film paradox: cutting back in winter but 22 hours airing now." *Variety* 303 (June 24, 1981): 40, 70.

_____. "TV nights are 'made' by movies." *Variety* 268 (October 25, 1972): 1, 59.

Knoll, Steve. "Mag Video launches cassette rent plan." *Variety* 305 (November 18, 1981): 39.

_____. "Warners revises homevid policy." *Variety* 305 (November 11, 1981): 1, 81.

"KNXT's enviable status: 7 years of first-run product still on tap." *Variety* 212 (October 1, 1958): 25, 45.

Koury, Phil. "Phonevision issue." *New York Times*, February 19, 1950, sec. 2, p. 5.

"L.A. indie gobbles up 26-title Columbia pic, package for $8-mi." *Variety* 317 (January 2, 1985): 25, 124.

Lafferty, William. "Feature films on prime-time television." In Tino Balio, ed. *Hollywood in the Age of Television*. Boston: Unwin Hyman, 1990, pp. 235–255.

Landry, Robert, "Exhibs fear 'motel movies.'" *Variety* 264 (October 27, 1971): 3, 40.

Lardner, James. "Romancing the cassette." *Video* 12 (October, 1988): 60–65.

"Leo's TV roar now a grunt." *Variety* 205 (January 16, 1957): 33.

LeRoy, Mervyn. "Motion pictures and pay-TV." *Atlantic Monthly* 200 (December, 1957): 84–86.

Leslie, Cy. "Doomsayers of yore, note: people are buying cassettes." *Variety* 333 (January 11, 1989): 89.

"Letters." *New York Times*, February 9, 1975, sec. 2, p. 27.

Levin, Gary. "Hit films form pricey platforms." *Variety* 363 (June 3, 1996): 25–26.

Lewis, Anthony. "TV block booking of movies barred." *New York Times*, November 6, 1962, pp. 1, 14.

Lewyn, Mark. "The networks vs. Hollywood: it's prime time for a truce." *Business Week*, April 9, 1990, p. 26.

Linderman, Lawrence. "Son of a buck, godfather! What have they done to you?" *TV Guide* 30 (July 17, 1982): 4–8.

Linfield, Susan. "The color of money." *American Film* 12 (January/February, 1987): 29–32, 35, 52.

Litman, Barry R. "The economics of the market for theatrical movies." *Journal of Communication* 29 (no. 4, 1979): 20–33.

Littleton, Cynthia. "Big-ticket C-deal." *Broadcasting & Cable* 126 (April 15, 1996): 67.

"Loew's sales to TV cited in trust suit." *New York Times*, March 28, 1957, p. 63.

Loftus, Jack. "H'wood starts indie film webs." *Variety* 317 (December 19, 1984): 1, 94.

Lohman, Sidney. "Radio and TV news." *New York Times*, March 13, 1949, sec. 2, p. 11.

"Long drawn-out legal hassle seen." *Variety* 206 (April 24, 1957): 22, 38.

Lubasch, Arnold. "ABC counters film trust suit." *New York Times*, April 15, 1971, p. 86.

Lydon, Christopher. "FCC puts limit on networks' TV." *New York Times*, May 8, 1970, pp. 1, 63.

MacDougall, William L. "Stampede to cash in on cable's new film market." *U.S. News & World Report* 94 (March 7, 1983): 49–51.

"Made-fors fill CBS movie nights as web stops buying theatricals." *Variety* 319 (May 22, 1985): 47.

"Major distribs picking up more indie productions." *Variety* 330 (February 24, 1988): 66.

"Majors face uphill fight to boost software sales, survey sez." *Variety* 309 (December 22, 1982): 26.

"Majors' race for TV dollar." *Variety* 205 (February 27, 1957): 27, 34.

"Majors release 600 post-'48s." *Variety* 224 (November 15, 1961): 25.

"Majors' 34 hours vs. Indies' 18 on webs for '72–'73." *Variety* 267 (Many 31, 1972): 34.

"A market-by-market telefilm appraisal." *Variety* 215 (July 8, 1959): 40, 42.

Maslin, Janet. "Cable TV, home video and chopping of movies." *New York Times*, March 25, 1982, p. 19.

Melanson, James. "Majors to share video rentals." *Variety* 321 (January 8, 1986): 1, 68, 70.

———. "Vid survey sez 41% rent tape in March week." *Variety* 326 (March 25, 1987): 1, 180.
"Meter TV films to end on June 6." *New York Times*, May 23, 1958, p. 46.
"Metro at 'bridge pic' crossing." *Variety* 240 (August 25, 1965): 25.
"Metro, NBC huddling on deal for pix stars to be worked into TV formats." *Variety* 191 (August 26, 1953): 3, 61.
Meyer, Nicholas. "Are the networks trimming more than just film?" *New York Times*, January 22, 1989, sec. 2, p. 27.
"MG's new flexible sales plan on features." *Variety* 206 (April 10, 1957): 35, 38.
Michie, Larry. "FCC: 'open door' for hotel pix." *Variety* 269 (January 24, 1972): 1, 62.
———. "New film box office horizons on cable TV." *Variety* 279 (May 21, 1975): 1, 78.
———. "New pay cable is breaking out in tiers." *Variety* 296 (August 29, 1979): 61, 72.
———. "Old films to ride pay cable cycle." *Variety* 287 (May 25, 1977): 1, 93.
———. "Pay cable pay-off on pix to pallid now: Columbia." *Variety* 280 (October 1, 1975): 83, 104.
———. "Pay-per-view as home video foe." *Variety* 322 (March 19, 1986): 1, 36.
———. "Shut out of U.S. pay–TV, Hollywood takes Europe for piece of the action." *Variety* 317 (January 9, 1985): 77.
———. "Stake claim to cable Klondike." *Variety* 282 (February 18, 1976): 1, 124.
———. "Television's 1973 'operation moneybag.'" *Variety* 276 (September 4, 1974): 39.
"Midseason primetime schedule 1995–1996." *Variety* 360 (January 8, 1996): 63.
Miller, Stuart. "Vid ad to head 'home.'" *Variety* 342 (March 25, 1991): 24, 100.
"More Fox films sold for TV use." *New York Times*, November 2, 1956, p. 54.
Morgan, Thomas, "Networks raise ratings by showing more films." *New York Times*, October 23, 1986, p. 26.
"Most stations don't go for extra premium on colorcasting of pix." *Variety* 205 (February 13, 1957): 67.
"Movie block-booking hit again." *Business Week*, December 10, 1960, p. 38.
"'Movie station (KHJ-TV) sprinkled with culture; parlay pays off." *Variety* 224 (November 22, 1961): 25.
"Movies-in-home TV is shown on coast." *New York Times*, March 22, 1957, p. 47.
"Movies come out of the dog house." *Business Week*, November 10, 1951, pp. 140–142.
"Movies: new sick industry." *Business Week*, November 25, 190, p. 26.
"Movies on home TV at $1 fee started." *New York Times*, January 2, 1951, p. 28.
"Movies on the tube." *Newsweek* 79 (April 10, 1972): 87–88.
"Movies ordered released for TV." *New York Times*, September 13, 1955, p. 63.

"Movies that never die." *Newsweek* 45 (March 7, 1955): 56.
"MPAA bids FCC suspend rules curbing pix, series on pay cable." *Variety* 275 (July 31, 1974): 37.
"NAB's new caution on post-'48s." *Variety* 224 (September 20, 1961): 25.
"NAS asks FCC to kayo movie and sports rules for pay cable." *Variety* 279 (May 14, 1975): 133.
Natale, Richard. "The pay-per clause for film & B'way preems." *Variety* 346 (February 24, 1992): 1, 271.
"NATO asks FCC to ban pay–TV pix on Warner's cable systems." *Variety* 273 (January 16, 1974): 51.
"NBC coughs up $70 mil for Par pix." *Variety* 311 (July 27, 1983): 43, 57.
"NBC-TV: Sat nite movie night." *Variety* 221 (December 21, 1960): 19.
"Nets bet bucks on pix appeal." *Variety*, January 12, 1998, pp. 79, 84.
"Networks cool to dubbed pix." *Variety* 242 (May 4, 1966): 175.
"Networks dominate home taping." *Variety* 339 (April 11, 1990): 39.
"Networks may open up prime time." *Variety* 205 (January 16, 1957): 33, 44."
New film is piped into homes." *New York Times*, September 4, 1957, p. 67.
Nichols, Peter M. "Movie rentals fade, forcing an industry to change its focus." *New York Times*, May 6, 1990, pp. 1, 34.
"1967 financial markets—top 50 U.S. TV markets." *Variety* 252 (October 9, 1968): 32.
"Non-movie movies." *Time* 89 (January 13, 1967): 42.
O'Connor, John T. "When films go under the knife." *New York Times*, July 16, 1978, sec. 2, p. 25.
"Oddity of AFM status re strike." *Variety* 217 (December 30, 1959): 3.
"Once fought ABC films, not got them." *Variety* 276 (October 30, 1974): 5.
"$100,000,000 syndie gross." *Variety* 233 (January 1, 1964): 25.
"O'Neil envisions TV film circuit in RKO buy." *Variety* 199 (July 20, 1955): 20.
"Orion home video provide P.P.T. to qualifying distribs and stores." *Variety* 331 (June 15, 1955): 30.
"'Ours alone to sell' position by majors presages TV-residuals showdown." *Variety* 217 (December 2, 1959): 3.
"Par sets *Airplane II* home video market debut at lowball $29.95." *Variety* 310 (March 9, 1983): 34.
"Paradise lost." *Time* 51 (January 19, 1948): 88, 90.
"Paramount films will go on pay–TV." *New York Times*, August 7, 1964, p. 55.
"Paramount in all-out build-up of pix, via use of stars on tv." *Variety* 177 (January 18, 1950): 2.
"Par's TV marriage vows." *Variety* 198 (March 30, 1955): 1.
"Pay cable finances & Showtime pre-buys." *Variety* 296 (August 29, 1979): 61.
"Pay–TV acquires first-run films." *New York Times*, July 23, 1964, p. 54.
"Pay–TV link accepted by U.S. after changes." *New York Times*, August 12, 1983, pp. 29, 32.

Peers, Martin. "Giants chow down indies." *Variety* 368 (September 15, 1997): 31, 33.

_____. "Satellite terror in cable sky." *Variety* 360 (January 29, 1996): 27–28.

"Phonevision block." *New York Times*, March 5, 1950, sec. 2, p. 4.

"Phonevision dials wrong no." *Variety* 177 (February 22, 1950): 3, 18.

"Pix biz sues TV: 'monopoly.'" *Variety* 260 (September 30, 1970): 1, 25.

"Pix pay-off in 2D play-off." *Variety* 248 (October 11, 1967): 71.

"Pix, punches power up pay-per-view." *Variety*, November 24, 1997, p. 43.

"Pix-to-TV dam." *Variety* 190 (April 15, 1953): 3, 25.

Polskin, Howard. "TV's love affair with the movies." *TV Guide* 38 (May 26, 1990): 16–18.

Porter, Russell. "3 companies sued as TV film trust." *New York Times*, April 11, 1958, pp. 1, 22.

"Post-'48s 'sure' for TV; Reade blasts exhibs." *Variety* 212 (September 17, 1958): 1, 22.

"Post–1950 films on TV in doses, and exhibs fret." *Variety* 229 (December 12, 1962): 1, 60.

"P.P.T. raises ire of store owners." *Variety* 332 (August 10, 1988): 33.

"Pre-'48's: $67,500,000 untapped." *Variety* 224 (November 15, 1961): 25.

"Pre-1948 sell-off was 'must'—Selznick." *Variety* 209 (January 15, 1958): 3.

"Preminger loses case on film cuts." *New York Times*, January 20, 1966, p. 71.

"Pressure majors on post–'48's." *Variety* 209 (February 5, 1958): 27.

"Primetime studio scorecard." *Variety* 323 (May 21, 1986): 61, 87.

"Probe Hollywood's video ban." *Variety* 182 (April 4, 1951): 3, 18.

Pryor, Thomas M. "'B' pictures facing new hurdle?" *New York Times*, March 27, 1949, sec. 2, p. 5.

_____. "By way of report." *New York Times*, February 6, 1949, sec. 2, p. 5.

_____. "Coast theatres fight toll video." *New York Times*, October 30, 1954, p. 14.

_____. "Columbia plans 39 movies for TV." *New York Times*, June 10, 1952, p. 23.

_____. "Film actors guild cancels contract." *New York Times*, September 6, 1951, p. 39.

_____. "Film groups seek pay–TV franchise." *New York Times*, July 20, 1957, p. 33.

_____. "Film studio to lease 104 movies to video." *New York Times*, December 31, 1955, pp. 1, 17.

_____. "5 film companies deny conspiracy." *New York Times*, September 23, 1955, p. 49.

_____. "Hollywood canvas." *New York Times*, June 15, 1952, sec. 2, p. 5.

_____. "Hollywood dilemma." *New York Times*, September 23, 1956, sec. 2, p. 7.

_____. "Hollywood edict." *New York Times*, June 13, 1954, sec. 2, p. 5.

———. "Hollywood ready for test with TV." *New York Times*, September 14, 1953, p. 24.
———. "Hollywood report." *New York Times*, November 7, 1954, sec. 2, p. 5.
———. "Hollywood sale." *New York Times*, January 1, 1956, sec. 2, p. 5.
———. "Hollywood session." *New York Times*, July 29, 1951, sec. 2, p. 3.
———. "Hollywood test." *New York Times*, November 8, 1953, sec. 2, p. 5.
———. "Hollywood trial." *New York Times*, September 18, 1955, sec. 2, p. 7.
———. "Movie companies upheld on TV ban." *New York Times*, December 6, 1955, p. 45.
———. "Movie producers oppose TV sales." *New York Times*, December 4, 1957, p. 52.
———. "Movies for video produced quickly." *New York Times*, August 21, 1952, p. 33.
———. "Movies on TV cut theatre business." *New York Times*, October 15, 1956, p. 28.
———. "Nassers sue U.A. over video clause." *New York Times*, December 15, 1951, p. 11.
———. "Skouras is heard at trial on coast." *New York Times*, October 27, 1955, p. 67.
———. "TV impact on films believed at peak." *New York Times*, July 26, 1951, p. 17.
———. "TV-movie tie-ins remain confused. *New York Times*, May 15, 1952, p. 39.
———. "Yates reassures theatres on TV." *New York Times*, September 15, 1955, p. 39.
"Radio and television." *New York Times*, November 10, 1948, p. 58.
"Radio decline seen with television rise." *New York Times*, April 6, 1949, p. 58.
"Rating TV pix on theatre box office." *Variety* 248 (September 6, 1969): 38.
"Reel attraction." *Newsweek* 66 (November 15, 1965): 116, 118.
"Rerun issue grinds away." *Variety* 277 (February 5, 1975): 45, 62.
"Residual deals on 17 more post-48s negotiated by SAG." *Variety* 215 (July 15, 1959): 39.
Richmond, Ray. "Encore pours pix into mix." *Variety*, December 23, 1996, pp. 31, 36.
———. "Race on for 21st century pix." *Variety*, August 12, 1996, p. 21.
Rosen, George. "New H'wood pix preem on TV." *Variety* 231 (June 12, 1963): 1, 44.
———. "Pix get second TV change." *Variety* 198 (April 20, 1955): 27, 35.
Rosen, George. "Pix-networks alliance in '50." *Variety* 146 (December 28, 1949): 1, 46.
Rosen, George. "TV readies a time bomb." *Variety* 202 (March 7, 1956): 23, 36.
Roth, Morry. "Pay-per-view: on the cutting edge of TV." *Variety* 307 (July 28, 1982): 43, 62.

"Roy Rogers in suit to bar films on TV." *New York Times,* June 24, 1951, p. 36.

"Roy Rogers ruling bars film sale to TV." *New York Times,* October 19, 1951, p. 24.

"SAG-majors peace pipe not figured to unleash post-'48's in a hurry." *Variety* 218 (April 6, 1960): 33, 54.

Salmans, Sandra. "Hollywood takes on HBO." *New York Times,* February 3, 1983, pp. D1, D4.

_____. "2 pay-TV services merge." *New York Times,* September 7, 1983, p. D15.

"Sarnoff doesn't mince words as he lashes at toll-TV system." *Variety* 199 (June 8, 1955): 29–30.

"Schary sees pix made for TV when sponsors pay $1,000,000 per film." *Variety* 190 (May 13, 1953): 1, 17.

Schoenfeld, Herm. "Home video systems spring up into likely billion dollar industry." *Variety* 289 (January 4, 1978): 118.

_____. "MPAA just now doubts home show biz." *Variety* 292 (October 25, 1978): 3, 40.

Schrage, Michael. "The perils of pay-per-view." *American Film* 8 (April, 1983): 17–19.

Schulze, Laurie. "The made-for-TV movie." in Tino Balio, ed. *Hollywood in the Age of Television.* Boston: Unwin, Hyman, 1990, pp. 351–376.

Shumach, Murray. "Movie men wary about TV deals." *New York Times,* February 1, 1960, p. 22.

Schwartz, Joe. "Americans go to the movies." *American Demographics* 8 (September, 1986): 60.

Schwartz, Tony. "Court halts pay-TV network." *New York Times,* January 1, 1981, pp. 27, 35.

_____. "3 top movie studios are expected to join pay-TV film project." *New York Times,* August 8, 1982, pp. 1, 28.

_____. "U.S. says 5 companies broke law in plan to limit movies on pay-TV." *New York Times,* August 5, 1980, pp. 1, D15.

"Screen Gems brochure an issue." *Variety* 241 (February 9, 1966): 7.

"See end of pix spiral era." *Variety* 243 (April 10, 1966): 35, 47.

"'See it soon on TV' misconception is murder for box office." *Variety* 208 (November 6, 1957): 1, 79.

Seideman, Tony. "Low-priced vidtapes as lure for big retail chains." *Variety* 310 (March 9, 1983): 34, 122.

_____. "*Star Trek II*: sales vs. rental fulcrum." *Variety* 308 (October 6, 1982): 31–32.

"7 Arts in $21,500,000 U buy." *Variety* 231 (July 17, 1963): 49.

"725 MGM movies leased for video." *New York Times,* August 15, 1956, p. 59.

Shanley, J.P. "Movies on video." *New York Times,* July 15, 1956, sec. 2, p. 9.

_____. "725 MGM movies leased for video." *New York Times,* August 25, 1956, p. 31.

Shayon, Robert Lewis. "David and the network goliaths." *Saturday Review* 52 (November 1, 1969): 52.

Shepard, Richard. "Movies on TV—the unkindest cuts of all." *New York Times*, October 7, 1956, sec. 2, p. 11.

"Showtime takes action with extreme plan." *Variety*, December 22–January 4, 1998, p. 28.

Sloane, Leonard. "Pay-as-you-view movies for hotels." *New York Times*, November 14, 1971, sec. 3, p. 5.

———. "TV movies new major factor in filmdom." *New York Times*, March 13, 1970, pp. 53, 56.

Smith, Sally Bedell. "U.S. will fight pay–TV merger by films studios." *New York Times*, June 11, 1983, pp. 1, 21.

"Something new, some old in HBO's marketing push." *Variety* 319 (June 26, 1985): 68.

"Speed of switch to Cinemascope will key 20th's pix flow to video." *Variety* 190 (April 15, 1953): 3, 24.

Spencer, Walter Troy. "Pay–TV is giving filmmakers reason to pause." *New York Times*, November 7, 1976, p. 27.

Spiro, J.D. "Hollywood and TV." *New York Times*, July 1, 1951, sec. 2, p. 3.

"Starz offers moon for big pix." *Variety*, February 16, 1998, p. 38.

Stein, Benjamin. "Hooked on television movies." *Saturday Evening Post* 246 (May, 1974): 30–33, 144.

"Stevens loses suit over his film on TV." *New York Times*, May 24, 1967, p. 95.

"Stevens sues NBC and Par." *Variety* 240 (October 27, 1965): 1, 24.

"Study reinforces depth-of-copy gripes & profitability of P.P.T." *Variety* 332 (August 10, 1988): 33.

"Suppose we sell-off to TV." *Variety* 216 (November 18, 1959): 3.

"Supreme Court rules California cannot prohibit pay television." *New York Times*, October 11, 1966, p. 95.

"Talent guilds' $30-mil stake-out based on post-'48 films $190–250-mil value." *Variety* 217 (January 20, 1960): 1, 4.

Taub, Stephen. "Sunny skies ahead for the old dream machine." *Financial World* 152 (July 15, 1983): 46–51.

"Television as theatre rival dominates Dallas meet." *Variety* 205 (December 5, 1956): 31.

"Television: boon to movies." *U.S. News & World Report* 27 (October 14, 1949): 21.

"Television: movies' friend or foe?" *U.S. News & World Report* 26 (January 7, 1949): 24–25.

"Texas exhibs design 'no-television' seal." *Variety* 209 (January 1, 1958): 17.

"That post–'60 residual pie." *Variety* 234 (February 26, 1964): 39.

"33% of recent pix tabu for TV." *Variety* 238 (a 21, 1965): 29.

"Though comparison lopsided cheapies made for television influence Paramount's ideas." *Variety* 212 (October 8, 1958): 5.

"Too wary of Theatre tele." *Variety* 179 (August 2, 1950): 1, 6.

Toy, Steve. "OTP draft blames network rivalry." *Variety* 269 (January 31, 1973): 33, 42.

"Trade unit hits toll TV." *New York Times*, June 17, 1957, p. 47.

"Turner's 1st major move at MGM: colorizing 24 pics for syndie." *Variety* 323 (May 28, 1986): 48, 58.

Tusher, Will. "Exhibs reject Hirschfield disk plan." *Variety* 298 (March 12, 1980): 7, 36.

"TV and film: marriage of necessity." *Business Week*, August 15, 1953, pp. 108–110.

"TV and films seen linking fortunes." *New York Times*, April 25, 1950, p. 26.

"TV and Hollywood sing a new duet." *Business Week*, April 16, 1966, pp. 107–108.

"TV-bird-in-hand lost $160-mil?" *Variety* 209 (December 18, 1957): 5, 18.

"TV cinematics' brisk biz." *Variety* 233 (December 11, 1963): 27.

"TV experiment held up." *New York Times*, November 10, 1954, p. 48.

"TV film ruling stands." *New York Times*, February 27, 1951, p. 22.

"TV films." *New York Times*, April 3, 1951, p. 26.

"TV films trimmed, FTC survey finds." *New York Times*, July 9, 1970, p. 75.

"TV gets 123 westerns." *New York Times*, March 23, 1955, p. 39.

"TV homes at 80-mil." *Variety* 303 (June 3, 1981): 1.

"TV-movie policy." *Business Week*, July 1, 1950, p. 21.

"TV official cites high cost of film." *New York Times*, October 5, 1955, p. 71.

"TV pays $2-million for RKO film library." *Business Week*, Dec. 31, 1955, p. 45.

"TV plan approved by actors group." *New York Times*, December 19, 1956, p. 62.

"TV webs paying less for pix." *Variety* 264 (November 10, 1971): 1, 39.

"TV's 10,427 features." *Variety* 232 (October 30, 1963): 31. "TV's $3½-billion '73." *Variety* 276 (September 4, 1974): 39.

"TWC-Viacom pay cable bow." *Variety* 271 (July 18, 1973): 26.

"$12,500,000 post-'48 pix sale." *Variety* 221 (November 30, 1960): 27.

"20th–Fox still has 300 pre '35s, but are they marketable?" *Variety* 219 (July 20, 1960): 27.

"20th's clearance pledge okay—D. of J." *Variety* 209 (January 22, 1958): 11.

"Two groups plan films in this city." *New York Times*, June 26, 1951, p. 25.

"200G Rep deal releasing 104 pix for TV seen breaking log jam." *Variety* 189 (December 17, 1952): 1, 63.

"$2,200,000 sales in UA's bundle of post-'48 features." *Variety* 205 (February 13, 1957): 67.

"Typical TV station profits top $1-mil." *Variety* 206 (June 9, 1982): 43.

"UA in unique status on post-'48 pix for TV." *Variety* 206 (March 20, 1957): 31, 52.

"U.S. drops suit against movies." *New York Times,* March 7, 1956, p. 38.
"U.S. to appeal TV film ruling." *Business Week,* August 13, 1960, pp. 53–54.
"U.S. wins decision in TV-movies suit." *New York Times,* December 3, 1960, p. 47.
"*Variety's* global 50." *Variety* 368 (August 25, 1997): 33, supplement.
Vianello, Robert. "The rise of the telefilm and the networks' hegemony over the motion picture industry." *Quarterly Review of Film Studies* 9 (no. 3, Summer, 1984): 204–218.
"Video can't pay for itself." *Variety* 207 (June 5, 1957): 3, 10.
"Video rentals dilute pay cable, new owners drawn by prices." *Variety* 311 (July 20, 1983): 34.
"Video rises on Par's horizon." *Variety* 205 (January 2, 1957): 5, 63.
"Video will aid films, theatre owner says." *New York Times,* March 19, 1950, p. 82.
"Video's 'movie-mad' audience." *Variety* 186 (April 30, 1952): 25, 30.
"VSDA reports sales up 4.3%." *Variety* 332 (August 10, 1988): 33.
"Wait for it on television." *Variety* 208 (October 23, 1957): 3–4.
Wall, James M. "Pornographic violence and public outrage." *Christian Century* 93 (December 15, 1976): 1115–1116.
"Wanna TV-sale watchdog?" *Variety* 241 (February 9, 1966): 7, 20.
"Warner is heard in antitrust suit." *New York Times,* November 1, 1955, p. 63.
"Warner's use of films on CATV not 'alternative theatre' to FCC." *Variety* 278 (March 19, 1975): 16.
Watts, Stephen. "British screen scene." *New York Times,* June 23, 1957, sec. 2, p. 5.
"WCBS-TV pays record $8,400,000 for Par's library of 700 pix." *Variety* 210 (May 14, 1958): 21.
"WCBS-TV posts billion-viewer mark for 7 years of late show." *Variety* 210 (May 28, 1958): 52.
"Webs '69–'70 feature rates." *Variety* 254 (April 30, 1969): 35.
"Wedding of H'wood-TV inviting bigger 'n' ever." *Variety* 206 (March 13, 1957): 1, 18.
Weiler, A.H. "7 movie companies sue ABC, CBS, over programming." *New York Times,* September 30, 1970, p. 39.
Weinraub, Bernard. "Warning: This movie is harmful to directors." *New York Times,* March 9, 1993, pp. C13–C14.
Wharton, Dennis. "MPAA members say they'll 'fess up' to altered states." *Variety* 353 (November 8, 1993): 17.
_____. "Scorsese plugs for artists' rights on hill." *Variety* 358 (March 20, 1995): 20.
"What they paid for features." *Variety* 241 (February 2, 1966): 32.
"What TV is doing to the movie industry." *U.S. News & World Report,* February 7, 1958, pp. 88–90.

"Whatever happened to that NAB screening of post–'48s?" *Variety* 228 (October 31, 1962): 31.

"Why do H'wood studios sell off pix oldies?" *Variety* 219 (July 13, 1960): 25.

"Will feature films reshape TV?" *Business Week*, November 24, 1956, pp. 131–132, 134, 136.

Woods, Mark. "Warner signing on in Oz." *Variety*, September 3, 1996, p. 32.

Woodstone, Art. "TV features' sound economy." *Variety* 220 (August 31, 1960): 25, 37.

Wright, Joseph, "Subscription TV may recapture lost audience for motion pictures." *Variety* 257 (January 7, 1970): 68.

Yarrow, Andrew L. "Debate heats up on coloring films." *New York Times*, June 22, 1988, p. 26.

Young, Stanley. "Cable TV's 'Porky's' syndrome." *Los Angeles Magazine* 34 (November, 1989): 246, 248–249.

"Zenith Radio sees Phonevision fight." *New York Times*, May 26, 1950, p. 35.

Index

ABC 22, 32–33, 36, 107–109
Abraham, Seth 162
actors: barred from TV 8, 10–11; on TV to publicize films 30–31
Adams, Val 84
Adler, Allen 121–122
admission rates 4
advertising 52–53; on TV 7; on videotapes 199
Advise and Consent 89–90
All About Eve 133
Aladdin 154
Allen, Woody 157–158
Altman, Robert 97
Alvarez, Christine 200
American Cinema Editors 93
American Civil Liberties Union 135
American Federation of Musicians (AFM) 12–13, 67–68
Anatomy of a Murder 79–80
Andrews, Dana 115
antitrust actions 4, 10, 37–39, 56–57, 61–62, 75, 119–120, 171–172
aspect ratio 132
Atkinson, George 184
attendance: effects of TV 6–7, 24–25; theatrical 5, 189
audience 46; effects of TV 53–54; for films on TV 78; potential 52; research 55, 100, 165; theater 54;
untapped by theaters 26
Austria, Ralph 7
Autry, Gene 14–15, 30

B films 7, 9
backlog: of majors 12; of majors, pre–48 13; post–48s 47–48, 49, 67–70, 72, 76; release, pre–48s 37–38, 42–43; sales vs. rental 41
Backman, Preston 139
Balaban, Barney 47, 65, 72
Bank of America 11
barker channels 178–179
Barnouw, Erik 43
Barry, Charles 45, 63
Bart, Peter 111
barter system 75
Bartlesville, Oklahoma 65–66
baseball, televised 101
Beatty, Warren 132–133
Ben-Hur 82
Bischoff, Sam 12
Black, David 96
Blay, André 183
Bleier, Edward 95, 178–179
block booking 4, 16, 41–42, 49, 55–60, 74, 79–80, 140
blockbusters 48–49, 85, 124–125, 127–128
books, abridged 93

252 Index

Boren, Charles 69
box office receipts, indie films 152–153
boycotts 1617 26–27, 66, 71–72, 114–115
Boyd, William 30
Brando, Marlon 30
Brandt, Harry 23
The Bridge on the River Kwai 85
Bronson, Edward 92
Brown, Les 100, 106, 116
Bryant, John 137
Business Week 8–9

C&C Super Corporation 40–41
cable TV 117–121; basic 173–176; capacity 145; ownership 118–119, 143; vs VCRs 166
Caine, Michael 138
Callenbach, Ernest 97–98
Capra, Frank 92, 156–157
Cassiday, Hopalong 17–18
Castell, Ron 153
Catholic Legion of Decency 51
CBS 107–109
Celler, Emanual 67
censorship 94–100; state 50–51
Chandler, A.B. 24
Chase, Stanley 84
Cheers for Miss Bishop 17
Cinemascope 11
Cinemax 162
Clark, Samuel 107
clearance windows 70–71, 125, 153–155, 174, 186
Close Encounters of the Third Kind 132
Cohn, Marcus 67
color TV 37, 60–61, 86
colorization of films 155–158
Columbia 4, 32
commercialization 14–15, 34
commercials 110; rates 77, 87, 102, 108; scheduling 91; time 60, 87
compression 134
The Constant Husband 51–52
Consumer Reports 6
content of films 91–97, 129–131
contracts, with actors 15
Cooper, Phil 56
copyrights 137, 183–184
Corey, Wendell 30–31

cost of films: to networks 81–81, 84–85; to TV 11, 17–18, 38, 48, 77, 80–81, 87, 123–124
cost of TV series 64
Cruise, Tom 199

Dales, John 105–106
The Damned 99
Dann, Mike 84, 113
David, Saul 93
Davis, Bette 10, 94–95, 133
Dawson, Archie 59
The Deer Hunter 131
deGraw, Harold 119
De Prez, Fred 180
deletions 92–97
Dempsey, John 146–147, 174
Dempsey, Michael 157
Depinet, Ned 38
The Depression 3
deregulation 144
Dinner at Eight 52
direct broadcast satellite (DBS) 181–183
direct to video release 153–154
directors, film, TV cutting 94
Dirty Harry 130
Disney studio 33
Disneyland 33–34
distribution 41, 46, 61–62, 88
distribution contracts, of indies with majors 18
divestment, theaters 4
double-shot versions 98–99, 131
Douglas, Kirk 31
dramatic anthology TV series 34–35
DuMont network 36
Dunville, Robert 50

Earthquake 129
editing of films on TV 50–51, 89–97, 129–137; legality of 14–15
Edwards, Blake 131
Emerline, Ernest 49, 76
employment, film industry 4–5
entertainment conglomerates, revenues 200
Erlicht, Lew 125
Eves, Jeff 183
exhibitors, opposition 12–13, 15–17,

24–25, 47, 54–55, 68–70, 82–83, 180–181

Famous Film Festival 74
featherbedding 13
Federal Communications Act 50–51
Federal Communications Commission (FCC) 4, 10, 22–23, 30, 35–36, 116, 117, 163–164
Federal Trade Commission (FTC) 93
Fellows, Harold 67
Ferguson, Warren 186
film clips 31
film networks, by majors 147
film production, by TV networks 107–109
Film Quarterly 97
film scheduling, strategy of 83–84
film series: made-fors 113; on TV 48–49
film telecasting contracts 81
films: on networks, reruns 85–86; on pay-TV, rules 121; publicized by TV programs 126–127; withheld from TV 9, 11
films on TV: implications of 52, 84, 100, 106–107; nonmajors 5, 17; number of 46, 48, 53, 55, 82, 126; old 49–50
final cut, right of 133
Fink, Morton 194
First Sale doctrine 186, 193
Flanagan, Al 56
flat rate vs. pay-per-view pricing 65
Fonda, Henry 115
Ford, John 92–93
foreign expansion 173
foreign films, on TV 18–19, 80, 138
Fox, Matthew 28
Fox studio 22, 46, 71
Fox TV network 147–148
Fuchs, Michael 165

Ganeless, Michelle 169
Garland, Les 144
Garner, Hugh 19–20
General Teleradio 19, 36, 39–40
Gephardt, Richard 157–158
Ghostbusters 125–126
Gilliat, Sidney 51–52
Gilula, Steve 181

Glick, Earl 156
global revenue, majors 192
The Godfather 96
Goettel, Gerard 172
Gold, Ronald 100
Goldenson, Leonard 74–75, 86
Goldsmith, Tom 187
Goldwyn, Samuel 6–7, 8, 23–24
Good Neighbor Sam 94
Gordon, Julius 71
Gould, Jack 5, 11, 18–19, 31, 48, 90–91, 94, 101
Grant, Donald 126
Greeley, Bill 87
Griffing, Henry 65–66
Gruen, Erica 199–200

Halpern, Nathan 24
Hansen, Victor 56–57
Harper, Richard 57, 60
Harrison, Ben 15
Hauser, Gustave 165–166
Hays Office 58
Herlands, William 62
Heston, Charlton 115
Heyworth, Jim 165
Hift, Fred 53, 66
Hill, Arthur 136, 158
Hirschfield, Alan 187
Hogan, Gerry 157
Holden, William 91
Home Box Office (HBO) 118–119, 160–161
home taping, from TV 183–184
homosexual themes 137
Horowitz, Murray 47, 48, 55, 78
Hough, Hal 89
household expenditures, films 5
How to Marry a Millionaire 82
Huggins, Roy 113
Hughes, Howard 39
Hyams, Jerome 60, 117

independent producers 12
industry decline 3–5
International Telemeter Corp 28–29, 64–65

Jaffe, Jerry 126
Jarmoc, Max 100, 112
Johnson, William 95

Kaiser, Henry 74–75
Kalmenson, Benjamin 39
Katz, Jon 127
Katzenburg, Jeffrey 135
KHJ 88
kinescopes 33
Klein, Arthur 90
Klingensmith, Bob 155, 188, 197
KMPS 50
Knize, Leon 193
Koening, Ben 91
Kramer, Stanley 9, 30, 31
KTTV 53
Kurnit, Scott 180

labeling, edited films on TV 134–137
labels, disclaimers 133–134
labor unions 12–14, 67–70, 105–106
Ladd, Alan Jr. 181
Landau, Ely 57
Lang, Jennings 99, 109, 112
The Last Detail 97
late shows 18
Launder, Frank 51–52
Lemieux, Barry 177
Leonard, John 188–189
LeRoy, Mervyn 67
Leslie, Cy 199
letterbox format 132
Levin, Gerald 119
Liberty Media 148
licensing terms 150
Life 16
Litman, Barry 124
live TV 20, 34–35, 42–43, 78
loan-outs 9
local programming 89
Loew, Arthur 46
Los Angeles 52–53, 88

McClennan, John 98–99
McDonald, Eugene 25–27
MacDougall, William 166
McGannon, Donald 74
McNamara, Paul 29
made-for-TV movies 109–114, 126, 128, 134, 138–140
Magnetic Video 184
Malone, John 173
Mamoulian, Reuban 6
Mann, Delbert 95

market research 52–53
Markle, Wilson 156
Maslin, Janet 130
Matranga, Jack 149
Maul, Richard 177
Mayer, Roger 158
merchandising, of videotapes 198
mergers 35, 128, 143, 172–173, 175–176
Metzenbaum, Howard 134
MGM 4, 22, 31, 46
MGM Parade 34
The Mickey Mouse Club 33
Midnight Cowboy 96
Miller, Paul 193
Million Dollar Movie 20, 50, 89
Minneapolis 50
Mitchell, Homer 38
Monogram 13
Moore, Thomas 84, 98, 102
Morrison, H.G. 10
Mosk, Edward 133
Motion Picture Association of America 68–69, 136
Motion Picture Production Code 92
movie channels 148–149
movie nights, on networks 86
Mrazek, Robert 134
multiplexing, of pay channels 167
Murdoch, Rupert 140
Murphy, George 93
Musicians Guild of America 67
Mutual network 22
Myers, Abram 70

Nasser, George 11
Nasser, James 11
National Association of Broadcasters (NAB) 91–92
National Association of Radio & Television Broadcasters 67
National Association of Theatre Owners 107
National Catholic Office for Motion Pictures 98
National Telefilm Associates (NTA) 46
Nelson, Ralph 94
Network 131
network structure 35–36
networking 6
networks, film 36–37, 75

New York City 53, 82
New York Times 10
Nuell, David 127
Nutter, Ralph 90

O'Brien, Donn 130
O'Brien, Robert 110
O'Connor, John 129–130
Office of Telecommunications Policy 122
Oldam, Phil 128
O'Neil, Thomas 40
Our Man Flint 93
output deals 141, 166
outtakes 131–132

package selling 41–42, 47, 56–57, 59–60, 76, 86, 103, 140–141
Palm Springs, California 28–29
Paramount 6, 21–22, 28–29, 34, 47
Pastore, John 99
Patton 96
pay-per-view 150, 176–183
pay-TV 64–67, 114–122, 160–173; in hotels and motels 116–117; opposition to 28–29, 66–67; in Santa Monica, California 114–116
Peck, Robert 135
Peers, Martin 145
Pemerantz, Charles 110
phone companies 155, 168
Phonevision 25–27
Pidgeon, Walter 115
The Pirates of Penzance 150–151
A Place in the Sun 90–91
plot additions, to films for TV 129–132
Porter, Paul 23
Potter, Richard 91
Powell, Charles 157
Premiere Network 146–147, 171–172
Preminger, Otto 79–80, 89–90
premium cable TV 118–120
pricing, of videotapes 190–199
pricing policies 49, 58, 76–77, 124
primetime access rule 120–121
primetime, network 53, 73–74; films, nonmajors 36; films on 74, 83–84, 124, 129; first majors release 78–79; reruns 102
profitability 60; profitability, of film airings 40; of film sales 48; of films on TV 61; of TV stations 81–82, 141
programming: by networks 141–143; of films 37
programming day, length of 17
promotion campaigns 168–169
promotion of videotapes 190–192
Proposition 15 (California) 115
Psycho 94

racism 51
Radnitz, Robert 129
Raiburn, Paul 7, 10
Ransohoff, Martin 109
Raphael, Allan 162
ratings 50, 73, 100, 101–102, 126, 145–146
Read, Roger 50
Reade, Walter Jr. 71–72
Reagan, Ronald 143
Reardon, Barry 181
Reds 132–133
reissues, theatrical 72–73, 77–78
release delays 125, 149
release patterns 149, 154
religious objections 99, 137
Republic 12, 37–38
reruns 4, 18–19, 32, 48, 60, 87–88, 103, 122, 139–140; pay-TV 161, 162
residuals 13–14, 41, 67–70, 75–76, 105–106
right-to-know, edited films 93
RKO 4, 39–41
Roberts, Steve 183, 185
Robinson, Hubbell Jr. 42
Rogers, Roy 14–15
Ross, Barney 136, 137
Roth, Paul 121
Rubens, William 101
Rubin, Miles 120

sales, package 18
sales strategies 80
Sarnoff, David 9, 30, 39, 52, 74
Sarnoff, Robert 73
Saturday Night at the Movies 82
Schary, Dore 11
scheduling of films 50, 82
Scheffer, Steve 70
Schenck, Nicholas 34
Scorsese, Martin 135, 137

Index

Screen Actors Guild (SAG) 13–14, 68–70, 105–106
Screen Gems 32
Screen Producers Guild 70
selling strategies 47
Selznick, David O. 48
series, branded 33–34
series from movies 106–107
Shakespeare, Frank Jr. 60
Shanley, J. P. 46
Sheinburg, Sidney 173, 183
Shepard, Richard 51
Sherwin, Howard 135
Sherwin, Wally 88, 93–94
Sidney, George 93
Simpson, Alan 134
Singlinger and Company 52, 54
Skiatron system 28
Skouras, Spyros 11, 24, 38–39, 68
soundtracks, film 12–13, 96, 131
Sponsor 32
Stand by Me 133
station allocation freeze 35–36
station ownership policy 35–36, 63
Stein, Benjamin 113–114
Stellings, Ernest 53–54, 72
Stengal, Rob 153
Sternfeld, Alan 139–140
Stevens, George 90–91
Stevens, George Jr. 157
Strebe, Earle 28
subscription TV 8, 25–30, 65–66
Sullivan, Ed 31, 42
superstations 159–160, 164–165
Swafford, Tom 96
sweep periods, ratings 101, 128
Synar, Mike 135
syndication 85, 88

talk shows 87, 126–127
telecasting of films, strategy 48–49
Television 34
Television: Code 58; material, non-movies 17; networks, by majors 145–146; ownership rights, of films 14–15; production, by majors 106; production costs 22; series, by majors 31–32, 63–64, 106, 142; sets, number of 5; station allocation 22–23; station ownership 21–23, 142; stations, number of 5, 82

Television Programs of America 20
Theater Owners of America (TOA) 15–16, 29, 66–67
theater ownership 142
theater TV 7, 23–25, 64
theatrical release, majors vs. indies 151–152
Thomopoulos, Anthony 133
Thurmond, Strom 67
ticket prices 5
Top Gun 199
Townsend, Bob 155
trailers 7
Turner, Ted 155
Two Minute Warning 129

UHF 35–36
United Artists 11
U.S. Commerce department 135
U.S. Justice department 4, 10, 36, 56–60, 107–108
U.S. News & World Report 7–8
USA network 174

Valenti, Jack 106, 116–117, 121, 143, 163, 173, 185, 187
van Volkenburg, J.L. 38
Variety 56, 69, 78
versions for TV 94–95
VHF 35–36
Viacom 144
videocassette industry 183–199
videotape exhibition 188–189
videotape rental vs. sales 184–199
Vincent, Francis Jr. 170
Vogel, Joseph 61
von Zerneck, Frank 139

Walt, Norm 84
War of the Roses 127
Warner, Jack L. 9, 39
Warner Bros. 22, 42
WATV 48
Wayne, Jeff 149
WBBM 50
WCBS 46, 50, 84, 88
Weaver, Sylvester "Pat" 12, 114–115
Wells, Richard 91
Wertheimer, Thomas 162
westerns 17–18
The Wild Geese 130

Wise, Robert 97
The Wizard of Oz 42, 70
WOR 20, 50
World Series 23–24
WTCG 159–160
Wynoski, Jim 154
X-rated films 95–97

Yates, Herbert 16, 37–38
Young Mr. Lincoln 92
Youngstein, Max 73

Zanuck, Richard 86, 110
Zinnemann, Fred 92–93
Ziv, Frederic 128

www.ingramcontent.com/pod-product-compliance
Ingram Content Group UK Ltd.
Pitfield, Milton Keynes, MK11 3LW, UK
UKHW041935140426
5217IPUK00014B/484